CHRISTIAN LIFE

IN THE

PRIMITIVE CHURCH

BY

ERNST VON DOBSCHÜTZ, D.D.

ORDINARY PROFESSOR OF NEW TESTAMENT THEOLOGY IN THE UNIVERSITY
OF STRASSBURG

TRANSLATED BY

The Rev. GEORGE BREMNER, B.D.

AND EDITED BY

The Rev. W. D. MORRISON, LL.D.

WIPF & STOCK · Eugene, Oregon

Wipf and Stock Publishers
199 W 8th Ave, Suite 3
Eugene, OR 97401

Christian Life in the Primitive Church
By von Dobschütz, Ernst and Bremner, George
Softcover ISBN-13: 978-1-6667-3428-7
Hardcover ISBN-13: 978-1-6667-2997-9
eBook ISBN-13: 978-1-6667-2998-6
Publication date 8/20/2021
Previously published by Williams & Norgate, 1904

This edition is a scanned facsimile of the original edition published in 1904.

Preface to the German Edition

For a long time theologians were specially attracted by the great thoughts which are connected with the objective content of Christian truth. Much earnest labour was expended upon dogma in the way both of working it out speculatively and investigating it historically. Within recent years, however, more attention has come to be paid to the subjective element in religion, viz., personal Christianity, religious psychology, and the various forms which religion assumes in the individual, in different ages or classes, and in particular peoples and periods. The need for an account of popular religious thought and feeling (*Volkskunde*) has been almost generally recognized. As a division of practical theology, it is concerned in the first instance with the present, but it will certainly welcome the assistance of history. The present study is an attempt to transfer the method to primitive Christianity.

To this end we choose the domain where, in our opinion, Christianity can adduce the best evidence of power—the domain of morals. At the present time theology shows a strong disposition to look for the special power of Christianity in a quite different quarter. There is a growing mysticism which seeks its essence in enthusiasm and in ecstatic spiritual phenomena, known to our fathers as union with God and to us moderns as demonism (δαίμων, δαιμόνιον). We are indebted to this current of thought for the light which it has thrown upon prophetism and for a far richer understanding of primitive Christianity. The operations of the Spirit and of spirits undoubtedly form an important chapter in the history of religion. But not everything in the history of Christianity turned upon these phenomena, nor do they determine the verdict to be passed on primitive Christianity. On the contrary, they may easily lead to an unjust estimate of history. They transform the restriction of an overflowing enthusiasm by the fixed forms of ecclesiastical development into the "fall" of primitive Christianity.

If we start not from general conceptions of religion, but from the thought that Christianity is the religion in which everything is defined by the historical person of Jesus Christ, it is clear that at once the ideal of Christianity and the standard by which its historical forms are to be judged must be sought not in ecstatic outbursts of feeling but in the doing of God's will. To begin with the moral proofs of Christianity, is an old and approved apologetic method. Gregory of Nazianzus says, πρᾶξις ἐπίβασις Θεωρίας ; and in an early Christian preacher we find "neither life without knowledge, nor sure knowledge without real life," *Ep. ad Diognetum*, xii. 4.

That being so, we are not concerned so much with the ethical theories set up by Christianity from time to time as with the actual effects which the impulse proceeding from the Gospel produced. We must ask how far it was possible to realize the ideal in practice.

How did things look in the early Christian communities? What was their actual moral condition? What was the individual's contribution to the moral life of the community? These questions indicate the problem with which we have to deal.

Strangely enough, it is a problem which has been dealt with hardly at all. Ritschl's suggestion that more attention should be devoted to moral conditions in the history of the Christian Church (*Litt. Centralblatt*, 1856, 454 f.) has only been very occasionally given effect to in the treatment of the apostolic age. It has been kept in view most by Lechler perhaps, and more recently by Weizsacker, who has followed up the beginnings of Christian morals with characteristic thoroughness. As distinguished from the idealizing method of the earlier period, it has now become easy to fall into the mistake of painting too black a picture. From all sorts of statements gleaned in the darkest corners and dipped in the deepest hues, Hausrath drew a picture so gloomy that one is compelled to wonder where Christianity ever found the power to conquer the ancient world. Harnack (*Theol. Litt. Zeitung*, 1884) replied by showing the proper standpoint for judging its moral standing, but the task itself has not yet been accomplished. Ulhorn's great work contains an exhaustive treatment of the main point, Christian charity; Zahn, with his well-known erudition, has considered other single questions in various lectures; quite lately some of the preliminary problems, the spread of Christianity, the social composition of the Christian communities, the Christian attitude towards national life, and the position of women have been dealt with by

Wohlenberg. I do not include works on moral doctrine and its history. Only one comprehensive treatment of our subject is known to me. It is to be found in Kähler's thoughtful lecture on "die richtige Beurteilung der apostolischen Gemeinden nach dem Neuen Testamente," which was called forth at the Sachsische Missions-Konferenz in Halle, 1894, by Missiondirektor Buchner's suggestive lecture on "die gerechte Würdigung der (modernen) heidenchristlichen Gemeinden." Both works bear some trace of their occasional character. For an exhaustive treatment more detail is necessary.

For our purpose single pictures are requisite. Their value for us will depend on their individual character. We purposely place the two compositions whose richer material calls for most attention, at the beginning and the end. As certainly as primitive Christianity is to be distinguished as a closed system from the Christian ecclesiasticism of the later period, so certainly within itself it is extraordinarily multiform. What a difference there is between the Christian life on Jewish and on Greek soil, where the synagogue had prepared the way or where the Gospel entered the heathen world immediately, in the metropolis or in an outlying Syrian village. What a difference it makes whether the first witnesses of the life of Jesus, with their decisive authority, missionaries with the power of a Paul, stood by the Churches to guide them, or whether these were dependent on themselves and the men of the second generation. Not to specialize means to paint an unfaithful picture. Even supplementary conclusions drawn from facts in one quarter and applied to another are hazardous, and to be employed only where inadequate sources demand some imaginative development. A comparison of the individual pictures will supply the material for a final verdict.

When we speak of Christian morality we frequently mean a definite theological and ethical system, or at least a complex of moral views which are familiar to us, and which our own settled convictions take for granted to be Christian. But history reveals very diverse views on this point. The actual morality of a people and a period depends on a variety of circumstances. It is affected by the geographical nature of the country, climatic and similar considerations, the racial character of the people, with its past history and present political condition ; in a word, by all that comes under civilization and history, and by its religion. The main point for us is to decide what value attaches to this last factor.

To that end regard must be had to the moral standing of the non-Christian world of the age. From it only can we learn why Christianity had such a hard fight to establish its fundamental moral thoughts. It alone makes clear to us that the morality of early Christianity, notwithstanding its imperfections, was unmistakably higher than all that Greek civilization could achieve. One who sets aside the history of the times deprives himself of the best aid to a vivid picture and a clearly-grounded verdict.

Our time-limits hardly require any justification. Primitive Christianity is a historical entity and includes the first century of development from the death of Jesus up to the time of Hadrian (30–130). It was the time when the Bar Cochba war actually made an end of the national Judaism of Palestine and deprived Jewish Christianity of any historical importance, when Aelia Capitolina came to stand on the holy place of Jerusalem, and a Gentile Church settled there; the time when Christianity began to covenant with Græco-Roman civilization with the view of establishing itself as the Church in the world, when speculative minds began to build bold systems out of it and apologists attempted to justify it to the civilized world as the best practical philosophy; the time, finally, when with the last who had themselves seen the Lord (Quadratus apud Eusebius, *Hist. Eccles.*, IV. iii. 2), the primitive Christian enthusiasm sank into the grave and men had the consciousness of belonging not to the second only but to the third and the fourth generations.

It follows from the historical nature of our task that all primitive Christian compositions belonging to this period are to be employed as sources, without any distinction between canonical and extra-canonical. In the same way we must proceed as chronologically as possible. Notwithstanding this, however, the Pauline are treated before the Jewish-Christian Churches. This is a procedure which is justified by the sources. It brings out the special character of each community better, and enables us to adopt a more material order towards the close.

It is only a section of the history of primitive Christianity with which we deal. The border-line between it and other parts is not always easy to draw. Constitution, worship, the whole life of the community and its usages, are forms in which the moral spirit of Christianity finds expression. But it is only from this point of view and not on their technical side (if I may say so) that these questions can here be handled. I must therefore be excused for only touching upon many an interesting problem and for making statements whose proof in detail I am here compelled to deny myself.

This difficulty will be most felt in questions of literary history. I have been compelled to introduce them; for only so could the sources be systematically valued. On the other hand it would have disordered my work, if I had yielded to the temptation to include a small introduction to the New Testament. The discussion of single problems which I handle in a way special to myself may be possible elsewhere.

I trust that the few supplementary notes, especially the last, will be found useful, and the detailed indexes helpful in using the book.

My study has a larger aim than the knowledge of primitive Christianity. However important a general investigation of this ground-laying and initial period is, it only acquires full significance when it is placed in relation to the present. Among religious questions in our eminently practical time, perhaps the most outstanding one is the extent to which Christianity demonstrates itself as a moral power in our people's life. It is a question that concerns statesmen as well as theologians. In his *Kirchengeschichte Deutschlands*, A. Hauck has shown the valuable contribution which the historian can make to its solution. Historical study clears the vision for our own time. Much that we do not understand in it, and do not even detect, can be observed when we take some object of consideration more remote from us. We live often in an ideal world, and hardly notice how little the world around us corresponds to it. But when we have once clearly recognized the contrast between ideal and real in the past, it will soon meet us in the present, and we shall learn what steps to take to remove it. Kahler concluded his lecture with a warm appeal to fructify the study of the New Testament through the reports of present-day missionary enterprize. I may surely say conversely that every clergyman, in order aright to estimate the circumstances of the flock entrusted to his care, ought to have fashioned for himself a clear picture of conditions in the early Christian communities. These were by no means ideal. For that very reason they can be typical.

Preface to the English Edition

"What is Christianity?" is the great question in the theology of the present day. Harnack tells us that the answer can be found only by historical research. Thus we come to ask what the beginnings of our religion were. What was the primitive Christianity?

It is with this problem that the present book deals. It gives a picture of early Christian life on its moral side. Possibly some of my readers may suppose that the question is already answered. "Christianity," they say, "is morality, moral renovation both of the individual and of society." Such a view, however, is far from being the author's conception. He lays great stress on this moral transformation. To his mind it constitutes the most effective proof of the truth of Christianity. But it is only a proof, a demonstration of Christianity, and not its essence.

Christianity is salvation by faith, faith in God through Jesus Christ, His only begotten Son. Apart from revelation such a faith cannot arise in mankind, nor can it be maintained in sinners without the assurance of forgiveness. It is this faith which gives life and happiness. Without fruits, however, it would be false. St James (ii. 20) says that "faith without works is dead." Our Lord makes faith the first requisite of all,[1] but He too seeks for its fruits.[2] When He says, "Not every one that saith unto me, Lord, Lord, shall enter into the kingdom of heaven; but he that doeth the will of my Father which is in heaven" (Matt. vii. 21), He emphasizes the duty of moral activity or practical Christianity. But He does not deny the necessity of calling Him Lord, that is, of having a religious attitude towards Himself. In speaking of "the will of my Father which is in heaven," He joins morality to religion, *i.e.* to faith in God and obedience to Him.

Much, however, depends upon the time and the nation. Every age has its own conception of the Gospel, and as human thought is always imperfect, there must always be one-sidedness to correct. Sometimes the idea of the Church is overvalued and the rights of the individual must be asserted. At other times individualism is excessive and requires to be balanced by bringing forward the thought of community. In the same way faith and morality are the two parts of religion. The one cannot exist without the other. But the one or the other is always gaining a dangerous supremacy.

It has been said that we are inclined to fall into a mere morality, and the reproach is made in especial against the Ritschlian school. What the author feels at present is the very opposite danger. Among the younger German theologians there is a great inclina-

---

[1] Mark i. 15, xi. 22, iv 40; v. 36, ix 22; v. 34, x 52; Matt xvii 20; Luke xvii 6; Matt. viii 10; Luke vii 9; Luke vii 50, xvii 19.

[2] Matt vii 10 ff, xii 33; Luke vi 43 ff, Mark iv 7 f., 28 f., xii 2; Luke xiii. 6 ff., Mark xi. 13 f.

tion towards mysticism. There is one school which makes Jesus Himself an ecstatic who lived in a Utopia of eschatological ideas. Others, who do not go so far, describe His apostles as men quite incapable of the sublime spirit of the Gospel, who fell back to the level of the surrounding religious world. No doubt there is some truth in these assertions, but they need to be counterbalanced by urging all that is lasting in Christ's teaching and by connecting His disciples with Himself and separating them from the world around them. Close examination will show this to be the predominant feature of His and their teaching, and not the fact that they took their stand on the inferior level of the religions of the time.

Considerations like these would seem to lead to a careful study of the ethics of Jesus and the Apostles. Notwithstanding many good works already dealing with the subject, it would be a task that would repay trouble. But the present writer has his reasons for going a step further. What he endeavours to investigate is not the ethical teaching of primitive Christianity, but its real morals. At the same time, however, he wishes to express his very distinct conviction that historical progress cannot be explained by forces originating in a collective way, but by eminent leaders or "heroes" as Carlyle calls them. The astonishing success of the Gospel during the first century is the work of St Paul and his fellow-labourers, not of the mass of Christian converts whom they brought together by their preaching. The character of the single communities owes more to the founder than to the former situation of the individual members.

Nevertheless the question whether Christianity

proved itself a moral force will not be answered by the study of Pauline ethics alone. We must also try to discover the standard of morals in the communities which St Paul founded. The task is by no means easy. In order to obtain a right impression of what the Pauline communities really were, we must carefully examine the Apostle's own opinion of them.

There is some difference too in national conceptions of the Gospel. In Germany the evolution of religious thought and feeling has always been highly theological, so that even historical investigation has been largely guided by dogmatic views. In England, where dogma is balanced by liturgical and practical interests, its influence would not seem to be so great. English dissent represents in itself the greatest variety of religious opinions. The most remarkable feature of modern development is that all differences of dogma and creed disappear before the great practical tasks of to-day. These tasks all endeavour to accomplish. This is just what we observe in primitive Christianity. It is the true spirit of Christian life.

This being so, I hope that my book will find a good reception in its new English dress, as it has already found a hearty welcome in England in its German form. May it do its work not only by diffusing exact knowledge of old Christian manners and morals, but also by disseminating the spirit of primitive Christianity, the earnest, strong and victorious spirit of faithful religious and moral activity.

E VON DOBSCHUTZ

JENA, *Whitsuntide* 1904.

Table of Contents

INTRODUCTION. THE PROBLEM AND THE SOURCES

PAGES

Christian life according to the Apology of Aristides, xxv. The counter-picture in Hermas, xxvii. The problem, xxviii. The sources, xxix Their inadequacy, xxix. The various groups of literature, xxix Limits of the evidence, xxxiii. Want of statistics, xxxiv. Trustworthiness, xxxiv Theory and fact, xxxvi. The significance of Jesus' moral thoughts, xxxviii . . . xxv–xxxix

BOOK I. THE PAULINE CHURCHES.

CHAPTER I. THE EDUCATION OF THE CHURCHES.

Moral training by the Apostle, 1. The ethical element of his preaching, 1 Enumerations of vices, 2 Table of domestic duties (Col iii. 18-iv. 2), 4. Detailed moral teaching (Rom. xii.-xiv), 5 Motives, 8. Pedagogy, 9 . . . 1–10

CHAPTER II. THE CHURCH OF CORINTH

The town, 11 Paul's labours, 13. The community, 13. The devotional life, 16. Participation by all, 16 Disorders, 17 False valuation of the Spirit's operations, 18. Baptism and the Lord's Supper, 19 11–22

TABLE OF CONTENTS

CHAPTER III. THE CHURCH OF CORINTH (*continued*)

PAGES

Christian and non-Christian, 23 Meat offered to idols, 26. Lawsuits, 29 Mixed marriages, 30. The question of slavery, 33. The position of women, 36 Marriage and celibacy, 40. The seventh commandment, 43 The case of incest, 44. Paul's intervention, 45. Refusal of the Church, 47 The culprit's penitence, 48. The Church's attitude criticised, 49. The Apostle's preaching lacking on the moral side, 51. Further training, 53 The isolation of this case, 54   23–55

CHAPTER IV THE CHURCH OF CORINTH (*continued*)

Property, 56 Lawsuits, 57 Unwillingness to give, 57 The collection, 58 Disorders at the common meals, 60 Drunkenness and slander, 63. The "strong" and the "weak," 64 Libertinism, 65. Asceticism, 68. Paul's attitude towards it, 69 Parties, 71 Their relation to the Apostle, 74 Judaistic agitation, 75. Final judgment, 78   56–80

CHAPTER V THE CHURCHES OF MACEDONIA: THESSALONICA AND PHILIPPI.

The towns, 81 Foundation of the churches and their intercourse with Paul, 82 The Epistles, 84 Common features, 84 Immature Christianity of *Thessalonica*, 86. Community of feeling, 87. Conspicuous Christian consciousness, 89 Overtrained expectation of the Parousia, 90, Its evil consequence, viz., disorders, 91 Mature Christianity of *Philippi*, 93 Close relations with the Apostle, 94 Missionary zeal, 95. Exhortations reminders, not reproaches, 95 Feeling of unity, 96. Organisation, 96 Final judgment, 98   .   81–98

CHAPTER VI. THE CHURCHES OF ASIA MINOR. GALATIA AND PHRYGIA

Paul's labours in Asia Minor, 99. *Ephesus*, 100. Conflict with superstition and trade jealousy, 100 *Galatia* and *Phrygia*, 102 Resemblances and differences, 102. Single instances of defect, 104 Good sides of the Church life, 105 Interruption

TABLE OF CONTENTS   xix

PAGES

of the normal development, 106. *Galatia :* Judaistic agitation, 106 Its nature and the grounds of its success, 108 The law seemingly a higher morality, 108 Evil consequence, viz, discord, 110 *Phrygia (Colossæ)* asceticism, perfect morality, 111 Causes of the tendency to asceticism, 113. Effects, 115. *Epistle to Philemon* The question of slavery, 115 . . 99–120

CHAPTER VII. THE CHURCH OF ROME

Paul's relation to Rome, 121 The *Epistle to the Romans*, 121. Origin of Roman Christianity, 122. House-Churches, 122. Doubts and antitheses, 124 Vegetarianism, 126. Its extent at the time, 126 Motives, 127. Legalism, 128 The Sabbath, 128 "Strong" and "weak," 129. Attitude towards the authorities, 129. Taxes, 130 *Romans xii –xiv* as expressing the Apostle's average experience in his Churches, 132. Survey of the Pauline Churches, 133 121–137

BOOK II. JEWISH CHRISTENDOM.

CHAPTER VIII THE PRIMITIVE CHURCH, THE CHURCH OF JERUSALEM

Jewish morality, 138 Significance of the law, 139. The Church of Jerusalem, 141. The ideal wholly Jewish, 141. Peculiarities of the Christians, 142 Community of goods, 143 Family character, 144. Joy of confession, 145. Moral troubles, Ananias and Sapphira, 146 Disputes between the Hebrews and the Hellenists, 147 138–148

CHAPTER IX FURTHER DEVELOPMENT.

Various tendencies, 149. Peter and the disciples, 150. The Hellenists, 150. James and enthusiasm for the law, 151. Victory of the Judaistic ideal in Jerusalem, 151. The Apostolic decree, 151. James the representative of the Jewish ideal, 153. The Jewish ideal found in the Lord's sayings, 155. Organisation, 157. Mission-work on Jewish soil, 158 149–159

xx TABLE OF CONTENTS

CHAPTER X. JUDAISTIC PROPAGANDA.

                 PAGES
Propaganda among Gentile-Christians, 160. Antioch, 162. Corinth, 163. Galatia, 165. Rome, 166. Criticism: a moral supplement to Paul's preaching, 166 160–167

CHAPTER XI. JEWISH CHRISTENDOM OF THE LATER PERIOD.

The altered situation, 168. Continuance of the two tendencies, 169. Sayings of the Lord in the Gospels of the Hebrews, 169. Final judgment, 171 168–172

BOOK III. LATER CHRISTIANITY AMONG THE HEATHEN.

CHAPTER XII THE CHURCHES STILL UNDER PAULINE INFLUENCE—ASIA MINOR.

Relation to the Pauline period, 174 The Christendom of *Asia Minor*, 175 Sources. *Ephesians* and *1 Peter*, 175 The moral aspect of Christianity emphasised, 176 Effect on devotional life, 177, and conceptions of faith, 178 Contrast with heathendom, 178 Heathen calumnies, 179 Missionary task, 181 Positive conception of duties, 181 Development of the ideal. Biblicizing. 183 Christianizing Jesus —Word and Pattern, 184 Maturing of the communities, 185. Advance in actual moral standing, 187. Relaxation of moral energy, 188. General estimate, 189. Dangers of developing hierarchy, 189. Dangers of developing heresy, 193 173–194

CHAPTER XIII THE CHURCHES STILL UNDER PAULINE INFLUENCE—ROME AND CORINTH

The Church of *Rome*: Sources, 195. The general situation, 195. *Epistle to the Hebrews*: Persecution and apostasy, 196 Moral earnestness, 200. Good sides of the Church life, 200 Constitution, doctrine, worship, 201. Advance on the Pauline period, 203 Further advance, 203. *1st Epistle of Peter* and *1st Epistle of Clement*, 203. Concern for all Christendom, 204. Principle of order in constitution and worship, 205. Practical Christianity, 207. Moral training, 208. Points

TABLE OF CONTENTS

of progress, 209 New dangers, 209 The Church of *Corinth*, 210. *1st Epistle of Clement*, 211 Former high standing, 211 Present decline, 213 Disorders, 214 Causes, 215 Effects, 216 Survey, 217 195–217

CHAPTER XIV. THE JOHANNEAN CIRCLE

John of Asia Minor, 218. His dominating influence, 220 Conflicts with particular Churches, 220. (*3rd John*), 220. Conflict with false teaching, 222 (*2nd John.*) The verdict upon the Churches in *Apoc ii, iii*, 225 Moral torpor, 228. Relaxation of moral energy and the conflict with it in *1st John*, 229 The *Gospel of John* as reflecting the age, 230 . . . 218–234

CHAPTER XV. THE JOHANNEAN CIRCLE (*continued*): THE CHURCHES IN THE TIME OF IGNATIUS.

Ignatius, 235. *Polycarp*, 239 Consciousness of unity, 240. Active intercourse, 241. Fixed organisation, 242 Strict separation from false doctrine; docetism, 245. Judaism, 246 Elevation of the average morality, 247. Final judgment, 250 235–250

CHAPTER XVI. THE BEGINNINGS OF GNOSTICISM.

Nature and beginnings of gnosticism, 251. Christianizing, 251. The beginnings—fluctuating boundaries, 252. Barren intellectualism, 254 Lovelessness, 254. Avoidance of confession, 255. Dualistic asceticism, 258 Its nature, 258; and stages, 260. Celibacy, 261. Position of women, 263. Surrender of property, 264 Withholding of sustenance, 266. Antinomistic libertinism, 268. Its forms, 268 Criticism, 271 Untruthfulness, 273. Impure propaganda, 274. Final judgment, 275 251–276

CHAPTER XVII. THE CHURCHES OF THE TRANSITION TO CATHOLICISM.

The nature of Catholicism, 277. Absence of local colour, 277. Sources, 278. The ideal: the new law, 278 Twofold morality, 279 Principle of order, 281. Repression of the free ministers

xxii   TABLE OF CONTENTS

	PAGES
of the Spirit, 282. The office: its dangers, requirements and rights, 284. Arrangements in the Church, 286 Worship, 287 Church discipline, 289 Missionary duty, 290 Duty of confession, 291. Loyalty, 292 Hatred of the Jews, 293 Unity of the Church, 295 Unity of the congregation, 296 Organisation of charity, 296 Private charity, 300 Rich and poor, 303 Labour, 304 Sustenance, 304 Family life, 304 Slaves, 306. Feeling of insufficiency, 306 Actual advance, 307	277–308

CHAPTER XVIII. THE CHURCHES OF THE TRANSITION TO CATHOLICISM (*continued*)

The Church of Rome according to the *Shepherd of Hermas*, 309   Hermas and his book, 310   His confessions, 310. Unchastity, 312. Dishonesty, 313. Want of discipline, 314. Joyous Christianity, 316. διψυχία, 318. Cheerfulness, 319. Inwardness, 320   Motives, 321. The Church, 323   Relation to the State, 325   Christian strangers in Rome, 326. Church-work, 327. Persecution, martyrdom and apostasy, 328 Half-Christians, 331. Secularisation, 332. Separation from heathenism, 334   The clergy, 335. Quarrels as to precedence, 337. Heretics, 337. Discord, 338. Devotional life, 339 Fastdays, 340. Baptism, 341. Preaching, 342. Meetings for edification, 344. Instruction of catechumens, 345. Practical requirements, 346. Family life: unchastity, 349   Divorce, 349. Differences in married life, 352. Position of women, 353   Discipline of children, 353. Order and cleanliness, 353. Slaves, 353 Business dealings, 355. Wealth, 356. Hospitality, 357. Charity, 358. Willingness in giving, 359. Final judgment, 360   .   .   . 309–362

CONCLUSION

The problem, 363. The proper standpoint, 363. Moral conditions of the age, 364. General picture of Christian morals, 368   Ideal and actual, 371   Development within the period, 372. Advance, 374   Later retrogression, 375 External influences. the Gospel and asceticism, 376   The victory of Christianity, 378   .   . 363–379

TABLE OF CONTENTS

NOTES

		PAGE
1	On ancient statistics (p xxxiv)	381
2	On slavery among the ancients (pp 33 ff, 115 ff)	383
3	On the divine judgment in Corinth (pp 44–52)	387
4	On James, the Lord's brother (pp 153 f)	392
5	On vegetarianism in the ancient world (pp 126–128)	396
6.	On the terminology of morality	399

INDEX OF PASSAGES REFERRED TO OR DISCUSSED	411
GENERAL INDEX	428

CHRONOLOGY.

	YEAR	PAGE
DEATH OF JESUS	30–33 (?)	
STEPHEN'S MARTYRDOM	31–34 (?)	
PAUL'S CONVERSION	34	
DEATH OF JAMES THE ELDER	44	
APOSTOLIC COUNCIL	51	99
PAUL IN MACEDONIA	Summer, 52	81
ARRIVAL IN CORINTH	Autumn, 52	13
,, EPHESUS	,, 54	100
COLLECTION JOURNEY	57, 58	102
IMPRISONMENT IN CÆSAREA	58–60	102
,, IN ROME	61–63	93
EPISTLE TO PHILIPPIANS	62	93
DEATH OF JAMES	62	
,, PAUL	63	169
,, PETER	64	

Introduction

THE PROBLEM AND THE SOURCES.

"THE Christians have received the commandments (of the Lord Jesus Christ), which they have engraved on their minds and keep in the hope and expectation of the world to come; wherefore, they do not commit adultery nor fornication, they do not bear false witness, they do not deny a deposit, nor covet what is not theirs. They honour father and mother; they do good to their neighbours, and when they are judges they judge uprightly. They do not worship idols made in the form of man; and whatever they do not wish that others should do to them, they do not practise towards others; they do not eat of food consecrated to idols, for they are undefiled; those who grieve them they comfort, and make them their friends; they do good to their enemies; their wives, O King, are pure as virgins, and their daughters modest; their men abstain from all unlawful wedlock and from all impurity, in the hope of the recompense to come in another world; if any of them have bondmen, bondwomen, or children, they persuade these to become Christians for the love that they have towards them; and when they have become so, they call them without distinction brethren. They do not worship strange gods; they walk in all humility and kindness, and falsehood is not found among them. They love one another. From the widows they do not turn away their countenance; they rescue the orphan from him who does him violence: he who has gives to him who has not, without grudging; and when they see a stranger, they bring him to their dwellings, and rejoice over him as over a true brother; for they do not call themselves brothers after the flesh, but after the Spirit and in God. When one of their poor passes away from the world, and any of them sees it, then he provides for his burial according to his ability; and if they hear that any of their number is imprisoned or oppressed for the name of their Messiah, all of them provide for his needs, and if it is possible they deliver him.

"If there is among them some one poor and needy, and they have not an abundance of necessaries, they fast two or three days that they may supply his want with necessary food. They observe scrupulously the commandments of their Messiah: they live honestly and soberly, as the Lord their God commands them, thanking Him always for food and drink, and all other blessings. And if any righteous person of their number passes away from the world, they rejoice and give thanks to God, and they follow his body, as if he were moving from one place to another. When a child is born to any one of them, they praise God, and if again it chance to die in its infancy, they praise God exceedingly, as for one who has passed through the world without sins. If, on the other hand, they see that one of their number has died in his ungodliness, or in his sins, they weep bitterly and sigh, as over one who is about to go to punishment.

"As men who know God, they ask from Him what is proper for Him to give and for them to receive. Thus they complete their life-time. And because they acknowledge the goodnesses of God towards them, lo! therein consists all the beauty that is in the world.

"The good deeds, however, which they do, they do not proclaim in the ears of the multitude, and they take care that no one shall perceive them. They conceal their gift, as one who has found a treasure and hides it. Thus they labour to become righteous as those who expect to receive the fulfilment of Christ's promises in the life eternal."

In these words towards the end of the primitive Christian era Aristides, the apologist, describes the life of Christians to the Emperor. No one can refrain from admiring the wealth of moral power revealed in the picture. But does it correspond with the facts?

We take up the Shepherd of Hermas, a Christian writing of about the same date. What do we find there? One of the most prominent Christians in the community has to be severely taken to task on account of the disorder existing in his home. His wife indulges in slanderous talk, his children have fallen away from the Lord; they have betrayed their parents and plunged into excess and unchastity, while the father does not move a finger. Nor is this state of things confined to one Christian household. Even in the case of the leaders exhortation to a more righteous life is required, and the Church cries to all the "saints," "Ye will not cease from your wickedness." The whole composition is one great sermon on repentance, intended not for the heathen but for the Christians themselves.

How does this agree with the beautiful description given by the apologist? Which of the two is right, Aristides or Hermas?

We shall not attempt in the meantime to answer this question. It raises wider issues. It brings us face to face with a problem of fundamental significance for the criticism of early Christianity and of Christianity in general. That Christianity possesses a moral ideal which makes it superior to most, if not to all other religions, is almost generally admitted. But has it also possessed the moral power to realise that ideal? Has it transformed its confessors into better men?

Greek philosophy also developed a high degree of moral perception. But it was just here that it failed: it believed that to know good meant to do it, and had little or no notion of the hostile forces of evil, of sin in men. When St Paul says, "For to will is present with me, but to do that which is good is not," he sums up the moral bankruptcy of the best in the pre-Christian world.

Christianity introduces a new spirit, the Holy Spirit, who creates both moral judgment and moral strength. It is no matter whether this spirit has succeeded in forming connected ethical systems—a New Testament ethic has of late become a frequently-attempted task;

INTRODUCTION xxix

the important question is whether in individuals and in communities it has manifested itself with power, whether it has made Christians of heathen and Jews, whether it has trained the immature into an intelligent and fully conscious Christianity.

Can we prove that it has done so?

It is well to state at the outset that the historical sources are far from sufficient; yet they always admit of a competent treatment of the problem.

In no source at our disposal is there any attempt made to accomplish the task we are undertaking. We have no account of the actual moral circumstances in all their variety. The Acts of the Apostles, which must naturally appear the chief source for the apostolic age, does not touch the question. Luke had absolutely no idea of writing a history of morals. His aim was to picture the victorious progress of the Gospel from Jerusalem throughout the world as far as Rome. He is entirely dependent on what his slender sources afforded him. Even where these contribute concrete touches, such as would be of the greatest interest to us, he presents them in such a rosy hue as to make it difficult to obtain from them any accurate information.

Much more important are the epistles of the New Testament, especially those of St Paul. They are genuine correspondence, and discuss all sorts of questions that then occupied the community, and these, owing to the nature of Christianity, were concerned not only with doctrines, but almost more with life, usage, and morality. The two epistles to the Corinthians in particular place an abundant supply of actual details at our disposal. Yet they fall far short of a complete picture. At best they are only dashes of colour lacking the unity and background of the finished work. How much, *e.g.*, lies behind occasional references like those in 1 Cor. i. 13 ff. and xv. 29, where Paul in passing speaks of baptism. It is due to a lucky chance that we hear of the presumptuous bearing of the women, yet it must have been an important fact in the Church's life. Naturally Paul writes only of what he had occasion to discuss. As a rule, it is the shadier sides of the moral life of the communities that are thus brought to light. Were we not to supplement the picture it must necessarily be distorted. Any aspect of the life of the community to which no allusion is made would seem to have given no occasion for reproach, to have been in no way reprehensible. We must not forget, however, that the argument *e silentio*, however necessary it may be as a corrective, would be exceedingly misleading if employed absolutely in generalising form. Further, these two letters to Corinth cover a space of something like six months. We can perhaps infer what preceded them. But what followed? Again may we apply what we know of Corinth to Thessalonica and Philippi, where our information is more meagre? By no means. This element of momentariness, this local colour lies in the nature of the letter, constituting and at the same time limiting its value as a source.

The Epistles of Paul are followed for a later period by other documents of almost equal evidential importance, because we owe them to individuals who were in actual touch with the concrete circumstances. We have the so-called first Epistle of Clement, in which the state of matters both in Rome and in Corinth is indicated, the two short epistles of John and the seven of Ignatius. Most important of all are the seven letters of the Apocalypse. Properly speaking they are the only real sources in our domain. They handle expressly the question we have raised and throw light in the way either of praise or of blame on the condition of individual communities. But how little is it that the seer indicates, how much remains concealed from us in absolute darkness!

Among the epistles of Paul and Ignatius, a special position belongs to those written to the Christians of Rome, as neither writer had any personal acquaintance with the facts there. Notwithstanding information which they may have received on certain points, most of the colour which they give to their account of matters there is without doubt borrowed from the impressions made on them by the communities which they already knew. The picture they present to us is not so much Rome as a representation of the average Eastern community.

This brings us to the so-called Catholic epistles, to which must be added those to the Ephesians and the Hebrews and the epistle of Barnabas. These "open letters," as we might more aptly designate them, are naturally lacking in exquisite freshness of spontaneity, destination to a distinct circle of readers and specific occasion. The impressions produced are perhaps more trustworthy as a whole, but the pictures presented are far less distinct.

These are all compositions of men who, though they had active relations with the communities concerned, were yet far removed from them. Occasionally Paul's knowledge rests on personal observation, but as a rule he is dependent on the reports of others. Much may have happened which he never heard of, and which, consequently, we have not learned. Moreover, his standpoint was far above that of the communities to which he wrote. To this extent it may be maintained that the epistles of Ignatius and Polycarp are more valuable to us than Paul's. In their own personality these writers represent a portion of the Christian community to which they belonged, a claim which cannot be urged on behalf of Paul to the same extent.

In some ways more importance would attach for us to writings originating from the communities themselves. Of these, however, we possess but few. Among those few we may perhaps reckon the gospels. Weizsacker has shown how these are to be employed as sources of information regarding the apostolic age. The traditions of the sayings of our Lord, the changes of form which these undergo, the emphasising or weakening of single words and whole passages, supply us with a means of discovering what the communities considered matter of vital importance. In this respect still more valuable is a work like the Shepherd of Hermas. In it we have two sides reflected. On the one hand Hermas is an average representative of the Christian community in Rome: on the other hand he is a man who from time to time rises above the community in the power of the prophetic spirit.

As a sermon in the special sense of the word belonging to this period, we may reckon only the so-called second Epistle of Clement. But the apologies, most of which, it is true, lie beyond it, may be considered as authorities here. As we saw in the case of Aristides, these attempt at least to give as comprehensive pictures as possible of life in the Christian communities, and call attention to facts which we have no other means of learning, but which are nevertheless integral parts of the picture, *e.g.*, the cordial participation of the whole community in the domestic events of individual members.

We shall return to the use to be made of the Didache and such literature as bears on the constitution of the Church.

However extensive the material at our disposal may seem to be (and for the later decades of our period it increases in amount, though not in significance), it does not provide us with a comprehensive picture. We possess much information about Corinth in the time of Paul, but only for a few years. The next time we come across Corinth in our sources is a full generation later. Of Ephesus in the Apostle's time we know almost nothing, and of Antioch still less. Yet these Churches must have had very great significance. Our greatest difficulties are connected with the Jerusalem Church. Direct sources are here so deficient that nearly everything is pure deduction. Deductions, however, are possible. The same may be said of the two main tendencies in the early Church which lie near the main current of its historical development, Judaism and Gnosticism. For what we know of these, we are indebted almost exclusively to those who combated them. For this reason we are justified in reading between the lines of the controversy, and in emphasising the few remnants of original sources in a way that would not be admissible were the material richer.

One of the chief blanks in our tradition is the absence of almost all that modern statistics demand. How large were the Churches? Almost nowhere do we meet with a definite number, and the few numbers which we do have are uncertain. Harnack has recently shown the complex combinations which the calculation of the spread of Christianity with some degree of accuracy involves. How, too, were the communities composed? From what social strata did they acquire their members? We have nothing but indications and unsafe conjectures. According to modern views, housing arrangements, rate of wages, and other questions of the same kind are of great significance for the development of morality. In that period which resembles our own so much, this must also have been the case to some extent.

No such question is ever once touched upon in our Christian sources; even secular works give us no adequate account of these circumstances. At present there is a very keen conflict of opinion among experts as to the fundamental questions of ancient statistics.

These deficiencies of our knowledge must not be lost sight of, otherwise we shall enter upon our investigation with too high hopes. Yet our task is not impossible, for there is much that our sources can reveal to those who know how to interpret them.

But are these sources trustworthy? The instances which we began with bring us face to face with this question. Has not the Apologist simply taken the Sermon on the Mount and set down as fact what is there traced out as the Christian ideal? Has he not represented Christians as in very deed what Christians ought and desire to be? We shall not stop to ask if he could have ventured on such a course, when the heathen were ready to charge him with falsification and to reveal the palpable breach between the ideal and the actual. There is no ground to doubt the reporter's integrity. Nor can we simply cancel the credibility of two contradictory reports. For it is far more probable that they provide us with two aspects of the same picture, the one emphasising its lights and the other its shadows. This is the case with our entire material. All these Christian writers have a definite end in view. A few of them, where the interest is mainly apologetic, have embellished the facts to impress "them that are without," but as a rule the writer addresses his work to his brethren in the faith, and throws light upon blemishes rather than merits. We must not expect an entirely objective treatment proceeding upon sober and disinterested observation. Such a representation could come only from the hands of one who stood apart. But in this case it is just the heathen writers that are most untrustworthy. Tacitus records on mere hearsay all the calumnies that were rife among the people; and when a man like Pliny came to be better informed on Christianity, he changed his opinion about it, but thought it beneath his dignity to do anything more in the matter. From the Jews no contribution at all is to be expected.

Thus we remain practically dependent on the sources mentioned above. Even these require to be employed with due consideration of their aim and point of view. The most important material at our command is without doubt that which these sources unconsciously supply, facts altogether independent of the writer's personal views. Such facts, however, are few, and we should deprive ourselves of substantial assistance did we consider nothing else. However poor we are in accurate information as to the moral standing of the communities, the moral views of primitive Christian writers are quite clear. It is by no means so difficult to construct a New Testament ethic out of these sources. There is a great temptation to write one. But as our desire is to present not theory but fact, not reflections but actual ethical forces, we must exclude all mere theorising and speculation. Yet whatever has a practical aim, whatever comes before us in the form of counsel, belongs in many ways to our theme. Exhortations, especially when frequently repeated, enable us to form conclusions as to actual defects. A passage like Rom. xii.–xiv. is in this respect specially instructive, as it is based upon the Apostle's observations in all his Churches. Conclusions of this kind, however, are not always justified. There are exhortations which have become so to speak stereotyped, belonging simply to the set form of Christian counsel. In the Didache (chaps. i.–vi.) and in the Epistle of Barnabas (chaps. xviii.–xx.) a pre-Christian Jewish catechism is incorporated. We cannot discover from its instructions the failings of the Christian communities in which it was employed. Yet here, too, we possess available material. For—and this is the second point—we can draw from it a picture of the living ideal of the Christians. This ideal we must know, or we shall be quite unable to estimate the actual state of matters. It would be unjust to measure the moral standing of a primitive Christian community by our own moral standard. It would be equally wrong to apply one and the same standard to the Church of Jerusalem and the Pauline Churches for the purpose of estimating their moral condition. We must always ask, what was it these Christians desired to be? Not till we know that can we decide correctly what they were. Lastly, the ethical ideas of leading men had great educational significance for the Churches. It was Paul that moulded the moral judgment of his Churches consciously and unconsciously. His personality operated directly in manifold ways, and perhaps features of it whose practical significance was not quite clear to the Apostle himself.

But along with his personality there were his exhortations whose richness is only partially reflected in his epistles. Oral instruction of this kind would not remain without fruit. Constantly reiterated, these admonitions must at length have passed into the moral consciousness of the Church, and to some extent become operative forces. The significance of literature bearing on the Church's constitution like the Pastoral Epistles and the Didache lies in this. They tell us what ought to be, and enable us to conjecture what must have been effected in course of time. In spite of their ascription to apostles, early composition, and great wisdom, these works would not have been preserved had they not proved themselves, amid continued use, to be an effective means of religious and moral instruction, of developing a moral judgment and liberating moral energy.

In a word, our material is much more copious than at first sight it seemed, only we must know how to procure it out of the sources. It is impossible to formulate general rules. The test of any method is its application.

One question remains to be discussed. If the ideal and the thoughts that determine it cannot be disregarded, should there not be set forth before everything the moral ideas of Jesus, the demands He made on men? I believe not. In the teaching of Jesus two distinctions are to be made. We have first of all the single utterances. These are not intended as a series of ethical injunctions, as a new law; what is great in them is rather the distinct separation of morality from the domain of usage (Mark vii. 14 ff.), and of law (Luke xii. 14). The later conception of them in this fashion, their varied effectiveness, and the interpretation put upon them, will each in its own place engage our attention. On the other hand we have the few fundamental ideas, the joyous earnestness, the sincerity, the inwardness, all reaching their climax in the cardinal point of the relation of children to the Heavenly Father. These require no further definition. Their greatness is their simplicity. Not so much spoken as lived, not so much handed down as felt, they have continued to operate as forces without any great consciousness of such operation on the part of men. We shall see that the different ideals of early Christianity have adopted them, but have not exactly sprung from them. The course of Christ's ministry was not at all adapted to form the basis of a Church or an ideal Church constitution.

INTRODUCTION

One of the most outstanding features of that ministry, the cause at once of the Pharisees' misunderstanding and hatred, was the attraction which publicans and sinners had for Him. He did not keep apart from them, neither did He condemn them. He sought the lost with yearning love, in the sure confidence that moral purity can never be polluted through contact with the impure, but that, on the contrary, a blessed influence streams from it upon the unholy, that good is mightier than evil, God stronger than the devil. Applied as it was by Jesus, this was something absolutely new compared with the terror of pollution adhering to all ancient religions. It is the glory of Jesus that He is the Saviour of sinners. Could He at the same time be the Head of a Church of the Saints? That His disciples must form one there was no doubt. The difficulty, as history abundantly testifies, was to reconcile those two facts. It was acutely set forth in Celsus' criticism (Origines, iii. 59), and is expressed shortly and clearly in the fact that into the mouth of Him Who said, "I am not come to call the righteous but sinners" (Matt. ix. 13), there was put this other word, "I will elect for myself the good; the good whom my Heavenly Father hath given me" (Gospel of the Hebrews, apud Eusebius, Theophania, p. 234, Lee).

Christian Life in the Primitive Church

Book I

THE PAULINE CHURCHES.

CHAPTER I.

THE EDUCATION OF THE CHURCHES.

ANYONE who desires to estimate the morality of the early Christian Churches must enquire first of all into the manner in which Christianity morally influenced mankind. The most important factor, of course, was the new Spirit which it communicated, and which in the domain of morals also constituted the enabling power. But this power required to be laid hold of, and guided to a definite end. A new ideal of life had to be imparted to men, while existing moral sensibilities and notions had to be radically transformed.

We know little of the nature of Paul's missionary preaching, at least in its ethical aspect. It is not improbable that this particular element was made very considerably subservient to the great fact of salvation, of which the Apostle felt himself to be the preacher (1 Cor. ii. 2). In particular, this is likely to have been the case in the synagogue and among those God-fearing heathen who had already received some degree of moral training in it. Moral instruction was not—could not be—entirely neglected. The two epistles which he wrote to the two churches as yet unknown to him personally, the Colossians and the Romans, bear witness to this. In the former, we have the famous table of domestic duties, iii. 18; while the latter gives us a still more comprehensive picture of Christian morality in hortatory form. To these we must add some passages in the other epistles, where Paul appeals to earlier utterances of his own. These form direct and telling evidence of the moral character of Christianity. The exhortations previously given to the Thessalonians deal with chastity and honesty (1 Thess. iv. 1 ff.). In writing to the Corinthians (1 Cor. vi. 9, *cf.* iii. 16, vi. 15) the apostle takes for granted their knowledge that those who are stained with heathen vices shall not enter into the Kingdom of God. The Galatians had already received the same warning (Gal. v. 21). In the same passage he recounts what he considers to be absolutely incompatible with Christianity. (*Cf.* also 2 Cor. xii. 20, Col. iii. 5, Rom. i. 29 ff.)

These enumerations of vices are not altogether new. Paganism knew something similar; in orphic circles this was the form in which ethics were treated. Paul was influenced chiefly by the method which the Jews followed in the instruction of proselytes; but he does not follow any one pattern slavishly. There are no two enumerations which entirely agree. Under the influence of his environment he was always able to bring forward new aspects of moral truth.

Bearing in mind the necessities of his readers, he emphasised now one point, now another. With keen eye he detected racial failings as well as those confined to special localities, and sought from the outset to combat them. It was, in the first place, sins of the flesh, unchastity culminating in "that which is against nature," that met the Apostle at every step, and especially in Corinth, as the characteristic of contemporary heathendom. Heathen ethic went far when it made adultery punishable. St Paul went beyond that, combating at once all unlawful sexual intercourse and all excesses of the life of pleasure tending thereto. In Jewish thought whoredom and idolatry are very closely connected. Paul represents covetousness also as equivalent to idolatry (Col. iii. 5). Self-seeking in all the various forms in which it disturbs the peace of church life makes the second category. More than once Paul had occasion to lay great stress on this. It was certainly his own experience he was recording when he characterised the heathenism of the time as impiety towards gods and men, and especially towards parents, and as destitute of truth and love (Rom. i. 30 f.). In all this he sees works of the flesh, movements of the natural man in his state of alienation from God. In a remarkable way he sets over against this condition the Christian ideal, as the fruit of the Spirit, the uniform sentiment of men bound to God through the Spirit of Jesus Christ, unfolding itself in love, joy, peace, long-suffering, kindness, goodness, faithfulness, meekness, temperance (Gal. v. 22 f.). That a corresponding outward demeanour shall accompany such inward disposition follows as a matter of course.

Naturally enumerations like these do not embrace the whole field of the Apostle's ethical teaching. With an "and such things" he gives the thoughts of his readers room to supply out of their recollection of his earlier instructions what appears to them to be important in the present case.

It is only when writing to churches where he has not as yet worked personally that he thinks it wise to state in rather more detail the moral ideal of Christianity.

In the first place we have the valuable table of domestic duties in the Epistle to the Colossians (iii. 18-iv. 2), which became the pattern for so many old and new systems. Here also we find in the forefront (iii. 5 ff.) a warning against the vices of fornication, uncleanness, inordinate affection, evil concupiscence, and covetousness which is idolatry. These are expressly represented by Paul as the main characteristics of his readers' pre-Christian life. He demands the putting away of all such vices, especially anger, wrath, malice, blasphemy, filthy communication, lying; and the putting on of a Christian character, a heart of compassion, kindness, humbleness of mind, meekness, long-suffering, forbearance and forgiveness, love and peace. To this end the effectual means are Christian teaching, common song and prayer: in a word, the decided turning of the whole community and of the individuals who compose it to God and to the salvation given to us in Christ. How this teaching is to find expression in Christian practice the Apostle indicates in a few powerful touches. The subjection of the wife to the husband, which in heathendom was a legal slavish relation enticing her to seek emancipation, becomes for Christians a voluntary submission which has its origin in Christian decorum. The wife, in return, has a claim to love and good treatment at the hands of her Christian husband. So too with the children. Their subjection to paternal, or as Paul, adhering to the decalogue, says significantly, parental authority, recognised by the whole ancient world as of the severest kind and amounting to absolute deprivation of rights, is regarded in Christian circles as a moral duty pleasing to God, while the obligation to loving and gentle treatment is laid upon fathers. Slavery is not abolished, but the condition receives a new moral aspect. The vision of the exalted Lord gives the slave joy in obedience, not in self-interested service, but in sincere endeavour to secure the true welfare of his master, even at the risk of earning punishment instead of recognition: Christian hope holds out the promise of future compensation.

On the other hand, with the consciousness of being answerable to the Lord in heaven, the Christian master feels the duty of justice and reasonableness towards his slaves quite otherwise than if that duty were grounded on Stoic teaching. The passage closes, as it began, with a recommendation to uninterrupted prayer, thanksgiving and intercession —a remarkable indication of the source which supplied the power for such a life.

The moral ideal of Christianity is gone into with more detail in the exhortations which form the second part of the Epistle to the Romans. Here in the most compressed form we have a multitude of the highest Christian obligations poured out in a manner without parallel in the whole field of Christian literature. In the front stands the exhortation to deliberate separation from the heathen manner of life by consecrating the whole man, even the physical being, to God (xii. 1 f.). Thus the entire moral demeanour of the Christian comes under the category of a "reasonable service." His highest motive and aim is the fulfilment of God's will which is identical with what is good, acceptable, and perfect. This involves a total change of the idea of worship. It is no theurgic action, which seeks to work upon the Almighty and so to extract something from Him, to turn His anger aside and to draw His saving power to one's own service. Moral conduct, the voluntary fulfilment of God's will is the "reasonable service." The essential equality of all adherents of the Church follows from this view. There is no longer any offering or any priest, but different forms of activity within the life of the community according to the variety of individual powers and tasks. To this there correspond the modest recognition of oneself as a member of the whole body and the joyous and loyal fulfilment of the duties that fall to one's share in the service of the Church, be it in word or in deed, in teaching or edifying, through a loan, legal assistance, or alms. Everything turns upon love, which, free from hypocrisy, abhorring evil, and cleaving to good, keeps fast hold of brotherliness as its *goal*, yields respectfully to others, and does not seek any haughty self-exaltation. Christian life is a restless eagerness, as if the Spirit seethed. The consciousness of serving the Lord brings joy in hope, patience in suffering, and constancy in prayer. It is an ardour which goes beyond one's own community, and renders to Christians, from whatever locality, needful support and hospitality. Even that does not suffice: Christian morality soars to a loftier level still, to an attitude towards enemies that contradicts all natural feelings.

The Apostle here expressly inculcates the Lord's command to renounce revenge; not evil for evil, but good and blessing instead of curse for the persecutor. The truly fine revenge of satisfying the enemy's hunger and thirst, which the wisdom literature of the Old Testament had already enjoined, here finds its still higher realisation in love for the sake of peace. This does not mean that all natural feelings are to give way to a stoical ἀταραξία or the callousness of a Buddhist saint. Everything truly human is to be sanctified; we are to rejoice with them that rejoice, and to weep with them that weep. The leading note here is not the thought of flight from the world, but the victorious conviction that good is stronger than evil. Hence follows a willing obedience to the "powers that be" which are recognised as God's servants even when making inconvenient demands for taxes. Hence above all we arrive at the supreme principle of love of neighbour, which transcends the decalogue as obedience transcends law. The further discussion of the relation subsisting between the weak and the strong is nothing more than the application of this principle to the special circumstances of Rome. The prospect of the *ever-nearing* salvation exhorts to ever-increasing eagerness, to avoid all that belongs to the works of darkness, gluttony, extravagance, anger, and all that fleshly desires excite in us, and rather to lead in union with the Lord Jesus Christ an honest life that does not require to shun the light.

This specifically Christian character is emphasised by Paul. The words of Jesus Christ form the Apostle's guide, even though it is the preaching of Christ and Him crucified rather than the words of the Lord that the Apostle has in his mind when he writes of the λόγος τοῦ Θεοῦ (Col. iii. 6). Christ, the fulfilment and end of the law (Rom. x. 4), is also and in a higher sense the founder of the new law of love, (Gal. vi. 2, *cf*. 1 Cor. ix. 21), not as the teacher of a profound exposition of the law, not only as the pattern for Christians, but above all as He whose spirit is become within them a new vital power. In mystical union with the exalted Lord (Rom. xiii. 14, vi. 3, Gal. iii. 27), the Christian attains the power to realise the ideal of Christian morality, while at the same time the prospect of the Lord's advent sharpens his feeling of responsibility.

The Apostle's thoughts are so fixed on the exalted Lord, that the Saviour Who walked the earth—apart from the few sayings of Jesus Christ received by him through oral tradition—is almost entirely lost. Even in his thought of Christ as the Pattern, it is not single features of the earthly career of Jesus Christ that float before the Apostle's eyes, but the great fact of His laying down the form of Godhead (2 Cor. viii. 9, Phil. ii. 5 ff.); the love that gave itself up to death (Gal. ii. 20); the forgiveness of sins (Col. iii. 13), and the adoption of the heathen world (Rom. xv. 7). It was the picture of the transfigured Christ that acquired a tangible form, so to speak, in the Apostle. Hence by way of supplement he can say, " Be ye followers of me, even as I also am of Christ " (1 Cor. xi. 1, *cf.* iv. 16, 1 Thess. i. 6, 2 Thess. iii. 7, Phil. i. 30, iii. 17, iv. 9). St Paul's example ranged itself effectively on the side of his teaching, and it was a picture of real Christian morality that the Apostle supplied to the communities which he addressed. Recall only the multitude of outward and inward troubles which he bore with patience and joy (2 Cor. xi. 23 ff., xii. 7 ff.); the unselfishness with which he toiled at night to maintain himself (1 Cor. iv. 12, 1 Thess. ii. 9), and the loving pastoral care with which he tended each individual (1 Thess. ii. 10 f.). Paul can claim to have fulfilled his Lord's commandment to bless and not curse one's enemy (1 Cor. iv. 12 f.).

Paul seldom appeals to the law in connection with the moral demands which he makes (1 Cor. xiii. 34). From Scripture he takes only occasional instances as examples or warnings (Rom. iv. 17 ff., 1 Cor. x. 1-11). All the more weight is laid by him upon the Christian consciousness of his communities. With all due regard for the judgment of them that are without (1 Thess. iv. 12, Col. iv. 5), they were nevertheless to feel their complete superiority to these and the fundamental distinction between them, while on the other hand they were to feel themselves members of the one community of Christian churches (Rom. xvi. 4-16), bound to the most consistent ordering of their manner of life (1 Cor. vii. 17, xi. 16, xiv. 36), to the maintenance of the tradition which had come to be formed (1 Cor. xi. 2, Phil. iv. 8 f.), and also to mutual support (Rom. xv. 27)—these things he continually emphasises.

Paul knows that the new moral ideal is not reached with a single stride; one requires to be trained to it wisely and patiently. For that very reason he lays stress on the necessity of growth: "Now is our salvation nearer than when we believed; the night is far spent and the day is at hand" (Rom. xiii. 11 f.; *cf.* Col. iv. 5), "redeeming the time." "Watch ye, stand fast in the faith, quit you like men, be strong" (1 Cor. xvi. 13).

Paul is little concerned with points of casuistry except when they are forced upon him. Then indeed he feels himself to be the authoritative law-giver of his communities. We shall find the first epistle to the Corinthians especially to be the forerunner of apostolical ecclesiastical ordinances (διατάξεις, *cf.* 1 Cor. xi. 34). But even here he leaves as much as possible to the independent judgment of the community (1 Cor. x. 15), and the individual (1 Cor. x. 27). He still relies unreservedly on the working of the Spirit. Everything turns upon Him in Christianity. He not only points the way (Gal. v. 25), but at the same time constitutes the enabling power (Rom. viii. 12 ff.). Such a Spirit is above law. He produces his results spontaneously in the love whose marvels Paul has celebrated in 1 Cor. xiii. "Inexhaustible in the creation of new forms and manifestations, He fills up all blanks in the code of duty and moulds the life from inner impulse" (Weizsäcker). Where this Spirit was a living power and found such eloquent expression through the words of the Apostle, we may be sure that the moral life would assume a form worthy of God, would be truly Life in the Lord.

Is this a confidence which the result justifies?

THE PAULINE CHURCHES.

CHAPTER II.

The Church of Corinth.

ALL towns bear an individual character, and the particular features of Corinth are familiar. Occupying an incomparably favourable site at the meeting-place of two seas, with magnificent harbours on both sides, and a towering fort to guard it, the town had been famous for ages as the wealthy and luxurious Corinth. Timàus (250 B.C.) is said to have estimated its slave population at 460,000. After a century of desolation Corinth quickly recovered its former greatness. Once more it undertook as the prized inheritance of the past the conduct of the Isthmian games. In the new Julian colony, it must be added, the vices of the ancient Greek town reappeared. Here the Proconsul fixed his seat. The temple of Jupiter Capitolinus and of Octavia recalled the Roman foundation of the city. But the freedmen of Cæsar were quick enough to adopt Grecian manners, although they did not become really Greek.

The great seaport, as is so often the case, was cosmopolitan in character. The motley population, thrown together from all the nationalities of the earth, lacked every bond which common religion and custom could give it. The Jew turned his steps towards the synagogue, the Egyptian towards the magnificent temple of Isis, while the Phrygian worshipped in the sanctuary of the "mother of gods." The greatest attractive power for all, however, belonged to the temple of Aphrodite, with its world-famous cult of unchastity. "To live in Corinthian fashion" was a bye-word for every kind of debauchery. "A journey to Corinth is not every man's business." Many a merchant lost the cargo of several vessels there.

The great commercial city was characterised also in dazzling social contrasts. Round those favourites of fortune whose riches had been quickly acquired, and those business men whose wealth had been painfully piled up, a proletariat gathered of sea-faring folk, porters, and others, who, living on the earnings of the day, lived only for the day. The main business was the transport of goods. No one great industry properly so called was possessed by the town to awake intelligence and at the same time to stimulate energy. In such unceasing excitement there was no room for science and art. Instead, artificiality and the flowery rhetoric of the Sophists prevailed. The name Corinthian denotes the most ornate of architectural styles. In the markets of the world the city was represented by its fine clay wares, antique bronze vessels (in most cases imitations), and its tapestry. It possessed the most lascivious of theatres, and listened to the shallowest of platitudes. Its philosophers were cynics. Along with memorials of Bellerophon, Medea, and so on, the grave of Diogenes was pointed out, and strange tales were related about him—how he had turned upside down all the ordinary ideas of civilisation and manners. The Corinthian's ideal was the unscrupulous enforcement of his own individuality. The merchant toiling upward by all possible means, the glutton yielding to his every desire, the athlete steeled by physical exercises and bidding defiance to every power—these are the real Corinthian types; in a word, the man whom none surpasses, to whom nothing is impossible and nothing denied.

A remarkable contrast was presented when somewhere in the autumn of the year 52 the Apostle Paul left Athens, a city which maintained the honourable tranquillity of ancient Greek custom and wisdom, and found himself amid the bustle of this modern town. Yet, strangely enough, what he sought for vainly among the philosophers of Athens—viz., responsiveness to the truth—he found here among a mass of proletariat driven together by purely earthly interests. His year and a half of activity must have produced rich results. A great church arose.

Three years had passed since then. In the interval Apollos had made the city the scene of his labours; Paul too had kept up his connection with the Church in many ways. It was now that he wrote to her the first of the two epistles which we now possess. A few months elapsed and the second was dispatched. Much may have occurred in the interval, but it is the same Church that is depicted in both epistles. What sort of picture then do they present ?

If only we possessed more information as to the inner circumstances of the community! We cannot estimate the numbers with any degree of accuracy. Only a very few names are known to us. Everything, however, points to the probability of the community's having attained a considerable size. It had outlying branches in other places of the province of Achaia (2 i. 1). In the port of Cenchreæ it is possible that there was an independent church (Rom. xvi. 1).

The picture usually formed of this community of Corinth represents it as composed of merely poor and uncultured people. I do not believe that correct. Paul, it is true, speaks of "not many wise after the flesh, not many mighty, not many noble." We must distinguish, however, between "not many" and "not any." On the contrary Paul indicates that people of superior rank, and no inconsiderable number of them, did belong to the Church. We shall see, too, how social distinctions cut deep into the life of the community. A man like Stephanas (1 xvi. 15) must have been well off. Lawsuits concerning property were certainly not raised by slaves and poor seamen. The Apostle asked the Church for a large contribution to the charitable fund which he was collecting. If, so far as he was himself concerned, he renounced all support from the Corinthians, it was not because the Church was poorer than others, but on special grounds. People who discussed the superiority of Alexandrine allegory or of a simple style of preaching, could not have been without considerable culture.

This community, indeed, must have presented a very motley appearance. As Paul says, there were Jews and Greeks there, but under the latter designation we must remember he includes all non-Jews, the heathen of all countries. There was only a small proportion in whose veins Greek blood flowed. Romans, Asiatics, Egyptians—all were there together.

What was the bond, we must ask, that held all these together? What was the new element that gave them something in common and lifted them out of the world that lay about them?

It was in the first place the name of Jesus Christ; they were baptised in it (1 i. 13); they confessed it (1 i. 2). The power contained in this name is indicated to us by Paul. It is the Shibboleth which reveals the man who possesses the Spirit of God and the man who does not. The glad confession, "Jesus is the Lord," and the hostile, "Let Jesus be anathema" (1 xii. 3), are the two antagonistic forces; two worlds part asunder on this name, two spiritual kingdoms.

In the second place it was the Spirit of God possessed by all of them, Who manifested Himself with demonstration and with power. It was not the knowledge, however important and rich in result, that there is one God, Maker of Heaven and earth, which was the distinguishing element. Many Jews and adherents of the synagogue already possessed this knowledge. Everything turned on the possession of the Spirit of this God, Who proved Himself to be mightier than all the Spirits and demons of heathendom. It was in the full sense of the word a communion of the spirit which consisted in a continuous and incredibly intensified enthusiasm, in an inspiration which exalted every faculty to the manifestation of miracle even in the natural domain. To this Spirit nothing was impossible. He found utterance in ecstatic speech, imparted hidden mysteries, and made prophets and teachers of the uncultured. He inspired every sort of manifestation of ministering love, of guiding wisdom, of self-sacrificing devotion.

He performed miracles, he healed diseases, moved mountains, and transformed men, who felt themselves miserable and oppressed, into a cloud of witnesses overflowing with strength and courage.

This communion of the Spirit found outward unity in the devotional meetings. We know practically nothing of the form which these assumed, when and where they came together, how often and for what various purposes. We may suppose that the house of one of the better-off members offered the community hospitality. At the outset, according to Acts xviii. 7, it was the house of a proselyte, Titius Justus, which was next the synagogue. For a later date Gaius has been thought of (Rom. xvi. 23).

From the notice concerning the collection (1 xvi. 2) we may assume that the first week-day (our Sunday), as distinguished from the Jewish Sabbath, and in commemoration of the Resurrection of the Lord, was fixed as the day of regular assembly.

Here, however, we must distinguish between meetings solely for edification and those which bore the character of a common meal. These latter certainly took place in the evening.

To appreciate the ethical value of this devotional life, it is an exceedingly significant fact that we have to assume a zealous and active participation of all members. There was no trace of the distinction between a ministering clergy and a worshipping people. Every one took part, every individual contributed to the common edification. "When ye come together, every one of you hath a psalm, hath a doctrine, hath a tongue, hath a revelation, hath an interpretation" (1 xiv. 26). The marvellous wealth of

THE CHURCH OF CORINTH 17

the Church, for which Paul praises God with thanksgiving, consisted in this manifold and effectual demonstration of the Spirit in its midst (1 i. 4 f.).

There was, however, danger involved, and first, the danger of disorder. Where there was no unified and authoritative management, where, too, the Spirit was revealed in such manifold fashion, confusion was almost unavoidable. While one stood prophesying before the congregation, another would feel himself seized by the Spirit, and without waiting, would move from his place and begin to speak aloud. Or there might be some ecstatic pouring out a flood of inarticulate sounds, after the fashion known as speaking with tongues. It was, to be sure, unintelligible, but there was profound significance in it, and some of the congregation possessed the gift of interpretation. But no sooner had one begun to reveal its real meaning, than another with the same gift, who thought he understood better, would interrupt with a cry (1 xiv. 27 ff.). In view of the excitability of these Southerners, it is hardly possible for us to imagine the animation of scenes like these. The fact that nothing worse took place is a good indication that the spirit was indeed of God. Paul bears excellent testimony to the Church, when, with all his insistence on order, he looks to its own intelligence and self-mastery to remove all these blots. He does not once think of limiting the general freedom of speech by concentrating the direction of worship in the hands of a single person or a few individuals, a means adopted in a later period. "Ye all can prophesy one by one." All he does is to prescribe that in each meeting not more than two or three prophets shall speak, and two, or at most three, ecstatics, each through an interpreter; but they are to speak one after another, not all at once.

If another is seized by the Spirit, then the first is to resume his seat—a wise precaution against too lengthy addresses. Those, too, who are moved by the Spirit can and must to some degree retain the mastery of themselves. "The spirits of the prophets are subject to the prophets."

A second danger consisted in the wrong valuation which was set upon these operations of the Spirit. The common notion that the more wonderful is also the more divine was to be met with within the Christian community as well as elsewhere. Indeed, when once the Spirit came to be looked upon as a divine power affecting the natural life in the first instance, it was only to be expected that the greatest demonstration of the Spirit should be found where the greatest disturbance of natural functions took place. Here the moral worthlessness of such a view came clearly to light. It recalled the old heathen *mantic* too vividly, which, out of lifeless things like the hollow of Jupiter's Oak at Dodona, or out of the mouth of priestesses in a state of narcotic stupefaction or ecstasy, claimed to know the oracle of God. Almost no value was set upon the simple form of sober instruction which Paul regarded as no less a gift of divine grace (1 xii. 28); this coveted gift must be either prophecy or glossolaly. The latter, however, on account of its unintelligibility, was ranked far above the former, so that all were fain to possess it, and probably many fancied that they did. Paul was constrained to emphasise in the strongest terms

THE CHURCH OF CORINTH 19

that while the charismata were all entitled to honour
(1 xii. 1-3), as manifestations of God's Spirit (1 xii.
4-30), the aim should be to strive after the greater
and more valuable of them (xii. 31-xiv 1). The
greatness of a gift did not depend on its miraculous
form, but on its value as a means of edification for the
others (xiv. 1-25). The speaker with tongues therefore was to pray for the gift of exposition (xiv. 13), and
prophecy was to be preferred to glossolaly (xiv. 1 ff.).
In the last resort this domain also was to be governed
by the duty of love (xiii.); it is the revelation of moral
energy which makes a deep impression upon those
without (xiv. 23 ff.). This wonderful development of
the moral judgment which Paul here describes from
nature is also warranted by later analogies.

The want of moral grasp which we detect in the
Corinthians' false method of estimating the charismata
by their external form appears again in connection
with baptism. The rite is already beginning to reveal
some trace of the sacramentalism which attaches an
external efficacy to it and afterwards led to the
development of a Christian system of mysteries.
How little anything of the kind was in the Apostle's
thought is shown us by the passage in 1 Cor. i. 14 ff.,
where he speaks of baptism.

It is a matter of secondary importance and is
entrusted to assistants. He had himself something
of greater moment to attend to, the preaching of the
gospel of the crucified Christ, contrary to the present-
day practice of giving every deacon or licentiate the
right of preaching, while the administration of the
sacraments is restricted to the ordained clergy. In
view of this I cannot believe that the Apostle

approved of a usage which he once mentions in order to draw from it an argument for the hope of resurrection among the Corinthians—the practice or malpractice of being baptized for the dead (1 xv. 29). As regards this usage we can only suppose that Christians, out of warm affection for departed relatives, had themselves baptized in the names of their loved dead, that is to say, had their dead friends initiated into Christianity, in order to secure for them also the blessings of Christianity and the future everlasting life. The significance of the act of baptism as a confession was thus abolished, and it was deprived of all its moral effect on the person it was intended to aid. It presupposes a magical efficacy such as we find in the purification-offering for the fallen (2 Macc. xii. 42 ff.), and in many of the Greek mystery rites, even if there is no sufficient analogy for vicarious consecration. It is remarkable that views like these should appear so early in the Christian Church, but in itself it is not to be wondered at. For they were only the adoption in the Christian domain of prevalent ideas, inner resemblance of the method of worship providing the cause and want of moral vigour the impulse. I believe that an injustice is done Apollos when he is made answerable for this exaggerated importance attached to baptism, as a sacrament which produces an *ex opere operato* effect. It lay in the nature of the case. Magic is the complement of mantic. The over-valuation of the "Spirit" avenges itself in a non-spiritual and morally indifferent treatment of worship. "Spiritualists easily become Spiritists" (Jülicher).

With regard to the Lord's Supper, or the meals

which they ate together, a similar distortion of the Apostle's conception was not impossible. In certain passages the language he employs can be understood to indicate a purely sacramental operation of the meal of bread and wine, and at a later date actually had this construction put upon it, *e.g.*, where he describes the cup of blessing as "the communion of the blood of Christ," and the bread as "the communion of the body of Christ" (1 x. 16).

By these words the Apostle himself understands a token of fellowship gathering round the death and resurrection of Christ as its palladium: but it would only be natural that the Corinthians should to some extent understand them in the sense of a "medicine of immortality," a real union with the glorified body and blood of Christ. He sees in the cases of sickness and death which occur in the community the divine punishment of the profanation of the Lord's Supper (1 xi. 30). They might conceive this to mean that the consecrated bread and the consecrated cup of themselves bring death and sickness instead of the hoped-for immortality to those who eat and drink unworthily. Where there is no proper moral insight, everything, even the highest, the purely moral notion, becomes transformed into a magical "something."

This, however, was not of much importance. On the contrary, what Paul has to complain of is the want of solemnity. The sacramental idea is still practically of no account. The Corinthians treated the Supper as a common meal, where they feasted and drank to the full, as was customary in the festive banquets of the heathen. We shall have occasion to return to these irregularities at the Lord's Supper in connection with the social blots in Corinth. Here it is sufficient to state that, along with the want of love, Paul had also to contend with a want of discipline and order.

Two points, however, are clear. The Church's worship is still securely based on the principle of a true service of God, in which the glorifying of God goes hand in hand with mutual improvement in spiritual edification. There is no indication of the desire to make an impression upon the deity, which constituted the kernel of every pre-Christian cult. It was a long time before Christianity lost its insistence on this point and allowed its worship of God to sink from a truly spiritual and moral elevation to the level of a theurgic act.

The second point is that this devotional life forms the only unifying bond of the community. We shall afterwards recur to the weakness of the Church consciousness. In ordinary life each one went his own way. It was the Spirit which was felt to be the new, the incomparable possession. But this Spirit appeared not as the moral principle which penetrated and glorified all religious relations, but as a power which in wonderful wise magnified the natural capabilities of man. He did manifest Himself also in the life of the individual, but the assembled congregation was the special field of His operation.

If we are to understand the moral standpoint of these Corinthian Christians, we must view them as Corinthians rather than as members of a Christian community. In spite of the many points which distinguished them as Christians from the surrounding world—and we shall come to see these with more precision and in different aspects—the non-Christian basis everywhere peeped through.

THE PAULINE CHURCHES.

CHAPTER III.

The Church of Corinth (*continued*).

There was no alteration in external relations. The Christians occupied the same house as before and had the same neighbours. They followed, most of them at least, their former calling. Those who were slaves remained so. Rich and poor were still there. So far was the Apostle from proclaiming a programme of social revolution, that on the contrary he declared, " As the Lord hath called every one, so let him walk" (1 vii. 17 ff.); whoever was a slave when converted was to remain a slave.

It is almost impossible for us to understand adequately the difficulties with which this was fraught for the earliest Christians. Even the mission-field of the present day (apart, perhaps, from Japan) does not supply anything similar, for, as a rule, the preaching of the Gospel is accompanied by a new and higher civilisation, which at the very outset raises the young Christian to another plane of existence. At the most we can observe an analogy in the new formation of Protestant congregations amid entirely Roman Catholic surroundings. The individual experiences a complete inward change. But the outward relations remain the same. How was it possible for the convert to avoid dealings with his former companions, neighbours or friends? The Christian slave had to obey his heathen master.

We are not greatly surprised that at first these Christians continued their social intercourse with friends who still remained heathen. How little even our own intercourse with one another is regulated by identity of confession or of attitude to the higher questions of life! They allowed themselves without any scruples to be invited to the house of a heathen family; some of them had no qualms in accepting such an invitation, even when the banquet took place in a public temple. In their view it was no more than social fellowship. Perhaps they knew, from their own past experience, that all the ceremonial observances, with their accompaniment of offerings and libations, were for the majority mere forms combined with more or less superstition, and not in any way an affair of true religion demanding a corresponding inward participation.

Why should they as Christians not adopt a similar attitude, and treat them as mere empty forms? They knew themselves to be inwardly far superior to the original significance of these rites, and to be wholly emancipated from the interpretation which superstition gave to them. They could not eschew intercourse altogether. Where was the limit?

Business also brought them into touch with the outside world. How was that to be avoided? It was impossible for the Christian to supply all his wants from companions of the faith, nor could the Christian merchant or artisan confine his customers to these. But wherever business was carried on by such a system of mutual fraud and over-reaching, as prevailed in the ancient world—and to this day in southern countries—disputes were bound to arise. And where there was a regular tribunal, an advantage which the Roman colonies enjoyed over many provincial towns, it was only natural that these disputes should issue in a trial before the public judge. If the quarrel was between Christians and heathens, no other course was possible; and that they should pursue the usual course even when the quarrel was between Christians, is not so strange as it appears to us who from the outset treat the matter in the light of Paul's expressed opinion.

Naturally, however, this continual contact with the outside world brought many dangers for the inward life of Corinthian Christians. One must howl with the wolves, and whoever lets himself quarrel with one who in point of culture stands beneath him sinks to the same level. Hence we can understand how the Apostle vigorously insists on the greatest possible separation from the surrounding world, in which insistence probably he himself represented a not inconsiderable part of the community. It is not to be forgotten that Paul was a Jew to begin with, and however much he had freed himself from all the exclusive prejudices of Jewish race and belief, his views of life were nevertheless quite different from those of the majority of his converts. A Jew looked upon aloofness from all heathen as a matter of course. He did indeed deal with heathen in the way of business, but even this in the view of the stricter rabbis was restricted to certain branches of commerce. Never might he enter with a heathen upon any sort of social intercourse if he was to preserve any trace of his Jewish character.

The closest ties, often ties of blood, bound him to his own countrymen. The synagogue offered him not only the right of outward protection, but above all an unconditionally recognised court for all disputes among its members. It is in views and notions so conditioned that we must find the key to the understanding of the opposition which Paul and one section of the Christian community offered to the probably more common procedure sketched above.

Complete separation from all that could in any way entail contact with idolatry was insisted upon. Entering a heathen temple, no matter whether with the intention of worshipping or only of taking part in a sacrificial meal, was considered total pollution, and, therefore, directly forbidden. Intercourse with heathen in their own houses was declared to be at least strongly suspicious. The question was raised whether the unconscious eating of flesh offered to idols was dangerous for the Christian. Here we must not mistake the fine distinction between the opinion of the Apostle and that of the Corinthians. The result is about the same, but the ground is quite different. The stricter section of the Corinthian Church appears to have been guided by a view borrowed from Judaism, but still quite intelligible to the converted heathen, to the effect that heathenism as such produces an outward stain, the work of the demons who are the objects of worship. The nature of this pollution is quite physically conceived. If an animal is offered to a heathen god, or, according to the Jewish-Christian method of expression, offered to an idol, then the demon that lurks in this idol takes possession of the animal and fills its every part. If any part is not used for the offering, but is exposed for sale in the market, it is still infested by the demon, and what is demoniacal in it passes over to the eater whether he is aware of its origin or not. The ancient ideas of both heathenism and Judaism, the material conception of religious operations, meet us here again upon a Christian basis, but elevated through a finer religious and moral sensibility. Paul himself indicates this very delicately when he says of such Christians (1 viii. 7): "they being accustomed until now to the idol, eat as of a thing sacrificed to an idol," that is to say, they attribute to it the same effects as they did when they believed on the idols; only now these effects are realised by them, not as rich with blessing, but as instruments of curse.

Not so Paul; he was moved by the inspiring impression that the prophets were right when they described the gods of the heathen as vanities (Elilim instead of Elohim). Wherever he came to know heathendom more minutely, the fact became clear to him. It was certain that demoniacal powers. bore sway in the whole of heathendom—their might was only too easy to trace,— but demon and idol are not identical. Meat offered to idols did not without more ado become demoniacally affected. It was a general truth which he had learned from his Lord, and had not brought with him from the rabbinical school in Jerusalem, that religious moral operations must not be conceived in an external and mechanical fashion; in a case of the kind everything turned on the consciousness. The meat offered to idols, so far as the market was concerned, he admitted without hesitation. From this it followed for the Christian who received an invitation from a heathen, that he might and should eat of everything set before him which was not expressly stated to partake of the character of meat offered to idols. The same reasoning made a visit to a banquet in the temple impermissible, for there the religious nature of the meal was clear from the first. He sanctioned social intercourse in the private houses of heathen, yet in a tone that resembles a strong dissuasion. For him it was always a matter of conscience, and in characteristic fashion he pushed the conscience of others into the foreground by his method of basing everything upon the obligation of love. Love called for forbearance with the weaker brethren; they were still a little afraid of meat offered to idols. If such a one sees his Christian brother partake of it without harm, either he is offended and the brotherly unity is disturbed, or, still worse, he joins the brother without the same inward justification, and acts against his conscience. That is the most grievous sin, and issues in death. For non-Christians also the Christian is obliged to have regard; what confusion must arise in a heathen's mind if he sees a Christian, who he knows abhors idolatry, eating of meat offered to idols. Let us suppose that a heathen has invited his old acquaintance, in spite of the inward alienation that has arisen between them since the conversion of the latter. He is glad his friend has come. The idea of injuring or provoking him is far from his thoughts. He considers it his duty, however, to notify him that one of the dishes is prohibited, inasmuch as it consists of meat offered to idols. The Christian says, "That makes no difference," and eats of it. It is not the flesh in itself, but it is the eating or the abstaining with its plain confession, "I am a Christian," that is the important point. Here, too, as Paul emphasises very strongly at the close, lies the great danger for the Christian's inner life. With all the inward freedom which lifts him above the suspicions that attach to the eating of meat offered to idols, there is the danger that, through a false connivance in respect of heathendom, he may himself become negligent in his Christianity and fall back to the heathen spirit. This is the reason why Paul, in spite of the freedom of his standpoint in principle, wishes for the greatest possible separation from heathen. "Be not unequally yoked with unbelievers" (2 vi. 14 ff.). His desire was to keep his Church like a chaste virgin, far from contact with the world's seductions.

This it was which kindled his zeal against the practice of going to law before heathen courts, and not any utilitarian consideration such as induced Greek societies to forbid the bringing into public of matters and disputes affecting themselves. It would be unfair to see here no other motive at work than the transference to the Christian Church of Jewish exclusiveness and independence. That thought, no doubt, was not absent from his mind. He sees in the frequenting of pagan tribunals by believers a failure to recognise the greatness of the Christian Church, which is called by its Lord to take part in the judgment of the world. In his eyes the practice is almost a denial of the Lord. The chief consideration with him, however, was the danger with which this contact with the heathen world threatened the Christian community. The Christian should not go to law at all. Paul demands of his Church no more and no less than the surrender of individual right. He repeats what the Lord in the Sermon on the Mount prescribed to His disciples as love's highest expression: better to endure wrong than to do wrong; better to let themselves be robbed than to deprive another of anything. This was the level up to which Christians must be educated. As a matter of fact, too, it might be effected if they came before the Christian Church with their disputes; mutual concessions might be made through the mediation of wise Christian brethren, and the highest Christian duty, brotherly peacemaking, involving even the giving up of one's supposed rights, might be inculcated. Such a course could not be expected from the heathen judge. On the contrary, at his tribunal the heat of the quarrel increased passions and desires still more. Out of self-defence there grew covetousness. desire for revenge, hatred—and whoever hateth his brother is a murderer. "Know ye not that the unrighteous shall not inherit the Kingdom of God."

The influence of paganism made itself felt even in domestic life. And no wonder: the young Christian Church was just about to lift itself out of the world, and could not possibly have already regulated all family relations. Here, *e.g.*, was a wife converted to Christianity. Her husband was far from the new religion. What was to be done? It was a case that must have been of frequent occurrence. So much we gather from the way in which Paul discusses the question of mixed marriages (1 vii. 12–17). There is no authoritative saying of the Lord to settle the question. Jesus was not a teacher of casuistry. He set forth broad ethical principles as self-evident expressions of true religion. The application of these principles to the circumstances of particular times as well as the conclusions to be drawn from them for the totally altered conditions of the new mission to the heathen, was left in the hands of the Apostles. It was not so with Judaism. Such questions had for long been matter of rabbinical discussion, and the fundamental principle was laid down that the change to Judaism did away with all former relations. The proselyte, male or female as the case might be, was under no obligation to his or her heathen spouse, and was strictly bound to enter into a new marriage with a Jew. It is questionable to what extent these theories were only pious wishes of the scribes grounded on the fiction that Israel was lord in his own land, with power to adjust his own legal relationships even with the heathen. Enough that the theory existed. It is conceivable that in the young Christian Church also opinions of this nature were expressed. Many a Christian may have felt uncertain whether his or her union with a pagan could continue. If one came to live in the belief that heathenism was impure and polluting, such sentiments were unavoidable.

It is equally clear, however, that those Christians, who, as we have seen, continued to maintain their intercourse with pagan acquaintances, would have found no difficulty in the continuance of wedlock with a heathen spouse. It was reserved for the Apostle's higher Christian insight to speak the decisive word. Here, too, he understands how to enforce the highest principle. Christianity demands that on the occasion of a new marriage community of faith shall be required (1 vii. 39), but the existing mixed marriage is of no doubtful validity. St Paul formulates his view in sharp antagonism to the existing Jewish-Christian idea of the polluting power of paganism, and maintains that there is a sanctifying power resident in Christianity. Paul's belief in the superiority of the good over the bad, a belief especially remarkable in one who had been a Pharisee, enables him to reverse the relation. Instead of timid flight from what pollutes, he leads a victorious attack on the evil. He finds the proof of his position in the holiness of the children springing from such a mixed marriage. Not the pagan but the Christian partner regulates the religious status of these children: they are holy.

Thus the decision lies with the heathen spouse. If he or she is content with the Christianity of the wife or husband, and puts no obstacle in the way, then the relation may remain. The mixed marriage becomes in this way a means of winning the souls of the heathen for the Lord. But in cases where the heathen partner will not tolerate a continuance of the marriage under the new conditions, then it may not be forced upon him or her. Neither the Christian principle of the indissolubility of marriage, nor the missionary sentiment, can in such a case be regulative. The point here is the spiritual welfare of the Christian partner, and his or her outward and inward peace. This it is which turns the scale: where such well-being can be preserved only by separation, then separation must be had recourse to. The whole discussion runs on the lines of two general principles:

"Christianity willeth peace," and "Christianity does not abolish existing relations; it sanctifies them" (*cf.* vii. 15, 17-24).

Outward relations remained the same, but inwardly everything had altered. We see this next in the case of slaves. We have already referred to the great significance which attached to this element of society in Corinth and the Christian Church there. How was it now with the slave who had turned Christian?

At the very outset his joining the Church depended, according to existing law, on the will of his master. The still imperfect organisation—there was hardly as yet a regular list of members, far less a formal control of them—probably made the evasion of this regulation possible. As a rule, however, permission was given. The custom was to allow slaves the free observance of their inherited religion, so far as it did not interfere with the cult which the house followed. In opposition moreover to Aristotle's view that the slaves are a lower class of beings, the continual and vigorous proclamation of the universal rights of man, slaves included, by the Cynics, and especially by Stoics, had probably already caused some alteration in the general view. We may presuppose that where permission was once given, no hindrance would be laid in the way of attendance at the meetings—so far as the arrangements of the master were not thereby disturbed. In other words, the house slave proper of a heathen master had less freedom in this regard than slaves employed in business pursuits or in trade. These enjoyed in many respects an extensive independence, subject, however, always to the goodwill of the master; and at any time the permission, after being given, could be revoked.

It may be readily believed that there were many slaves who, to secure freedom for the exercise of their religion as well as to avoid many moral dangers that threatened them in the place which they filled, thought of acquiring their freedom. That might come in the shape of a gift from the master as the reward of particularly good service, or for special reasons, such as the death of a master, conspicuous honour at the hands of the state, and so on. Emancipation could also be attained by ransom, providing that the master agreed. In this case the Church or individual members of it might have to raise the ransom, because the private means which the law of the time admitted slaves to earn was not always sufficient for that purpose.

It may have been due to this in the first place that Paul dissuaded from ransom, even where it was possible (1 vii. 21), as his principle was not to burden the Church unnecessarily; but there was also a higher moral motive—the maintenance of Christendom in its existing social relations as these had been appointed by God.

The moral strength of the new Christian spirit reveals itself in the fact that there are faithful, obedient, and conscientious slaves. The aspiration after emancipation was often only the manifestation of an impulse which, though excited or strengthened by Christianity, had essentially as little to do with it as the social rising of the peasants in the sixteenth century had to do with Luther's preaching of Christian freedom. In contrast to mere external emancipation, Paul shows how Christ has brought the slave an inward, even although no outward, deliverance. The idea is analogous to the conclusion of Epictetus, himself a slave, that the good slave is on a higher moral level than the evil master. But the thought of the Apostle has an additional force— quite another practical significance. In the Christian Church the slave can really feel assured of his personal equality of rights, which is also his guarantee that in the future the Lord will bestow on him equal rights, equal glory and blessedness.

Thus slavery lost its terror. Paul is fond of employing it as a picture of the Christian as God's property (Rom. vi. 18, 22). "Ye are bought with a price" (1 vi. 20, vii. 23).

In the case of a Christian master the relation assumed a different form. Nothing is said of the duty of setting the slave free, and we shall see that Paul never thought of demanding it. But the freeman is brought to the consciousness that he is himself a slave of Christ, and so is answerable to a higher Master, not only for his own body (vi. 19), but also for the souls entrusted to him. Nowhere in the epistles is there any mention of the treatment of heathen slaves by Christian masters. We have an instructive exemplification, however, of the position of Christian slaves in a Christian household in the case of Stephanas, Fortunatus, and Achaïcus. I assume that the two latter belonged to the household of the first-named, to the family in the Roman-legal sense of the word. They accompanied their master on the journey to Paul at Ephesus. The master of the house is named first certainly (1 xvi. 15), but the two others are mentioned alongside; as Christian brethren they were all equally dear to the Apostle.

A similar state of matters existed in regard to women. It is to be regretted that we know so little about their status in the public life of the closing period of antiquity.

Rohde is right in maintaining that here too, for certain, usage differed much in different towns. From motley Corinth, with its advanced views, we expect less strictness than is attested in the case of the old-fashioned Athens of those days. Custom varied also with the different ranks of society. The strict discipline which was maintained for the honourable matrons and daughters of the upper middle classes was as little in force among Princesses as it was feasible for the women of the working-classes. In addition to this, all slaves were released from such control, not to speak at all of those—mostly also slaves—who lived in dishonour. If the respectable married woman was forbidden to visit the theatre, if she went to the heathen temple only when veiled in Oriental manner, the woman of loose morals was found everywhere. And Corinth was full of prostitutes. The temple of Aphrodite on the fort alone possessed over a thousand "hierodules," a dedicatory gift to the goddess from men and women, as Strabo tells us.

We cannot discover the character of the female element in the Christian Church. It is certain that many honourable women of better standing were Christians, just as these formed no small portion of the proselytes of the synagogue. But the Christian community could not have entirely lacked persons who before their conversion followed dishonourable pursuits any more than it lacked slaves. The gospel was preached to sinners, and just in these circles did it often find most acceptance.

This consideration shows us the difficulty which the Church had to face in the female question: should the honourable matron, used to a strict morality, sit, not only next her slave, but also next a former prostitute? Should the former lay aside the veil, which she was accustomed to wear outside the house, or should the latter assume it? Were the freedom and equality with men, which were conceded in public life to the hetaira, to hold good, or the chaste seclusion and subjection prescribed by usage for the honourable wife? The gospel recognised the full equality of man and woman in regard to religion, more clearly perhaps than was the case in the pagan cults, or even in Judaism itself. Did not the claim of women to equality of position within the Church follow?

As usual, the freer and more progressive tendency gained more acceptance. Among the Libertines, with whom we shall afterwards become more fully acquainted, emancipated women must have played an important part. They were evidently the least trustworthy element in the Church, the soul of the opposition against the Apostle and his earnest discipline. He becomes impassioned whenever he has to speak of their "emancipation," which nothing could bring to reason (1 xi. 16, xiv. 36 f.). The first point is their appearance in the assembly (1 xi. 2–16). Paul insists on veiling, at least as soon as the woman comes forward with spoken prayer or prophetic address

(4 f.). He produces as motives, custom (13), the order of nature (14 f.), but above all, the relation of woman to man, as fixed by the creation, which gives the woman the same relation to the man as he bears to Christ, and Christ to God. This involves a subjection of the woman to the man, which in turn demands an external sign, "because of the angels," lest they should lust after the woman, who belongs to her husband alone (10). The question, however, goes further. Should the women speak at all in the Church (1 xiv. 34–38)? Paul determines the question by an appeal to usage (35) and to law (34); they are to remain silent. If they wish to learn anything, they are to ask their husbands at home. Undoubtedly, with this strict prohibition, Paul introduces something new into the circumstances of Corinth, a sharpening of discipline which its deterioration necessitated. This explains why at first he tolerates the open prayer and prophecy in the Church by the women, and then forbids all speech by them in the congregation. The whole question seems to have been a specifically Corinthian one. It is worthy of remark that in the two passages quoted, the Apostle appeals to the usage of the rest of the Churches (1 xi. 16, xiv. 36). In places where stricter custom on the whole held sway in regard to the women, nothing similar to these Corinthian disorders appeared within the Christian Church. It was altogether something new to the Apostle, which he learned only by degrees how to overcome.

However pointedly he affirms here in opposition to a false emancipation, not only the steady preservation of good usage, but also the subjection of the wife to the man, it is yet characteristic of him, as also of Christianity, that at the same time he does not forget to assert the religious equality of the two sexes. This reveals his broad and liberal spirit, which, even in the case of an error that called for such strenuous opposition, allows no slackening of principle. It also shows to what an extent this tendency to level existing distinctions—in this particular case, to raise woman—prevailed in the Church.

When Paul, in connection with the story of creation, lays emphasis on the fact that the man is not of the woman, but the woman of the man, and that the man was not created for the woman, but the woman for the man (1 xi. 8 f.), he adds, improving what he has said, or at least supplementing it, "Howbeit neither is the woman without the man, nor the man without the woman in the Lord; for as the woman is of the man, so is the man also by the woman; but all things are of God" (11 f.). The natural order already typified what was realised in Christ. Paul designedly emphasises in his discussion of marriage (1 vii.) the complete equality of the two parties. What he says of the man he repeats word for word of the woman (2, 3, 12 f., 14. 32 ff.); three times he even gives the wife the first place (4, 10 f., 16). And he indicates that it is Christianity which is to be thanked for this equality when he calls husband and wife brother and sister (15).

In sharp contrast to the libertine craving for emancipation on the part of single individuals are the ascetic tendencies which distinguish others. Not only debauchery is prohibited, but all sexual intercourse, even within the sphere of legal marriage. Surrender of full marital relations is demanded of married people, further marriage on the part of widows is interdicted, while the single are not to marry at all.

To understand this line of thought, we must clearly realise that the ancient world as a whole saw something supernatural, something demoniacal in the act of generation. Sometimes it was deified—as in the Phrygian cults, the cult of the Phœnician Astarte, and the Aphrodite cults influenced by it; sometimes it was held on this very ground to be pollution. The idea of the Mosaic law that copulation causes one day's levitical pollution was widely spread in heathendom. Alexander Severus in such a case set aside his morning worship in the Palace chapel. We shall afterwards see what a strong ascetic bent obtained at this time throughout the whole world. It is quite conceivable that this idea found support in the young Christian community of this city of excesses. In view of the immorality dominant in heathendom, and the ceremonial fostering which it received, every earnest moral movement was constrained to urge the other extreme of perfect abstinence within as well as without the marriage state, the renunciation of marital relations, and a vow of chastity on the part of the single.

These subjects had become familiar to the Apostle in the form of questions put to him by letter, very likely as debated points upon which no agreement could be come to in the community; hence there was a desire to hear his opinion. In his treatment of such topics Paul furnishes the best illustration of his method, founded on principle, and at the same time characterised by disciplinary wisdom. " He does not leave the Church in any doubt as to what his opinion is." " Weighing each case separately, he endeavours to settle what was attainable, and to hold open the prospect of what was worth striving for " (Heinrici). His position was all the more difficult, as he was himself not free from ascetic tendencies. The demands made corresponded with his innermost desires, and perhaps the advocates of this view were able to appeal to express statements of his own in this direction. Yet he clearly recognised that the view did not agree with the principles of Christianity. He shows himself to be an Apostle of Jesus Christ in subordinating his own view, his own ideal, to the Lord's authority. A word of the Lord confirmed solemnly the indissolubility of the marriage tie. Paul declares this as absolutely binding. It was a simple consequence of this, when in the regular marriage he demanded the consummation of the same. Marriage is for him an ordinance of God, if only for the prevention of licentious satisfaction of the sexual impulse. To release oneself from this divine ordinance, there was required a special gift of God's grace—continence. Paul takes his stand—we must not omit to observe—in sharpest opposition to the Encratism of a later period, when he makes any temporary renunciation of the marital relation for the purpose of more intense devotion dependent on mutual consent and limited to a short time. He knows too well the danger of temptation to which later ages boldly thought they could bid defiance, only too often to yield to it. He is able to speak with more freedom in regard to the unmarried, be they widows or single. No word of the Lord constrained to marriage where marriage had not yet taken place. So the Apostle can say, " It is good for them if they abide (single) even as I " (8). The father who is firmly determined to keep his own daughter a virgin, does well (37). The widow who does not marry again is happier (40). But he never forgets to represent this only as his view; it is not binding law: the widow is free to marry again whom she will; only let her marry a Christian (39). The father who believes that he brings a disgrace on his daughter, if she remains permanently unmarried, is to do as he will. He commits no sin if he causes her to be married (36). Marriage is no sin (28). Anyone who cannot maintain his chastity does better to marry.

However much Paul prefers celibacy, however much he commends it on the ground of the necessity of unreserved devotion to " things of the Lord " and the nearness of the Parousia which demands the utmost possible separation from all earthly ties—this tone, however, is not nearly so strong as has been often maintained—yet he constantly emphasises that his object in thus writing is solely the welfare of Christians, that he has no wish to lay any snare for them (35), and that he speaks of celibacy as permitted, not as commanded (6). In the end the discussion always comes back to the principle, " As the Lord hath apportioned to each man, as God hath called each, so let him walk." " Art thou bound unto a wife? seek not to be loosed. Art thou loosed from a wife, seek not a wife " (27).

This is not the place to consider in detail the great significance of the whole discussion for the Pauline ethic, but it indicates to us that the Apostle, while considering the danger of unchastity in Corinth a very real one, did not, in spite of all his leanings to asceticism, suffer himself to be deluded by encratite tendencies in the Church. He had in truth good cause to set little store by the moral strength of these Corinthian Christians. There must have been not a few of them to whom the significance of the seventh commandment was not yet clear.

If there was no rending of Christianity from contact with the surrounding pagan world, neither was heathenism at one stroke to be rooted out of the hearts of the Christians. We shall not be astonished if the Christians of Corinth continue to be moved by ordinary human lusts and passions, nor shall we even wonder greatly if we find vice among them in the specially aggravated form which it had assumed in the pagan world of the time, nay, if their whole method of moral judgment was still in many cases pagan.

The seventh commandment is, "Thou shalt not commit adultery." We are not directly concerned here with the manner in which the Lord, in opposition to the externalism that then held sway, brought this commandment into relation with sinful desire. "Every one that looketh on a woman to lust after her hath committed adultery" (Matt. v. 27 f.). What we have to note is that this commandment, which was generally restricted to marriage, had already received a wider application in the late Jewish literature through the prohibition of fornication or sexual relations outside the marriage-bond.

We are accustomed (or ought to be) to look upon adultery and fornication as equally sinful. The Grecian world of that time had quite another view. The respectable wife of a citizen brought up in strict seclusion remained shut up in her special apartments almost like an oriental, and in her case adultery hardly ever occurred. But on the streets hetairæ were continually moving about in crowds, and they practised unchastity as "hierodules" in the service of a heathen temple. A man's intercourse with them, whether he was married or unmarried, was hardly reckoned any offence at all. In addition to this we must add the specific vice of that age, the sodomy, which had eaten its way so far into human thought as to have found philosophical justification. All this Christianity opposed with an inexorable "Thou shalt not commit adultery." But its insistence on moral purity met among the Christians of Corinth with the most vigorous opposition.

In the foreground of the Corinthian misconduct there stands a special case. A Christian has entered the marriage relation with his step-mother, the wife of his father, who is evidently dead. Paul condemns this as incest of the worst kind, and supports his view by the consideration that it is considered such even among heathen. As a matter of fact both Jewish and Roman law forbade the marriage of a son with his step-mother, and only seldom have instances of it been historically attested. Yet one case would not in itself signify much: it would be unjust to conclude as to the moral condition of the Church from the aberration of a single individual. The occurrence, however, assumes the greatest significance through the attitude which the community adopted to it. The Church must have been engaged for a considerable time in dealing with this scandal. It gave rise to a lengthened correspondence with the Apostle, of which, however, only a small part is still in existence.

In the first place, the news which reached the Apostle while he abode in Ephesus must have been to some extent indefinite. Under the impression that the moral condition of Corinth was not quite in order, he had let them have, in a letter now lost, an exhortation in general terms "to have no company with fornicators" (1 v. 9, *cf.* 2 vi. 14 ff.). The Church was offended, and replied by asking how that was possible? If all contact with immoral men was to be avoided, then it would be necessary to retire from the world (10). We must assume that this was an intentional misunderstanding of the Apostle's words.

He had alluded to circumstances within the Church; they behaved as if everything was right there and only the relation to the world outside could be thought of. Paul desired to purge the community of impure elements: the community assumed the appearance of perfect purity. We do not consider here the kind of tone which they allowed themselves to adopt towards the Apostle. Everything turns on the want of self-knowledge, or, as we might better express it, the conscious palliation of a serious moral offence. In the meantime Paul had obtained more accurate information concerning the case, presumably through the Corinthians' own envoys, Stephanas and his companions. We perceive his indignation deepened twofold by the tone of the Corinthians to personal exasperation, not only at the special case, but above all at the conduct of the Church in the matter. The immediate expulsion from the Christian community of such an incestuous person, which was a matter of course for the Apostle, the Church had delayed, and had not taken a single step towards it even when the Apostle in his former epistle had at least hinted at it. Instead of meeting the offence in heavy sorrow and moral indignation, the Church was puffed up and set itself in opposition to the Apostle. That indeed throws a very suspicious light upon the moral judgment and sentiment of this community. But there was worse to come. When he became aware of the facts the Apostle demanded a kind of Divine Judgment. He is not content with mere expulsion from the Church, but requires the Church —in spiritual communion with himself in solemn assembly—in name and in the power of Jesus Christ, to pronounce the curse over the sinner concerned. The Apostle expects as the effect of this the sudden death of the guilty person, with which, however, he connects the hope of his escape from everlasting perdition, delivering him unto Satan for the destruction of the flesh that the Spirit may be saved in the day of the Lord Jesus (5). This can only be understood through a knowledge of contemporary ideas of the curse and its operation, which were in essence the same among Jews and Greeks. From these ideas the conception of the Apostle is distinguished only by the positive moral element. The temporal destruction of the sinner is for him not the end itself, but a means to the end. The end, moreover, is not merely the preservation of the

Church's purity, but the personal salvation in a higher sense of the sinner himself.

What attitude now does the community adopt towards the offence brought thus clearly to light and to the very definite demand which the Apostle makes regarding it?

Paul experiences what he hardly thought possible, a direct refusal. When it was no longer possible to deny the facts, an attempt was made to justify them. We have, unfortunately, but very imperfect information about this stage of the matter and what followed. I think it most likely that it was as follows. The sharp tone which the Apostle adopted in the epistle conveyed to Corinth by Stephanas only provoked more violent opposition. At least, the people who gave the Church its tone would not hear of consenting to his request. Of this humiliating failure Paul is informed, as we may suppose, by Timothy, who arrived in Corinth soon after the letter. The Apostle's whole authority was at stake. He resolved upon a decisive course. He proceeded by sea direct to Corinth, to secure order by his own personal appearance. But now he met with a new and far more bitter disappointment. In consequence of physical weakness he was unable to intervene so impressively as the occasion required. The demand which he had made he could not enforce. Still the Church took the side of the misdemeanant. As suddenly as he had come Paul returned to Ephesus, deeply shaken inwardly. But now came a reversal. What his advent in anger had failed to do, his departure in grief accomplished. The Church came to its right mind. Loyalty to its faithful and fatherly counsellor again won the upper hand. The majority at least of the Church decided, late enough indeed, but still eventually, to agree to his wishes. The curse was pronounced. It is true the penal miracle did not appear. The curse bound up of necessity with excommunication had, however, manifestly an effect of another kind. The sinner came to see his guilt, and repented. In the interval Paul had sent Timothy to maintain his authority in Corinth, and was now awaiting his return restlessly in Macedonia, whither he had gone by Troas to meet him. There he heard of the complete revolution which had taken place, and proceeded immediately to adopt a new method of dealing with the matter. Instead of sternness he lets gentleness have sway, and proposes that the Church should receive back the repentant sinner. That, indeed, is a course which has been declared impossible, and on that account it has been sought to connect what is discussed in 2 Cor. ii. and vii. with a quite different occurrence than the case referred to in the first epistle— a personal insult, namely, which the Apostle received from a member of the Church. There is here, however, a misconception of essential points in the view which antiquity took of the curse. The prophets of the old covenant never weary of affirming that God's anger will turn aside and His threats stop short of fulfilment if Israel repents. The case of Nineveh in particular in Jonah's history is designed to teach that repentance and turning away from sin may undo the effect of the curse. This was also the view of the Apostle and his time. Hence we have the practical consequence that the withholding of the divine judgment amounted to a reinstatement of the sinner by God. As the result of this twofold outcome, the manifested repentance of the sinner and its divine acceptance revealed in the non-fulfilment of the curse, there was nothing left for the Church to do but to concur with the divine acknowledgment. If God forgave, so must the Apostle; and the Church must combine readmission with its forgiveness. Holding this view, the Apostle was quite justified in demanding the readmission of the sinner. And so, in a better way than he himself had thought possible, the ultimate aim of saving the offender's soul, which he took to be the motive of the supernatural punishment, was achieved.

We have gone with considerable detail into these circumstances, because it is only on the ground of all these considerations that the significance of the one case of incest for our question can be made clear. The first impression is very unfavourable. That a thing of the kind could occur in one of the churches still in the first wave of inspiration and so richly endowed is a sad fact which shows a lack of moral discipline. It may be said by way of extenuation that perhaps the guilty person, stupefied by rabbinical theories or cynical views, was not aware of the incestuous nature of marriage with a step-mother. Still the community cannot evade the reproach of inadequate development of moral judgment. Worse still, it tolerated the incest, even excused it, and in the last resort sought to justify it. Is this not a total perversion of all moral notions? If the Apostle was right in affirming that the height of moral depravity is reached when sin is not only committed, but also applauded (Rom. i. 32), how can we look upon these Christians of Corinth as anything but the most reprobate and immoral of mankind? For the action of the Corinthians was no momentary aberration and confusion. It was a deliberate attitude, maintained for weeks in strenuous opposition to the Apostle. It would be a waste of pains to search for motives connected with the offender's social standing or wealth. That would only make the conduct of the Church more contemptible. It is hardly credible, particularly as nothing of the kind is ever mentioned, that apart from this one error he was a specially zealous Christian and conspicuous minister of the Spirit. The personality of the offender is quite a secondary matter; his name is not once mentioned, Paul employing only the reproachful "such a one." But this silence makes the Apostle's personality and opposition to his authority more prominent. We must beware of a too hasty judgment. It would certainly be entirely wrong to represent the Corinthian Christians as fornicators and adulterers. Had they been so, Paul would not have taken such pains with them. He would simply have broken off all connection with them and withdrawn his few true followers from their midst. His continually-renewed efforts bear on behalf of the community a more telling testimony than that contained in the appreciative words at the beginning of the first epistle. The Apostle must have been of opinion that the community's defence of a case of gross immorality was not an error that deprived it of its Christian character. To one with his strict ideas on the point this was an admission that meant much. The behaviour of the Corinthians

THE CHURCH OF CORINTH

was not due to any tendency to immorality among them. It was, so to speak, a purely academic thing. They would have thrust it from them with anger had anyone believed that they were actually capable of exemplifying the conduct which they defended in theory. Cases often occur even in our own day of individuals becoming blindly enthusiastic in behalf of theories, whose application to themselves or their households they would very strongly deprecate. Freedom appeared to be at stake, the very point upon which the greatest fanaticism and intolerance are developed. Probably the purpose was to fight for the Apostle's original views against his own restrictions.

The " All things are lawful unto me " with which Paul opposed Jewish narrowness had become a catchword, and was now made to cover gross licentiousness. In determined constancy to the view which they had once fought for, they met every effort on the part of the Apostle with that uncontrollable defiance which the feeling of power so easily gives where thorough adequacy of judgment fails. For it is just the half-mature and half-cultured who boldly rebel against all usage and order, trusting blindly in their own power. This will demand our attention later.

Thus much is certain. The community's conduct reveals a grievous want of moral insight, but there is no reason to trace it to immoral principles. [In speaking of community we must not overlook the fact that only a section, though at the outset the majority, was concerned, and that the leaders are to be distinguished from those who simply assented.]

This defect of moral insight was perhaps a

consequence of a defect in the Apostle's first preaching. At first (and it could hardly have been otherwise with Apollos) he had not laid any great stress on the moral principles of Christianity. What he had to preach was the Gospel, the glad tidings of the kingdom of God, of Jesus the Crucified, and the salvation which became available for man as the consequence of His death on the cross. That message burned in his soul. The moral aspect was for him almost a matter of course. We must not forget also that to these Corinthians Paul was not only an Apostle of Jesus Christ, but also a born Jew among heathen. They and he had grown up with quite different ideas. He brought presuppositions which they entirely lacked. As surely as he was shocked by the gulf of moral depravity into which he gazed in Corinth—the description of the moral decay of heathendom (Rom. i. 18, 32) is the echo of his intense abhorrence—so surely did he trust, like all great preachers of faith, that the power of the Gospel would produce a direct moral effect. Thus it was with Luther. He did not trouble himself about the moral or immoral consequences that could be drawn from his gospel of Christian freedom until iconoclastic peasants with murder and fire brought home to him the necessity for making the moral inference clear.

The want of clearness in the moral notions of the Church is indicated in the Apostle's remarks in 1 vi. 12, 20, where he is compelled to fight expressly against the idea which represented sexual intercourse as belonging entirely to the natural sphere. *Naturalia non sunt turpia.* This was exactly what was preached by the popular philosophy of the Cynics and of the ancient Stoics, who with their fanaticism for nature, contributed to the dissolution of all moral distinctions. There was a lapse of human civilisation to the animal standpoint when they spoke of sexual intercourse. Zeno and Chrysippus did not shrink from representing incest as permissible. Corinthian Hellenism, misshapen through centuries of habit and altogether distorted through such philosophy, dominated the Christians of Corinth. Into the inward freedom that Christianity brought them, they must first be educated.

Christianity accomplished this task, as we see in Paul himself. With what loving insistence does he discuss the moral responsibility which attaches to men in respect of chastity of the body. "The body is not for fornication but for the Lord, and the Lord for the body: and God hath both raised up the Lord and will also raise up us by his own power." The body is a member of Christ; shall it be given to a harlot? Shall the spiritual union with Christ be lost through fleshly union with such an one? Fornication is the most heinous of all sins, because it is a sin against a man's own body; and the body is a temple of the Holy Ghost which we have from God, through which we have become God's well-won property.

It is wonderful how Paul in this passage makes everything turn upon the most elevated Christian ideas. They were the thoughts in which the Corinthians, as we saw, mostly lived, and constituted the something new that lifted them above their former environment: Christ the Lord with His almighty power, as would be proved in the awaking of the dead, and the Holy Ghost, the principle of freedom, which involves the obligation of a higher standard.

Let us not forget either that Paul established this principle. It cost him much pains, many a hard fight —the motto of this chapter might be chosen from Isaiah xliii. 24. But the final adoption of his view by the majority was a victory not only for his own personal authority but also for the cause of morality. It was the triumph of painstaking instruction.

Let us try to determine from this trend of thought the actual state of morality in the Corinthian Christian community. The method of thought which we have found characteristic of that community in its obstinacy as well as in its conception of moral questions made much immorality possible. But from its possibility we cannot immediately conclude its actual existence. It is true Paul appears to take for granted that there are among the Christians all sorts of immorality and vice when he proceeds to explain the statement of his first epistle, "I wrote unto you not to keep company if any man that is named a brother, *i.e.*, a Christian, be a fornicator, or covetous, or an idolater, or a reviler, or a drunkard, or an extortioner; with such a one, no, not to eat" (1 v. 11). But this enumeration of heathen vices, to a certain extent stereotyped, will not prove the actual occurrence of all these within the Church: it was one case with which Paul was concerned. Much less may the evidence of cases of unnatural unchastity be found in the extended enumeration of vi. 9 f.: "Be not deceived: neither fornicators, nor idolaters, nor adulterers, nor effeminate, nor abusers of themselves with men, nor thieves, nor covetous, nor drunkards, nor revilers, nor extortioners shall inherit the kingdom of God." Paul expressly adds, "Such were some of you—as heathen; but ye were washed, but ye were sanctified, but ye were justified in the name of the Lord Jesus Christ and in the Spirit of our God (again the two principles), vi. 11. He warns them against lapsing to the sub-Christian level and tries to quicken the Christian conscience. If such things had been of more frequent occurrence, and Paul knew of them, he would certainly have condemned them with the same severity as in the one case discussed, and demanded the intervention of the Church. The detailed and vigorous treatment of this special case, as against the few and merely general warnings we find elsewhere, shows that other concrete cases of this kind could not have been known to the Apostle.

It would be just as precipitate to employ these considerations to prove that as a matter of fact the case was quite unique. I do not go the length of saying that it would be unnatural to imagine the Corinthian Church as a pure spot in the slough of immorality which the town itself was. But we must be advised to caution. Such moral depravity as seemed to be indicated in the defence of its incestuous member cannot have prevailed in the Church. It was better than it made itself out to be.

THE PAULINE CHURCHES.

CHAPTER IV.

THE CHURCH OF CORINTH (*continued*).

THE question of Corinthian notions of property seems to call for a less favourable reply. It is true Paul has not so much to say on this point, but the method in which he handles it reveals that he is dealing with a defect of much greater range. The reason why it did not come to be a question of first importance was that it had not the same close connection with the hotly-contested principle of freedom.

At the outset it must be stated that private property in the Christian community was maintained intact. Paul had not the slightest idea of appearing as the representative of communistic ideals in Corinth. Neither do thoughts of the kind seem to have occurred to the community. What we have to observe is rather the opposite extreme of blindness to the Christian duty of love which ought to manifest itself in communicating within the Christian body, and what was still worse, an adherence to the most doubtful heathen practices in business affairs. Paul expressly mentions the covetous and robbers along with fornicators as absolutely excluded from the kingdom of God (1 vi. 10), and therefore to be rigorously kept outside the Church (1 v. 10 f.). That this is no general admonition is shown by the law-suits of the Corinthian Christians. The case mentioned in VI. 1 (τις) of a man bringing a suit against a Christian brother before a heathen tribunal was not an isolated one. We have already discussed the view to be taken of this. Here we are concerned with the process as such, the dispute as to mine and thine. Paul tells them it is a sinking to a sub-Christian level. Christianity is not content with the mere forbidding of everything unlawful in the practice of business. It demands more, the giving up of one's rights where one experiences injustice from another, especially among brethren of the faith.

For these supreme principles of Christian ethic which originated with the Lord himself, the Corinthians, with their conspicuous individualism and their insistence on the rights of every single person, had but little understanding.

Few of them had quite grasped that the Christian of means has a duty to perform to the community. We see an illuminating instance in Stephanas, whom the Apostle praises for having voluntarily placed himself and his household at the service of the Church (1 xvi. 15). What the full meaning of this is we cannot apprehend. One service, however, lies before us. Stephanas, by commission and in name of the Church, has journeyed to the Apostle with Fortunatus and Achaïcus, evidently his slaves (17). Naturally this was done at his own expense. This is a genuinely Greek thing. Athens looked to her rich citizens for λειτουργίαι or services on behalf of the state, and her societies to their well-off members for the defrayal of extraordinary expenses. The reward was a decree of honour. It is also a decree of honour which Paul claims here for Stephanas, though in a quite different sense. He claims from the Church not the mere verbal recognition, but the practical gratitude of voluntary subordination to those who have willingly dedicated themselves to her service. The Church does not seem to have showed such gratitude, and it is doubtful whether the Apostle's desire was gratified.

How little the Church as such was ready to contribute to common purposes we learn from the incident of the collection. This collection engaged attention for a long time. Already in the first lost letter of the Apostle the impulse to it must have been given. The Corinthians entered cheerfully upon the proposal, but begged for further instruction as to how to carry it out. Paul had evidently appealed to their honour—the very point where Greeks were most sensitive. Perhaps the Corinthians thought that the collection was meant to be made all at once. Then the rich members would do their part and the honour of the Church would be saved. What Paul desired, however, was a general participation. So he arranges—following his recommendation to other churches—that every Sunday each shall lay by something for this purpose, so that at his visit the total sum may not have to be got together. This shows great wisdom on the part of the Apostle. He has in view the circumstances of the majority of the members, whose scanty earnings did not admit of large outlays; in small instalments something might rather be asked for.

But indeed this procedure made still higher demands on the individual's energy. Every one knows that men prefer giving a larger sum once than keeping up the regular payment of even a small sum. Had the collection been levied at least as often as they came together for their Sunday meeting, success might have been attained earlier. But a common fund seems to have been wanting as well as a person authorised to take charge of it. To save at home for such a purpose was quite beyond their range of thought. However much the goodwill was present, it failed in practice. How was the individual profited by Paul's promise that if the amount was respectable enough, the Corinthian Church should be represented in the deputation which would accompany him to Jerusalem? The Corinthians did not possess so much congregational ambition.

Paul became convinced that no progress could be made this way. After his short visit to Corinth, he sent Titus (2 ii. 13, vii. 13, viii. 6), evidently with the idea of supplying the want of some competent person to manage the common funds. This step appears to have been of some practical use, although it gave occasion for base suspicions against Paul and his representative Titus. Paul considers it the only method of bringing the matter to an honourable conclusion, and therefore sends back Titus, who, in the meantime, had returned (2 viii. 6, 17). In the epistle which the Apostle gave him, he wisely appealed to the honour of the Corinthians. The zeal of the much poorer Macedonian Churches puts them to shame. They (the Corinthians) abound in every demonstration of the Christian spirit. Why is it otherwise in regard to this grace? They have experienced the love of Christ (again the two motives). Their readiness is admitted. But they must give more practical proof of it. The matter must have engaged the Apostle's attention for quite a year; as time went on he came to lay more and more stress upon it as the solemn outcome of his mission to Greece. This makes his want of success in Corinth all the more painful. Hence the repetition and detail. Once more he acknowledges the readiness and zeal of the Corinthians, which he had lauded to the Christians of Macedonia, who had been stimulated by their example. Once more he insists that at his arrival all shall be in order, lest he and the Corinthians themselves be put to shame when the strangers who accompany him observe that the real facts in the Corinthian community do not warrant his boast. Once more he emphasises the grace of perfect voluntariness, but also the need for cheerfulness, pointing out that liberal giving finds also liberal reward. Everywhere we detect the enormous struggle it required to make the collection a feature of the Church at Corinth, although, according to all that the Apostle says, the congregation was quite capable of undertaking it. Both regard for the Apostle and the Christian feeling of community should have been in themselves sufficient to ensure its accomplishment.

This want of readiness to give, or sense of community, is also to be found in the inner affairs of the Church. It finds its way into the communion-meal, which afforded the highest manifestation of brotherhood in the Church. It was the custom—presumably every Sunday—for the community to come together in the evenings for a common meal. The place in all likelihood was put at their disposal by some better-off member like Gaius. Every man brought his own portion—as opposed to the custom of the Greek guilds, where the cost of the meal was defrayed out of the guild's treasury or by individual members—but the idea was that all the contributions should be put together and then equally divided. In this way the Lord Himself, to whom the gifts were brought, was made to appear the host (κυριακὸν δεῖπνον, 1 xi. 20). Prayer and edifying addresses would consecrate the meal. In reality it had assumed quite another shape. We cannot indeed admit that Christians neglected what was the custom even among heathens and Jews, the consecration of the meal by a libation or a prayer. But the characteristics of a common meal were wanting. Everyone kept what he brought with him for himself, without caring whether the others were all come or had enough to satisfy their wants, and began upon his own supply. Thus even in this common meal the social differences which were felt within the Church itself were painfully acute. While some made a great display with rich, too rich, banquets, others must stand by with empty stomachs and envious glances. Paul considered that this deprived the meal of its essential character. In reality, not only was brotherhood violated and the equal standing of all members before the Lord lost sight of, but the behaviour of those who feasted and revelled even to drunkenness—the reproachful "one is drunk," is not likely to be an exaggeration—profaned the solemnity of the Lord's supper.

There may have been many who attached to it the

character of a joyous banquet, looking more to the glorious second coming of the Lord than to the commemoration of his sacrificial death. Still, there was something offensive in the view, and Paul combated it vigorously. He sets the relation of this meal to the death of the Lord in a clear light, and enforces the view with all his might. He groups these disorders in connection with the Lord's Supper, along with the case of incest, as the worst features in the circumstances of the community. To such irregularities he traces the numerous cases of sickness and deaths (xi. 30), which are a divine punishment for the slighting of the Lord, involved in the profanation of the supper. At this stage he takes the first step towards raising the character of the supper, towards its transformation into a symbolic act of worship, in prescribing that extreme physical hunger is to be appeased beforehand at home. Much of the blame for these disorders in the common meal must be attributed to the want of a fixed constitution, a definite organisation. At a later date, when all offerings were first brought to the bishop to be blessed and divided by him, an effective preventive of such occurrences was discovered. So long as the Apostle was himself in Corinth, it was natural that he should himself direct affairs; in all probability Apollos also enjoyed a natural authority of this kind in the community. But now, when it was deprived of all such authorities, and left to itself, the community no longer knew where to look for the right balance. The truth is, this too was moral weakness; the Church should now have organised itself. Individualism was still too strong, though indeed possessing its valuable correlative in religious enthusiasm. It would be possible to reproach Paul himself with having left an immature Church of this kind without the support of a fixed organisation. Here again, however, the Apostle's greatness is revealed. He is a preacher of the Gospel; a Church organiser only in cases of necessity, and only sparingly obtruding his authority. We saw how he endeavoured to establish the authority of Stephanas in the community as one of the first converts, and as a devoted Christian who voluntarily dedicated himself to the community's concerns. That, however, is done only by way of exhortation.

In regard to these irregularities in the Lord's Supper St Paul speaks with the greatest firmness: "The rest will I set in order when I come." It is the prelude of the apostolic constitutions of the later period (diataxeis), and without doubt the Apostle had a good claim to speak thus authoritatively. He possesses a sort of fatherly authority over the Churches which he has called into life (1 iv. 14 f.). But like a wise pedagogue he spares the feelings of the Church; in jest he threatens them like bad children—shall I come unto you with a rod? (1 iv. 21)—but in earnest he seeks ever to prevail on them by loving persuasion rather than by asserting his authority. Thus he sharply reproached their unbrotherliness, but almost more effectively he continued to address the Corinthians as " brethren," and warned them finally not to neglect the brotherly kiss (1 xvi. 20).

There are other defects than these, also intimately connected with Corinthian peculiarities. If the Corinthian drunkard was a constant figure in the civic comedy, Paul will be in dead earnest in those passages already touched upon, where he names also the evil speakers. We can hardly attach to these the importance of merely preventive warnings, when we see that even in the communion-meal some drank to excess, and when we consider the shameless tone which they allowed themselves to adopt towards the Apostle.

These observations do not emerge into the proper light until we give due heed to the deep gulf that extended throughout the Church. Everywhere we come upon the distinction between strong and weak, if we may so describe the two tendencies, following the Apostle's epithet provoked by the former (1 viii. 7 ff.). We could also employ the terms emancipated, libertines, freethinkers, and, as opposed to them, the narrow party. A clear perception of the nature and origin of these two tendencies is of fundamental importance for the judgment of the community's moral standing.

They do not at all coincide, as has been maintained, with the two elements, out of which the Christian Church was formed, heathens and Jews. About the numerical relation of these two constituents we know nothing. If Paul began his work in the synagogue (Act xviii. 4), it came quickly to a rupture (6 f.).

Probably he was followed into the neighbouring house belonging to the proselyte Titius Justus, the head of the synagogue, by Crispus and his household, as well as many other Jews, *e.g.*, Aquila and Priscilla, and above all by proselytes. Yet the majority of the Church must have been composed of former heathens. These Jews were by no means identical with the "weak": the breach with the synagogue and adherence to Paul and his gentile-Christian community presuppose a great degree of inward strength and freedom. We even find among them people who were so disposed to break with their Judaism as to be ashamed of the mark of circumcision (1 vii. 18). On the other hand Paul mentions former heathen as "weak," when he speaks (1 viii. 7) of their "being with conscience of the idol unto this hour.'"

What, then, does the distinction rest upon? On the one hand we find liberty viewed as the essential of Christianity, as the new principle upon which everything turns; on the other hand, sanctity. Both to be sure are central ideas of Christianity, yet they can become in the highest degree dangerous through one-sided emphasising and mistaken interpretation.

"Am I not free?" So the Apostle begins his self-defence, adopting their tone (1 ix. 1–19). "All things are lawful for me" he frequently repeats out of their mouth (1 vi. 12, x. 23). Perhaps these were words which he had himself used in his preaching at Corinth. But to what use were they put? They were now to justify intercourse with heathen even to the extent of participating in their sacrificial banquets in the temple (1 viii. 9 f.). They were to warrant the abolition of all distinctions between the natural and the moral in sexual intercourse (1 vi. 12 f.). Under this party cry there was pressed forward the emancipation of women, and all morality was laughed to scorn (1 xi. 3 ff.). When actions were in process, when irregularities occurred in the Lord's Supper, "all is allowed to me." The joyful confession of the free gospel was turned into the catchword of a "Libertinism" tending towards lasciviousness.

We have already seen that here and there this

conduct was not so evil in intention; it was more a theoretical defence of the unconditional right of freedom than a frivolity that wished to further immorality. But these Christians were self-deceived. Involuntarily this freedom proclaimed so vigorously as the one underlying principle, stimulated to a licentious use of it. Its true inner nature was mistaken; it was sought for in externalities of every kind. The slave, instead of joying in the freedom which Christ gave him, hankered after outward liberty. The Jew, instead of gratefully recognising his freedom from the constraint of law, exerted himself to secure release from circumcision: others sought also and found the freedom only in things which were unbecoming Christianity and morally impermissible.

In view of later phenomena, the connection which this insistence on liberty established with rationalism is worth noting. As justification for the misuse of the Christian freedom, there was adduced enlightened knowledge or γνῶσις (1 viii. 1). The nature of this rationalism we learn from the discussion of the Resurrection, which is denied because no human conception of it could be formed. This bare rationalism, reminding us of sophistic scepticism, with which, however, almost magical views as to the effect of baptism could go hand in hand, was also regarded as the essence of the Christian doctrine of God. It was a simple matter to take out of the Gospel the thought that there is but one God; it followed that "an idol is nothing in the world" (1 viii. 4). There was no realisation of the fact that there is much between heaven and earth which cannot be explained by this smooth formula—there be gods many and lords many, says Paul (1 viii. 5); that there are invisible powers of which men must beware—Paul names these, after the notions of his time, demons, though our method of more abstract thought would call them the spirit or the tendencies of heathendom; that there is a devil who makes it his object to take advantage of the saints of God (1 v. 5, 2 ii. 11). And so with this rationalism the Corinthians cast both themselves and the weak brethren whom they treated with such contempt into perdition.

Paul employed a twofold argument against "libertinism." In the first place it involves a danger for the strong himself, who, intoxicated by "liberty," becomes careless and falls under the sway of those dark powers of heathenism. " I would not that ye should have communion with devils" (1 x. 20). "All things are lawful for me; but not all things are expedient; all things are lawful for me, but I will not be brought under the power of any" (1 vi. 12). In the second place it is a violation of brotherly love towards the weak, a want of consideration which burdens the strong himself and at the same time brings great danger to the weak through the temptation to act in a way contrary to the dictates of his conscience.

" All things are lawful for me; but all things are not expedient: all things are lawful for me; but all things edify not. Let no man seek his own, but each his neighbour's good" (1 x. 23 f.). "Knowledge puffeth up, but charity edifieth" (1 viii. 1). The conclusion was obvious; the weak must be enlightened. Let it be the duty of love for the strong to raise them to their own high level. Paul replies, not without irony: " For if any man see thee which hast knowledge sit at meat in the idol's temple, shall not the conscience of him which is weak be emboldened to eat those things which are offered to idols? And through thy knowledge shall the weak brother perish for whom Christ died." It is a sin against the brother, a merciless wounding of his conscience, and at the same time a sin against Christ (1 viii. 10–12).

How now about these "weak"? Did they really occupy, as was supposed, a lower level of Christianity? Could they be helped by rationalism? Their weakness was their earnestness. They had learned from the Gospel that here there was something new given them, something quite opposed to their whole former life and requiring the complete renunciation of all that was in any way connected with heathenism. Everywhere they feared pollution, not only through the immorality of heathendom, but equally through contact with demons and their worship. We have already seen that this agreed with a widespread view among the Jews, we may almost say the prevailing view. Jewish Christians were, therefore, so far predisposed to the notion. But not less must the earnest heathen, who felt an aversion to the heathenish immorality and worship, have come to adopt such ways of thinking.

We know only too well the length to which these went. That fornication was forbidden, and that a case of incest like this raised great excitement, follows as a matter of course. Those "weak" in all probability came afterwards to form the kernel of that majority which Paul at length helped to victory. That meat offered to idols was disdained was a plain consequence of the Apostle's utterances—the "weak" of Corinth had the practice of the whole later Church on their side here. But apparently exception was taken—at least some went so far—to the eating of flesh which might possibly have come from a sacrifice to idols. From that it was only one step further to the total renunciation of meat—not out of Buddhistic Pythagorean motives nor out of Jewish scruples, but out of this fearfulness and dread of demons.

But when Paul says, "Therefore if meat maketh my brother to stumble, I will eat no flesh for evermore, that I make not my brother to stumble" (1 viii. 13), he may only be expressing with some exaggeration the unconditional renunciation of all that causes the brother to stumble, without justifying us in drawing conclusions of the above kind from it.

Further, it may have been from these "weak" that the questions touching celibacy emanated. In that case the disinclination to marriage would have to be regarded as a similar increase of the abhorrence of immorality. Above all the aversion to continuing a mixed marriage was in keeping with the abandonment of all that was heathen (1 vii. 12 f.). Perhaps ideas of this nature found expression against the glossolaly which recalled much that was pagan. When Paul establishes the significance and the right of these manifestations of the Spirit among Christians in opposition to the service of dumb idols (1 xii. 2 f.), when he closes the whole discussion with the exhortation, "Wherefore brethren, covet to prophesy and forbid not to speak with tongues" (1 xiv. 39), it surely presupposes that a certain feeling against these was not first of all due to him, but was already felt by some of them in intelligible opposition to the over-valuation of these amidst the Christian community. It is not by any means impossible that here the more sober view is connected with the strict view of the "weak" against that of the rationalists and the desire for wonderful effects. In any case the contrast between "strong" and "weak" was the fundamental one for the Church life of the time.

How are we to judge it? It is remarkable enough to see the Apostle incline now more to one side, now more to the other. In the marriage question his heart was with the ascetically inclined; but he acknowledges the rightness and conditional obligation of the opposite standpoint. However urgently in matters of immorality and emancipation he opposes the libertine positions, in the matter of the meat offered to idols he gives the strong the principal right, only, however, to defend the claim of the weak to forbearance more warmly, and at last to reach a position totally distinct from the attitude of the strong.

It is no uncertain wavering, no indefinite balancing of opposite standpoints; Paul stands above parties. He has the Gospel, "my Gospel" (Rom. ii. 16): they have each only a fraction of it. The whole occurrence shows us the immaturity of this Christian community. Probably not without some thought of this great contrast the Apostle ends by finally calling to them, "Watch ye, stand fast in the faith, quit you like men, be strong. Let all your things be done with charity" (1 xvi. 13 f.).

If we must acknowledge that the "weak" were possessed of the greater moral earnestness, we must also admit the greater moral power of the "strong." The earnestness was dissipated in unevangelical fearfulness, the misguided power turned into unchristian licentiousness. Neither dread nor defiance could lead to the goal, but only liberty hand-in-hand with love.

Up till now we have intentionally kept back one defect, which in many cases has been regarded as of fundamental importance—the existence of parties in the Corinthian Church. It is, however, only one manifestation among others of the defective moral attitude of the community and not the source of its shortcomings. The old view that all Paul says in the first epistle must be referred to one of the parties indicated in the first four chapters attaches far too much importance to the matter. Paul is moved to discuss the parties first, probably by the proper consideration that the important demands which he has to bring before them presently cannot make their due impression until the Church is a unity. For the rest, however, he treats the matter rather as stupid childishness than as a radical defect. The fact that he asserts the highest motives is only in keeping with his invariable method of dealing with things.

The impulse to these disorders was unconsciously given by Apollos, an Alexandrian Jew, who, through his eloquence and familiarity with the Scripture, had proved himself a valiant defender of the Gospel against the Jews. Thus it came about that after the Apostle's departure he arrived in Corinth with a recommendation from Paul's missionary companions, and carried on an active and fruitful ministry in the city. There was no material difference between him and Paul. Paul treats him as an entirely like-minded fellow-worker, not only placing no hindrance in the way of his paying a second visit to Corinth, but even advising him warmly to that course (1 xvi. 12).

Only in form was there any difference, because the brilliant rhetoric of the Alexandrian and his profound allegorical interpretations of Scripture soared far above the simple method in which Paul purposely set forth the chief points of the Gospel. Apollos came quickly to find a circle of ardent admirers. But evidently it was only after his departure that the glorification of this master assumed such a pronounced form as to offend another section of the Church. This latter party maintained that it was Paul, the founder of the Church, to whom the greatest debt of thankful respect was due. As usual, contention sharpened the antithesis, so that the claims and the merits of the opponent were denied. "I hold to Apollos," met with the sharp rejoinder, "I hold to Paul." And when once there were such party cries, it is not astonishing that others should come in, and a Jewish Christian party rally round the cry, "I am of Cephas (Peter)" (1 i. 12, iii. 22). On this matter they may have come to very great differences. But the devotional unity of the Church was not interrupted by it. Paul writes not to the one party, but to the Church of God in Corinth. He does not demand the adherence of all to the one party, but the giving up of every division in the higher unity of the Church; in opposition to the three party-cries originating in the names of men, he sets "I hold to Christ," as the only permissible one. The whole discussion is filled with this thought of the subordination of all human authority to the only valid authority, that of the Lord Jesus, which itself rests on the authority of God. His details as to the proper way to preach the Gospel, the distinction between the "wisdom" and the simple preaching, and the relation between his work and that of Apollos, always reach a climax in the reference to Christ, and beyond Him to God.

An attempt has been made to explain these disputes as a natural expression of the party-spirit so characteristic of the Greeks. A law of Solon forbade impartiality. It was the form which the passion for debate and discussion took on the basis of the new Christian society. This is certainly correct. But Paul sees something different in it: a want of Christian consciousness, to some extent a denial of the Lord. And that is in very deed what this party-machinery in Corinth chiefly teaches us. These Christians were sadly—not to say entirely—lacking in a clear Church consciousness. The individualistic trait which we have repeatedly observed assumes great prominence here.

The enjoyment of unrestrained freedom in private life was insisted upon. In the Church, too, personal taste and individual inclination were followed. Behind the glorification of the authorities there was in the last instance personal vanity, the elevating of themselves above all authority, as Paul very clearly recognised and severely reprehended.

We do not know if there existed a closer connection between this party division and the great antithesis between strong and weak, already referred to. It is not wide of the mark to say that the followers of the richly-endowed Apollos were to be found among the libertines proud of their gnosis, while the followers of Paul, with his tendency to asceticism, were to be found among the members of the narrow party. But it is as impossible to make Apollos answerable for the bald rationalism of every freethinker as to hold Paul responsible for the fearful anxiety of their opponents, not to speak of the Cephas-party, which cannot be suitably accommodated to this view. It is by no means impossible that these divisions in the Church's life crossed each other, some of the Apollos-party being narrow, some of the Pauline party liberal, and *vice versâ*. One thing, however, is clear: both defects arise from one root, viz., the confident, self-sufficient vanity with which they set themselves above all higher considerations.

The exaltation of self is most noticeable in their conduct towards the Apostle. It was only a little thing that in the controversy as to the merits of their preaching they placed Paul and Apollos on the same level, and to a large extent decided against Paul. The Apostle explained, " With me it is a very small thing that I should be judged of you or of man's judgment." But the arrogant tone which they had employed he lashes sharply in the bitterly ironic sentences : " Now ye are full, now ye are rich ; ye have reigned as kings—without us." " We are fools for Christ's sake, but ye are wise in Christ: we are weak, but ye are strong : ye are honourable, but we are despised " (1 iv. 3, 8, 10). We have already met instances of this in their intentional misinterpretation of the Apostle's words, in order to upbraid him in quite unbecoming fashion : " What you desire is impossible "; in their simple refusal of the Apostle's urgent demand ; and in their venturing on personal defiance of him when he appeared in Corinth.

The opposition which had grown to large dimensions within the Church was combined in the course of time with a new and foreign element, the Judaistic agitation. It was only when the two came in contact that the position became dangerous. There may have been some few such Judaists in Corinth at the time when Paul wrote his first letter, and these even as Christians may have retained so much of their Judaism as to adhere to the synagogue instead of to the Pauline Church. Paul attempts to help them with brotherly hand over this barrier. Only in the interval between the two letters can occasion have been given, probably through reinforcements from Jerusalem, to a real aggressive agitation directed against the Church. Our source here is almost exclusively the second epistle. We have elsewhere to speak of the nature of this Judaism. Here its interest for us is confined to the influence which it exerted on the Church of Corinth and its relation to the Apostle.

The attack was aimed directly against the personality of the Apostle. To undermine his authority, his cry of adherence to Christ was taken out of his mouth by the Judaists, only for the purpose of contradicting him and vindicating themselves in a more special sense: "How can Paul say to you, 'I hold to Christ—viz., as pupil?' He has not seen the Lord any more than you. Only we have a right to speak so (2 x. 7), for we are His immediate disciples." Thus the Gospel of Paul could only be imperfect and in need of being supplemented still more. His own moral character was assailed. The collection gave occasion to question the honesty of himself and his associates (2 xii. 16–18). The fact that he had never accepted any support from the Church of Corinth was misrepresented as tending to the support of this suspicion (2 xii. 13–15); here, too, a sign of want of love was sought. His imperious nature was effectively pictured to the Corinthians, already so sensitive to every semblance of tutelage (2 x. 9). The strongly-contrasted weakness which he shows when he appears in person is referred to (2 x. 10 f.). He was not straightforward, not true; that was shown also by the contradictions in his announcements and promises (2 i. 13). As his uprightness, so at the last even his moral purity was questioned (2 iv. 2). The illness which they had seen attack him on his short visit to them came to be looked upon as a divine punishment (2 xii. 7). The revelations boasted of, the vision of the Lord on which he based his claim to Apostleship (1 ix. 1), showed that he was mad (2 xi. 16, xii. 11).

It was a systematic attack which did not allow any point of weakness to escape. It must have had success too, at least to a certain extent. When Paul sets himself to refute in detail the charges raised against him, it is because they must have made an impression on the Church. With one section this was certainly the case. There is to be observed here, as so often in life, a co-operation of entirely opposite extremes; the suspicions to which the Apostle was exposed from the zealous Jews, as an apostate from Judaism, found willing ears among those libertines who were rebels against all law and all morality. It may be regarded as a suspicious indication of the immatureness of their moral judgment, even of the immoral tendency of many members, that there could be any talk at all of doubt about the Apostle's disinterestedness, honesty, and purity. At any rate it shows that their relation to the Apostle was not so respectful as it ought to have been. Paul feels like a father towards the Church, but it had none of the child's unquestioning trust of his father.

Yet here, too, there must be no one-sided treatment. It will be remembered that the Church continually appeals to the Apostle's knowledge. The letter of the Corinthians which replies to our first epistle was no private communication emanating from individuals or a group of individuals: it came from the Church, and in spite of the unsuitableness of the tone it adopts, there is nevertheless something naïve and childlike revealed in their asking him for direction upon all the disputed points in the Church. All the sections—those inclining to asceticism as well as the libertines—are at one in that. They even ask Paul himself to use his influence with Apollos to get him to come to Corinth again. Notwithstanding all the fanaticism for Apollos there must nevertheless have been present an almost jealous love for Paul in the Church. What else could be the meaning of the enemy's taking advantage of his renunciation of pecuniary support to throw suspicion on his love? But at last this love conquered. After grieving him sorely, they suddenly become conscious of wrong. In the second epistle of the Apostle there sounds through all apologies the gentle tone of a reconciled love raised above all doubt and all conflict. The visit which in anger he refused to make (2 ii. 1) he was able to make in joy (Acts xx. 2 f.).

We shall do justice to this attitude towards the Apostle, with its wonderful mixture of attraction and repulsion, only when we reflect how young and immature the community still was. The Apostle tells them plainly that they are still mere babes. Yet how mature, how grown up they believed themselves to be, like a boy who has outgrown the clothes of childhood, and in the proud consciousness of manhood is no longer satisfied to endure paternal discipline. He has not yet learned from experience that a man needs some authority. He feels so uncertain that he is always grasping after some authority, too often, alas! delusive.

The conduct of the Corinthians towards the Apostle, however much it pained him, is ultimately only a sign of moral strength yoked with immaturity.

It is certainly no very pleasing picture that this Christian community presents to us. It is well calculated to destroy at the outset all illusions about ideal circumstances in the apostolic age. Men were then just what they are now. Christianity had to reckon with the same difficulties. "The flesh lusteth against the Spirit." The directness with which the new element here operated while it strengthened the impression it made, liberated undreamed-of powers; but the shortness of the time prevented a complete leavening or permeation of the old material. The ancient usages, malpractices, and vices of the heathen past life continued to make themselves painfully felt. The want of moral discipline is in pronounced opposition to the rich spiritual gifts of the community.

THE CHURCH OF CORINTH

One of the characteristic wants of the Christians of Corinth is the consciousness of being members together of the same congregation. United for worship, they followed for the rest every man his own way, without reflecting that the Christian can participate in all the blessings of the new faith only as a member of the Christian community, that combination offered the best defence against all dangers coming from without, and that accordingly the individual came to acquire obligations towards the Church.

Instead of this they took their stand with all insistence on the principle of unrestricted personal freedom. Their disregard of the brethren, their want of respect for the Apostle, are only consequences of this characteristic individualism and independence. What did any one care for the other Christian Churches to whose customs Paul repeatedly appealed ? (1 vii. 17, xi. 16). Why should they give money for the necessities of the Christians of Palestine ? They were sufficient for themselves, and would neither let themselves be directed from without nor themselves recognise duties to the outside world. The attitude they adopted to Christianity was not very different from the earlier one to the cults of Poseidon, Isis, and the Mother of gods; it was something necessary to life, but life itself was not defined by it.

If the circumstances of Corinth are viewed from this standpoint, then all the errors and confusions are quite intelligible. But just as the single defects which appeared so considerable at the first glance appeared not so dangerous on a closer survey, so in the finished picture they become still less prominent.

How much honourable striving is revealed alongside of licentiousness even if we only think of the "weak"! And the most and best naturally escape our notice. It is the nature of the good not to shine. Paul did not write his epistles to eulogise the virtues of his Churches; only necessity, the defects that he knew of, induced him to write at all. So our final opinion of the moral standing of the Church cannot be so bad. There were at any rate life and vigorous effort there. That occasionally—or perhaps we must say often— these fell out of the right way is an indication of excess of power. The Church still required Christian education. It found this too. When we consider the wild motions of these restless spirits in the days of Paul, we cannot but think that the weak bonds of the Church were bound to be rent, that it was bound to disappear again from the earth, broken up into a number of smaller circles, and decimated through the complete retrogression of these half-heathen. Instead of this we shall again find the Church of Corinth, after about forty years, shaken it is true by hot conflicts, but nevertheless in such a position that its continuity is placed beyond doubt, and that it receives the most commendatory testimony for practical evidence of Christianity. In it was fulfilled the Apostle's promise (2 xiii. 11), "Finally, brethren, farewell; be perfect; be of good comfort; be of one mind; live in peace; and the God of love and peace shall be with you."

THE PAULINE CHURCHES.

CHAPTER V.

THE CHURCHES OF MACEDONIA.

THESSALONICA AND PHILIPPI.

IN the summer of 52, before coming to Corinth Paul journeyed through Macedonia. Landing at Neapolis, he proceeded first to Philippi, and then reached Thessalonica by way of Amphipolis and Apollonia, to work some weeks there. He fled further inland to the remote Berea, whence, driven to a hasty departure through renewed persecutions, he reached Athens by sea, and afterwards Corinth (Acts xvi. 11 f., xvii. 1, 10, 15, xviii. 1). I am inclined to doubt the ordinary view that Paul did no missionary work in Amphipolis and Apollonia. Of Berea also we learn almost nothing. Neither of the Epistles to the Thessalonians mentions it at all. We might easily believe that the foundation of a permanent Church was not laid there, were it not that Sopater, son of Pyrrhus from Berea, appeared among the deputies who accompanied Paul. Certainly, however, among the Churches of Macedonia, those of the two towns Thessalonica and Philippi were most prominent.

Thessalonica, rising picturesquely on the sloping

bank of the Thermaic Gulf, was the capital of the province, then as now a very important commercial centre and place of traffic communicating with Italy by the Egnatian road, *viâ* Dyrrachium. "Lying in the lap of the kingdom" and populous, it was not far behind Corinth in importance. The mixture of peoples was similar; among them Jews were especially numerous. Living seems to have been dear: Paul and his companions (1 Thess. ii. 9) could not maintain themselves adequately by the labour of their hands.

Philippi, now a deserted ruin, situated about three hours' journey inland, in the well-watered, fruitful hollow between Pangæus and Hæmus, and connected with Thessalonica by the Egnatian road, was of considerable extent. Renowned since ancient times for the gold mines that lay close by, the scene in 42 B.C. of one of the decisive battles in the civil wars, it was built anew as a Roman colony under Augustus.

As inscriptions show, the Latin element predominated. The few Jews and proselytes had no synagogue of their own. Their place of prayer lay on the river bank before the town-gate.

The labours of Paul, who was accompanied by Silvanus and Timothy, cannot have been of long continuance at either place, although the periods given us in the Acts seem to be rather under-estimated: "certain days" (xvi. 12); a second Sabbath in Philippi (16); three Sabbaths in Thessalonica (xvii. 2). In Thessalonica Paul receives monetary help at least twice (Phil. iv. 16). This lively intercourse was continued. From Athens Paul arranged that Timothy

THE CHURCHES OF MACEDONIA 83

should return to Thessalonica. From Corinth he wrote the two epistles preserved to us. These followed quickly upon one another, Paul having learned first from Timothy, and then through other channels, what the state of matters in the young Church was. In Corinth he received from Philippi further assistance, which was brought to him by Christians of the place (2 Cor. xi. 9); Paul could say that with that Church, and it alone, he was always on terms of giving and getting (Phil. iv. 15). His last visit to Corinth—the collection journey—brought him in the autumn of 57 and the spring of 58, both going and coming, through Macedonia (1 Cor. xvi. 5, 2 Cor. i. 16), 2 Cor. ii. 13, vii. 5 = Acts xix. 21 f., xx. 1; Acts xx. 3. Timothy (1 Cor. iv. 17, xvi. 10), and afterwards Titus (2 Cor. ii. 13, vii. 6, 13 f., viii. 17), had previously gone the same way in connection with the same matter. On the journey to Jerusalem he was accompanied by Sopater, the son of Pyrrhus, as deputy from Berea, and by Aristarchus and Secundus, as deputies from Thessalonica. The representatives from Philippi are included in the "we" (Acts xx. 4 f.). It must not be forgotten that there were some Macedonians who belonged to the permanent retinue of Paul, Aristarchus, Gaius, otherwise unknown to us (Acts xix. 29), and the author of the "we" sections (not Luke). Aristarchus remained with Paul in Cæsarea (Col. iv. 10, Phm. 24), and accompanied him in the year 61 on his passage to Rome (Acts xxvii. 2). At that time we find Epaphroditus, a special representative of the Philippians, with the imprisoned Paul. He had again brought the Apostle support (Phil. iv. 10 ff.), and because through sickness he could no longer be of service to the Apostle, he took our epistle with him on his homeward journey (Phil. ii. 25, 28); soon afterwards Timothy proceeded thither on the Apostle's commission (ii. 19). In case of discharge, Paul hoped to visit Philippi himself (i. 26, ii. 24). I hardly think this actually happened, notwithstanding the mention in 1 Tim. i. 3 of another visit, which cannot be made to harmonise with the sequence of events known to us.

Out of this extensive intercourse only three little letters are preserved for us. Two of these, addressed to Thessalonica, stand at the beginning of Paul's correspondence; the other, written to Philippi, constitutes, so to speak, the Apostle's will. An interval of ten years separates them. In spite of this, however, we are entitled to treat the two Churches together. Paul himself speaks (2 Cor. viii. 1) of the "Churches of Macedonia," and (Rom. xv. 26) even of "Macedonia," as if his little Christian Churches formed the Koinon, or diet of the province. Although Philippi occupied the leading place in his eyes, as we learn from a comparison of 2 Cor. xi. 9 with Phil. iv. 15, the Macedonians (2 Cor. ix. 2, 4) are certainly not to be confined to Philippi.

The Churches must really have had much in common. Paul speaks of their great poverty, which is united with great joy in giving (2 Cor. viii. 2 ff.). Both Churches were distinctly Gentile. The total withdrawal of the Jewish element will cause us less astonishment in Philippi than in Thessalonica. Lydia, the dealer in purples from Thyatira, was a proselyte. But her family, which, along with the family of the jailer, formed the foundation of the Church, would show no trace of Jewish character in their life. The other names which we hear, Epaphroditus, Euodia, Syntyche, Clement (Phil. iv. 2 f.), bear no Jewish stamp. Jason, Paul's host in Thessalonica, may have been a Jew (his name being a hellenised form of Joshua, Jesus), Acts xvii. 5 ff., and Aristarchus certainly was, Col. iv. 10 (Phm. 24). Demas, who has been connected with Thessalonica on account of 2 Tim. iv. 10, was a Gentile (Col. iv. 14 and Phm. 24), as was also Secundus (Acts xx. 4). The Gentile character of the Church is indicated still more clearly by direct and unmistakable statements of the Apostle (*cf.* 1 Thess. i. 9, ii. 14). These confirm indirectly the report in Acts, that besides certain Jews a great many God-fearing people, among them especially the chief women, were converted (xvii. 4). The adverse and hostile attitude of the Jews there, who pursued the Apostle into the neighbouring town of Berea, where the synagogue was differently disposed (Acts xvii. 5 ff. 13), can be detected in the sharp sallies of the Apostle against the Jews (1 Thess. ii. 15 f.).

Nowhere does Paul employ the same sharp tone, except in Phil. iii. 2 ff., where he speaks of his unbelieving countrymen, who, notwithstanding his love and readiness to sacrifice himself for them (Rom. ix. 1 ff.) constantly caused him so much trouble (Rom. xv. 31). It is a remarkable conformity between the first and the last letter of the Apostle, that in both of them, instead of the anti-Judaistic opposition, it is anger against the unbelieving Jews that breaks through. Certainly that is not to be explained by saying that the opposition was restricted to certain years. It was a permanent thing—according to Phil. i. 15 ff.—although Paul had learned to take a less severe view of it. Rather it was the circumstances of the Macedonian Churches themselves which induced Paul on both occasions to turn his attention to the unbelieving and persecuting Jews.

This fact, however, makes a comparative treatment of the two Churches very interesting, for here we can observe the effect of Christianity under similar conditions, in the one case immediately after the foundation of the Church, and in the other after ten years of trial.

In the letters to the Church of the Thessalonians (1 i. 1, 2 i. 1) the immaturity of their Christianity is very evident. The Apostle lays stress on the fact that their faith is not yet complete (1 iii. 10); their love must increase (iii. 12, iv. 10), and their Christian demeanour improve generally (iv. 1). He employs the tone of loving advice and counsel which a father adopts towards a still immature son (1 ii. 7, 11). The Apostle is well aware that his affection is returned by the Thessalonians. Timothy had convinced him of that (iii. 6). If he lays stress upon his disinterestedness (ii. 5 ff.), and his honest intention of coming again (ii. 17 ff.), his defence against the suspicion of restless and impoverishing charlatanry is evidently due to his own grief at the premature cessation of his work, and to sorrow for the consequences of that cessation rather than to the general tone of Thessalonian Christianity.

Certainly the Apostle warns them to hold fast to

THE CHURCHES OF MACEDONIA 87

the traditions which they have been taught (2 ii. 15). But the danger which threatened the Christianity of his readers was not a denial of the faith. On the contrary, Paul can only praise their constancy in the midst of much tribulation. At the outset they received his preaching in the midst of great distress, and yet with a joy that was of the Holy Ghost (1 i. 6), and they have continued loyal, following the example of the Jewish Christian Churches of Palestine (ii. 14).

Paul was well aware that persecution brings temptation, and that there was always a danger of their being shaken in faith. This he feared in particular from the report of his own ceaseless sufferings. For that very reason he sent Timothy to them and reminded them that he had never left them in any doubt as to this result of Christianity, and especially of Apostleship (iii. 3 ff.). In Thessalonica, too, there were faint hearts which must be encouraged. Yet on the ground of further information, Paul can boast to other Churches of the patience and the faith of the Thessalonians (2 i. 4).

Community of feeling among the members was exceedingly warm. Paul's insistence that his letter should be read to all members of the Church (1 v. 27) is no proof of disputes. It is the first time that Paul has epistolary communications with a Church; to himself it is something unaccustomed, and he is troubled as to whether his message will reach all. That he begs them to give effect to his greeting in a mutual kiss of brotherhood (1 v. 26) is, like the request for their intercessions (1 v. 25, 2 iii. 1), part of the training, which endeavours not to abolish defects but to strengthen good habits. There must have been real life in a community that could be told to "Exhort one another and build each other up, even as also ye do" (1 v. 11). Here is to be observed the exercise of the pastoral duty by every member of the Church, just as Paul claims to have taken fatherly concern for every individual (1 ii. 11). As was natural, the next step was that those persons whose gifts and circumstances specially fitted them, took over this duty of edifying and improving, so that a kind of educational staff began to be formed within the community. The exhortation to acknowledge these voluntary servants of the community—the management is also a service, and often a right hard one—with particular respect and loving trust (1 v. 12 f.) we have found already in Corinthians 1 xvi. 15 f. We come upon it again in Phil. ii. 29 f. (*cf.* Gal. vi. 6). It is like an anticipation of the conflicts which were to arise later from the consolidation of this Church management in ecclesiastical officialdom, when Paul here says, "Preserve peace with them." Their brotherly love within their own congregation, as well as towards Christians of other towns, is exceedingly exemplary (1 iv. 9 f.). Paul goes into no further detail on this point. He sees that in this respect they have been taught directly of God (*i.e.* His Spirit).

Undoubtedly this great brotherly love is the most genuine expression of Christian sentiment. Their sorrowing and grieving for the fate of departed brethren is particularly characteristic of the nature of this brotherhood, this feeling of close interdependence. The value of this sentiment is brought home to us when we see that according to the contemporary Jewish apocalyptic creed "those who remain are far more blessed than those who have died" (4 Ezr. xiii. 24), and that Paul himself explains the numerous cases of death in Corinth as a divine punishment (1 Cor. xi. 30). Should the Lord appear suddenly to establish the kingdom of God, it was really a burning question whether those who did not live to see it should not lose thereby the blessed participation in the kingdom of glory. The Church waiting the Lord's speedy advent had not reckoned on the possibility of cases of death. These deaths shook the whole community, which would not give up any of its members. How differently was the question of the resurrection from the dead dealt with in Corinth. In the spirit of rationalism, with no feeling of community, the possibility was simply denied, and that, too, after many of the members of the Church had died. Nowhere more clearly than in this contradiction is there revealed the conspicuous individualism, the religious superficiality of the Corinthians. There the Apostle adopts (1 Cor. xv.) a tone of reprehension; here he takes pains to comfort, and he does it by pointing to the difference from "others which have no hope" (1 iv. 13).

The remarkable Christian consciousness of the Thessalonians shows itself also in the special questions of ethics. Paul has only to remind the Church that their adoption of Christianity meant an abandoning of idols, and turning to the service of the living God (1 i. 9). Complete separation from everything pagan in their way of life was consequently a matter of course. Paul touches specially only on the specifically Grecian sin of fornication and the temptation to dishonesty and imposture, which was probably a serious one to the Thessalonians engaged in commerce (1 iv. 3, 6), and in both cases he refers to former statements of his own. This procedure shows how well he could discover the weak points, and by diligent exhortation effect their improvement. Again we must observe that it is only the highest demand of Christian ethics that Paul finds it necessary to impress upon them, the duty of renouncing the avenging of suffered wrongs.

It is remarkable that Paul here looks to the Church to see that none of its members fall short in this respect (1 v. 15). Only the feeling of communion gives the individual the strength to overcome the selfish desire for revenge.

Otherwise the two Epistles are throughout brilliant witnesses for the Church, the reality of its faith, the joy of its love which fears no pains, and the continuance of its patience, 1 i. 3 (*cf.* iii. 6, v. 8). The Apostle can call the Thessalonians an ensample to all that believe in Macedonia and Achaia (1 i. 7), his hope, his joy, his garland of pride before the Lord when He comes (ii. 19), a ground of never-ceasing thanksgiving (iii. 9). These Epistles, as distinguished from those to the Corinthians, are marked by the special prominence of the general and genuine recognition which accompanies every special exhortation with an " as ye now do."

Only one point is lacking in this otherwise ideal picture. We are reminded that we are standing on the rude basis of actuality. It is a symptom specially characteristic of youthful immature Christianity.

THE CHURCHES OF MACEDONIA 91

We have already seen what a large part speculation as to the future played. To some extent this must have been occasioned by the nature of the preaching of Paul, who, apart from the express discussion of the Parousia (1 iv. 13 ff., v. 1 ff., 2 ii. 1 ff.), refers to it three times in the first short letter (1 ii. 19, iii. 13, v. 23). On the other hand, it was probably affected by the social condition of the Christians of Corinth, who sighed for freedom from the load that burdened them. The harassing poverty which Paul (2 Cor. viii. 2) bears witness to probably caused him to avoid being a burden in any way in Thessalonica (1 ii. 6 f., 2 iii. 8). If the first factor in the Christianity of the Thessalonians was the service of the living God, then the next was the expectation of the return of the exalted Lord (1 i. 9 f.). The intensity of this expectation was due to the Apostle's preaching; every moment, it was believed, they should be looking for His coming: He would come like a thief in the night. In reminding them of this, and exhorting them to watchfulness (1 v. 1 ff.), Paul poured oil on the fire. In the second Epistle he is compelled to defend himself against misunderstandings; he can explain his position only by falsification of his own words (2 ii. 2, *cf.* iii. 17), and by producing from the armoury of Jewish eschatology those lines of thought, which, without putting aside the speedy coming of the Parousia, point to certain precursors of the same, apostasy, Antichrist, and so forth.

Here we have to deal only with the moral consequences of this over-strained Parousia expectation. It was the cause of a restless and unwholesome condition among the Christians, which resulted in a disordered life. Many deserted their work in expectation of the coming end; why should they trouble themselves uselessly? The genuine Greek contempt for the labourer ($\beta\acute{a}\nu a\nu\sigma os$), the opinion that work is only a thing for the necessitous, and not in itself honourable, lent its aid. In most of the towns the free citizen of the poorer class preferred the miserable living which the state gave him to earning his bread with his own hands. Above all, however, the pressure of outward circumstances seemed to have become intolerable at the very moment when the prospect of freedom appeared. The consequence was that the people fell completely into necessity, and became a burden to the other members of the Church, at the same time bringing Christianity into an entirely false light among those without the Church. For their idleness was combined with a great outward officiousness; the imminence of the Parousia intensified the zeal for conversion. They interfered in public affairs which did not concern Christianity, and again excited public feeling against the Church. At the outset Paul had probably not had in view the seriousness and extent of this state of affairs; in the interval both had perhaps developed. In the first epistle he exhorts them to tranquillity and retirement ($\dot{\eta}\sigma\nu\chi\acute{a}\zeta\epsilon\iota\nu$), and special regard for the judgment of the outside world (iv. 10 ff.); he lays stress on watchfulness and sobriety (v. 6–8). But with an "Admonish the disorderly," he dismisses the whole affair (v. 14); he is so cautious that, avoiding all one-sidedness, he immediately speaks on behalf of the enthusiastic element, and says, "Quench not the Spirit; despise not prophesyings" (v. 19 f.). Quite different is his procedure in the second epistle: he de-

THE CHURCHES OF MACEDONIA 93

mands from every man not only quietness, but work to maintain himself. Here, for the first time, clear expression was given to the moral value of labour, as surpassing the old Jewish view of Gen. iii. 17 ff. Any one who resists is threatened with temporary exclusion from the Church, though in the hope of improvement (2 iii. 6, 14 f.); not a harsh rejection, but brotherly admonition is to bring about the offender's reinstatement (15). Here, too, the highest aim is the peace of the community (16).

This occurrence, in itself so interesting as a pathological symptom in the enthusiasm of those early days, is the more significant in view of its frequent repetition in the course of Church history. Social oppression and strained expectation of the end always work hand-in-hand to drive whole crowds from house and home to an aimless vagrancy. As in Thessalonica, the desertion of work always meets us as the chief feature. On the other hand, Paul's word to the Thessalonians, "If any would not work, neither should he eat," has proved its educational value in the history of Christian monasticism.

Some ten years later Paul addresses a letter from his prison in Rome to the Church of Philippi. It is, so to speak, his last greeting, far less a letter of exhortation to the Philippians than a pouring out of his heart to the Church which lay nearest it. There does not lack concrete detail; Paul had just received news of Philippi through Epaphroditus. But the Church is hardly mentioned—a fact which is certainly to be regarded as excellent general testimony on its behalf.

Naturally the Apostle speaks here also of the need

for perfection; He who began a good work in the Philippians will also perfect it; their love will abound yet more and more (i. 6, 9). But the Apostle himself, so near his end, confesses even of himself, "Not as though I had already attained, either were already perfect" (iii. 12.) In general he treats the Church like an independent grown-up son, who has earned his father's complete confidence by proofs of his reliability and obedience (ii. 12). He trusts that the congregation's own insight, guided by God's Spirit, will discover what is right (iii. 15).

The loving relations between Paul and the Church are similar to those subsisting between him and the sister Church at Thessalonica, but still more intimate because tried by time. We have (Phil. iv. 1) almost the same terms of endearment as in 1 Thess. ii. 19, "my joy and crown." The Apostle longs to go to them (i. 8), and in the meantime sends his best-beloved assistant (ii. 19). He is guided in all his emotions and feelings by regard for the weal of the Church: death would be dear to him, because it would unite him with the Lord; yet it is more necessary that he should remain alive for the Church's sake (i. 24); should death come, however, he will be an offering for the faith of the readers (ii. 17).

He knows, too, that he is borne up by the intercession of his Philippians (i. 19) as well as by their material support (iv. 10 ff.), which latter found special expression in the appearance of Epaphroditus as representative of the Church. Evidently he was not only to bring over to the Apostle a sum of money, but in name of and on commission from the Church, to do for him all those personal services which a father may look for from his son. Illness had prevented that, and so the Apostle sends him back (ii. 25, 30). The same feelings bind Apostle and Church together: one with him in obedience (ii. 12), it is to be one with him also in joy (ii. 18).

Among the few features in the picture of this Church which we find in the Epistle, the foremost place is given to praise of its active participation in the preaching of the Gospel, "from the first days until now" (i. 5.) This was proved in monetary support of Paul and his missionary assistants; but the Apostle certainly did not mean to confine his praise to that. They preach the Gospel with word and deed: hence he reminds them—we can hardly say exhorts—to walk worthy of the Gospel (i. 27). It may be that Paul, who in imprisonment had had many sad experiences, fears a falling away in zeal, when he writes to them, "Work out your own salvation with fear and trembling" (ii. 12). But who would conclude from that, that in Philippi a spirit of assurance and indifference had spread? Nor can murmurings and disputings have been a leading feature in this Church; yet the sorely-oppressed Apostle writes, "Do all without murmurings and disputings" (ii. 14). Again it is only the Apostle's own feelings, and the desire to strengthen himself, that make him three times write, "Rejoice ye" (ii. 18, iii. 1, iv. 4); he heartens himself thus, and shows his beloved Philippians the all-compensating value of the Gospel, which he had himself so clearly experienced (iii. 7 ff.). And when, in view of the Parousia, which is somewhat postponed probably by the prospect of his own death (i. 23) but is by no means far distant (iii. 20, iv. 5), he repeats the Lord's exhortation, "Be careful for nothing" (iv. 6), he indicates, perhaps, the point where the Philippians differed from the immature Thessalonians, but gives no proof of any appearance of incipient wordliness.

On the contrary, the Church stands there like a light in the world, clearly separated by its blamelessness and harmlessness from the crooked and perverse generation (ii. 15 f.), yet influencing the outside world by its gentleness (iv. 5). Let the adversaries threaten never so much, the Philippians do not need to fear; for they know that all suffering for Christ's sake is a proof of divine grace, a token of salvation (i. 28 f.). They do not depend on themselves. It' is God who works in them both to will and to do (ii. 13); Christ, by virtue of the authority bestowed on Him, will lead them to perfection and glory (iii. 21). Everywhere it is clear that the Apostle is only recalling thoughts which lived in the Church.

The consciousness of unity is largely developed. When the Apostle prays that evermore they may recognise the differences between themselves and others—a thing on which the Jew grounded his pride (Rom. ii. 18)—his desire is to strengthen their consciousness of superiority in face of the heathen, and above all of the Jews (iii. 2 ff.). As a matter of fact, among all the Pauline Churches the Church of Philippi appears from the first to have been the best organised and most efficient. It is certainly not altogether because the Epistle to the Philippians is the latest of all that we find episkopoi and diakonoi mentioned only here in one of Paul's Churches (i. 1). It is rather an indication of a strong feeling of common interest, that it had fashioned organs for its various activities. The mention of officials in the salutation is obviously connected with the main purpose of the Epistle, acknowledging receipt of the money sent. Still it is always open to suppose that these contributions proceeded in the first place from private people like Lydia, the dealer in purples. That Paul (2 Cor. ii. 9) speaks of "the brethren who came from Macedonia" rather favours this view, and the "ye" of Phil. iv. 15 f. does not contradict it. It is Paul's way to generalise thus, and instead of naming individuals to name the Church, instead of the Church the province (*cf.* 2 Cor. xi. 8 f. with Phil. iv. 15). At the time of the Epistle it was no private matter any longer, but a piece of Church business (ἐκκλησία, iv. 15) performed by the officials on the commission of all. It presupposes a consolidation of Church interests such as we do not find elsewhere. The character of the town, as one of no very great size, somewhat remote and used to the strong discipline of Roman administration, may have made consolidation easier; yet it remains a sign of vigorous Church consciousness that this office was created.

On the other hand the exhortations to unity (i. 27), to mutual love and respectful subordination (ii. 2 f.), do not attain any great importance. The employment in them of the example of Christ (ii. 5 ff.) shows how high the moral standard was. Paul may have been thinking of actual circumstances in the Church, and we learn (iv. 2 f.) that there was a special quarrel between two women which may have caused dispeace. We know nothing further about the dispute. It cannot have been serious. It is interesting to note that apparently a single individual, perhaps the husband of one of them, perhaps one of the Church officials, is held to be specially responsible for their behaviour—another proof of their consciousness of interdependence.

In this Epistle there is no other indication of special defects. Paul's exhortation in iv. 8, "Whatsoever things are true, whatsoever things are honest, whatsoever things are just, whatsoever things are pure, whatsoever things are lovely, whatsoever things are of good report, if there be any virtue and if there be any praise, think on these things," only reveals his high estimate of the Church. When we remember, too, that he was accurately informed about it through Epaphroditus and others, we may conclude, without fear, that the life of the community must really have been an exemplary one.

The Christian communities of Macedonia are indeed exemplary and typical (2 Cor. viii. 1 ff.). We found it so in the young Church of Thessalonica (1 Thess. i. 7), and we find it even more clearly in the mature Church of Philippi. In the one case we observe a characteristic defect of immaturity, the evil consequence of over-strained Parousia expectation; in the other we observe the proof of Christianity in the power to give itself a form corresponding to its needs.

Here we will not deny facts which indicate that a very different state of matters might arise even in these pattern-communities. Discord and worldliness were lurking at the door, and unfortunately, as we shall afterwards see, they gained admission.

THE PAULINE CHURCHES.

CHAPTER VI.

THE CHURCHES OF ASIA MINOR.

GALATIA AND PHRYGIA.

THE European mission of the Apostle is, so to speak, framed by his work in Asia Minor. Under that I do not include his labours in Pisidia and Lycaonia. For the so-called first missionary journey, undertaken along with Barnabas, which brought Paul by way of Cyprus into these southern parts of Asia Minor (Acts xiii. 14), belongs to the first period of his labours—the fourteen years described by himself (Gal. i. 21), as the Syrian-Cilician period with Tarsus and Antioch as centres. It is clearly distinguished from the second or Asia Minor-European journey with centres in Ephesus and Corinth. The Apostle is thinking of the latter when he writes to the Romans (xv. 23) that he has no longer any scope in these regions, and intends to seek a new sphere of activity in the far west. The apostolic conference of the year 51, and his separation from his old missionary colleague Barnabas, mark the transition from the first to the second period. After a short visit to the Lycaonian-Pisidian Churches (Acts xv. 40, xvi. 5), which do not afterwards appear again, he sets out for his new field of activity, detained at first against his will in Galatia (Acts xvi. 6, *cf.* Gal. iv. 13). Thence he reaches the coast at Troas (Acts xvi. 7 f.) and so finds his way to Europe. But in Corinth he looks again towards Asia. The newly-won fellow-workers Aquila and Priscilla become his pioneers for Ephesus, while he himself makes a visit to Jerusalem and Antioch. Then—avoiding Lycaonia-Pisidia—he proceeds northwards through Galatia and Phrygia to Ephesus, the new centre of a three years' activity (Acts xviii. 18 ff., xix. 1, xx. 31). How far from here Paul himself undertook missionary journeys we do not know. It is a remarkable fact that in Phrygia, which is only a few days' journey east, communities arose which had never seen his face (Col. ii. 1), but were nevertheless, as founded by his pupils, subject to his counsel and control.

For information about the Ephesus Church, the most important in this mission circuit, we are dependent on the report in Acts. The so-called Epistle to the Ephesians, whether Pauline or not, certainly does not deal with the special circumstances of this community so well known to the Apostle.

Ephesus, the ancient and renowned sanctuary of Diana, long a link between Greek and Asiatic civilisation, had, as the capital of the province at the beginning of the empire, grown to an immense extent. Notorious for its sensual and luxurious life, it was at the same time a centre of religious charlatanry and magic. Alongside of the ancient Artemisium the worship of the Emperor and all sorts of other religious movements established themselves. Among those to be found there were Jews following the

THE CHURCHES OF ASIA MINOR 101

lucrative profession of enchantment and demon-exorcism, disciples of John, Hypsistarians, and other precursors of Christianity. Paul himself, whose great activity there seems to have made itself felt in the highest circles, was looked upon by outsiders as a "Goete" of this kind: things which touched his body were said to possess healing power (Acts xix. 12), and the name of the God of salvation preached by him was used also by non-Christian exorcists (xix. 13 ff.). Not without great pains was this superstition overcome by Christianity. We may be quite sure that Paul, if he possessed the gift of healing (1 Cor. xii. 9, 28), laid no stress upon it. He was a preacher of the Gospel, and this message of God's grace in Christ was at the same time a power of moral renewal. This is expressed in those words of farewell which he is said to have spoken to the representatives of the Church of Ephesus in Miletus (Acts xx. 17–38). A pattern of humility and patience, he had taught publicly and from house to house; he had maintained himself by the work of his hands, without desire for silver, gold, or fine garments, wholly devoted to tending the Christian Church, warning each separately and making known to all the whole will of God. And if any significance attaches to the accounts given in Acts xix., it is the moral effect proceeding from Christianity and its victory over superstition, as proved by the burning of the books of enchantment (xix. 18 f.).

In the same way the moral purity of Christianity comes into a clear light in the rising of the heathen followers of Diana and the local patriots against the preaching of the Apostle, due to the greed of some artisans and organised by Demetrius the silversmith (Acts xix. 23 ff.). The Christians cannot be reproached either with robbing temples or with blasphemy (xix. 37). However much their activity may have damaged the heathen cult and the trades depending upon it—as Pliny shows later in the case of Bithynia—they kept themselves from all tumult, and laboured peacefully. If there are disturbances, the other side is to blame (xix. 40).

We should have been glad to learn more here of the development of the community which we shall afterwards find to be still a centre of Christianity. But the sources are exhausted.

On the other hand, for the Churches of Galatia and Phrygia we possess in the Epistles to the Galatians and to the Colossians most instructive witnesses. In point of time they do not lie far apart. The Epistle to the Galatians was written after Paul's second visit to Galatia (iv. 13), that is to say, after the summer of 54 (Acts xviii. 23), probably, however, not during the following three years' stay in Ephesus, but on the subsequent European collection-journey in the year 57–58. The Epistle to the Colossians came from the imprisonment (iv. 10), evidently the Cæsarean imprisonment in the years 58–60. Only the Epistle to the Romans lies between them. Otherwise, however, they are separated by an event fraught with importance. After coming to terms with the leaders of the Jewish Church of Jerusalem, Paul had fallen a victim to the attacks of the unbelieving Jews, and though rescued by the Roman military, had lost his freedom and his activity.

There is a more important distinction in the fact

THE CHURCHES OF ASIA MINOR 103

that Paul in the one case has to do with churches which he himself founded and had already visited, while the churches of the Lycus-valley, Colossæ and the neighbouring Hierapolis and Laodicea, were personally unknown to him (Col. ii. 1). Founded by pupils and friends, they were known to him only through the reports of others. Yet here, too, intercourse seems to have been active (*cf.* Col. iv. 10, the earlier commandments touching Mark). Epaphras (i. 7) is with Paul when he writes the letter. It is perhaps not a mere chance that this epistle to strangers contains more personalities than the Epistle to the Galatians, highly personal as it is.

It matters little that the people addressed are of different nationalities. It is true we look for the Galatians of Paul in a country occupied by Celts, while the Lycus-valley belongs to Phrygia. But at that time no deep-going distinction can have existed for the Christian Churches. Paul preached and wrote Greek in the one place as in the other. These districts had been long hellenised: at least the towns were, and these alone are concerned in the Pauline mission.

In Ancyra there were Helladarchs as well as Galatarchs. It may be that the Greek element was to some extent a mere external varnish, but there was similarity also beneath the varnish. For the Asia Minor Galatians, in spite of their adherence to their Celtic speech and laws, must have been strongly influenced in religious affairs by the kindred Phrygians. But little in the Epistle of Paul finds its explanation in Celtic peculiarities, not to speak of the unfortunate attempt to discover a Teutonic element here. The type is quite similar to that in Colossæ; it is Asia Minor nature-religion with its extravagances and its asceticism which, excited by Judaistic agitation, asserts itself in the Christianity of these communities. Not the character of the people but the way in which they were influenced must have varied in these places; hence the differences. This agitation, introduced from without, which threatened to destroy the Pauline foundation of Christianity, is the most interesting and most important feature in the picture of these communities. Here, however, we have not to do with foreign agitators; they will occupy our attention later. Rather the point here is to note the moral presuppositions within the Churches which gave entrance to the agitation, and the moral consequences which it had.

Fortunately in these two epistles Paul speaks of the moral instruction he had imparted. Of this we have already spoken. The result is that these directions admit no conclusions to be drawn as to the actual state of morality in these communities, so that we can affirm neither that the ideal set up by Paul there was realised, nor contrariwise that his exhortations were occasioned by particular defects, apart, perhaps, from single features like the enchantments among the Galatians (v. 20). These sorceries, it is true, seem to have constituted a real danger for the Christianity of the place. So late as the year 312 a synod at Ancyra had to issue orders against Christians practising them. Perhaps, also, in the extravagant banquetings Paul had a specific Galatian fault in view (v. 21). The Phrygians were from ancient times a slave people, infamous for their evil speaking; Paul may therefore have had reason to warn the Colossians against calumny and slanderous gossip (iii. 8), and to commend gracious speech seasoned with salt (iv. 6); at the same time he warns the slaves against eye service and the masters against cruelty (iii. 22 ff.). In general, all we can learn from these many directions is how the forces of Christianity must operate in communities of normal development.

Normal development, however, is a rare thing. History is not guided according to our logic. It is much too rich, and the powers which it brings to development are far too complex to enable us to anticipate the course that a sequence of events must take. Only seldom can we grasp it by reflection when the whole course of events lies completed before us. In these communities also we find normal development checked by external influences.

In any case, in both letters Paul bears in general good witness to the communities. The Galatians " ran well " (v. 7); they have even suffered for their faith (iii. 4). They contributed to the collection (1 Cor. xvi. 1). The churches of Galatia evidently form a closely-bound communion (i. 2). No blemishes except the one which claims all Paul's thoughts, are spoken of at all. So also in Colossæ: Paul can address them as saints and faithful brethren (i. 2), boasting of their faith and their love to all the saints (i. 4); he rejoices at the sight of their order, the steadfastness of their Christian faith (ii. 5), and the news of their love towards him (i. 8). And when he prays that their knowledge of God's will may be increased and they themselves strengthened unto all patience and long-suffering with joyfulness (i. 9 ff.), it is only what we found in the pattern church of Macedonia. Still more clearly than in the case of Galatia the close connection between the neighbouring churches of Colossæ, Hierapolis and Laodicea is revealed; the greetings of the Apostle are for all; he arranges for the exchange of his letters. The conditions within the Church are still the old loose ones : naturally there are teachers and taught, older and younger Christians (Gal. vi. 6). But this seems a condition of free choice rather than of official ruling, which of course involves an obligation of fellowship in both spiritual and material things. In the Phrygian Churches a man of the name of Archippus took over a diaconate, evidently a kind of voluntary ecclesiastical office, of the particular nature of which we know nothing.

We shall think rather of the position of Stephanas in Corinth than of the "bishops and deacons" of Philippi. But let us observe that here Paul's concern is not to strengthen the authority of these officials, as in the case of Stephanas, and to a certain extent also in the case of Epaphroditus of Philippi, but to exhort Archippus to loyal fulfilment of the task he has voluntarily undertaken. The form, "Say to Archippus," which Paul gives his exhortation shows the extent to which the community was regarded as responsible.

Upon this pleasing development there now fell the mildew of strange doctrine. In Galatia we have to face the same Jewish agitation as we have already seen in Corinth, only here the material aspect is more in evidence than the personal. Naturally, however, success was impossible until the Apostle's

THE CHURCHES OF ASIA MINOR 107

authority was first shaken. Paul meets the attack with an elaborate demonstration of his independent Apostleship. It was authorised by God Himself, vouchsafed to him through the vision of Christ, exercised in independent mission-work, recognised by the authorities in Jerusalem, and maintained against them (Gal. i. 2); hence he reminds them of their earlier enthusiastic and self-sacrificing attachment (iv. 13 ff.). It even seems that doubt was expressed as to the Apostle's uprightness (i. 20) and the sincerity of his preaching (v. 11). Paul is roused to the highest pitch. He begins the Epistle with "I marvel" instead of the usual thanksgiving (i. 6). He addresses them as "foolish Galatians" (iii. 1). It is true he endeavours to avoid conveying the impression of a feeling of personal injury (iv. 12, *cf.* with 2 Cor. ii. 5, vii. 12): but his cursing of the perverters (i. 7 ff., v. 10 ff.) and his own signature, with the weighty and almost violent *résumé* (vi. 11 ff.), show the vehemence of his anger against the alien incomers. In a burst of rhetoric he explains the sudden apostasy of his communities as the effect of enchantment (iii. 1).

What is the general theme? The Galatians, because of the urgency of Jewish agitators, have recognised the obligation of Old Testament ceremonial law for Christians also. They have begun to observe the Jewish feast days (iv. 10), probably also to order their life according to the commandments touching pure and impure meats (ii. 11 f.). The demand for circumcision was still under discussion (v. 2). We can understand the Apostle's excitement. This "different Gospel," in his eyes, did away with the

Gospel of Jesus Christ (i. 6); to him law and grace were contradictory, not complementary; he viewed the Old Testament as the book of God's promises—the law it contained was only a temporary ordinance of passing significance; the efforts of the agitators were explicable to him only on the basis of lower selfish motives; he looked upon the apostasy of the Galatians to the Judaists as slavery to human authority, a denial not of him, for human authority was of no consequence (ii. 6), but of the authority of the Lord Himself.

He considered it a weakness, a letting of themselves be hindered from running well (v. 7), a falling back to the sub-Christian level (iv. 8 f.), and there he was right. Pagan inability to understand a pure, reasonable service of God, a worship of God in spirit and in truth, pagan customs of festivals, of meat observances, and similar things may have been unobservedly helping to dispose the Galatians to the ready reception of Judaistic doctrines. But though Paul was right in making this his main ground of reproach, it was certainly not the ultimate cause. What impressed the Galatians in the Gospel of the Jews was just its morality. However paradoxical it may sound, the acceptance of Jewish law by the Galatian Church which Paul combated so vigorously is a proof of the morality of their Christianity. The "Thou shalt" of Jewish law impressed them. If faith was obedience, and if the Old Testament was God's revelation, as Paul had taught them it was, the fulfilment of God's commandments must be the perfection of faith. The Judaistic doctrine presented itself as a completion of Christianity and its moral supplement. To be sure, from the Pauline standpoint, and also from that of the Reformation, their conduct showed weakness. It revealed failure to appreciate the value of evangelical freedom (v. 1), undervaluation of the moral power of faith (v. 22 f.), denial of that which constitutes the essence of Christianity, viz., the possession of the Spirit (iii. 2 ff., v. 25). But shall we despise these Christians for their inability to follow up the profound thoughts of Paulinism? That the law works only curse (iii. 10 ff.); that the scripture hath concluded all things under sin, that the promise by faith in Jesus Christ might be given to them that believe (iii. 22)—who that has not had Paul's experience, can quite understand that? Pelagianism, Pietism, we dare say the whole doctrines of Roman Catholicism and a large part of the Lutheran theology, combine to support the Galatians here.

That the moral motives by which the Galatians allowed themselves to be guided were really creditable is shown, however little it may be admitted, by the whole nature of Paul's argumentation. With all his excitement, the tone he adopts is quite different from that of the second epistle to the Corinthians. It is only with want of judgment, and not with wickedness, that he reproaches the Galatians, and he takes pains in an elaborate argument to show from their own premises their perverted and sub-Christian standpoint. The nature of Galatian Christianity is made quite clear by comparison with that of the Corinthians: nowhere here is there any mention of such moral disorders; everywhere only honest, although misjudged, moral effort. When Paul warns them of the misuse of freedom (v. 13), it is only the necessary supplementing and safeguarding of his exhortation to stand fast in it (v. 1).

Only one serious defect eating into the life of the Church can be inferred from the Apostle's exhortations. It is the immediate consequence of the above agitation—viz., discord. Although Paul, following his usual practice, always addresses the community of the Galatian Churches, it is certain that all of them have not equally accepted the ideas and demands of the agitators. Groups were formed; those zealous for the law formed the party of progress, while the supporters of Paul were the conservatives. Things must have gone pretty far, when Paul, evidently on the ground of reports which have reached him, employs the words, "If ye bite and devour one another, take heed that ye be not consumed of one another" (v. 15). Every party impulse lets loose the passions, and excites ambition, love of quarrelling and jealousy (v. 26). We can understand why Paul in his catalogue of vices occupies so much space with terms expressive of dispeace (v. 20), why he so emphasises love within and without the Church (vi. 10), why he puts love as the true "law of Christ" (vi. 2, *cf.* "faith working through love" v. 6), on the side of liberty as its supplement (v. 13 ff.), and represents in this epistle the death of Christ as above all a service of love (i. 4, ii. 20, *cf.* iii. 1). With this is closely connected the fact that Paul asks for gentleness towards the fallen (vi. 1), the keeping together of disciples and teachers, and the supporting of the latter by the former (vi. 6 ff.). The restoration of love and a respectful attitude to himself (iv. 19), and the stress

THE CHURCHES OF ASIA MINOR 111

which he lays upon close union with the whole of Christianity (i. 2, cf. iv. 17), lie in the same direction. These phenomena are analogous to those which we observed in considering the parties in Corinth.

If the Judaistic party had succeeded, the life of the Galatian Churches would have assumed quite a different character. The painful observance of external and trifling duties then inevitably connected with the law would have defeated the free spirit of Pauline Christianity. From the ethical standpoint the Churches would perhaps have become more "moral," better, holier; but they would have lost in moral power. For moral power is developed only under the protection of freedom. That that did not happen is proved by the preservation of this epistle, as well as by the later history of the Asia Minor Churches, to which we shall afterwards return.

Similar, and yet with some points of difference, was the state of matters in Colossæ. In Galatia it was simple legalism; here the ideal of asceticism, widely diffused at the time, united with Old Testament ideas. The result is about the same. In Colossæ, too, the Jewish festivals were observed, and the Old Testament regulations as to meats followed (ii. 16, 21); even circumcision seems to have been suggested (ii. 11 ff.). But the tendency, the moving force is quite different from what we observed in Galatia. There, in spite of certain connecting points in the pre-Christian religion of the readers, it is an essentially Jewish, we might almost say Pharisaic, ideal that is pictured to the people; here elements springing from heathen nature-religion and oriental Dualism appear with some slight amount of Old Testament framing. The very mention of drink as well as meat (ii. 16) goes beyond Old Testament regulations. The "touch not, taste not, handle not" (ii. 21), shows a tendency directed less to single pollutions than to abstinence as such. The Christians of Colossæ aim in this arbitrary worship at self-humiliation and mortification of the body (ii. 23). Essenism has been detected by some writers, and indeed it does contain a similar blend of Jewish legalism with an oriental-hellenistic Dualism. But I do not see what ground there is for ascribing to this self-absorbed Jewish monasticism a propaganda extending to Asia Minor and Rome. Dualism, with the asceticism inseparable from it, was, so to speak, in the air; it was the strongest spiritual tendency of the time, almost equal to Christianity in power. We shall afterwards see the varied connections which it established with Christianity. Here it is enough to point out that the Apostle Paul himself had to pay it his tribute (1 Cor. vii. 8 ff., 26).

Can we wonder that in Churches which were only indirectly touched by his spirit this tendency flourished still more vigorously? It is quite intelligible that recourse was had to the Old Testament as authority for ascetic demands of this kind; the Old Testament was the Holy Scripture. Much more significant is the attempt to give the movement a speculative-theosophical foundation, in which the angels, as an intermediary species of beings between the transcendental God and the material creature, played a leading rôle. Belief in angels and angelolatry were integral parts of the Jewish piety of the time. Even the Christians—Paul included—shared the belief. Angel worship is very much subordinated to the

THE CHURCHES OF ASIA MINOR 113

thought of God's revelation in Christ, yet not rooted out. Paul indeed knows, apart from the "Lord," only ministering powers, as does also the writer of the Epistle to the Hebrews ; but elsewhere the angel-cult comes much in evidence. Heathenism found in this a means of adjusting its idea of good and evil spirits which are everywhere active, to monotheism. Under the pressure of dualistic views, when the purely transcendentally-conceived God was strictly separated from matter as the seat of evil, the connection through beings of this intermediate nature was unavoidable. That ethical notions were thereby disturbed is a matter of course. Paul combats the system as a philosophy which has nothing to do with Christianity, and an empty deception which, in spite of its alleged support in the Old Testament, rests only upon human authority. He sees in it the authority of Jesus Christ, the only mediator of salvation, wronged, (ii. 9 ff.), and this was his chief argument against it (*cf.* with 1 Cor. i.–iv.). He reproaches asceticism, in that while it pretends a pitiless discipline of the body, it really serves only to still the desires of the flesh (ii. 23), leads only to haughtiness (ii. 18), and reveals an earthly character (iii. 1 ff.). As opposed to that he wishes the Christians of Colossæ to direct their minds upwards to Christ (iii. 1 f.), rooted fast in Him, and building upon Him (ii. 7, *cf.* i. 23). He reminds them how alienated from God their former heathen condition was (i. 26 ff.), and emphasises the separation which Christianity has effected from the power of darkness (i. 12 f.).

But in all this we fail to discover anything that points to immoral motives in their inclination to that

8

doctrine: it is a misguided moral effort similar to that which we found among the Galatians. Asceticism is the form in which the moral earnestness engendered by Christianity will find its first expression in immature heathen converts. Pure legalism in the Pharisaic sense took for granted the whole Judaism of the time as it had developed through centuries of custom and education. On that account a permanent success of Jewish propaganda in Gentile Churches was extremely unlikely. To this legally-regulated asceticism, however, the heathenism of the time was wholly predisposed. The sensuality which dominated its worship demanded such a desensualising as a reaction. Yet its realisation always required a religious moral impulse. The extent of this impulse can be measured by the amount of energy spent upon asceticism. Still greater must the moral force be which overcame this tendency and guided the energy back to the paths of positive Christian morality. Paul did that. In the light of those ascetic movements in the Churches, the Apostle's simple and plain directions, which sanctify all natural relationships (marriage, children, slaves), become particularly significant. They introduced the Christians of Phrygia to a quite different ideal from that to which some of them aspired. Paul does not in any way refuse to recognise the Spirit: he encourages them to produce spiritual psalms, songs and hymns (iii. 16), and he emphasises his spiritual union with them most strongly (ii. 5). He lays no small stress on the Christian's renunciation of the world; his "mortify therefore your members which are upon the earth" (iii. 5) makes perhaps a still greater demand than the asceticism of his enemies; but he looks upon everything inwardly, not externally: the evil desires, not the bodily members, are intended.

In Colossæ there were fewer immediate consequences of the agitation than in Galatia; the opposition was evidently not so keen, for Paul himself speaks with less sharpness. Nevertheless Paul may have this opposition in mind when he praises Love as the bond of perfection, and exhorts them, where one has any complaint against another, to follow willingly the example of the Lord and to forgive (iii. 13 f.).

The relations were less strained; but it may be questioned if Paul had such a thoroughgoing success as in Galatia. His letter made an impression. That is shown, as in Galatia, by its preservation, and also by its later elaboration in the Epistle to the Ephesians. This fact is an indication that an effective vindication of the Apostle's thoughts was considered necessary. We shall at any rate see that ascetic tendencies of the kind are continually cropping up in Asia Minor. The Pharisaic ideal of the Galatian agitators was an exotic growth, that did not permit of being long cultivated on that soil; the asceticism and speculation of the Phrygian heretics was here, if not native, long acclimatised.

Special interest attaches to these Phrygian communities, however, on account of the short Epistle to Philemon belonging to them. This epistle not only affords us a glimpse of circumstances within a Christian house, but also brings before us the great slave-question which exercised men's minds for centuries, and shows us how Christianity approached the problem.

In one of the three Phrygian towns—Colossæ, as we may suppose—lives Philemon with his wife Appia; Archippus also, whom we have already had occasion to mention, must have belonged to the household. Philemon was comfortably circumstanced; his house was entirely Christian, and a rallying-point of the Church. Paul will dwell there (22) when he comes to Colossæ. Philemon appears to have been one of his own converts (19); his wife also is Christian, and Archippus occupies a leading position in the Church (Col. iv. 17). Paul calls him his fellow-soldier (2). Philemon is also keenly interested in the spreading of the Gospel, as we may gather from the honourable designation " our dearly beloved and fellow labourer " which Paul gives him (1). The Apostle bears excellent testimony to his faith in the Lord and his love towards all the saints (5). He must have devoted himself to suffering Christians joyfully (7). In some respects he might be classed with Stephanas of Corinth. People like these show us the higher average of morality among Christians.

From this Christian a slave Onesimus has escaped; we do not know from what cause or under what circumstances. It almost seems not only that he had run away from his master, but that he had embezzled a sum of money. That any sort of bad treatment drove him to flight is quite improbable. Had it been so, Paul would not have failed to reproach Philemon; besides, in the letter to the Colossians, the obligation of masters to be just and reasonable to their slaves is passed over in a few words. Much more probable is it that the still heathen slave had taken advantage of his Christian master's mildness.

To be sure he had deceived himself lamentably as to what awaited him in the outside world. The lot of a runaway slave was not an enviable one: the best that could happen to him was to fall into new slavery. If he was recaptured—and the magistrates were obliged to assist in this—the severest punishment waited him, perhaps a death so cruel that many voluntarily presented themselves to fight with the wild beasts. Only when he was fortunate enough to secure the protection of a friend of his master might he hope for a better fate. That being so, the conjecture has some appearance of probability that it was no accident which led Onesimus to Paul, but that he purposely sought out the Apostle in the hope of securing his influence with Philemon. At any rate Paul converted the fugitive. For some time the slave was with him in prison and did him personal service (*cf. supra*, p. 94). Then, however, Paul sends him back with a letter of recommendation to his former master. It is not our business here to show the wonderful delicacy with which Paul discharges the task of beseeching Philemon for a favourable reception of the runaway. He indicates, yet does not enforce, his right as an Apostle to command. He desires to retain the slave for his own service, but parts with him for Philemon's sake. He jestingly offers compensation for the wrong done by Onesimus, and then refers to the immeasurable debt of gratitude owed by Philemon to himself. He calls Onesimus his child whom he has begotten in his bonds. He plays upon the name, laying stress on the change for the better which has transformed Onesimus from uselessness to usefulness. The short deprivation of his services will be amply compensated by eternal possession. What we have to note is that in the case of this runaway—and, as we may suppose, embezzling—slave, who, after the ideas of right of the time, had nothing to expect but severe corporal punishment, perhaps penal servitude and branding for life, Paul prays for full forgiveness by his master, and that in a tone which clearly shows that he was making no vain request. The Apostle's action was due not to considerations of general humanity, and still less to the thought of a utilitarian morality which would mean the quiet letting-go of a wicked slave, but to the fact that the slave was a Christian, and because the master was also a Christian he could count on success. The solidarity of the Christian brotherhood is the main point here.

In the second place we see how the social relation was altered. There is indeed no suggestion that the Apostle set up slave-emancipation as a demand. That would have entailed a social revolution, and within the small Christian circle would have been hardly practicable either for the masters, whose property might to a large extent consist of slaves, or for the slaves themselves, who were most of them dependent on the means of subsistence which they received from their master. In the Empire even the testamentary manumissions usual in noble houses were restricted in order to prevent the growth of the proletariat. In the case of the Therapeutæ and similar conventual religious societies we find a repudiation of slavery, the attempt to put into practice the equal and universal rights of men. Christianity did not strive for this. Christians retain slaves and remain slaves.

That continued into the Christian empire in the fourth and fifth centuries, and then only gave place to other forms like bond service. Nevertheless Christianity made an alteration, eloquently attested by this little Epistle of Paul. Though the Stoics spoke much of the universal rights of man, and highly-educated slaves like Epictetus declaimed upon the theme that they only are truly free who make themselves inwardly free, the practice really corresponded with the well-known question of the Roman matron, "Is the slave a man?" Mommsen says that, "compared with those of the Roman slaves the sum of all the negro-ills is a drop." We must remember however that this statement holds good only of the crowds of land-slaves on the great estates. It may be maintained that the well-known stories of refined cruelty towards even the slaves who were most intimate with their masters, are few and, perhaps, also exaggerated. It may be pointed out that many slaves were highly educated, and that these usually stood on a friendly footing with their master, like Tiro with Cicero, and that the law of the empire began to provide the slave with a certain legal protection. Still the fact remains, he was a thing without rights, given over to the will of his master. Even liberation did not change matters much.

But the Christian spirit did, for it saw in the slave not only the equal man with equal rights, but the beloved brother. That is the decisive element in the Apostle's treatment of the question; in that this little letter is in complete agreement with the other passages where the author touches upon the matter. The main point is that the relation becomes changed inwardly through a new spirit. Mutual love, demonstrating itself as willing obedience on the part of the slave, and as just, fair, mild treatment on the part of the master, creates within the old legal form a new moral system. That it was not lasting, that it exposed the slave constantly to the occasions of a change of master, that in an only one-sided Christianity difficulties of every kind came in, are considerations which do not trouble the Apostle. He is not writing a programme, but only a little letter of recommendation for a Christian slave to his Christian master, and in it he gives wonderful expression to the Christian fundamental thought of the surrender of one's rights. Philemon has indisputable right to punish Onesimus in any way he chooses, and to indemnify himself for the injury he has suffered. If he renounces this right, he acts like a Christian.

THE PAULINE CHURCHES.

CHAPTER VII.

THE CHURCH OF ROME.

AMONG the Pauline Churches, the Church of Rome occupies a special place. It was not founded by the Apostle; in his own opinion it does not quite belong to his field (xv. 20 ff., in spite of i. 15). At the time of writing, Paul and the Roman Christians are still personally unacquainted, although bound together in the communion of prayer (i. 10, xv. 30). He had indeed many acquaintances in Rome, and his name was often mentioned with respect among them. The view which would find distrust of the Apostle in i. 9, 11 ff., and xv. 22, is probably wrong. He purposely seeks out all personal connections, and concludes his Epistle with the long list of greetings, the numerous names on which give us, nevertheless, only a very incomplete picture of the composition of the community. Was Paul at all informed as to the circumstances of this community, and can his letter serve us as a source of information on its moral standing?

My view is that the Epistle to the Romans is distinguished from the other writings of the Apostle by the fact that he does not handle questions which were suggested to him by the Church; he elaborates trains of thought which were at work in himself.

It contains the clarified expression of what was inspired in the Apostle's mind by the Galatian disorders. Hastily committed to paper in the Epistle to the Galatians, it was now dedicated in riper form to the Church of the metropolis, whose sympathy the Apostle of the Gentiles was trying to win.

Nevertheless it is no abstract doctrinal work, but a real letter. Paul did not lose sight of his readers. He knows how to enter into the particular requirements of the Christians of Rome, and has probably heard of some of the points discussed among them. At the end of the letter, where we find the list of greetings, we come upon individual traits which cannot be explained by the Apostle's experiences in other communities.

We know no more about the extension of Christianity in Rome than about its beginnings. Certainly the number of the Roman Christians was already not small. It would seem that we are not entitled to speak of a Roman Church; at least Paul avoids this name (Rom. i. 7, Phil. iv. 22). As the Jews of Rome lacked a unified organisation, so Christianity in the capital of the world seems to have appeared in the form of separate circles, so-called house-churches (Rom. xvi. 5, xiv. 15). In his letter Paul presupposes, indeed, that these feel themselves to be one. He treats them (like his own Churches) as consisting essentially of Gentiles. To find a Jewish minority indicated in the apostrophe to the Jew (ii. 17), is hazardous. Naturally there were Jews among the Christians of Rome—certainly Priscilla and Aquila, Andronicus and Junia, also Mary (xvi. 3, 7, 6), and probably many of the others named.

Pilgrims returning from Jerusalem, Palestinians emigrating to Rome, may have spread the first seeds of the Gospel in the circles of the synagogues and among the proselytes associated with them. There may have been people among them who observed the law strictly, but undoubtedly there were also people of a liberal spirit, like Andronicus and Junia. These seem to have acquired particular importance in the spread of Christianity in Rome; they were intimately connected with the Apostle Paul, and had on one occasion even shared his imprisonment. The edict of Claudius, which drove the Jews out of Rome (Acts xviii. 2), and was caused perhaps by the tumultuous scenes which the preaching of the Messiah come in Jesus called forth in the synagogues, may have helped to bring about the separation of the proselyte circle from the mother-soil of the Jewish synagogues, so that the Gentile element gained the upper hand.

Alongside of these, again, a special circle of strict Jewish Christians may have arisen, just as a special synagogue of Hebrews existed along with the synagogues of Greek-speaking Jews. The various forces represented still later among the Christian missionaries in Rome are shown in Phil. i. 14 ff. A very keen missionary activity developed there under the eyes of the imprisoned Apostle. In many cases indeed he believes that the Jewish Christians wish only to anger him. But he had friends among the missionaries, who were spurred on by love to him. He had some sad experiences to endure; there are many whom he can look upon only as enemies of the cross, who follow after only earthly desires (Phil. iii. 18 f., *cf.* Rom. xvi.

17 f.). But on the whole he can rejoice in the progress of the Gospel (Phil i. 12–18). In the pretorium and in the palace it has secured a footing (Phil. i. 13, iv. 22). We shall have opportunity later to return to the further development of Christianity in Rome.

As the mission history of our own times often enough teaches us, nothing disturbs the moral consciousness of young Christian communities more than the adherence of professional preachers of the Gospel to different principles when a question of practical conduct is raised. If that was the case even in the Churches where Paul's authority was supreme, how much more must it have been so in Rome, which lacked a dominating personality like his? So there arose also inside the circle addressed by Paul certain doubts and antitheses, which were calculated to disturb the Roman Christians' consciousness of unity. That is the one special feature, the one concrete thing which we hear about them. That their faith is known all over the world (i. 8) does them great honour; that the news of their obedience, *i.e.*, their willing acceptance of the Gospel and their subordination to its moral demands, has reached everywhere, gives the Apostle great pleasure (xvi. 19); but we do not learn much in the way of detail from these facts. The particulars concerning the moral consequences of justification by faith, which he gives in the sixth chapter, are purely theoretical and have no connection with Rome. The same holds good of his spirited declaration about the peace of God accompanying justification, and the boldness to rejoice in hope of the glory of God and in tribulation (v. 1 ff.). All that is spoken of the working of the Holy Spirit in the Christian (v. 5, viii. 2, 12, 23, 26) belongs in the first place to the Apostle's own grateful confessions. One might be tempted to consider also "those divisions" (xvi. 17) pure hypotheses of the Apostle. They are concerned with differences in regard to the observance of feast days and commandments touching food (xiv. 5 f.), exactly as we found among the Galatians. The only advance is that Paul mentions the limitation to the eating of herbs (xiv. 2), and includes drinking (probably the rejection of wine; xiv. 17). We might suppose that Paul's statement about the meat offered to idols during the dispute at Corinth, "If meat maketh my brother to offend, I will eat no flesh while the world standeth lest I make my brother to offend" (1 Cor. viii. 13), had called forth in Corinth itself a vegetarian movement which now cast its shadow upon this letter written from Corinth. But the detail with which Paul handles this question, as distinguished from all his other exhortations (xiv. 1–xv. 13), and the fact that he recurs to it again and emphasises it strongly (xvi. 17 f.), show that in Rome the question was a burning one. It was not quite like the question of meat offered to idols in Corinth, nor like the conflict as to the observance of the law in Galatia. The nearest parallel to it was the feeling in Colossæ. Here as well as there Essenism has been suggested. Only in Rome the matter seems to have had still less Jewish Old Testament colouring. In connection with this, Paul does not go into the question of the law at all. He even emphasises the significance of the Old Testament as a lesson-book for Christianity (xv. 4), without by a single word guarding against false nomistic exploitation of it. In Rome he represented the right of the weak to have their standpoint considered as he had done before in Corinth, while in the Epistle to the Colossians he argues hotly against rules being made in these things at all.

To understand what it was the Christians of Rome were concerned about, we must make clear to ourselves the significance of vegetarianism at the time. Pythagoreanism was revived and took over the repudiation of all animal food, as a main rule of its method of life from the Orphic societies which flourished in Egypt especially. Once Empedocles had philosophically justified vegetarianism, and now once more the question was eagerly discussed in the schools. Peripatetics, Stoics, Epicureans declared for the eating of flesh, while the teachers who were guided by Plato maintained the opposite view. Plutarch in the second century, and Porphyrius in the third, wrote against the use of flesh.

The theme was treated in romances. Appolonius of Tyana is described as the saint of this new-pythagorean method of life involving vegetarianism and abstinence from wine, as is also the Egyptian priest and prophet Kalasyris in the Ethiopica of Heliodorus. Whether Indian influences also contributed, as the Gymnosophists of Heliodorus' Ethiopica seem to suggest, may remain uncertain. The influence which the whole mode of thought exercised on the young Christianity is clear. Its effect on Judaism was less, especially in Palestine (in the case of Essenes, *e.g.*, we cannot speak of vegetarianism); only the abhorrence of the unclean and of the eating of blood leads there under certain circumstances to temporary abstinence from all eating of flesh. We meet with a repudiation of it on principle, only in cases like the Philonic Therapeutæ, who stood on the borderland between Jewish and Greek life. It is in Egypt that we find it most conspicuous among the Christians: it dominated the Gospel of the Egyptians. The majority of the gnostic masters defended encratism. The Christian tales glorify it in the person of the Apostles. The line between Church and sect is here a fluctuating one, although the Catholic theologians as a rule defend the position that all God's gifts can be enjoyed by Christians with thanksgiving.

Usually abstinence from flesh is combined with abstinence from wine. The motive of this is clear. Wine contains an intoxicating element, something which excites sensuality. Less clear is the motive of vegetarianism. Dietetics play some part, but the influence of this is not solely operative any more than the Platonic philosophers' physiological and psychological theories of the enchaining of the soul in the material body, which is therefore to receive only the nourishment absolutely necessary. What Plutarch and Porphyrius have to say usually creates the impression of having been elaborated. Even the thought of the *Universal Soul* is hardy decisive, where it does not, as in the case of Empedocles, adopt the definite form of transmigration of souls. Views like these, which directly affected human piety, the demoniacal mystery with which the act of procreation was surrounded by the ancients, who either deified it or held it accursed, and finally the universal tendency to asceticism and renunciation, must have been determinative for the majority. The last point of view certainly formed the Christian motive. Occasionally we meet with a limitation to the eating of plants as a grade of fasting and of penance.

Thus it may have happened in Rome also, that zealous maintainers of the strict moral character of Christianity demanded the renunciation of flesh and of wine. The Christian hope, with its thought of eternity, had to superficial observers a certain resemblance to the Platonic idea.

When, in addition to this, we meet with a preference among Roman Christians for special days, *i.e.*, evidently the observance of the Jewish Sabbath, we shall be little surprised. The satirists teach us clearly the superstitious respect which this custom of the otherwise despised Jews enjoyed in all circles of Roman society. How could the repute in which it was held fail to increase, when a direct union was formed with a society in which the sacred law of the Jews was the normative book? An inner connection need not have existed between the observance of the Sabbath and abstinence from flesh, although we may suppose the same people observed both. That these were Jewish Christians is nowhere indicated, and Judaists are, in a case of the kind, directly excluded.

Certainly those who observed the Sabbath and renounced flesh considered themselves better Christians. In their judgment the others were lacking in proper moral earnestness. On the other hand, the latter considered the abstinence of the former a weakness; with a right understanding of the Gospel, they maintained freedom from Sabbath regulations, and the right to partake of every kind of food with thanks to God. Therein lay the difference which endangered brotherly love. When we look more closely, Paul appears to presuppose people of the latter kind in the circle to which his letter first goes, and he designates them briefly, as in Corinth, the strong. The weak may have belonged, to some extent, to other circles. But Paul insists that the unity of Christian brotherhood shall be maintained, even at the sacrifice of knowledge and liberty, and above all at the expense of odious and damaging judgment.

In Rome it was of great importance that the Christians gave no external offence. Paul enters vividly into the circumstances of Rome, where the increasing size of the proletariat made the police power much greater, and the suspicious method of the imperial government made the supervision much more strict.

The Jews, whom the imperial government had consistently favoured since the time of Cæsar, had recently had to pay for noisy disturbances in and around their synagogues, with expulsion from the city. Still more easily could the Christians be made to undergo similar and still worse things, if they made themselves in any way unpleasantly conspicuous. The July days of the year 64, the burning of the town and the persecution of the Christians in consequence, showed clearly that only a suspicion was needed to set extreme measures in motion against them. They were abandoned as outlaws to all sorts of violence. This made it the more important that on their part they should avoid every suspicion, and that they should be aware of the duty of implicit obedience to the magistrates. It is very possible that this was not everywhere the case, but that here and there ideas of opposition were excited. As in Thessalonica enthusiasm called forth a distaste for labour, so in other quarters it might give rise to revolutionary notions. In these circles, usually composed of insignificant people like freedmen and slaves, the fanatic idea that they were called to play a leading political rôle in the world, and in some way or other to help to hasten the coming of God's kingdom on earth, could easily be fostered by the influence of the prophets and the apocalyptic literature. Here in Rome, "the sight of the might which ruled the world compelled them to reflect upon its nature and its divine right," and Christianity offered impulse enough to deny the latter. It may be due to this that they were charged with hatred of humanity. In the days of Nero, on the admission of Tacitus himself, they were not the incendiaries they were given out to be (Ann. xv. 44), and the alleged crimes which had made them hated among the people were evidently wicked calumnies like those against which, at a later time, the apologists had to defend themselves. Unfortunately we know nothing definite about the sentiments of the Christians of Rome, and must beware of concluding from Paul's quite general exhortations that there were special defects in Rome. Paul does indicate something which might easily lead to conflict—the taxes and customs.

The Roman citizen was free from taxes: the provincial was not. How it was with the settlers in Rome, who were not citizens, we do not know. After

THE CHURCH OF ROME

the year 70, every Jew had to pay into the Roman treasury the old temple-tax of a didrachmon; there is no evidence of a taxation of Jews in Rome during the Julian-Claudian period.

Again, it is possible to think of the conflicts which might arise from the demands for these taxes from Christians, as Jews or adherents of the synagogue. But Paul had evidently in mind rather the circumstances of his provincial Churches. Customs on goods imported were exacted in Rome, as well as in the other revenue districts of the empire. That the Christians were in any way specially disinclined to pay these is hardly credible. The complaints about duties of this kind were naturally quite general. It is a criterion of the moral spirit of Christianity, that instead of complaining, it required its followers to pay readily all such due claims. And this is all the more remarkable, as the Christians were to a certain extent entitled to feel themselves the citizens of another higher kingdom, free from all earthly burdens (*cf.* Matt. xvii. 25 f.). Every inner bond which would have united them to the authorities was wanting. Paul himself adopted no positive attitude to the state. He even sought to avert every influence on his Churches, *e.g.*, in legal cases; far less did he entertain any idea of making the Christians a power in it. His conduct reveals no limited vision, but a magnificent clearness and consciousness of aim.

What else Paul mentions in these last chapters of the Epistle to the Romans has still less relation to the special circumstances of Rome. We have already spoken of this section as an example of the moral education of the communities by the Apostle. It is possible, at the same time, to see in it a precipitate of the experience which he had gained in his Greek-Asia Minor communities. It is worth while to glance again at chapters xii.–xvi. to find out the points which Paul considers worth mentioning, and lays his finger upon. These will be the defects which he has come most in contact with.

In the first place there are the sins of the flesh, which he has everywhere to combat as the chief evil, especially in Corinth. There is sometimes no trace of the knowledge that the body of the Christian should be a consecrated instrument, a temple of the Holy Spirit (xii. 1). With unchastity are very closely associated excesses in eating and drinking (xiii. 13). Next come selfishness and pride, which do not permit the consciousness of unity and mutual obligation to develop (xii. 3 ff., xiii. 13), and which everywhere give occasion to disorder, disputes, and contentions.

Paul already knows the lukewarmness, the slothfulness which is unable to hope joyfully, to suffer patiently, and to continue in prayer (xii. 11 f.). In particular, however, he has to quicken the love, which embraces even the strange brother, which repays the enemy with blessing instead of curse, which shares the joy and suffering of others, and does not withdraw haughtily into itself. We see that the great rule of the giving-up of all revenge needs always to be laid anew to the heart of the Churches, and we see in the closing thought, " Be not overcome of evil, but overcome evil with good," all the greatness of this Christian morality, which, certain of

THE CHURCH OF ROME

victory, seeks its proof in fighting, not in flight. It can do this because its first and only principle is love (xiii. 8 ff.), a love which surrenders its own freedom and right for a brother's sake (xiv. 1-xv. 7). The state of owing no man anything, which was considered by the heathen the condition of happiness, was here held to be obligatory in a much deeper sense: the debt of love is unending.

Paul here enforces the grandest thoughts of the Sermon on the Mount. The warnings against heathen vices assume no prominence. It is equally honourable for the Roman Christians and for his other Churches that he gives no more detailed exhortations. The dark picture of heathendom, as he drew it in the first chapter, lies behind them. He takes it for granted that the Christian consciousness is strong enough among them to effect a complete break with the former method of life (xii. 2, xiii. 12).

Such is the picture of the Pauline Churches, very incomplete it is true—our sources offer no more—yet rich enough to admit of an answer to the question, "To what extent did Christianity become effective as moral power?"

To reach the right standpoint we must put ourselves into the conditions that Paul met with. This we can best do from the picture which the Apostle himself gives of the decadence of heathendom (Rom. i. 21 ff.): "Because that, when they knew God, they glorified him not as God, neither were thankful; but became vain in their imaginations and their foolish heart was darkened. Professing themselves to be wise, they became fools, and changed the glory of the uncorruptible God into an image made like to corruptible man, and to birds, and four-footed beasts, and creeping things. Wherefore God also gave them up to uncleanness through the lusts of their own hearts, to dishonour their own bodies, between themselves: who exchanged the truth of God into a lie and worshipped and served the creature rather than the Creator (Who is blessed for ever. Amen).

"For this cause God gave them up unto vile passions; for their women changed the natural use into that which is against nature; and likewise also the men, leaving the natural use of the women, burned in their lust one toward another, men with men working unseemliness, and receiving in themselves that recompense of their error which was due. And even as they refused to have God in their knowledge, God gave them up unto a reprobate mind to do those things which are not fitting; being filled with all unrighteousness, wickedness, covetousness, maliciousness; full of envy, murder, strife, deceit, malignity, whisperers, backbiters, hateful to God, insolent, haughty, boastful, inventors of evil things, disobedient to parents, without understanding, covenant breakers, without natural affection, unmerciful; who knowing the ordinance of God, that they which practise such things are worthy of death, not only do the same, but consent with them that practise them." Although this gradual demoralisation involving the religious and the moral consciousness may be called a philosophical presentation of history, yet how much truth there is in it. Although the colours of the moral picture are purposely chosen of a sombre tone, it was not a pessimism which despised mankind that guided the brush, but the moral indignation of a man whose whole heart was given to the task of raising the Gentile world from this slough of sin and vice. The picture which he paints is the result of actual observation; Corinth in especial gave him material enough, and what we discover from ancient sources teaches us that this description is perhaps one-sided, but right in the main. Humanity had really lost sound moral judgment; sin was not only committed, but approved and glorified. The sense of sin was lost, and philosophy even set herself to cover wicked practice by more wicked theory. Individual moral teachers may have striven after something better; in the upper grades of society a fine tone may have concealed much; in the country and remote small towns the ancient honour may have been still to some extent preserved, though even the pastorals of Longus were affected by the demoralisation inseparable from the civilisation of the time. For the circles in which Paul worked and from which he gathered his churches together, he was unquestionably right. What we have observed in these young churches only confirms what was said of the non-Christian world, for it is the aftermath of ancient habit.

For the rest, however, the churches shine as lights in the world (Phil. ii. 15), however little the Apostle thought or we may think of idealising them. The time is long past when it was thought necessary to remove every stain and shadow from the ideal picture of Christianity in apostolic communities. Historical reality here also asserted itself. We see now that even in the mighty throes of the Spirit of God, in those days things went on still in a very human way, and that the law of growth, which the Lord Himself recognised as holding also for the kingdom of God, has here been confirmed. Not complete Christian communities with perfect knowledge and proved in every detail fell to the Apostle in his mission-preaching, but with painful labour on individuals and communities, he had slowly to train the small groups of those laid hold of by the Gospel into Christian Churches.

Everywhere in these Pauline Churches we meet with youthful immaturity. This is least so where we observe a Church after lengthy development, as in the Epistle to the Philippians. The sensuality of the Corinthians, the excessive spirituality of the Thessalonians, the hasty fall to every new doctrine which we observed in Corinth and in Galatia and Phrygia — all are but signs of immaturity. Men were only half-conscious of their own dependence. They adhered to authorities, whether Paul and Apollos, or the Jewish agitators.

It is not so much weakness as immaturity that we observe, immaturity with which a superabundant energy, the sign of youthfulness, is bound up. All the Corinthians' boasting of liberty, their parties, and similar facts in the other Churches, are outflows of this unrestrained and partly misguided power. But this power reveals itself also in good: in the joy of sacrifice, in the feeling of community, especially, in the case of the Macedonians, in confidence of faith and in readiness to suffer.

And lastly there is an expression of this power also in that moral earnestness, which we occasionally found described as weakness, the anxiety concerning meat offered to idols, eating of flesh and drinking of wine, and even avoidance of marriage. There is therein a power of renunciation, and yet it is still a weakness. It is as much a residuum of the ancient mode of thought as the traces of excess in the different domains of the sensual life. The flesh is not overcome by denying the senses, but by the Spirit's sanctifying power.

To sum up. It is astonishing what Christianity in a relatively short time made out of these motley and confused heathen groups; earnest men working out their salvation with fear and trembling, saints fully aware of the moral tasks of their consecration. If their judgment was often immature, their goodwill and vigour were great; and, besides, there stood by them the Apostle and his assistants training and advising them. We never see more than isolated sections of their development, but our main impression cannot fail to be that the Churches were making great progress.

Book II.

JEWISH CHRISTENDOM.

CHAPTER VIII.

The Primitive Church—The Church of Jerusalem.

We break quite different ground when we turn to the Jewish Christian Churches of Palestine. The Jews, too, were men, subject to the same desires and impulses as others. In the Gospel we meet with the public prostitute and the adulterous woman. In His parables the Lord pictures the rich miser and the wanton spendthrift, the unfaithful steward and the deceitful servant, the thief and the unjust judge. The so-called Testaments of the Twelve Patriarchs chastise the spirit of fornication, of greed, of anger, of coquetry, of pride, of lying and deceit in the twelve tribes. The very worst was said even of the priests (Levi. xvii.). While he fully acknowledges their zeal for righteousness (Rom. x. 2 f.), Paul reproaches his countrymen with the transgression of every commandment, especially the seventh and the eighth (Rom. ii. 21 f.). Following after the law of righteousness, Israel did not attain to that law (Rom.

ix. 31). Here, then, there is no distinction between Jews and others. All are sinners (Rom. iii. 9, 22). In Israel the general conditions of morality were similar to those among the peoples round about.

And yet it makes a great difference that the Jews had long lived under the civilising influence of their divine law. They were protected from the danger of lapsing into sensuality. The days of Antiochus Epiphanes, when paganism seemed to enter Jerusalem in the nakedness of its sins and vices, were past, since the Maccabees had again won for the law absolute supremacy. With constant and increasing zeal, the scribes sought to protect the people by a fence of law. The ideal was the Pharisee who separates himself entirely from all heathen or even semi-heathen impurity. But the very word Pharisee is sufficient to bring before us at once the other danger of this moral ideal. The Pharisee of the Gospel we know well enough as the type of pride, lovelessness, insincerity, and hypocrisy. And not only the Pharisee, but the whole Jewish piety which was demanded by the scribes of the time was in conflict with that of the Lord: their externality, which almost stifled the moral sentiment; their casuistry, which in the multitude of trifling pedantries neglected the main commandment of love, and the hypocritical artificiality with which they evaded the law while observing all its precepts.

Naturally there were in Israel other currents of thought as well. The aristocratic worldlings and politicians known to us as Sadducees, who under the pretence of conservatism repudiated the best impulses of the traditional religion and did not scruple to meet with heathen rulers on equal terms, hardly concern us at all; no more do the Essenes, who are not mentioned in the Gospel. These latter lived for the most part in monastic seclusion in the district east of the Jordan, and, probably not uninfluenced by the asceticism which dominated the world of the time, sought to realise the negative side of Pharisaism to the utmost. Yet we may suppose that here and there in the land there were groups of pious people, who still had some understanding of the greatness of the moral view of the prophet. " He hath shewed thee, O man, what is good; and what doth the Lord require of thee, but to do justly, and to love mercy, and to walk humbly with thy God " (Micah vi. 8); " I will have mercy and not sacrifice " (Hosea vi. 6, Matt. ix. 13). These formed the circles in which Christ's preaching had most success. But here, too, the law was the highest aim in life. The question, "What was God doing before he created the world?" met with the answer, " Sitting and studying the law," and though this may indicate a deification of legal learning, nevertheless the ideal of every pious Jew was to find his delight in the law of the Lord, and to meditate therein day and night (Ps. i. 2, cxix. 27; *cf.* Test. XII. patr., Levi. xiii., Rom. ii. 17 ff.).

Thus from the beginning a quite different turn was given to Christian morality on this ground, and a much more precise character was stamped on it. We can realise this when we read the description of the really pious in Ps. xv., or Job's self-defence (chap. xxxi.), with which the characteristics of the Patriarchs in their " Testaments " are in complete agreement. Still more detailed is " The Two Ways," soon appropriated by Christianity, but originally a Jewish

THE PRIMITIVE CHURCH 141

catechism, which adds to the commandments of the Decalogue the extract of Israel's experience contained in the wisdom-literature. The commandments are indeed most of them negative, but they show the great heinousness which was attached to sins of thought. Great weight was laid on duties towards the community. Beneficence is the crown of morality. In a Jewish Apocalypse (Steindorff, *The Apocalypse of Elias*, p. 152) we even find neglect of charity considered the only sin that matters, just as in the parable of Jesus (Matt. xxv. 41 ff.). Close beside it, however, we find purely external precepts like the strict keeping of fast-days and hours of prayer. The moral consciousness has not yet reached a clear separation between what is essential and what is not.

Here lies the new element contributed by the Gospel. It can be sought only in the subordination of all externalities. Relation to the person of Christ and the certainty of God's fatherly grace supplied the power of realization.

If we wish to appreciate justly the earliest Christian Church which gathered at the beginning in Jerusalem round the Twelve, we must think of all its members as pious Jews. The certainty that the Messiah had appeared in Jesus of Nazareth, and that though carried away to Heaven for a short space He would come again very soon to set up the kingdom of God (Acts iii. 21), only impelled them to redouble their pious zeal and strive after the realisation of the Jewish ideal of piety. Their attitude towards the law was quite naïve. That Jesus set man above the Sabbath, and love above all ceremonial duties, abolished these institutions just as little as the similar prophetic utterances which were recognised alongside of the law as holy and divine abolished it. Jesus' exposition of the law was only fulfilment, not dissolution. He deepened the comprehensions of the commandments and gave them a more profound inward content. They remained binding, and the whole law with them. It was a simple matter, of course, that Jesus' disciples, like all pious Jews, offered the ordinary prayers, observed the Sabbath, shared the pilgrimages, frequented the Temple, and brought their offering there. In their worship and in every relationship they were faithful to the law. Their Christianity, if we may speak here of such a thing, and their belief in the Messiah, found expression in increased devotion to duty and in redoubled zeal.

From the very outset, however, the disciples of Jesus formed a community, which, bearing in the first instance a family character and later always growing, was knit closely together and was to a certain extent outwardly distinct. In this narrow circle customs were developed, partly, it is true, unconsciously, which bore in them the seed of new formations. In Acts ii. 42 it is said that those who were received into communion through baptism—that is, through a purificatory bath—continued steadfastly in the Apostles' doctrine and fellowship and in breaking of bread and in prayers. It is a way of forming a communion that was not quite unheard of in the Israel of the time. The best analogy is offered by the common houses of the Essenes. But it is not at all necessary to adopt Essenic influence in order to explain the development of Christian forms of

THE CHURCH OF JERUSALEM 143

that kind. For these lack above all the main feature of Essenism—monastic communism.

It is true we are accustomed to associate with the early Christian Church the thought of community of goods. And it ought not to be denied that in the Acts of the Apostles it is to be found. But it is clearly shown to be only one of the features with which the author idealises the picture of the early Church. Luke himself, like many of his contemporaries, was strongly inclined to communism. The faint traces of it which he brought into his Gospel are still more distinct in the Acts. But the facts which he himself reports contradict it. The same idealising process took place among the Pythagoreans. While all older sources presuppose private possessions, the later Neo-Pythagoreans, whom we may call contemporaries of Luke, maintain that Pythagoras introduced community of goods from the very beginning. The real truth is that an active spirit of great mutual helpfulness did reveal itself, κοινὰ τὰ τῶν φίλων. But it is wrong to say there was a rule demanding the surrender of private property for the common good. It was exactly the same with the early Church. Brotherly love knew no limits; no one said, as Luke very properly describes the state of affairs, that anything was his own: they had everything in common (Acts iv. 32). The delight in giving went in some cases so far that property was sold, and the proceeds placed at the disposal of the community. This was done by Barnabas (iv. 36 f.), and by Ananias and Sapphira, who coveted his fame (v. 1 ff.). These, however, were exceptional cases and attracted particular attention. There was no rule on the point.

We cannot speak of any obligation to surrender private property in behoof of the community such as Luke describes.

The life of these first Christians must have borne a markedly social, even family character, which is expressed in their favourite designation of one another as brethren. They assembled regularly and probably had frequent common meals. In particular the poor were cared for. That there was much poverty in the Church is shown by various circumstances, *e.g.*, this very "daily ministration" (Acts vi. 1). It is also rendered likelier by the consideration that in the understanding between Paul and the authorities at Jerusalem the latter deemed it necessary to seek assistance from the Gentile Churches of the former. Poverty may have been due partly to the Galileans having abandoned their possessions when they migrated to Jerusalem, and partly to their having given up work, and gifted away their possessions in their first enthusiasm. Still there were Christians of means in the early Church. Mary, the mother of John Mark, possessed a fine house and servants (xii. 12). We learn, too, that there were men- and maid-servants belonging to the Church of believers (*cf.* ii. 18). The joy of the doorkeeper Rhoda at the unexpected appearance of Peter shows how closely this slave reckoned herself to belong to the family. Differences of position were levelled by the common faith. The women, too, enjoyed complete recognition as members of the Church, or, better, of the Family (*cf.* ii. 17), *e.g.*, Mary, the mother of the Lord (i. 14) and the Mary just named. Sapphira also appears as an independent member along with her husband (v. 7 ff.). Peter is the head of the family, and the Twelve stand by him. Otherwise there is a complete lack of organisation. When there was anything to be done, as, *e.g.*, in the burial of a fellow-member, the younger members of the circle offered their services voluntarily (v. 6, 10, viii. 2).

In the course of time, however, the family idea was found insufficient. A community of from three to five thousand is a school, a sect, an order, like other Jewish ones. Thus we find the Christians designated as disciples, men " of the way " (Acts ix. 2, xxiv. 14), and saints. The last, which is simply a term like " separate " (Pharisee) and " pious " (Essene), is applied by Paul specially to the Church of Jerusalem, and indicates that the Old Testament ideal of a people holy to God was to be realised within it.

We may gather also from the report of the first years of the early Church given in Acts that a great enthusiasm filled the young and constantly-increasing Church, and the joy of confessing Jesus continued even in the midst of suffering. For the rest, we are not entitled to speak of a persecution of the Christians in this early period any more than of a brilliant public activity on the part of the disciples. The latter must have had the former as a consequence, and the Church would have been very quickly effaced. That the leaders of the people did not in their turn recognise the movement that was supposed to be checked by the death of Christ, and did not think of vigorously combating it, is due to the consideration that this small band of believers in the Messiah did not differ outwardly in any way from other Jews, and that it had made the ideal of the law-zealous Judaism of the time quite its own.

We may, however, ask if the ideal was realised. Luke, who clearly endeavours to set this early Church in the fairest light, has preserved for us two incidents which show that everything was not as it should have been.

In the forefront there is the story of Ananias and Sapphira. Urged on by the ambition to emulate Barnabas, who had earned high praise for his heroic self-denial on behalf of the Church, they resolved to take the same step. But they could not bring themselves to hand over the whole purchase price of their land to the Church. Without mentioning it, they reserved a part of the sum-total for themselves, while desiring to create the impression of the same generosity which Barnabas showed, and to be thought worthy of the same honour. The matter is accordingly one of simple lying, not the keeping back of a gift that was owed; the lie is all the more hateful since to cover its ambition it avails itself of the cloak of self-sacrificing love. In the strength of the prophetic spirit Peter discovers the deceit, and the sudden death which comes as a miraculous judgment upon the pair rids the Church of the offenders. This was the consideration which decided Luke to adopt the story. The holiness of the Church reacts spontaneously upon every offence, however trifling. Without questioning this, however, we can view the matter in a somewhat different light. It indicates that in the early Church all the members were not saints, but that much human sin found its way into it. Yet we shall not fail to observe that a moral spirit ruled within

THE CHURCH OF JERUSALEM 147

the Church, and did not neglect the punishment of things which often went unavenged outside it. It is the Holy Spirit's retributive intervention against sin.

The second instance in Acts is the internal differences which arise between the Hebrew and the Hellenist sections of the community. To the former belonged pure Jews, who, without leaving the holy soil of Palestine, maintained their fathers' speech, Aramaic, and their fathers' customs; while the latter consisted of those who, whether of free will, or under compulsion, as prisoners of war or merchants, had settled outside in the heathen world, had some of them been for generations there, had adopted the universal language Greek, and had allowed themselves much relaxation in the strictness of Jewish usage. Piety and love of home had again drawn them back to the holy city, not to a hasty visit to one of the feasts, but in certain cases at least to a stay of some length. Now, however, they adhered to the usages of foreigners, to Greek language and custom, and had therefore to tolerate being viewed askance by the real Jews as only half-Jews and being placed to some measure on the same level as proselytes. In ordinary life the antagonism did not find any great expression. The Hellenists kept by themselves and had their own synagogue. But the Christian Church united both in one, and so brought the antagonism to light. The Hellenists complained that at the "daily ministration" less attention was paid to the poor of their ranks. It would appear that the complaint was not without justification: for the community chooses from among the Hellenists the seven who were entrusted with charge of the distribution. Here again the most important point for the author of Acts is the quick and effective settlement of this disturbance of the common peace by the introduction of the new institution of the seven through the Spirit of God working in the Apostles. In this arrangement we shall recognise a proof of the powerful moral Spirit which regulated the existing forces, and employed them wisely for the general good, each after its kind. Then, too, we shall have to honour the character of this first "office" in Christendom, the care of the poor. Evidently it is like the "preaching office" of the Twelve, quite a voluntary dignity that did not keep its holder fully occupied. Stephen finds time for a rich evangelical ministry as well. Of most importance for us is the proof which it gives that divisions and discords were already known in the early Church.

Luke's ideal picture presents only these two shadows. It would be historically as unjust to conclude that there were no other troubles in the moral life of this Church as it would be vain to set forth considerations that might have given rise to them. The condition of the early Church under the immediate guidance of the Apostles was no ideal one, but it was a time of pious Jewish zeal and quiet growth in Christian spirit.

JEWISH CHRISTENDOM.

CHAPTER IX.

Further Development.

The Hellenists brought a new element into the Church. They were far removed from Pharisaic legalism. Much even that belonged to their law was weakened and set aside for them by allegorical interpretation. If Jesus' preaching of the Kingdom of God had an aspect that went beyond legalism, it fell here upon understanding ears. Apart from Jesus' foes, these Greeks were the first to appreciate and give expression to the fact that the attitude of Jesus to the Sabbath, and His words regarding the Temple, represented in principle a higher stage than Old Testament worship and an abolition of the law itself. On the early Church that had a twofold effect. Externally it led to the first greater conflict with the Jews. Stephen, the leader of the Hellenists, suffered martyrdom, and the Church was scattered. Internally it rendered the former naive attitude to the law impossible. At least all the most vigorous thinkers were exercised as to whether the law was an external order of God and still absolutely binding on the new Church, or whether it was abolished through Jesus. Was Christianity the true Judaism, or something different, something new? We see the conflict in its most pronounced form with Paul, who fought Christianity as rebellion against the law, but simultaneously with his conversion became the Apostle of the law-free Gospel.

Yet there was a section of the early Church, its very kernel, composed of immediate disciples like Peter, which still adhered firmly to the former view. That can be easily explained from the impression which, with all His liberty, Jesus had made on them by His loyal observance of the law.

They felt themselves inwardly free from the law, but the idea of outward emancipation never occurred to them. At the first glance Peter thought the proposal to go into a heathen house strange and even offensive. It required a Divine encouragement to persuade him (Acts x.). Soon afterwards in Antioch, when the same Peter wished to join the company of Paul, Barnabas, and other Gentile Christians, he again felt some scruples and withdrew (Gal. ii. 11 ff.).

On the other hand, the Hellenists, including as the most energetic champions Barnabas and Paul, the Hebrew of the Hebrews, represented with increasing clearness the complete separation of Christianity from Judaism. They preached in Samaria, they went even to Antioch and brought the news of salvation to the God-fearing heathen. With that, however, the former moral ideal of Jewish Christianity, unconditional obedience to the law of Israel, was given up. A special ideal of Christian morality required to be formed in opposition to the heathen one. How this was done, and how it quickly began to be realised under the powerful influence of Paul in his churches among heathen and Jews, we have already seen.

As opposed to this, however, there began in Jerusalem itself a reaction of increasing consciousness, sustained chiefly by such as had not belonged to the circle of Jesus' own disciples and were not touched by His free Spirit. The chief representative is James, the Lord's brother, who had not joined the Church till after the death of Jesus, but who, as the Lord's brother and by his own strong personality, quickly attained a leading position. These people deliberately support the unconditional obligation of the law: the Pharisaic ideal is also the Christian; perfected holiness in communities loyal to the law prepares the way for the Lord's return.

In Jerusalem this movement appears to have gained more ground. Luke explains it by the coming over of numerous Pharisees (xv. 5). It is more likely that the others left Jerusalem: first, the Hellenists (after the Stephen persecution), in order to carry the Gospel, whose far-reaching significance they had come to recognise, into the wide world; then, probably as the result of steps taken against them by Herod Antipas in the year 44, Peter and perhaps also other members of the original band, who grew more attached to their view as time went on.

The stricter section remained behind; James retained the power in his hands. We see him at the so-called Apostolic Council, in the year 51, occupying a leading position with Peter and John (Gal. ii. 9, *cf.* Acts xv. 13), and by the year 58 he stands alone at the head of the Church (Acts xxi.

18), the recognised leader of Palestinian Christendom until his death, probably in the year 62. The sentiment of the circle which rallied round him, the spirit which guided the early Church in this later period, we learn clearly from the so-called apostolic decree. This decree, indeed, as it is reported in Acts, chap. xv., cannot be accepted as a resolution of the original Apostles and the assembled Church, passed in the presence of Paul and Barnabas in the year 51. Probably, in accordance with the unmistakable notice in Acts xxi. 25, it was issued in the course of the following years by James and his people to the Syrian-Cilician mission-field long abandoned by Paul. Here the demand is made of Gentile Christians that they should abstain from the eating of meat offered to idols, from blood, things strangled, and fornication, out of regard for the Jews, with whom they lived in the mixed Christian churches (*cf.* xv. 21). On the one hand it may be maintained that in this decree no dogmatic views were laid down, but only precepts which aimed at practical conduct, precepts that regulated morality. The fact speaks well for the spirit of this Jewish Christianity. On the other hand, however, it reveals the true Jewish contempt of heathen : while the morality was simply presupposed as existent among the Jews, it was not believed that the Christian spirit would lead the Gentiles to chastity without an express commandment. Again, the combination shows a want of right moral appreciation. This eminently moral commandment is coupled with—nay, comes after—demands of an essentially ceremonial kind, an eloquent testimony to the Pharisaic spirit of these Jewish Christians. Even though the omission of the demand for circumcision may signify a withdrawal of the sole adequacy of their special form of Christianity, the fact that such regard was demanded from heathen Christians shows how sensitive the Jewish Christian conscience was in these things, and how anxiously Jewish Christians themselves observed them. If meat offered to idols and fornication alone had been named! These two things constituted for ages the special temptations of paganism.

That a special point was made of blood and things strangled, shows the characteristic quality of this Christian rabbinism. Here in the circle of James— on this point there can be no doubt—the Jewish ideal of holiness is made the universal Christian ideal.

The reverence of later ages for this man, who, as the Lord's brother, occupied an altogether special position, not only raised him far above Peter and the Twelve, and made him the first witness of the resurrection, but also drew a picture of him, which, though largely fanciful, enables us to recognise clearly the ideal of these Jewish Christians. Hegesippus writes of James, "whom all call the just. From his mother's womb he was holy. Wine and must he did not drink, neither did he eat flesh. A scissors came not upon his head; he put no oil upon him, and made no use of a warm bath. He alone might enter into the holy of holies; he also wore no woollen thing, but garments of linen. And he went alone into the Temple, and was found on his knees praying for the forgiveness of the people, so that his knees were hardened like a camel's, because he always bent them praying to God and imploring forgiveness for the people. On account of the exceeding measure of his righteousness, he was called the Just and Oblias, *i.e.*, being translated, guardian of the people and righteousness."

In this picture there are different features mixed up. In the first place there is the Nazarite consecrate to Jahweh. He abstains from all intoxicating drink, and lets his hair grow. He is described as "devoted to Jahweh," and is connected with the Rechabites. At the same time he is also the high-priestly intercessor for his people. Clad only in linen, he entered the holy of holies, and here, stretched before God till his knees were hardened, prayed for the forgiveness of his people. These two characteristics are not widely separated. The Nazarite, who realised in himself the ancient ideal of one consecrate to God, is as holy as the priest. He is at once the votary and the intercessor.

This Christian high-priest is certainly only an ideal picture — as impossible, historically, as individual touches in the martyrdom attached to it. But it shows us how perfect righteousness was conceived among the Jews. It is no new ideal, but takes its colour entirely from the Jewish piety of the Old Testament.

It is vain to ask to what extent this ideal found its realisation in the single personality of the Lord's brother. The honourable title of "the Just" was applied to him not only by his brethren of the faith, but also by unbelieving Jews. But there is no good evidence to show that such weight was laid on his high-priestly character as to lead the people to bring him forward to witness against Jesus. Enough, the picture of James shows us the line of moral effort within the Jewish Christian circles of Palestine—righteousness within the law which was viewed with a strictness at least equal to if not greater than that of the Pharisees. The law was taken seriously; there were no such attempts to evade it as were made by the Pharisees.

We are certainly entitled in support of this to cite the tradition of the Lord's words, which were collected and edited with special care in these circles. It is indeed no simple matter to value these aright. To what extent can they be traced back to the Lord, and how much has the Church added? Do the alterations which we certainly come across reflect the views of broader circles, or are they more or less unconscious licences in the statement of them? It lies outside the limits of our task to follow out these points in detail. At any rate, in Jewish Christian circles the Lord's sayings had a different and greater effect than in the Pauline Churches; not that they were less authoritative for the Gentiles, but that they were less known, and were less suited to the circumstances among them. Much that he found in his source was omitted by Luke as unessential and unintelligible to his readers. The Gospel of Matthew, though in its present form exclusively suited to Gentile Christians, retained much more of the Jewish background. A saying like Matt. v. 17, which is mentioned in the Talmud as springing from the Gospel, and cited by Jewish Christians, whether really a word of the Lord or not, had the effect of one. It strengthened Jewish Christians in their loyalty to the law, and later caused the Gentile Christians to establish a new law. The beatitudes, the exposition of the law, the directions as to right giving of alms, praying and fasting, trusting to God and having no care, not judging others, and preserving discipleship even in the outward deed, also influenced the ideal. Too light a view of them was prevented by sayings like that of the strait gate. All this points in one direction, the deepening of and giving inward content to them. Any freer utterances bearing on the Sabbath, the Pharisaic purificatory usages, the temple-tax and sacrifice, would be similarly understood: " These ought ye to have done and not to leave the other undone," " Cleanse first that which is within the cup and platter, that the outside of them may be clean also " (Matt. xxiii. 23, 26).

A saying like that, contained only in the Codex Cantabrigiensis (Luke vi. 4), on the Sabbath-breaker, " Blessed art thou, O man, if thou knowest what thou art doing; but if not, then cursed art thou as a transgressor of the law," can, if genuine, have been only, so to speak, rescued for the Gentile Church. More probably it is a result of later reflection. It was already much that those independent sayings of the Lord were kept in memory; every occasion was lacking in these pious Jewish Christian circles to assert their authority in action. On the other hand we possess in the Stephen narrative, and in the report of the martyrdom of James, two equally beautiful instances of the delight with which the request of the Lord for fearless confession was obeyed, and how precisely His command to pray for enemies, supported by His own example, was observed. In these things, with all their conservative attitude to the law, they had become conscious of the special character of Christian faith and conduct. This constituted the new element which was also at once the unifying and the distinguishing factor.

Naturally a community so wide, so distinctly separated from its environment, could not continue to live in the former family manner. Tolerably early a fixed organisation was here developed. This was facilitated by the natural position of James as the Lord's brother and by his energetic character. How the presbytery arose alongside of him we do not know. But it can hardly be wrong to say that here there was a conscious imitation of Jewish, or, better still, Old Testament arrangements, Num. xi. 16 f. (*cf.* the pseudo-Clementine Epistle of Peter to James, i.). Paul left the development of an organisation as well as the realisation of the moral ideal to the working of the Spirit. The Jewish Christians had both organisation and ideal when they took up a decided position on the main principle, " We Christians are the true Israel." Jewish Christianity was spared the conflicts as to constitution which played such an important rôle in Gentile Christianity. Already the very tradition of the Lord's words revealed the early origin and the high appreciation of the close organisation. In Matthew the idea of the Church is found twice. It occurs in the famous words to Peter (xvi. 18), for whom the later Jewish tradition would, so to speak, gladly have substituted James, and in connection with a regulation of Church discipline (xviii. 17). The reference to discipline reveals to us the serious view taken of the duty of forgiveness and the difficulties which beset its practice. If the offender is not to be moved by any kindly counsel, the only means left is excommunication. As an organised Church, too, Christendom preserves still the character of brotherhood. For the rest, even here ministers of the Spirit were not quite lacking. The five Jewish Christian prophets and teachers in Antioch, the prophet Agabus, and the four prophetically-gifted daughters of the evangelist Philip, are instances in point. These latter also show that women took a prominent place in the Jewish Christian communities. Such an influence, however, on the moulding of the general views as they exerted in the Gentile world, could not have been attained by the prophets here. The importance of the law and all that hung on it was too great.

Christian confession involved the obligation to spread the Gospel. Missionary work in Israel did not at any time cease, though we know little about it in this later period. Wherever there was a national Judaism, conventicles of Christian believers were formed as far as Damascus. But in regard to morality these did not differ specifically from their surroundings. The people who, following the Lord's directions, moved about in the land from place to place, from house to house, clad in only one cloak, without shoe or staff, without purse or scrip, and living on hospitality, did not desire to realise a new moral ideal and establish it among their compatriots. There was not to be any glorification of beggary or a new order of Essenes. Rather they acted as the Lord bade them, because time pressed and they were called to address a message to Israel; nothing was to prevent or hinder them in this. Nor did the message which they brought of the near Kingdom of God bid the Jews now cease to be Jews. On the contrary they were to be true Jews, loyal and conscientious in the discharge of all the religious and moral duties that pertained to all such. But, as distinguished from the Pharisaic ideal and from Pharisaic practice, there appeared in the foreground here humility, uprightness, purity of heart; and brotherly kindness, readiness to help, and hospitality were extended to all without distinction. Thus the Christian houses here and there in the land may have differed somewhat from what people were used to till then. But, as a matter of fact, it was only the ancient ideal set up already by the prophets and wisdom teachers that was realised through faith in Jesus of Nazareth as the divinely-chosen Messiah.

JEWISH CHRISTENDOM.

CHAPTER X.

JUDAISTIC PROPAGANDA.

THE Jewish Christians who were convinced of the unconditional obligation of the law did not restrict their labours to their native land, where the observance of the law had a historical claim upon the Christians, in so far as it was conceived to be national duty. They carried on a propaganda in the heathen world also. We know only too well the confusion which this Jewish agitation caused in the Pauline communities. In the light of Pauline polemic, we are inclined to look upon its leaders as underhand and self-seeking peace destroyers, and consequently not to place any great trust on the Jewish Christianity from which they proceeded. But we are not to forget that we possess only one-sided reports of the quarrel. Paul was partisan in the matter. He may have been materially right and may have had occasion enough to complain bitterly of his opponents' procedure, yet the fact that he refused to recognise among them anything but the lowest egoistic motives shows that something of the old Pharisaism still clung to the Apostle. It would be impossible to grasp the whole activity of these Judaists apart from their being moved by some sort of ideals.

The law was absolutely binding. The Christian moral ideal was identical with that of Judaism. The condition of being without law, heathendom, was, as such, sin (Gal. ii. 15). The Gospel had now penetrated into the Jewish διασπορά and the heathen world. That might have sufficed; but Judaism, and especially the Pharisees and those zealous for the law, was eagerly concerned to make proselytes. Now, however, the heathen must become genuine proselytes of Jewish Christianity, zealous disciples of the Christian rabbis.

Instead of this Paul and his companions had accommodated themselves to the heathen; they not only renounced all observance of the law in the case of new converts, but themselves denied the law, and caused the Jews whom they won to do so, to live together in closest connection with the polluted heathen as with Christian brethren, and to share their meals. Paul did not even protest against meat offered to idols, and he permitted mixed marriages. In addition to all that he propounded a theory of faith and grace, which in its practical consequences could only be summarised," Let us do evil that good may come." Here was a cry to heaven. Steps must be taken for the salvation of these Christians and the native Jews among them. They must be showed that this conduct cannot be allowed; that at least the Christian Jew must still observe the law and must keep far from the uncircumcised, even when these are Christians; and that even the heathen, to gain the full righteousness which alone leads to salvation, must adopt the law, be circumcised, keep the Sabbath, avoid unclean meats, and so forth, in a manner corresponding with Jewish custom and the ideal of these Jewish Christians.

The first storm occurred in Antioch, a Church, to be sure, strongly pervaded with Jewish elements, in which, however, the liberal views of Paul must have governed the intercourse of all Christians. Here the Judaists immediately came on the scene and made the direct demand that all Christians shall be circumcised, for circumcision is necessary to salvation (Acts xv. 1). This attack having been beaten off through the firm attitude of Paul and Barnabas, and an acknowledgment of uncircumcised heathendom in the person of Titus wrung from the authorities in Jerusalem (we are not concerned further with the nature of the mission distribution and the outward proof of unity in the collection made by the Gentile Christians for the poor of Jerusalem, Gal. ii. 9 f.), the convinced representatives of the legal standpoint attempted to save at least the Jews in the Antioch Church. Here they surprised Peter, the most notable disciple of the Lord, sitting at table with heathen without scruple and in contempt of the law. In Corinth we saw Paul exercised to free his Christians from unlimited intercourse with the heathen; here these Judaistic fanatics erected a similar wall of division within the Christian Church itself.

We learn what impression was made by their arguments from the fact that not only Peter, but also all the other Jews in the Church, including Barnabas, Paul's comrade of many years' standing in the mission-field and his companion in trials, yielded to them and formed an exclusive body alongside of the Gentile Church. This naturally involved an indirect attack on the Gentiles. It required the whole of Paul's clearness of principle and moral energy to oppose the onset, and if for the moment he did secure the upper hand he was nevertheless driven out of Antioch, his former scene of labour. He sought a new and essentially pagan basis for his work. Here, too, his opponents followed him; and as he everywhere connected himself with the synagogue and everywhere to a certain extent formed mixed Churches, he himself gave them an opportunity of attacking him. In Corinth, in Galatia, and in Rome we meet them, always with the same intention even if with varying tactics.

In Corinth they at first adhered entirely to the synagogue and endeavoured from this basis to influence the Pauline community. They sought to attract to themselves the Jewish element there, rallying round the party-cry of Cephas. Perhaps it was they who quickened the people's anxiety in the matter of meat offered to idols. They took advantage of the case of immorality and of the Church's insubordination towards the Apostle; their first concern was to shake his absolute authority. To this end they appear to have employed means which justly raised the anger of Paul. Nothing can justify their daring to calumniate him as a deceiver who reimbursed himself out of the collection for his renunciation of support (2 Cor. xii. 16), and as an immoral person who did shameful things in secret (2 Cor. iv. 2). They cannot be excused for throwing suspicion upon the sincerity of his language and the purity of his intentions, nor for employing his bodily weakness against him and laughing at his visions. But we must remember that for them he was an apostate, and that from the earliest times men have always been inclined to look for the lowest motives among heretics and to turn even the good into evil. We cannot, indeed, free Paul from having repaid them with like coin. In Antioch he speaks only "of false brethren unawares brought in who came in privily to spy out our liberty which we have in Christ Jesus that they might bring us into bondage" (Gal. ii. 4). Just as in the case of Peter and Barnabas he sees only vile hypocrisy due to fear of man (Gal. ii. 12 f.), so he treats the Jews in Corinth with the most scathing scorn:—"Such an one" (2 x. 11), "without understanding" (12), "glorying beyond measure in other men's labours" (15). With biting irony he names them "the very chiefest apostles" (xi. 5, xii. 11), and compares them to the serpent which seduced Eve (xi. 3); they are false prophets, lying workers, who change themselves into apostles of Christ, as Satan transforms himself into an angel of light (xi. 13 f.); they enslave the Church and drain it of its strength. Thus Paul employs against them the use which they made of the apostolic right recognised by him, because he does not acknowledge their apostolic calling. It is in the last instance always a conflict of principles. We may regret that it is carried on with such personal bitterness, and blame the agitators as the originators; but however much we may defend the assailed and injured Apostle, especially in view of his admirable conduct towards his Church, to which he is always showing fresh tokens of love, mildness, gentleness, and forgiveness, we must direct our attention in the first instance to the principle. It is the question of righteousness.

As ministers of righteousness—the real true righteousness, and not the heathen semblance of it that Paul preached—the Judaists came among the Corinthians, and those Corinthians who thought they could not take their stand upon the right of Christian freedom too strongly towards Paul, let themselves be impressed by this "righteousness." What they understood by that the agitators do not appear to have at once expressed quite clearly; of the dispute about the law Paul speaks here hardly at all.

The opponents in Galatia come forward still more explicitly with their demands. The law, with circumcision, regular festivals, and commands touching meats—these external and main considerations of Judaism—is binding upon all Christians. That was not established here either without an attack on the authority of Paul, whose Gospel had to be represented as at least imperfect and in need of supplementing. But here personal insinuation seems to have been avoided. All that was probably indicated was that his system was calculated to please men and to catch the greatest possible number (i. 10), that he himself occasionally preached circumcision (v. 11), and that he sometimes rebuked his Churches (iv. 16). Here, also, Paul employs the most pungent and biting severity: he thunders one anathema after another upon the disturbers of the peace (i. 7 ff.), and hands them over to the judgment of God (v. 10). He sees in their labours among the Galatians only the egoistic attempt to secure a following (iv. 17), to make a fair show in the flesh, and to escape the persecution of the unbelieving Jews (vi. 12); he goes so far as to say, "I would they were even cut off which trouble you" (v. 12). But these are only single utterances in the middle of a discussion which has regard only to principle. The question here too is, "Can there be perfected righteousness without the law?" From their own point of view the Judaists acted quite consistently when they demanded from the Gentile Christians of Galatia the recognition of the law as an indispensable and divinely-ordered means of salvation.

Even when imprisoned in Rome, Paul had not done with these conflicts. He still sees at work in the activity of Jewish missionaries personal motives directed against him (Phil. i. 15 ff.): he describes such persons as enemies of the cross of Christ who only seek their own (ii. 21), men of earthly intention, whose God is their belly (iii. 18 f.). But he had fought his way to the acknowledgment that here, too, Christ is, to a certain degree, preached, and for that he rejoiced (i. 18).

This brings us to the proper point of view for forming an opinion. The Judaists were concerned with a real propaganda in favour of Christianity, the full complete Christianity as they understood it; and that was the Christianity of righteousness in the exercise of obedience towards God. It was a supplementing of Paul's Gospel on the ethical side—in modern phraseology, justification by faith through sanctification. It shows more than one parallel to Pietism in its fight against orthodoxy. The Judaists were no more just to Paul than the Pietists were to genuine Lutheranism: they denied the moral strength which comes with faith as such, according to Paul and Luther. On this point Paul's doctrine requires no

JUDAISTIC PROPAGANDA

supplementing; only a stronger emphasising of the moral effect of the Spirit could help where there were real defects. Paul, as we saw, did emphasise it more and more. The way, however, in which the Judaists wished to supplement his teaching was indeed as unfortunate as possible. By simply adding the old law they dragged back their new religion, which was developing with great vigour in its independence, to the standpoint of the old. Besides, as is the way of all sects, they worked within the Pauline Churches less for Christianity than for their own particular ends. When we consider what they achieved, the unrest, the strife, the wrangling, and the bitterness in the Churches, and the tension which they caused between them and the Apostle, we shall indeed feel inclined to apply to them the doom which the Saviour pronounced against the Scribes and Pharisees, makers of proselytes (Matt. xxiii. 15). The truest judgment passed on these believing Jews and their propaganda is that which in a great hour Paul pronounced upon his unbelieving compatriots: "They have a zeal for God, but not according to knowledge; being ignorant of God's righteousness, they seek to establish their own" (Rom. x. 2 f.).

JEWISH CHRISTENDOM.

CHAPTER XI.

JEWISH CHRISTENDOM OF THE LATER PERIOD.

THE Jewish agitators form only a part, probably a very small part, of Jewish Christendom, which ought not to be judged by its extremes in a one-sided way. That of itself it could give birth to a propaganda of this extent is remarkable. The energy which was thrown into the movement deserves notice. But for the bulk of Jewish Christians we shall have to look for the practical demonstration of their moral strength in another sphere.

The "sixties" deprive them of their leaders and their centres. James, we may suppose, was martyred in 62, Paul in 63, and Peter in 64. Before Jerusalem was besieged the Christians fled into the district east of Jordan to Pella (Euseb., Hist. Eccl., iii. 5). As to what became of them there we are but poorly informed. We hear of relations of Jesus, who earned a scanty living as peasants: they showed the Emperor Domitian their horny hands (*ibid.*, iii. 20). In these circles, as we learn, there was still some stress laid on family relationship with the Lord. We have here to seek the source of the ideal picture which Hegesippus gives us of the Lord's brother. Certainly the Spirit of James was cultivated. Here also joy in confession was highly valued (*ibid.*, iii. 32, iv. 22).

We learn that about the middle of the second century two tendencies existed side by side, which can be looked upon as the continuation of the distinction represented by Peter and James. There were those who adhered to the traditional law of their people, but did not consider it as belonging to Christianity, and those who declared the law binding upon all Christians. Justin, in his dialogue with Trypho (chap. xlvii.) recognises the former, but will not admit that the latter belong to the Church. How far and in what spirit each of these divisions has actually fulfilled the law we cannot tell. The transformation of the law into a system of rules of conduct without temple or holy city must have been easier for them than for their non-Christian companions. A story about Rabbi Elieser and the Christian miracle-worker Jacob of Kephar Sekhanji, preserved for us in the Talmud (Ropes, *Words of Jesus*, pp. 149 f.), leaves the impression, that these Christians in their treatment of the law were quite as trivial and perverse as the Jewish rabbis. But if it is admitted that there was a real kernel there, what guarantee do we have that in the Rabbinical Tradition the Christian saying retained its true form?

We possess a better source in the fragments of the Gospel of the Hebrews, which unfortunately are very scanty. Here we come upon a quite different spirit. Active brotherly love, assistance, and compassion are insisted on exactly as in 1 John iii. 17, iv. 20. " Behold many of thy brethren, sons of Abraham, are wrapped up in filth, and dying of hunger, and thy house is full of rich goods, and nothing comes from it for them." To trouble a brother's spirit is considered among the worst of sins: "Never rejoice except when ye see your brother united with you in love." These are, in fact, true developments of the fundamental thought of Jesus, and if the Jewish Church gave birth to them, we may be assured that it was also concerned to realise them. The strange variants in the account of Christ's baptism show that stress was laid on the consciousness of sin and guilt—just as in 1 John i. 8 ff. The disciples of Jesus were to be the good. Begging is forbidden. Manual labour is esteemed. The position of women is raised, if the citation from the Talmud is right, according to which the Gospel as distinguished from the law decrees that daughters shall inherit equally with sons. It is indeed a serious misapprehension of the main thought, when in the parable of the pounds the man who buries his pound is merely reproached for it, while the weight of punishment falls upon the man who squandered his with prostitutes and flute-players. The introduction of this feature from the parable of the prodigal son certainly weakens the effect, and it throws a sad light upon these Christian Churches, that an express warning such as we find quite natural in the heathen world was here conceived to be necessary. That everything was not pure and clean here is self-evident. We should believe it even without the Talmud's story of an unjust, corruptible Christian judge. But that this hostile source has not more to say about the wickedness of the Christians must certainly be regarded as creditable. Even more than the first decades had done, the excitement of the Bar Cochba time had given

JEWISH CHRISTENDOM—LATER PERIOD 171

them opportunity to prove in martyrdom their belief in the Messiah Jesus of Nazareth and his unpolitical Kingdom of God, and thereby to give that proof of the strength of Christian morality, which even the Gentile Christians of the second and third centuries considered most decisive.

Later on some of the Jewish Christians approximated more and more to the Gentiles. In Ælia Capitolina, on the ancient and holy ground of Jerusalem, a Gentile-Christian Church arose. Aristo of Pella wrote in the Greek tongue a dialogue against an Alexandrian Jew. Hegesippus is in principle a Catholic Christian. Those who did not share in this development, who still adhered to circumcision, legal usages, and the Jewish mode of life, were considered heretics, as early as the time of Irenæus (Hær., 1 xxvi. 2). The view may be considered severe, but it is historically justified.

In these Jewish Christian circles of Palestine also, Gnosticism and its accompaniment of asceticism entered. With it came a complete alteration of the old legal ideal of a righteousness like that of the Pharisees, but superior to it. That, however, belongs to another chapter.

Let us conclude with a short summary of our view of Jewish Christianity in the first century. In the matter of morality it had a different task from that of the Churches of Paul in heathen lands. For Jewish Christians it was not a matter of developing an entirely new ideal in opposition to the traditional and popular one, but of deepening and strengthening the existing one. This they did to the best of their power, and thereby rendered a real service to Christianity as a whole. We were struck with the immaturity of the young Gentile Churches; they were in the growing stage. The Jewish Christianity on Jewish soil bears to some extent the features of something old and complete.

The Jewish Christianity of Palestine trained by the law was, so to speak, the backbone which supported the moral consciousness of the whole. We must never forget that Paul himself was sprung from Judaism. And the Judaistic agitation in his Churches, in spite of all the injury it did, still achieved the result of laying more stress on the moral side of Christianity. The apostolic decree affected perhaps only a narrow circle directly; but indirectly, through its reception in Acts, it influenced the whole of Gentile Christianity. Later, too, men of outstanding importance sprang from Jewish Christendom —perhaps more than we suspect. Jewish Christianity bequeathed to the Gentile Church the very precious treasure which it possessed in the collection of the sayings of the Lord. At the same time it gave the Bible of the Old Testament to the Gentiles. Because of this, Gentile Christianity approached ever nearer to the ideals of Jewish Christianity—whether under the direct influence of Jewish Christianity or not is quite indifferent. When that was attained Jewish Christianity had fulfilled its task. It had only temporary significance and was bound to perish. That it remained alive till the days of a Jerome is astonishing. And we should certainly be still more astonished at the services it rendered in this period in the field of moral education, if history were not so thankless in dealing with quiet, earnest work in small things.

Book III.

LATER CHRISTIANITY AMONG THE HEATHEN.

CHAPTER XII.

THE CHURCHES STILL UNDER PAULINE
INFLUENCE—ASIA MINOR.

WHEN we turn again to the Gentile Churches on Graeco-Roman soil, we find a far greater variety. At first the influence of the Apostle Paul still dominates; it is possible to speak directly of a post-Pauline phase of Christianity. Then, however, other persons and powers come into view. In the front of these was John of Asia Minor, a man of quite different mould from Paul, of different origin, with a different development, and a different position, but nevertheless the most powerful influence in his circle. There remained, however, reminiscences of Paul, and so a mixed picture comes to be developed. Both influences, however, are crossed by a third, a current which came from outside, but quickly secured a place for itself in Christianity—Gnosticism. Gnosticism is only one among many currents; but it cannot be treated as a mere foil to the development of ordinary Christianity. Its significance claims a special treatment. And lastly, in the conflict with this strange tendency the development comes to a relative conclusion in what we might call Catholicising Christianity, which, though primitive Christian in its ground principle, and still imperfect in its outward form, nevertheless already anticipates material features of the later Catholicism. This chapter divides accordingly into four sections. Only within the first is a geographical division possible.

In the period immediately following the time of Paul we find the picture only slightly altered. We have still small communities scattered here and there in the larger towns. They were connected with one another only by the spiritual bond of faith and mutual love, and as single communities were only weakly fastened together by an organisation just in process of formation. The want of a ruling personality like the great Gentile Apostle is distinctly noticeable. They had all looked to him as to their spiritual father, and had recognised his authority absolutely, though sometimes unwillingly. Now, indeed, there were not wanting true leaders and advisers for the Churches. But these felt themselves to be descendants. They covered themselves, if they appeared as authors, with the name of Paul, Peter, Barnabas, or James, and when they desired to be impressive, they repeated with trifling modifications some such thing as the table of domestic duties from the Epistle to the Colossians.

The communities themselves had gained in compass and also in tasks. Continually widening circles had to be educated in Christianity, while at the same time the danger of a large stream of impure elements winning admission or supremacy in the Church had to be guarded against. On the other hand we must not neglect a fact usually undervalued, viz., that in the interval a class of old experienced Christians had been formed. For years, in some cases from earliest youth, these had been under the discipline of the Christian spirit, and represented, so to speak, the conscience of the Church, reacting against all degeneracy quite otherwise than the Apostle, with all his authority, had been able to do from without. Such excesses as those in Corinth during Paul's time are no longer heard of. The moral demands are perhaps somewhat lessened, but the average morality, the moral consciousness of the whole, is raised. There no longer breathes that mighty spirit which accomplished extraordinary things in the first enthusiasm; they have become smaller and more petty, but at the same time more painstaking and more faithful in small things.

The difficulties which the scantiness of our sources causes in this section are increased by the fact that these are so difficult to understand: we do not usually know even the author; we are in doubt as to the time and place of origin. Nevertheless a local classification alone, however subjective it may be, will make it possible for us to avoid a false generalisation and to estimate correctly what is special to each case.

We begin with the Christendom of Asia Minor. Thence comes the precious meditation upon the mystery of divine economy in the uniting of a humanity formerly divided, which we know as the Epistle of Paul to the Ephesians. The epistle is most intelligible when we understand it as the effusion of a profound Christian thinker whom Paul's Epistle to the Colossians had excited to such thoughts. Asia Minor is also indicated in the letter under the name of Peter, which, originating in Rome after his martyrdom, is directed to the Christians of the mission-field worked by Paul in Asia Minor and adheres strictly to his way of thinking. These two epistles are very different in nature. The one is profound speculation set forth in the hymning tone of exultant devotion; the other sober exhortation to practical demonstration of Christianity with a clear outlook on the circumstances of the time. But the conditions which they presuppose agree entirely in their main features. Both epistles contain in these common features many echoes of the Johannean world of thought still to be discussed. But they are not to be interpreted as if already they were influenced by John; they show us rather the basis upon which John's peculiar comprehension of Christianity could become fruitful.

In the first place it is remarkable how strongly the moral aspect of Christianity comes into evidence. Christianity is the practical ordering of life according to the principles of a new moral spirit. There is here, indeed, a greater divergence of the two lines, knowledge of the mystery of divine salvation and exercise of obedience towards God's will, which Paul binds fast together in the word faith; but the practical bent of piety maintains the supremacy throughout. The Epistle to the Ephesians, penetrating in prayerful devotion into the mystery of the union of the two halves of humanity in Christ, emphasises knowledge above all (i. 9, 17 ff., iii. 3 ff.) ; next to that, however, stands love as the ground principle of Christian life (i. 4, iii. 17, v. 2), which, while surpassing all knowledge, is yet in the last instance the object of it (iii. 19). It is speculation, but no unfruitful speculation, when, in Eph. ii. 10, the good works which are the special feature of the Christian condition are prepared by God beforehand, that the Christians should walk in them, and it is conceived as the end of their being chosen before the foundation of the world that they should be holy and without blemish before Him in love (14).

All through the first Epistle of Peter, which with great clearness turns its attention to the practical questions of life, in view particularly of the persecution that threatened on all sides, the leading thought is obedience to the will of God (i. 2, 14, 22)—instead of want of faith we find disobedience (ii. 8, iii. 1, 20, iv. 17)—, in joy (i. 6, 8), and hope (i. 3, 21). Christian conduct was comprehensively expressed in the characteristic word ἀγαθοποιία, doing good.

The moral spirit shows its effect on the conception of Christianity in very varied directions. There was a real devotional life not only in the author of the Epistle to the Ephesians with its prayerful tone, but also in the Churches (Eph. vi. 18 f.). There is no disposition to check the free motion of the Spirit: " Be filled with the Spirit " (Eph. v. 18). But we do not hear any more of those eccentric occurrences of a too tense enthusiasm which happened at first. " Be ye therefore of sound mind, and be sober unto prayer," " Be sober, be watchful," run the warnings in 1 Pet. iv. 7, v. 8. Even the married life is to be regulated by the practice of prayer (1 Pet. iii. 7).

The statements in the first Epistle of Peter (iii. 19 f., iv. 6) on the preaching of Christ to the dead have been much disputed. To estimate these properly they must be set alongside of the superstitious view of the influence of vicarious baptism on those already dead, which we came across among Corinthian Christians in the time of Paul. Both have the same end in view: the discovery of some comfort for the fate of those who were warmly loved, but must, it is feared, be for ever lost, because the blessing of the saving Gospel had not been attained by them in life. In Corinth the attempt was to secure it through a holy magic; here, by the idea of a missionary preaching which reached even to the dead. The advance in moral conception is unmistakable.

The Christian conduct of life is still defined by its opposition to surrounding paganism. "Given over to lasciviousness to work all uncleanness with greediness" (Eph. iv. 19), "having our conversation in the lusts of our flesh" (Eph. ii. 3, *cf.* 1 Pet. i. 14, ii. 11), lasciviousness, lusts, excess of wine, revellings, banquetings, and abominable idolatries (1 Pet. iv. 3), malice, guile, hypocrisies, envies, and evil speakings (1 Pet. ii. 1)—such being the nature of heathendom, Christianity stands in complete opposition to it.

Heathendom is ἄγνοια, *i.e.*, it lacks all sure moral knowledge, because it is alienated from God. Christianity brings this knowledge (Eph. iv. 17 f., 1 Pet. i. 14). There was darkness, here was light (Eph. v. 8, 1 Pet. ii. 9). Heathendom is moral death; Christianity is life (Eph. ii. 1 ff.) or effective power

(Eph. i. 19, iii. 20). And this is so not in spite of, but because of the Christians' acute consciousness that not this life but the next is all-important for them: in Heaven they are at home; on this earth they feel themselves strangers (Eph. i. 3 f., ii. 6, 1 Pet. i. 1, 17, ii. 11).

However much the opposition to heathendom was emphasised, it was very difficult in practice to separate the Christian Churches from contact with the surrounding heathen world. That is shown by the exhortations which are introduced and always repeated, above all by 1 Pet. iv. 3 f. Old and good friends are offended at the sudden cessation of earlier relations and retaliate with the same weapon. Men who naturally do not judge their life as the Christian convert now does, and are conscious of being honourable citizens, cannot but think that behind this Christian brotherhood which withdraws so anxiously into itself some abominations or other lie hid, which have to fear the light: and so they calumniate the Christians.

At this time, as the notice in Tacitus (*Ann.*, xv. 44) shows, there must have been current all those suspicions of the Christians, against which the apologists of the second century had unceasingly to defend their companions of the faith. It was said that they did the most horrible things in their secret assemblies, including unnatural unchastity and ceremonial sacrifice of children. Begotten of the filth of a corrupted people's fancy, and nourished through religious fanaticism, these charges repeatedly appear in the history of religion. The figurative speech of the Christians seems to have given them some ground. That the rabble of Rome set them going is not to be wondered at; that a historian like Tacitus spread them without investigation is a lamentable indication of the lack of understanding of the fact of Christianity on the part of a noble-thinking and eminent Roman. The sharp censor of the corrupted old world did not recognise that here there were to hand in kernel the moral forces which would shape the world anew.

Especially valuable witness is borne to the groundlessness of that report by his contemporary the younger Pliny in his report to Trajan during the period of his governorship of the Province of Bithynia. The Christians, even those who forswore Christianity before the pro-consul, solemnly declared that among them nothing in the nature of crime happened. On the contrary, at their Sunday assemblies they laid vows upon one another to commit no theft, robbery, or adultery, and not to embezzle property entrusted to them. When the pro-consul, after putting two deaconesses to the torture, could not come to any other conclusion than that he had to do with a perverted and gross superstition, the question was forced upon him, which he put to the Emperor, whether Christianity as such was punishable, or only in case of crime being proved also. It is the same question which the Christians had plainly stated and clearly answered: "But let none of you suffer as a murderer, or as a thief, or as an evil-doer, or as a busybody in other men's matters; yet if any man suffer as a Christian, let him not be ashamed, but let him glorify God on this behalf" (1 Pet. iv. 15 f.). It cannot be untrue that possibly in single cases

Christians were actually guilty of such crimes, and were therefore condemned. The ἀλλοτριεπισκοπεῖν especially, meddling in things that did not concern them, intervening in politics from the standpoint of Christian eschatology, or pressing forward with their own confession during the trial of another Christian, might be, for many, a great temptation. From the words of 1 Peter we cannot prove that murderers, thieves, and other evil-doers were actually to be found in the Christian Churches, nor even that the author reckons much on the possibility of Christians being condemned for such crimes. They are charges of the enemy, and everything that even appears justification of them is to be avoided. In this sense the warnings are intended as prophylactic.

There was, however, another aspect of the opposition to heathendom. Christians have a missionary task to perform, and the moral life is a means to it (*cf.* Matt. v. 16). It is not enough, instead of participating in the fruitless works of darkness, only to reprove them (ἐλέγχετε, Eph. v. 11, *cf.* John xvi. 8), and through doing good to put to silence the ignorance of foolish men (1 Pet. ii. 15, iii. 15 f.); they must win unbelievers by the silent preaching of a blameless Christian walk in the fear of God and in chastity (1 Pet. ii. 12). In especial this is the task of the Christian partner in mixed marriages (1 Pet. iii. 1 f.). Here again we see that the separation from the outside world was still by no means complete, however much it was aimed at.

We are reminded of Paul and conditions in the Pauline Churches by the positive way in which the different questions of the Christian moral life are handled. The first Epistle of Peter, written in Rome, discusses the attitude to the magistracy quite in the method of the Epistle to the Romans: unconditional submission is commanded for the Lord's sake (ii. 13 f.). Here, however, it becomes clear that the Christians had had occasion by this time to become acquainted with the organs of the Roman administration in their different grades as adversaries of Christianity. However much they are made to stand for justice "for the punishment of evil-doers and the praise of them that do well," the feeling throughout is that for the most part they are persecutors. It is all the more remarkable that the principle of respectful recognition of their divine appointment is maintained without alteration. An Old Testament word lends its aid. The Christian exhortation, "show honour to all and love the brotherhood," goes hand in hand with Prov. xxiv. 21: "Fear God, honour the king." This is not the language used where a revolutionary spirit prevails. Similarly the relations of the family life are treated in close connection with the table of domestic duties in the Epistle to the Colossians, but with much more breadth, first, in the Epistle to the Ephesians, and then in the first Epistle of Peter. We miss here the brevity and clearness, the insistence on the things of great practical significance, which distinguishes Paul. Instead, the Epistle to the Ephesians gives a series of lengthy appeals, while the first Epistle of Peter multiplies references to the heathen world. The special warning against drunkenness is new (Eph. v. 18). The repetition of the warning to women to be respectful to their husbands (Eph. v. 33, *cf.* 21) can

CHURCHES UNDER PAULINE INFLUENCE 183

hardly be taken to mean that any particular efforts after emancipation had made this necessary. There is a remarkable warning in the first Epistle of Peter against toilet luxuries. Even outwardly the Christian woman is to be distinguished by chaste simplicity, and is to seek her ornamentation in a meek and quiet spirit (iii. 3 f.). Here we have a proof not so much that the desire for ornaments had won the upper hand among Christian women as that more regard now began to be paid to those outward things. The Christian moral ideal assumes more definite and, to some extent, narrower forms.

As a matter of fact we have to observe here a double and very important advance on Paul. He had entrusted everything to the working of the Spirit of Christ, guarding only against the influences of the heathen spirit. He hardly ever appealed to the law. The pattern which guided him was the image of Christ, the Lord of Glory, Who had humbled Himself.

Now we find, first, a Biblicising of the Christian ideal, if we may say so. The Old Testament is adduced in stronger terms as the foundation of the demands of Christian morality. Eph. v. 31 refers love of husband and wife to Gen. ii. 24, vi. 2 f., and love of children to the Decalogue (Ex. xx. 12). The first Epistle of Peter (iii. 5 f.) holds up to Christian women the pattern of the holy women of the old Covenant, in particular Sarah, and summarises its exhortations in the words of the 34th Psalm (vv. 13–17 = 1st Pet. iii. 10–12). The conduct of the Christians is to conform (1 Pet. i. 13, 22) to the Passover (Ex. xii. 11) and the Covenant (Ex. xix. 10). From the prophet Isaiah the picture of the spiritual armour is taken (Eph. vi. 14 ff.). The Epistle to the Ephesians propounds a theory, that the Gentile Christians have become fellow-citizens with the saints and of the household of God (ii. 19). Then, too, it is acknowledged that the πολιτεία τοῦ Ἰσραήλ, *i.e.*, the Old Testament morality, however little the actual Judaism corresponded with it (ii. 3 f.), supplies the ideal. What was a matter of history in the Church at Jerusalem is here attained by the roundabout method of a historical-philosophical speculation apart from all Judaism—the law is abolished (ii. 14 f.)—simply on the ground of the authority of scripture, as the Gentile Christendom of all time acknowledged it. Christian morality appears as the completion of the Old Testament Jewish morality, "built upon the foundation of the Apostles and Prophets" (ii. 20); in the same way the Epistle to the Ephesians knits together the exhortations of the Apostle Paul to the Colossians with the utterances of the Prophets.

Yet the specifically Christian character of this morality is preserved, "Jesus Christ Himself being the chief corner-stone" (ii. 20). This is the second new factor in the conception of the moral ideal; it had received through the operation of the evangelical tradition of the words and deeds of the Lord, a much more definite stamp; they learned Christ, heard Him, and were taught by Him (Eph. iv. 20 f.). Not the self-humiliation of the transcendent Son of God, but single features of Christ's human life and passion, serve as pattern even in Eph. v. 2, 25 (*cf.* 24, 29), and still more in 1 Pet. ii. 21 ff. (where, it is true, the passion of Christ is described with words taken from

Isaiah liii.), and in iv. 1; we may also adduce here Heb. ii. 17 f., iv. 15, v. 7 ff.

Besides, the words of the Lord, to which Paul attached unique authority though they left no clear traces of extensive influence, begin now to be collected and spread abroad in many forms, and to determine the thoughts and judgments of Christendom. They become a kind of new law for the Christian Churches and also for the Gentiles, as they had already been for Jewish Christianity in another sense. This brought to Gentile Christendom an abundance of new moral knowledge. At the same time the danger grew, that what was spoken against a perverted legalism should itself become law when separated from its context. No Jewish propaganda was required for that. It is human nature to view the principles of morality not as inward impulse, but as external law.

The fact that several writings agree on this point shows that the matter is not the peculiarity of a single author. Then, too, the circumstances correspond with the altered situation. The Churches of Paul were in reality pure mission Churches; only a small percentage of the members had brought with them from the synagogue any previous moral education. Now we are dealing with Churches which had already a history behind them. Probably every day saw new members added. We are amazed at the extension which Pliny reports Christianity to have won in Asia Minor by the time of Trajan. Many of all ages, of every standing, of both sexes, in the town as well as in the villages, confess the name of Christ. The temples stand almost forsaken; their solemn services have ceased; no one will now buy the meat offered to idols. These crowds had to be introduced to the Spirit of Christianity. It is to them these warnings not to walk longer like the heathen are directed (Eph. iv. 17). Christianity cannot endure lying, theft, fornication, covetousness, and so forth (Eph. iv. 25 f.). That the permeation of the Christian Spirit was only partly successful is shown by the great apostasy in the first serious interference of the Roman governor. Pliny feels certain of being able to bring the contagion of this superstition to a cessation, and even to do away with it altogether. Most of the people quietly offered to idols and cursed Christ, while many declared that, if they had ever been Christians, they had given it up three, and sometimes twenty, years ago.

How far these people had been laid hold of by the moral spirit of Christianity, and retained as the most important relic of their Christian days, the feeling of obligation to avoid theft, robbery, adultery, to keep true, and not embezzle property entrusted to them, we cannot tell. We are concerned with the communities. And here the new addition is not so important as the old race of people grown up in Christianity, who, so to speak, represent the Church's conscience. Through constant use of the Old Testament, these became filled more and more with the moral spirit of the prophetic, and partly the legal religion of Israel. They give an increasingly constant form to the tradition of the Lord, and more definite shape to the moral ideal. In this way the general moral tone undoubtedly came to be raised. We found the later letters of Paul laying stress on the fact that an inward growth must go hand in hand with the longer existence of Christianity; and here (Eph. iv. 13 f.) the picture of growth from childhood to manly ripeness and perfected character is vividly worked out. 1 Pet. v. 10 prays for the preparation, the perfecting, the stablishing, and the strengthening of the Churches.

Comparison also enables us to observe an advance in the shape of an increase of moral requirements. Fornication, unchastity, covetousness, shall not only not exist (Col. iii. 5), but shall not once be mentioned (Eph. v. 3). Everywhere the negative is joined by the positive. Putting away lying (Col. iii. 8), let every man speak truth with his neighbour (Eph. iv. 25); the thief, instead of stealing, is to give his hands something to do, that he may have to give to the needy (Eph. iv. 28); instead of corrupt talk, they are to speak that which is good to the use of edifying (Eph. iv. 29); instead of filthiness, foolish talking and jesting, let them give thanks (Eph. v. 4). In the discipline of children, not only is severity repudiated, but there is an express demand for a Christian moral training. The social relations are already so equalised that the author can say to the Christian masters of Christian slaves, " And ye masters, do the same things unto them (*i.e.* strictly, obey them in fear and trembling!), forbearing threatening" (Eph. vi. 9).

The various reasons, " For we are members one of another" (Eph. iv. 25), "as becometh saints" (v. 3), and the mention of the relation of Christ to the Church, show that a definite Church ideal is forming. Christ offered Himself for the Church to cleanse it by the washing of water, and to sanctify it by the word, that He might present the Church to Himself, not having spot or wrinkle or any such thing, but that it should be holy and without blemish (Eph. v. 25 ff.). Holiness is conceived as a moral demand (1 Pet. i. 15). There is already a double designation of the community; from the outside they are "Christians" (1 Pet. iv. 16), from the inside, a "Brotherhood" (1 Pet. ii. 17, v. 9). The feeling of community is much fostered. Every one has his particular task in the service of the whole (Eph. iv. 11 ff., 1 Pet. iv. 10 f.). The Christian virtues of lowliness, meekness, long-suffering, all aim at mutual and loving forbearance, at zealous upholding of the unity of the Spirit in the bond of peace (Eph. iv. 26). "Finally, be ye all of one mind, having compassion one of another, love as brethren, be pitiful and courteous," is the summing up of 1 Pet. iii. 8, and there is added as climax of the Lord's demands, not to render evil for evil, but to repay cursing with blessing.

We cannot fail to observe a certain relaxation of moral energy. The exhortation, "Use hospitality one to another without murmuring" (1 Pet. iv. 9), hints that the ever-increasing demands for brotherly assistance began to be felt burdensome by many. Some perhaps sought their own profit; hence the demand for "unfeigned love of the brethren" (1 Pet. i. 22). The author exhorts not to love merely but to fervent love from the heart (1 Pet. i. 22, iv. 8), just as nowadays it is often thought necessary to speak of warm, living, strong Christianity—always a sign of relaxation.

Then, too, there seems to be some danger of perverted liberty. Like Gal. v. 13, 1 Pet. ii. 16 contains a warning against the misuse of freedom as a covering for wickedness. Christianity is the service of God.

Nevertheless the general estimate is entirely favourable. Paul's boast of the faith and love of the Colossians (Col. i. 4) can be simply transferred to these Churches (Eph. i. 15); and 1 Pet. v. 12 affirms solemnly that they stand in the true grace of God. On this account we must not draw false conclusions from the exhortations of the epistles: their insistence on the practical demonstration of religion has been necessary in every age of Christianity.

The first Epistle of Peter had special occasion to emphasise hopeful boldness and patient endurance of suffering in view of the persecution everywhere revealing itself. It was a stern probation of the Christian condition (i. 6 f., iv. 12 ff., v. 8 f.). The Epistle to the Ephesians, again, had every reason to exhort to unity in love, for, as we shall presently see, this unity was threatened by a danger that arose in the midst of the Churches.

While Christendom kept separating itself more and more from the world, and defining its own ideal with increasing clearness in dependence on the Bible of the Old Testament and the tradition of the Lord, there appeared two new internal dangers, which sorely threatened, if not the existence of Christianity, at least the purity and tranquillity of its moral life. These dangers were hierarchy and heresy.

We saw that in the first period the danger of disorder hindered free development under the Spirit. Therefore it was that Paul insisted on the recognition of the authority of those members who had voluntarily taken over the service of guiding and managing church affairs. These were probably most of them persons whose outward social position made it possible for them to make gifts to the Church. As people who had belonged to it since its foundation, or had been converted in other places, they enjoyed a natural authority. That was bound to change with time. Those "firstlings" died away like the apostles who had created and founded their office. Their place was taken by others who did not possess the same special significance. An exclusive circle of church elders (Presbyters) arose gradually in the Church. These might easily be in many, or even most, cases long-standing members of the Church, men whose age gave them a natural claim to authority; but without such justification it was possible for specially energetic persons to attain to leading place. Spiritual ambitions were developed. What formerly was praised as voluntary service was now coveted as something valuable, something rich in honour and material advantages. What reaction it was that called forth this procedure on the part of the Churches, accustomed as they were to the free development of all spiritual gifts and powers, we shall afterwards see. Here we are concerned only with the moral defects which the new office, if we may speak so of something so entirely incomplete, brought with it for its occupants.

What these defects were we learn from the exhortations which a Roman Christian conceived it necessary to give to them in the name of the Apostle Peter, their fellow-presbyter already glorified through martyrdom (1 Pet. v. 1 ff.). There is first the exhortation to voluntariness: "Feed the flock of God

.... not by constraint, but willingly." These words recall those of the Lord about hirelings, who, instead of laying down their life for the flock, flee in haste when danger comes. The office might, in fact, be felt by some not only as a burden but also as a danger; it exposed its occupant more than others to the magistrates in times of persecution. If we several times observe in the Christianity of this period a certain reluctance to suffer and a tendency to apostasy, nothing is more likely than that the tendency was quite as frequent in the case of persons of leading position. We know parallel instances belonging to a much later time, when a fixed organisation prevented apostasy but directly encouraged flight. Think of Cyprian of Carthage and Peter of Alexandria, who both wiped out the stain afterwards in the bath of blood. Now, too, we begin to hear of difficulties in internal management, opposition proceeding from the ministers of the Spirit, disorders in the presbytery itself, irregularities in the receipt of contributions, differences in doctrinal opinions, and so forth. It is easy to conceive that less strong, less ambitious, and less dominating personalities felt the office to be a burden, and tried to rid themselves of it. "Not by constraint, but willingly"; the warning shows the one side of the matter.

The other warning is still more significant. "Not for filthy lucre, but of a ready mind; neither as being lords over God's heritage, but being examples to the flock." A task of that kind releases the noble forces, but also passions and desires. One would suppose that the love of money must have been quite foreign to the first Christians with their separation from the world and entire concentration on the future glory. But they were men. The charm of power-bestowing gold is ineradicable. The desire to rule is a passion which can quite overcome many a gifted and vigorous mind. So it is not unintelligible that temptations of the kind appeared within the presbyteries. We shall see afterwards how even the prophets lost their authority by such human frailties breaking through in a very serious way; can we wonder that, where instead of the free Spirit there was only the thought of office, some succumbed to those temptations?

That, however, was not the rule. Men of the stamp of Callixtus, the best example of this type of hierarch, at the beginning of the third century, were not very numerous: on the contrary, his opponent, the strict Hippolytus, would have found at that time many of his way of thinking. The apostolical exhortation of the first Epistle of Peter to the effect that the office of elder involved in the first place the task of a pattern Christian walk, shows that they were still conscious of the high responsibility of this position in the moral aspect, and also of the significance which was attached to morality even in questions like organisation. When obedience to the elders is demanded of the "young men," what is intended by making it refer to the whole Church may be the enforcement of official authority in the sense of 1 Cor. xvi. 16, 1 Thess. v. 12. But apparently under young men, as under "elders," Christians with special services in the Church are to be understood, a lower stage of the clergy, so to speak, acting on the commission of the elders; hence the warning to obey them. Here, too, a comparison with later occurrences shows how easily insubordination could occur. The 18th Canon of Nicæa, *e.g.*, deals with the communicating of elders and deacons. But while ceremonial and hierarchical considerations are responsible for the arrangements there, in the first Epistle of Peter the moral idea alone is of importance. The warning closes, " All of you gird yourselves with humility, to serve one another." Hierarchical ideas cannot be more pointedly repudiated than by this saying, based, it is true, upon an Old Testament saying (Prov. iii. 34), but immediately recalling Christ's pattern act in the washing of the disciples' feet (John xiii. 4, 12 ff.).

More critical than the moral danger which threatened the Christian Churches through hierarchical endeavours was that which proceeded from heresy. This is spoken of in the Epistle to the Ephesians, but in such general terms that it is hardly recognisable what the matter really is, and one is tempted to adopt the view that the conditions treated of in the Epistle to the Colossians are simply re-echoed here. But not only is this short treatment in the Epistle to the Ephesians entirely new ; when we follow up the indicated line of development, we come across both hierarchical and heretical antitheses in the Johannean literature. It is perhaps not too bold to set the indications of the Epistle to the Ephesians in a more remote relation to these. If this view be correct, it is gnostic speculations of docetic tendency against whose seductions our author will arm his readers. This, however, is not our concern further. We are concerned only with the important consideration, that, exactly as we shall find in the Johannean writings, so also the Epistle to the Ephesians sees in the seducing arts of the false teachers (iv. 14), in which it detects the devil himself at work (vi. 11), moral dangers which are to be met by moral conduct. Instead of being tossed to and fro and carried away with every wind of doctrine, by the slight of men, the demand is simply to be true in love (iv. 15). Therefore the spiritual equipment of the Christian, which the author describes with the free employment of a picture out of Isaiah (xi. 5, lix. 17, lii. 7), is truth, righteousness, readiness to serve the Gospel, faith, certainty of salvation, the Holy Spirit, supplication, and intercession (iv. 14 f.). The false teacher lacks all these. His is a worldly form of Christianity, which, in its pride and superiority, despises the simplest commands of Christianity, and that of love most of all. Where there is genuine brotherly love, the danger which threatens from the seductions of heresy is removed. The practical Christianity of love meets the dissolution of religion in speculation and proves itself victorious.

LATER CHRISTIANITY AMONG THE HEATHEN.

CHAPTER XIII.

THE CHURCHES STILL UNDER PAULINE INFLUENCE
—ROME AND CORINTH.

THE CHURCH OF ROME.

WE are somewhat more fortunate as regards the sources for Christianity in Rome. Apart from the Gospel of Mark which originated in Rome, we possess in the so-called Epistle to the Hebrews a work of consolation and exhortation, which is indeed of the highest degree of individual colouring, but gives us clear glimpses into many circumstances of the Christian life. The first Epistle of Peter already employed for Asia Minor is here again to be introduced on account of its Roman origin. Besides these, we have the letter of the Roman Church to the Church of Corinth of the year 95. Here we see more clearly than in the Epistle written to Rome the spirit which inspired the Christian Church of the world's capital.

Of a Christian Church in Rome we may and must now speak; because in the year 95, the Christianity of Rome describes itself as the Church of God, which enjoys the right of sojourn in Rome. It might easily be supposed that the incorporation of the single circles which existed at the time of Paul was connected with the new organisation after the Neronic persecution. Nevertheless, the continuation of single congregations within the Church is, considering the extension of the town and the presumably large compass of the Christian Church, only natural, and can be proved for a later period. This is why the Epistle to the Hebrews gives the impression of having been written not to the whole Christian body of Rome, but to a definite circle, a house-church. For the rest, there lies between the Epistle to the Hebrews and the so-called first Epistle of Clement a development which presupposes perhaps a lapse of two decades. We shall treat each separately, and begin with the Epistle to the Hebrews.

The very fact that a λόγος παρακλήσεως of the kind (xiii. 22), a letter of consolation and exhortation, was necessary, gives food for thought. In that circle things were very far from being as the author wished, as, indeed, in consideration of the fact that the members were already Christians of very long standing, he was justified in expecting them to be (v. 12). The explanation lies in the hardships to which these Christians were always being exposed afresh. It is true they have already heroically endured one persecution—clearly the Neronic: they have some of them themselves endured reproaches and afflictions, and become a gazing-stock (perhaps an allusion to the employment of Christians in the Neronic games), while others have endured in inward participation with their fellows. They have visited prisoners and have themselves joyfully endured the confiscation of their goods in view of the future

CHURCHES UNDER PAULINE INFLUENCE 197

glory (x. 32 ff.). But now because afflictions are being continually renewed, their endurance begins to give way (xii. 3). Apostasy threatens (iii. 12). Many are already forsaking the assembling of themselves (x. 25).

What is the nature of this apostasy? According to analogous complaints in other epistles, it is not a falling away to heathenism or Judaism, but only a withdrawing into themselves. Holding fast certain principles of Christianity, monotheism, the moral ground thoughts and faith in future reward, they would live for themselves without exposing themselves through union with this persecuted body or through a public profession of Christ. Hence the continued exhortations of our epistle, not only not to forsake the assembling of themselves together (x. 24), but to hold fast to the confession of faith (iv. 14), and hope (x. 23), and the warning against letting themselves by such a withdrawal from the living God (iii. 12) fall back to heathenism with its service of dead gods (ix. 14).

But even where no direct apostasy threatened, a certain lukewarmness was to be observed. There was a lack of proper boldness ($\pi\alpha\rho\rho\eta\sigma\iota\alpha$, x. 19). If it did exist (x. 35), it was at any rate not much in evidence, was not firm unto the end (iii. 6, 14). The author has to be continually exhorting his hearers not to despise his word (xii. 25), but to hearken to the call to repentance (ii. 1 ff., iii. 7 ff.). Infidelity in his view is unbelief (iii. 18, iv. 11), transgression, and disobedience (ii. 2). Here, too, oppressions are the cause of torpor. They could not see how it was that just those chosen by God should suffer so much.

They had been deceived, they believed themselves injured (iv. 1). Hence the author repeatedly refers to the sufferings of Old Testament saints (xi. 35 ff.), and, above all, of the Lord Himself, whose dishonour they must bear (xii. 2 f., xiii. 13); hence he shows that suffering signifies divine discipline. It is a proof of fatherly love on the part of God (xii. 5 ff.).

This point even his loyal readers did not understand. In genuinely ancient fashion they saw in this sum of evils which overtook them, a proof that God was in some way or other angry with them. The deep feeling of guilt and need for reconciliation which was characteristic of the time arose among them in undreamed-of strength. Far from feeling satisfied with this Christianity of theirs, they sought everywhere for a means of atonement, and found it chiefly in the ceremonial sacrifice ordained by God in the Old Testament. The difficult problem which Paul left to Gentile Christians, in at once preaching the abolition of law and placing in their hand the Old Testament in which it stood as the holy word of God, had to be faced. It cannot be our task here to show how our author attempts to explain the difficulty by his beautiful conception of the shadowiness and ineffectiveness of the Old Testament types and their realisation in the Melchizedec high-priesthood of Christ and His one sacrifice of obedience, nor how by help of the peculiar character of Alexandrine exegesis he achieves his end. Its interest for us is only in showing what a burning question the problem had then become. We have no occasion to assume the operation of Jewish Christian and Jewish influence in this Roman body of Christians. If we follow up the indications in the letter, we find the renewal of the expiatory and ceremonial sacrifice to be due to thoughts raised purely by the Old Testament. The external occasion was given by the necessity of the time, the unceasing persecutions, in which it was believed God's anger was to be observed, and perhaps also by the consideration that the Jews had to face fewer such troubles. The internal ground, however, is rightly detected by the author in a want of Christian knowledge, which causes him all the more pain, as from brethren of such long standing in the Christian faith better was to be expected (v. 11 ff.). Without persevering further into the essence of Christianity, they were standing still at the very beginning (vi. 1).

His description of this stage is worth noting: turning away from the dead works of heathendom, monotheism, teaching of washings, laying on of hands, resurrection and eternal judgment. The moral elements are here strongly to the front. The Christian ideal of life is still defined through its contrast to heathen life, the determining motive is the prospect of future recompense. We can understand, however, that from this standpoint they could not reach the cheerful and confident Christianity which Paul had fostered in his Churches even in the midst of great tribulation. This "belief in God" has no more efficacy than the mere intellectual belief; it brings Christianity to no elevating and liberating consciousness of salvation. Belief in a recompense is not a cheerful longing for the heavenly fatherland (the author wishes to make it so, xi. 13 ff.), but it is a thought that excites fear, and thereby weakens. The

Christian characteristic of other-worldliness, so strongly emphasised by the author, seems to have become unfamiliar to his readers. Thoughts like those which Paul set forth in Rom. viii. 18 ff. had become strange to them; hence the aversion to suffering and the dread of confession.

The picture of these Roman Christians reveals, on the one hand, a sincere conception of morality. The whole search for other supplementary forms of religion proceeds from a deep moral idea, the idea of guilt and atonement. On the other hand it lacks the very feature which gives Christian morality its peculiar value, the fact that, based upon an immovable faith in God and God's love, it draws therefrom the power to overcome all difficulties.

The author of the Epistle to the Hebrews recognises these two aspects of the conduct of his readers. On the one hand he sharply reproaches their backwardness in Christian knowledge (vi. 1, xii. 1), while on the other he praises their moral achievements highly and sees therein a guarantee that God will not let them fall. He cannot forget their works, *i.e.*, the whole practical demonstration of their Christian standing, and the love which they have shown His name, in that they served the saints (*i.e.*, Christian brethren for Christ's name's sake), as indeed they still do (vi. 10). In one respect he bears them very favourable testimony: the Christian spirit of communion and its willingness to make sacrifices are strongly developed among them. He could only wish that every single one of them might show this zeal unto the end. To himself this would be exceedingly helpful, because his hope would be

CHURCHES UNDER PAULINE INFLUENCE 201

strengthened to joyful assurance. They are therefore to urge one another on to love and good works—another motive for regular attendance at divine worship (x. 25). Much is acknowledged in the short sentence, "Let brotherly love continue" (xiii. 1); and in the others, "Forget not to show love unto strangers" (xiii. 2); "To do good and to communicate, forget not" (xiii. 16). The exhortation to "remember them that are in bonds as bound with them, them that are evil-entreated as being yourselves also in the body," is required only as a reminder. Care for the sick and imprisoned—this is in the foreground because the most important in view of the greater danger attached to it—was still universally regarded as Christian duty (xiii. 3). Communion with the brethren far away is maintained by correspondence, e.g., the news of Timothy's release from imprisonment (xiii. 23), and by prayer (xiii. 18 f.).

The organisation of the Church is still quite free; there are leaders (ἡγούμενοι). Their duty is, in the main, teaching and pastoral work. While the author strengthens their authority among his readers, we do not require to find in his warning, "Obey them that have the rule over you, and submit to them" (xiii. 17), a proof of any disorder. The leaders are examples, especially the earlier ones, who, perfected through martyrdom, had maintained their constancy even to the end.

Heresy gives as little ground for fear as hierarchy. The exhortation, "Be not carried away by divers and strange teachings" (xiii. 9), appears to be given only in connection with tendencies of an ascetic nature, such as we found already combated in the

Epistle of Paul to the Romans. In union with the Biblicism of these Roman Christians, the question whether this or that might be eaten took on an Old Testament colouring. It was thought that the heart was specially fixed when the greatest possible abstinence was practised. The author is of the same opinion as Paul, though the motive is entirely different. Everything depends on the grace of God.

It cannot be maintained that there was any connection between these ascetic tendencies, on the one hand, and the inclination to greater emphasising of belief in angels, the temptation to an unchristian angelolatry combated by the author on the other. Be that as it may, we see in this wavering of Christian faith a new proof that it lacked clearness, and, above all, sure knowledge of the central truths. Such a lack always exerts an evil influence on moral conduct.

Worship is still maintained in essence at the former high level, although the great danger which its guidance by Old Testament ideas involves becomes clear. When the Christian life is viewed, not as a bond-service to God (1 Thess. i. 9), but as a liturgical service consecrated to God (Heb. ix. 14), the religious-moral ground thought may remain, but the centre of gravity is removed. When prayer and confession, charity and communicating (Heb. xiii. 15, 16), are described as the offering well-pleasing to God, then the spiritual moral basis of this divine service is still noteworthy, but the way is prepared for the conception of this natural outflow of Christianity as something special, well-pleasing to God, and therefore meritorious.

Compared with the communities of the Pauline period, this Roman Church has undoubtedly made a considerable advance. Those ground-questions of practical morality, the avoiding of unchastity, purity of marriage, honesty in business, contentedness, freedom from all greed of money, are indeed touched upon by the author (xiii. 4 f.). But we get the impression that he was following a catechetical custom, and only meant to remind his readers of what was self-evident rather than to inculcate demands that were necessary. What he conceived to be the main task was not the training of the Church in Christian morals, but the strengthening of its faith and its courage for confession.

All this throws a new light upon the first Epistle of Peter, which shares the background, the general views, and many single motives of the Epistle to the Hebrews. It was the common sufferings of the whole Christianity which caused the author to emphasise the Christian hope so vigorously. His doing so shows that even in Rome there were not wanting men who held fast the confession of faith to the end, even in oppression and persecution. The Roman Christians especially have felt more than others the call to be strong in faith, and also to strengthen the brethren. The first Epistle of Clement bears this out. Oppressions continue. The Church excuses itself for not having bestowed attention upon the conditions existing in Corinth earlier. Blow succeeded blow unceasingly; the persecution did not spare them a moment (i. 1). Yet the Church stood perfectly intact. We hear no complaints of apostasy. The Church forms an organism whose combined parts care for one another (xxxviii. 1, 2). She remembers all her members in intercession before God, especially the oppressed, the captives, etc. (lix. 4). She even expressly states that many of her members have had themselves shut up in prison to set their brethren free; others have even sold themselves into slavery to feed the poor with the proceeds (lv. 2). Secularisation has given place to the other-worldliness demanded by the Epistle to the Hebrews. The Roman Church describes itself officially as a Church of sojourners. Its most prominent characteristic is its concern for Christendom everywhere, as Ignatius also (Ad. Rom., iii. 1) bears witness. It was felt in Rome to be a duty to intervene with advice and action where there was any word of disorders in another church. Accordingly this letter was written, and with the letter an embassy went to Corinth (lxiii. 3, lxv.). We do not learn that there had been any request on the part of Corinth for support from Rome. It is true that towards its close the tone of the letter shows something of the imperativeness of the imperial chancery, or of the later papal secretariat; obedience is demanded for that which the Romans in the Holy Spirit have written (lviii. 1, lxiii. 2); the disobedient are threatened with eternal damnation (lix. 1). But this insistence is not so intended, and is designed to give weight to the counsel of lviii. 2; "not to us but to God's will are they to submit" (lvi. 1). Not desire to rule, but brotherly love and zeal in duty dictated the letter. The Romans are placed in genuine grief (xlvi. 9) by the conscience-confusing, soul-endangering circumstances in Corinth, and will not rejoice till they hear that peace and unity are again restored.

Christendom feels itself to be a unity, but it is a unity in love. The Romans pray that God may maintain undiminished the number of the elect in the whole world (lix. 2). What a difference there is between the statement that the ringleaders voluntarily exiled from Corinth could everywhere reckon on a good reception (liv. 3) and the episcopal procedure against heretics and schismatics characteristic of the beginning Catholicism! How very different is the solution here, reckoning as it does on freewill, from what we find in the episcopal schisms at the time of the Christian empire, when military power and the fists of monks, sometimes amid unheard-of cruelties, decided the question and "restored the peace of the Church"! There is still some trace of the power of self-denying love which we admire in the Gentile Apostle and his concern for his own people to be detected (Rom. ix. 1 ff.), when there is here set up the example of Moses, who would have himself blotted out of the book of life, were God not to forgive the people's sin (liii., *cf.* Exod. xxxii. 32).

Yet the ideal of Christian life had already been materially altered. It is not due to the purpose of the letter alone that the principle of order assumes such importance. Paul, too, desired order, but an order that admitted freedom of spiritual development, order arising from free self-limitation. Here, subordination to the divine ordering is the main Christian duty, "Let us fear the Lord Jesus, be humble before our leaders, and honour the elders" (xxi. 6). The organisation of the Church is not yet based directly on the Old Testament legislation. The latter appears only as an analogy, as a proof that generally speaking there must be order (xl. f., xliii.). The order spoken of here is firmly grooved, and, what is even more eloquent, there is already a finished theory of it, viz., apostolic succession. In view of the coming struggles and disorders, the apostles not only settled Church leaders for their time, but also arranged that in every age these should have proper successors. Every deviation in the organisation, and reactions of free spiritual activity above all, thus come to be regarded as heresy. This lowers the ideal much; but in this limited form the ideal is evidently realised by the Roman Church: a constant groove with powerful supervision, and the subordination of all members to the same.

The worship has also undergone some alteration. The conducting of it is now confined to constant hands. With these official leaders of the service some degree of formality in prayer and teaching was developed. Whether chapters lix. 2–lxi. hand down to us the Roman common prayer of the time, as is often said, or are constructed by the writer with the free employment of the formulas familiar to him from the Church services yet with reference to the purpose of the letter (von der Goltz), they show that there were already fixed forms of prayer, that these were rich in words (*cf.* the numerous doxologies, lxiv., lxv. 2), and had lost much of the simplicity, straightforwardness, and modesty of the ancient time. Still it is a prayer which does all honour to the earnest moral spirit of the praying Church. It betrays no want of the consciousness that purity of heart is a pre-condition of prayer (xxix. 1). Similarly with the didactic and hortatory passages of the letter; to some extent they are only in loose connection with the letter's purpose; they are lines of thought which the author did not first enter upon for the sake of the Corinthians (Knopf). Yet my opinion is that he worked them all over again afresh in their bearing on the questions that confronted him. In writing to a foreign church he adopts the method familiar to him in his own preaching (vii. 1). The sermon had assumed certain stereotyped forms. The extent to which Old Testament examples, after the manner of Hebrews xi., are enumerated in order to inculcate the various ethical notions, and the bringing together of so many passages, may be tiresome, but we recognise the high moral earnestness and the impressiveness with which, as a rule, ethical questions, much less purely doctrinal ones, were handled in preaching.

On the whole it is a Christianity with an eminently practical bent that this Roman Christian represents, quite in the style of the first Epistle of Peter and the Epistle to the Hebrews. The Pauline formulas of justification by faith, not through themselves or their own wisdom, understanding, piety and works, are repeated, but they have become formulas. The righteousness which Paul taught the whole world (v. 7) is a righteousness of deed and of conduct, a right-doing (δικαιοπραγία, xxxii. 3, *cf.* xxx. 3, xxxi. 2, xxxiii. 8). Faith is obedience (ix. 6); and alongside of it hospitality takes its place (x. 7, xi.). Joy in doing good is the most important feature in Christianity next to that subordination to divinely appointed authority (xxxiii., espec. xxxiv. 2) which firm belief in God's might and goodness works in men (xi. 2, xxxiv. 1 f.).

Christianity still knows that God calls sinners to salvation: Rahab the prostitute found grace (xii.). It is conscious of its own sinfulness, and prays God for forgiveness (lx. 1 f.). But it feels itself also a Church of God (*inscr.*); the pure and the righteous, these are the chosen of God (xlvi. 4). We are forcibly reminded of Hebrews vi. 1 f., when, as the chief elements of catechetics, first repentance (vii. 4–viii.), then faith (ix.–xii.), then moral conduct (in view of the circumstances in Corinth there are here specially mentioned humility, contentedness, unity, xiii.–xx.) are treated (*cf.* lxii. 2). There is a Christian moral training of youth, an instruction in the fear of God; it is the duty of the Christian who is head of a house to guide his wife in the right way. In the bringing up of children precept and example are to be united. From their parents the children are to learn the power of humility and holy love with God, the beauty and greatness of the fear of God, and the salvation it brings to all who with pure thought walk holy therein (xxi. 6, 8). A Christian is judged essentially by the testimony borne to him by others, and this refers in the main to his moral conduct (xliv. 3, xlvii. 4, *cf.* xxxviii. 2, xvii. 1). A fixed principle of judgment is thus presupposed. And as a fact the Christian moral ideal is already fixed; there is a "traditional standard" (παραδόσεως κανών) to be observed. It alone is "beautiful, joyous, pleasant with God our Creator" (vi. 2 f.). It is defined on the one hand by the examples and precepts of the Old Testament, and the author already applies the Old Testament expressions, "statutes and ordinances of God" (ii. 8, lviii. 2) to these commands of Christian morality. On the other hand it is based upon the words and the example of the Lord Jesus Christ (ii. 1, xiii. 1, xvi. 1, 17). The divine order of nature is also adduced, and gives the general tone a certain rationalistic stamp (xix. 2 ff.). Christian hope, though less strongly to the front than in the earlier period, still forms an effective motive for the practical demonstration of Christianity (xxiii.-xxvii, xxxv. 4).

There is one advance to be recognised here. Moral demands now go deeper, are more inward. Sanctification was shortly defined by Paul (1 Thess. iv. 3 ff.) as abstinence from heathen unchastity and deceitful practices in business. Here, not without regard to affairs in Corinth, it is described as fleeing before calumniation, unchaste and unholy unions, and drunkenness, lust after what is new, and abominable desires, hateful adultery, and disgusting pride (xxx. 1).

We are not concerned with the single points, nor with the order which, like that of the list of vices put together from Paul's reminiscences (xxxv. 5), shows want of systematic aptness. What we must note is that the thoughts always turn from the gross forms of heathen sin to what is inward (*cf.* xxi. 3). Moral judgment must have advanced, ripened, and become fixed, where this is done so plainly.

New dangers, it is true, do come to light, especially that of spiritual pride. Already there is a wisdom which is fond of talking instead of revealing itself in practice. Paul had once to defend the claim of the weak to consideration; now there is shown a pompous humility, *i.e.*, a kind of asceticism which, in the most striking opposition to the thoughts of the Lord, renews the hypocritical method of Pharisaism; a vain-glorious chastity which would have its abstinence admired as a wonderful achievement, forgetful that it is God who lends such a gift to men (xxxviii. 2). Nevertheless, the Church still remembers that Paul once wrote to the Romans about the duty of the strong to care for the weak and of the weak not to judge the strong (Rom. xiv. 1 ff.), and she makes a wise application of the exhortation to the different presuppositions of the present by introducing a practical offset: the rich are to care for the poor, and the poor to pray for the rich (xxxviii. 2). The Church has also laid to heart the subordination to authority as of divine appointment, which Paul inculcated on the Romans of his time. She remembers the worldly rulers in prayer before God, praying for their health, peace, unity, prosperity, and exhorting Christians to willing obedience. In spite of all the oppressions which proceed from them there is no thought of rebellion. In the glorification of her martyrs (v., vi.) she herself learns the joy of confession even in suffering.

Here too, therefore, Christianity took its essential form from Paul. The way in which he was looked up to, and the importance which was attached to his letters, show that the Christians were modestly aware of their own inferiority. Yet the Church knows herself still to be filled by the Spirit of God, and the fact that she was able at least to imitate (xlix.) the Pauline hymn on love (1 Cor. xiii.) is a brilliant proof of her moral spirit.

The state of matters in the Corinthian Church about the same time is in complete opposition to the consciousness and solidity of the Roman Church. Here, too, the first Epistle of Clement gives us very valuable testimony. The characteristics of this Church in the year 95 are most interesting, as they constantly challenge comparison with the peculiarly accurate presentment of the early Christian life which we possess in the first Epistle of Paul to the Corinthians. We observe here the truth that every separate Church has an individual character. However much the circumstances have changed in the forty years since the Apostle's epistle, it is still in ground the same features which meet us again, want of steadfast Church consciousness, individualism which makes itself felt in licentiousness, rebellion against every authority, extravagant valuation of spiritual gifts and their free utterance. We are not to suppose that the irregularities which occupy the first Epistle of Clement stand in any outward relation with that party-spirit in Corinth already combated by Paul. But the roots are the same, and out of them there are always wild shoots issuing afresh.

The letter of the Romans starts from a picture of Church life in Corinth as it was before the unwholesome chill of discord destroyed its bloom. This passage is worth quoting in its entirety: "Who," the Christians of Rome write (i. 2), "that sojourned among you, did not approve your most virtuous and steadfast faith ? Who did not admire your sober and forbearing piety in Christ? Who did not publish abroad your magnificent disposition to hospitality? Who did not congratulate you on your perfect and sound knowledge? 3. For ye did all things without respect of persons, and ye walked after the ordinances of God, submitting yourselves to your rulers, and rendering to the older men among you the honour which is their due. On the young, too, ye enjoined modesty and seemly thoughts, and the women ye charged to perform all their duties in a blameless and seemly and pure conscience, cherishing their own husbands as is meet; and ye taught them to keep in the rule of obedience, and to manage the affairs of their household in seemliness, with all discretion. ii. 1, And ye were all lowly in mind and free from arrogance, yielding rather than claiming submission, more glad to give than to receive, and content with the provisions which Christ supplieth, and not wishing for more; ye laid up His words diligently in your hearts, and His sufferings were before your eyes. 2. Thus a profound and rich peace was given to all, and an insatiable desire to do good. An abundant outpouring also of the Holy Spirit fell upon all; 3, and being full of holy counsel, in excellent zeal, and with a pious confidence, ye stretched out your hands to Almighty God, supplicating Him to be propitious, if unwillingly ye had committed any sin. 4. Ye had conflict day and night for all the brotherhood, that the number of His elect might be saved, with fearfulness and intentness of mind. 5. Ye were sincere and simple, and free from malice one toward another. 6. Every sedition and every schism was abominable to you. Ye mourned over the transgressions of your neighbours: ye judged their shortcomings to be your own. Ye repented not of any well-doing, but were ready unto every good work. 8. Being adorned with a most virtuous and honourable life, ye performed all your duties in the fear of Him. The commandments and the ordinances of the Lord were written on the tables of your heart."

Truly a precious picture, doing honour as much to the Roman as to the Corinthian Church! It shows in the first place where the excellences of Christianity were conceived to lie. We may be sure the choice of what is specially praised is partly determined by its opposition to the conditions of the time. But the whole compilation remains a valuable document of the ordinary conception of the moral ideal of life in a Christian community. The moral activities are entirely practical. It is no longer a matter of getting rid of heathen scandals and vices. The Christian ideal is thoroughly positive, determined on the one hand by Old Testament thoughts (i. 3, ii. 8), and on the other by the words and pattern of the Lord (ii. 1). The whole brotherhood is the subject of intercession, and hospitality has the leading place among the virtues. The Church life has assumed constant forms; subordination to leaders, here, for special reasons, made especially prominent, is Christian duty. The Church exercises a pedagogic influence on the individual members, especially the young and the women. The life of prayer is pure; brotherly love is maintained; the highest effort is doing good. Everywhere we feel ourselves strongly reminded of the first Epistle of Peter.

But our passage is also a witness that this ideal was no Utopia. In Corinth it had been at least occasionally realised. The intention to idealise always prevails, in order that on the brilliant background of the past the present hateful stain, the unholy and filthy disturbance which some perverse and impudent persons have caused, may appear all the more distinct. We must not, without further ado, put the witness aside as untrue. We have to take by way of supplement the development which, according to the Roman letter, followed. The sad state of the present is not, as Clement represents, simply the perversion of the earlier; it is only another and gloomier side of the same picture, which now comes into the foreground.

In iii. 1 we have a repetition of Deut. xxxii. 15 : " The beloved ate and drank, waxed fat, grew thick, and kicked. (2.) Hence came emulation and envy, strife and contention, persecution and disorder, war and captivity. (3.) So the dishonest exalted themselves against the honourable, the worthless against men of note, the wise against the foolish, the young against the old. (4.) So righteousness and peace departed far away, because every man abandoned the fear of God, and became blind in his faith, neither walked in the precepts of his appointment, nor acted as becomes the Christian, but proceeded each after the desires of his wicked heart in unrighteous and godless envy."

This is a picture, in the language of the Old Testament prophets, of the falling away from the right fear of God, of the rebellion of individualism against the authority of divine law, and of subjectivity against every objective standard. But what actually happened?

If we gather together the scattered indications of the epistle, the following picture is the result.

Some of the Church leaders—Presbyters they are called (xliv. 4), who probably presided over divine service—have been removed from office by the Church. Yet the Church had not taken this step out of free impulse. Behind it lurk some few individuals, of whom the Romans speak with a certain amount of contempt, calling them ambitious busybodies (i. 1, xiv. 1, xxi. 5). On the other hand it must not be overlooked that not simple excommunication is claimed against these; a cessation of the conflict is looked for from their own good sense; they are voluntarily to depart from Corinth, and so bring the quarrel to an end (lvii.).

It may be questioned if only personal ambition, passion for affairs, and evil tongues are to blame for this confusion. Among the numerous new explanations, the one which seems to me to be best in accordance with the sources, is that which sees in these Corinthian errors a significant moment in the great crisis which was caused in most of the Churches by the establishment of a fixed ecclesiastical constitution. Such a consolidation of management was bound to come. That we learned already from the defects of Church life combated by Paul. The transition from purely voluntary service on the part of single individuals, which at the same time involved more or less a leadership of the community, to a regulated responsible management through a Church council and Church officials, was necessary, and therefore justified and useful. But indeed it could not happen without great injury to the enthusiastic element. The ministers of the Spirit were forced out of their leading position; they had to renounce the unconfined freedom of their spiritual utterances. That did not happen without a struggle.

The quarrel in Corinth is a sequel to this. The matter is not one of the introduction of the Presbyterian form, but of the attempt, in a reactionary assertion of the ancient privileges of the ministers of the Spirit (xlviii. 5), to overthrow the already existing and adopted order.

The Romans can throw into the scale a theory which presupposes the longer existence of the combated regulation. Therein lay, treated from the moral point of view, the wrong of the momentarily victorious opposition. The enthusiasm which it represented, once justified as the natural form of primitive inspiration, became morally dangerous, when the historical development had gone beyond it to a more fixed form of Church organisation. Thus we are compelled to count it to the credit of the ringleaders who are so sharply combated by Clement, that they were fighting not out of—or not only out of—selfish motives, ambition, love of dominion, and so forth, but in the interest of a definite principle. It is proved in ground indeed, as Clement shows, that in the main it was through their fault that disorder entered the Church, disturbed the unity, inflamed the passions, and so did serious harm to the whole body of the Church. Entirely occupied with the conflicts in their own midst, they could no longer discharge satisfactorily the duties of hospitality or care for strange brethren. All that formerly made Corinth famous was now looked for in vain.

On the other hand we are not to forget that this conflict is the only thing with which fault is to be found in the Church of Corinth. With all the detail of the letter, it goes into no troubles that are not connected with that main defect. On the contrary the author concludes with real praise of the Corinthians. They are trustworthy and highly-respected men, deeply versed in the words of divine discipline (lxii. 3). We have no right to look upon all the more strongly-pitched tones of the exhortation as signs of defects among the Corinthians, and to push aside those explanations which are to their honour.

There is no longer any word of the insufficient moral judgment in questions of sexual life which Paul had once to combat, of the fondness for going to law, of the want of modesty in the appearance of the women, and in the celebration of the Lord's Supper. Only the love of disputes, the impulse to assert their own individuality, has remained.

Up to this point we find within the Pauline Church a quite normal development, a moral maturing and gaining strength, in which something of the old freedom and joy was lost, but which exerted a favourable influence on the whole body. The development naturally is not one of simple progress. Times of elevation were followed by periods of depression. Quarrels as to constitution and doctrinal errors break over the Churches. These continue to bear a very different local character. At bottom, however, there was agreement in spite of all the variety, and that is the more to be wondered at, because as yet there was lacking the unity of direction which existed in the time of the Apostle Paul.

Now, however, other factors appear in the midst of Gentile Christendom, and these must be valued before we can rightly understand the development of those communities.

LATER CHRISTIANITY AMONG THE HEATHEN.

CHAPTER XIV.

The Johannean Circle.

Towards the end of the century we again find a dominating personality similar to Paul, whose influence extended over a whole circle of Churches and impressed its mark on them. This was John of Ephesus. Whatever the real facts about this much-debated individual may be, there can be little doubt that for the Christianity of Asia Minor he was of decisive significance. John, like Paul, was a Jew; I believe we may say more definitely, a Jerusalem Jew. But his line of development was quite different from Paul's. In the first place he had seen the Lord Himself, and in His last period had come into contact with Him, although he did not belong to the twelve regular companions of Christ. He continued, however, in that Jewish Christian circle, which, as we have seen, had its home in Jerusalem; certainly not so zealous for the law as James, but just as little following the free, bold flight of the Hellenists. Later on, and in advanced years, he came to Asia Minor, where, like Peter, he made himself at home with the already fixed Gentile Christianity. He lived in closest communion with the Christians, without enquiring whether they were heathen or

Jews. But a heathen, as such, still repels him. He insists that the missionaries who go out from him shall not accept anything from the heathen (III. 7). The thought of meat offered to idols is quite horrible to him (Apoc. ii. 14, 20, I. v. 21). Here we trace the spirit of the so-called apostolic decree, not that of Paul. As the presbyter, the teacher, the man who looked back to the primitive age of Christianity, he stands in the midst of a Christianity which already clearly betrays signs of a new period. An upright pillar of the past, he saw his chief duty to lie in the conservation of the old, the maintaining of Christianity in its original form. "That which was from the beginning" (I. i. 1), he will hand down to the Christians of his time: he will strengthen them in what they have heard from the beginning (I. ii. 7, iii. 11). "That which ye have, hold fast" (Apoc. ii. 25, *cf.* iii. 3, 11). This old Christianity, however, is to him the practical Christianity, the religion of brotherly love. The old and yet ever new commandment which we have received from Him, Jesus Christ, the Son of God, is that we should love one another (II. 5 f., I. ii. 7, iii. 11, 23, iv. 7 ff., 21). The presbyter is a prophet: he views the future in mighty pictures. But the prospect of the end, the longingly-expected appearance of the Lord (Apoc. xxii. 20), only serves to strengthen loyalty in obedience to commands, and to stimulate the repentance of the erring (I. ii. 18, 28, Apoc. ii. 5, 16, iii. 11, 20), as with Paul (Rom. xiii. 11, Phil. iv. 5). The whole Apocalypse only serves as foil to these exhortations. The prophetic spirit shows its power in exhortation. A note of victory runs through the whole: Christ is the ruler of kings (Apoc. i. 5); our faith is the victory which overcometh the world (I. v. 4 f., *cf.* ii. 13 f.). The conqueror receives the reward (Apoc. ii. 7, 11, 17, 26, iii. 5, 12, 21).

Moving about himself and despatching his messengers, this John dominated from Ephesus, as centre, the greatest section of the Asia Minor Churches. He formed a school, as we shall afterwards see. Yet there were not wanting conflicts here.

We look first at Diotrephes, the leader of one of these churches (III. 9). He will not recognise the authority of this Ephesian John. He withholds John's letters from the Church, does not receive his messengers, and even demands that others shall turn them away. The attempt, to be sure, was not altogether successful. The presbyter has a circle of true followers there, who rally round Gaius. This Gaius receives messengers from John, shows them hospitality, and will, as the presbyter confidently hopes, take good care also of the Demetrius commended to him. But these followers form only a small circle of people forced out of the Church by Diotrephes, personal friends, who are greeted by name (III. 15). What in all the world causes Diotrephes to adopt this rôle? Of difference of doctrine we hear nothing. Could it have been only personal ambition that would not grant priority to the distant presbyter and his ambassadors? Did Diotrephes do something worse for which he did not wish to be brought to account? The disgraceful works, which the presbyter will expose at his next visit, are probably no more than the speeches which Diotrephes makes against him, and the way in which he treats his ambassadors, in short, his opposition to the presbyter's authority. But what is the explanation of this? Harnack has discovered the key. It is an attempt to withdraw the independence of single communities from the over-reaching guardianship of the charismatic itinerant preachers. It is a small part of the great constitutional conflict, which, as we saw, and shall presently see more distinctly, moved Christianity towards the end of the century and matured very doubtful moral consequences.

Personal ambition may, of course, have contributed in single cases. But it is as little to be denied that real interest demanded a more fixed consolidation. In the special case before us it was anxiety about the authority of the "inspired," which in some measure was uncontrollable. "Trust not every spirit" held good in the circle of the presbyter too, and a definite confession was required as criterion (I. iv. 1 ff.). Only one step further and there was rebellion against all utterances of the Spirit. Everyone did not possess the greatness of Paul, who at once warns against over-spirituality and exhorts, "Quench not the Spirit, despise not prophesyings" (1 Thess. v. 19 f.). To the Christians of Asia Minor, it was easier and it seemed surer to keep these uncertain spirits from themselves and their Church. To be sure this was a one-sided step, and the one-sidedness was punished through the dispeace which it brought into the Church, perhaps still more by a certain stagnation. Diotrephes is a type of that ecclesiasticism which will not for anything have the peaceful development of the Church disturbed by excitement from without, and so loses impulses of the greatest value. On the other hand, the presbyter is himself no less one-sided when he judges the opponents of his authority only by the evil side, and increases the tension through deliberate magnifying of the opposition between the circle of friends and the Church, *i.e.*, the majority which holds by Diotrephes. It is the way of pious itinerary preaching to strive ever to chain its conventicles more narrowly to itself, even at the expense of the Church's unity. We shall not be shaken in this judgment by the charming picture which Jerome gives of the old John, as, in his age and weakness, he has to be borne to the assembly repeating always the one word, "Children, love one another." Certainly John is the apostle of love. But the peacemakers are often the keenest shouters in dispute.

The motives of both sides become entirely clear when we take note of a second conflict which has nothing in common with the former, but still must have exercised a significant influence on it.

It is not quite clear how far the propaganda issuing from the presbyter and spreading over a wide circle of Asia Minor, aimed at missionary work among the heathen or only at confirming Christians, but there was also a propaganda of false teaching, the caricature, so to speak, of the other.

What makes this second movement so suspicious is that it is a divergence of the Johannean school itself. "They went out from us, but they were not of us" (I. ii. 19). The presbyter had fashioned a speech peculiar to his school. Christianity was the truth, God must be known (I. ii. 3). To that end it was necessary to be born of God; then God shall be seen as the only-begotten saw Him (I. iii. 2). God was light, and the Christians are to be children of light (I. i. 5). That was all conceived in the Spirit of the Old Testament, and moral in intention. In the Gentile mind, however, it must have called forth quite different thoughts. The Gentiles supposed a light-nature in God to be meant, and therefore only one who bore something of that light in him could enter into God's secret essence. The truth which had to be known was to them speculative; everything was natural and metaphysical. We are not concerned here with the way in which this influenced Christology in causing a separation between the non-suffering spiritual being called Christ and the man Jesus. The presbyter and his followers defend against this "progressive Christianity" (II. 9), the old confession of Jesus Christ as a historical personality, Who in full and real manhood brought us the complete revelation of God's nature. More important for us is the difference in the moral domain. Here in the hands of false teachers John's remark, " The Christian does no sin," became something entirely different. "The man of light cannot sin; whatever he does is no sin" (I. iii. 6, v. 18). The moral conscience of Christendom reacts against this in the most express way, as we clearly perceive from a number of passages in the first epistle (I. i. 6, 10, ii. 4, 9, iii. 4, 6 ff.). It is a similar situation to that which arises in the polemic of the Epistle of James against the misuse of Pauline formulæ. The original sense, which has become entirely perverted through the reversal of the main notion, must be guarded by correcting or supplementing the formula itself.

So the two tendencies stand in hostility to one another, feeling a relationship and yet more strongly an antipathy. The presbyter's contribution was to bring things to an open breach. He demands simple excommunication of any one who is not correct in the main point of doctrine, the uncompromising confession of Jesus Christ; even the brotherly greeting is to be denied him (II. 10 f.).

This harshness may have been demanded by the circumstances: the presbyter may have thought it impossible to become master of the enemy in any other fashion. Paul also employs the greatest severity against the Jewish agitators. But this procedure of the presbyter reminds us more of the attitude of the Epistle of Jude towards gnostic antinomianism. It reveals the painful dread of the contagious power of heresy, which is shared by so many Church theologians of the later centuries with the Pharisees; it goes hand in hand with the abhorrence of everything heathen. The best illustration we have of this is the well-known narrative of Polycarp. John and Cerinthus meet in the bath: "Let us flee," shouts the former, horrified at seeing the heretic, "the house might fall where Cerinthus, the enemy of truth, is." (Irenæus, III. iii. 4.) We should more easily understand this debarring of false teaching if one of the lascivious forms of gnosticism which we have yet to become acquainted with were concerned, for in that case it would be of importance to avoid contact with the shamed garment. But however likely a theory like that of the light nature which is incapable of sin might make such a thing, we have no indication of it in the Epistles of John. The evil works in which the Christians are not to partake (II. 11), are, as in the case of Diotrephes, the intrigues of those who were unfriendly to the author. Otherwise he reproaches them only with want of brotherly love (II. vi. f., I. ii. 9, iii. 10, iv. 8, 20). That lies in the nature of the thing: conflicts of the kind were bound to break up the community; the presbyter makes the breach complete. Again, it is quite intelligible that those gnostics, while zealously carrying on propaganda among the Christians, looked down in a very superior way on these ordinary Christians. Here, too, the truth of Paul's word that gnosticism puffeth up must have been verified. It is a fact always to be observed that one-sided intellectualism with its speculative inclinations causes practical unfruitfulness. Johannean Christianity, with its emphasising of practical activity and of thoroughgoing brotherly love, was indeed a different thing.

A somewhat modified, or at any rate very much more detailed, picture of this Johannean Christianity is given by the seven apocalyptic letters (Apoc. ii., iii.), one of the most valuable documents which early Christianity hands down for our particular purpose.

In these letters we possess short but comprehensive descriptions of seven Asia Minor Churches, entirely from the moral point of view; the seer pronounces a regular verdict on each. It is to be noticed that of the seven Church towns only two are known to us from the Pauline time; Christianity has spread widely. Each one of these Churches has had a separate development. Five of them receive praise, though with limitations; only two are directly censured. On the whole the result is favourable. The Churches appear as shining lights (i. 20). What does the seer find to praise? In the Metropolis Ephesus, he lauds the works, the afflictions, the patience, and the turning away from all false teaching; in Smyrna, the inward wealth in spite of outward oppression and poverty, and fidelity in suffering. Pergamum, the town of emperor worship, is praised for steadfastness of confession even in martyrdom. Thyatira is credited with works: love, faith, readiness of service, patience, an increase of Christian activity, and, in one section, conflict with heresy. This applies also to the otherwise reproached Sardis. In Philadelphia there is united with joyousness of confession an active missionary zeal in spite of little resources; it is evidently the pattern Church. Then comes the censure: Ephesus has forsaken its first love and must be awakened to repentant return to its earlier works. Smyrna needs only to be exhorted to further fidelity and steadfastness in suffering. In Pergamum a small minority has given itself over to heresy. In Thyatira, this plays a great rôle. Things are worst of all in Sardis and Laodicea: the former is dead in all its limbs, sleeping without any signs of life, while the latter, not cold and not warm, imagines itself to be rich, and does not know how miserable, pitiable, poor, blind, and naked it is.

Thus the Spirit of God judges the Churches by the mouth of the prophet, and from this point threats and promises are distributed. Before all, there is a twofold fight to be waged. The external conflict is the less dangerous. Hatred of the Jews (ii. 9, iii. 9), and the intolerance of emperor-worship (ii. 13), threaten with persecution and martyrdom. In most instances this serves only to confirm and strengthen faith. Joy in martyrdom finds repeated and spirited expression (*cf.* vi. 9 ff.). The special danger threatens from the side of heresy, which is described symbolically as the works of the Nicolaitans, the doctrine of Balaam, and Jezebel-doings.

It may indeed be questioned if the same thing is everywhere meant; the false Apostles (ii. 2, *e.g.*) may be other teachers. In the fundamental features, however, there will be agreement. What the seer has in view is a speculative gnosticism (ii. 24), which he considers only in its practical aspect of licentious libertinism, which had no scruple in entering heathendom with all its usages and abuses. The author speaks of eating meat offered to idols and doing fornication. This expression, it is true, belongs to the Old Testament symbolic. It is the description of how God's people forgot its holiness and yielded to the religion and usages of the Canaanites. It may be figuratively intended; or the actual words may connect themselves with something different. It is indeed possible that we have here to do with one of those forms of gnosticism which exalted the filthiest immorality to a principle—the speculative foundation points that way; but just as easily it can be a freer attitude to heathendom, such as we saw adopted by a section of the Corinthians, and due to a one-sided comprehension of Pauline teaching. A connection with Pauline thoughts is evident in Asia Minor and is made more likely by the fact that here and there influences of Pauline terminology are revealed. As in Corinth, emancipated women, who gave themselves out as prophetesses, appear to have played a leading rôle; and it is quite possible that this free-thought had immorality as a consequence. The seer at any rate faces the whole movement with the greatest suspicion. The great harlot symbolises for him the world-power hostile to God (xvii. 1 ff.). His ideal is the complete antithesis of everything heathen. He even goes so far as to count it Christian perfection to abstain altogether from sexual intercourse (Apoc. xiv. 4, *cf.* iii. 4 : I. iii. 3 is perhaps to be taken in the same sense). Ecclesiastical tradition rightly celebrates John of Ephesus as the apostle of virginity. How wide his ideal was then spread we do not know. The number 144000 (xiv. 3) is, of course, taken from the apocalyptic tradition, and is to be understood in an ideal sense. But the picture presupposes the existence at this time of no small proportion of Christian ascetics.

If this antithesis in the moral domain answers to the conflict which forms the subject-matter of the second and smaller letter of John, then we shall find the counter error discussed in the third letter to be a feature of the Churches of Sardis and Ephesus. These have become torpid, they have turned aside from prophecy and its enlivening spiritual utterances; there is only a dead ecclesiasticism.

"I counsel thee," says the Spirit through the seer, "buy of me gold tried in the fire, that thou mayest be rich; and white raiment that thou mayest be clothed, and that the shame of thy nakedness do not appear; and anoint thine eyes with eye-salve that thou mayest see" (iii. 18). This is an appeal to them to make use of the charismatic prophecy. In other places also there is talk of standing still and retrogression (ii. 4); only in one place of advance (ii. 19), and in one passage of missionary zeal (iii. 8). In spite of all the apocalyptic tone, a certain worldliness is certainly to be observed. But the prophetic spirit reveals itself as moral power in the Churches. Can we imagine that this mighty summons to awake passed over the Churches of Asia Minor leaving no trace behind?

A certain lassitude, such as the seer has to censure in Ephesus especially, can be recognised in the exhortations of the first and larger epistle, whose two poles are the repudiation of gnostic speculation and the inculcation of the brotherly duty of love. The high strain of the thoughts which speak of laying down life for the brethren must be moderated to the practical direction, at least to give some money for the hungry (iii. 16 ff.). The love of God, which had become a mere phrase, must be balanced by the demand for practical continuance in brotherly love (iv. 20). "My little children, let us not love in word, neither with the tongue; but in deed and truth" (iii. 18). This love is no longer an all-inclusive love, that extends beyond the limits of their own communion; always they speak only of loving "one another," and of "loving the brethren." The Christian withdraws timidly from the world, and restricts himself to his own circle. We observe a weakening of the feeling of sin, not only in the express requirement of a confession of sin (i. 8 ff.), but also in the way in which a distinction is drawn between sins of death and those for which intercession can be made before God (v. 16 f.). That presupposes, where the distinction is left to the judgment of men, an outward standard such as was adopted in the Church of the second and third centuries. Apostasy, adultery, and murder are past forgiveness.

On the other hand we must not fail to observe how powerfully the Christian conscience reacts against the relaxation of moral energy. With all imaginable variations, and with the most complex grounding, the essence of Christianity as a religion of practical morality is set forth. Truth, the nature of God the Father wholly and completely revealed in Jesus Christ the Son, is here made the weightiest practical requirement of Christians: communion with God in love to the brethren, turning away from the world, the lust of the flesh, the lust of the eyes, and the pride of life (ii. 16). Only "he that doeth righteousness is righteous" (iii. 7). It is the ideal of the primitive Church without its Jewish national characteristics which is here so vigorously held up to the Gentile Christianity of Asia Minor.

Now, however, everything which was essential to the old Judaism is removed: circumcision, Sabbath keeping, commandments about food. In the apocalyptic picture the altar appears in the heavenly temple, but only the prayers of the saints are laid on it; the slain lamb is not sacrifice, but rather priest. In regard to ceremonial, everything is altered; worship is spiritual: prayer and song, followed by reading of Scripture and exhortation. There is a special day set apart; but the Lord's day, on which the Church assembles and the seer becomes ecstatic, is nevertheless something different from a delayed Sabbath.

In addition to the severe attacks in Apoc. ii. 9,

iii. 9, the Gospel according to John shows how foreign everything Jewish is to this circle. The synagogue itself has torn asunder the bond between it and the new Church (ix. 22, xii. 42), while the heathen crush in (xii. 20 ff.). The Jews will not and cannot hear the voice of Jesus because they are from beneath, of the earth (iii. 31, viii. 23); their father is the devil (viii. 44). Jesus does not keep the Sabbath (v. 9 ff., 17 f., vii. 22 f., ix. 14 ff.). He does not attend the feasts regularly (vi. 4, vii. 8). He has dealings with Samaritans without any scruples (iv. 9, 40). Already prayer to God is not offered in a ceremonial which is restricted to special places, but in spirit and in truth (iv. 23). In Christ, as the only-begotten of the Father, His nature has appeared full of grace and truth (i. 14, 17). So they that are His are sanctified, and become more and more sanctified in the truth (xvii. 17). The Truth is the Word which he has spoken from the Father. It reveals His holy nature, and, at the same time, constitutes the moral demand made of the disciples. In the last instance it is His commands. So there is mirrored in the Gospel, in spite of the lofty speculation of the prologue, that thoroughly practical Christianity which is especially characteristic of the Johannean circle (xvi. 23).

What Christians have to do is to keep the word (viii. 51 ff.). That means to do God's will, as Christ Himself does what is well-pleasing to the Father (viii. 29, ix. 31). "If any man will do His will, he shall know of the doctrine, whether it be of God, or whether I speak of myself" (vii. 17, *cf.* xvii. 6 f.). The transformation of Christianity into practical conduct is the best apologetic, and proves its divine origin, just as Christ's own works are the most perfect witness of His having been sent by God (v. 36, x. 25, xiv. 11, 31, xv. 24, xvii. 4). That His disciples bear much fruit is the best glorifying of the Father (xv. 8, 16). The early Christian belief in the victorious power of the good that is rooted in God here finds clear expression (x. 29, xvi. 33). The view that some small amount of sin does not matter is directly contradicted. He who commits sin is the slave of sin (viii. 34). Evil works are a cause of unbelief (iii. 19). "If ye love me, keep my commandments" (xiv. 15, 21, xv. 10).

The living mission-interest is portrayed in the account of the winning of the first disciples. One tells the good news to the other, "We have found the Messias" (i. 41, 45). We are most favourably impressed by its simplicity and its contrast to later apocryphal missionary pictures. "Rabbi, where dwellest thou?" "Come and see" (i. 39). The Church is conscious that whoever approaches her abandons all hesitation, and is won (i. 46). In the figure of John the Baptist we are presented with a pattern of unselfish humility and truth (i. 20 ff., iii. 27 ff.). Every effort to secure honour among men, such as marked the Greek sophists and gnostic teachers, is strictly repudiated (v. 44, vii. 18, xii. 43). The ideal is that saving love which the Lord exemplified in the washing of the disciples' feet (xiii. 1 ff., 12 ff.). The disciples of Jesus are to be known by their brotherly love (xiii. 34 f.). This love goes so far as to lay down life for a brother (x. 17, xv. 12 f.). Love to the Lord does not fear to go to death with Him

(xi. 16), and to give up life for Him (xiii. 37). Martyrdoms have been predicted by Him (xvi. 2 f., xiii. 36, xxi. 18), but He has shown that they mean only following Him and going to the Father. Everywhere there is a feeling of confidence. Consciousness of uninterrupted communion glorifies the departure (xiv. 27 f., xv. 11, xvi. 20 ff., xvii. 13), while certainty of early reunion causes all the oppression of the world to appear trifling: "Be of good cheer, I have overcome the world."

The disciples, it is true, still live in the world, but they are distinctly separated from it; they form a community of the same inward unity which exists between Father and Son (xvii. 21 ff.). There is not lacking the painful experience of a great apostasy; but the true kernel draws together and to the Lord all the more joyfully and the more consciously (vi. 66 f.). The different generations are distinct; the immediate disciples of the Lord precede the believers won through their preaching (xvii. 6, 9, 20). The most prominent of all is John the presbyter, who lived to a great old age in Ephesus, and is now dead (xxi. 22 f.). Everything depends on the witness of the disciples (xv. 27, xix. 35, xxi. 24); but there is no word of hierarchical forms. The ideal of womanhood is presented in the figures of Mary the mother, the Samaritan woman, the sisters of Bethany, and Mary Magdalene. Love of children and care of the mother find their most beautiful expression in one of the words from the Cross (xix. 26 f.), though a false filial affection which interferes unduly with the pursuit of one's calling is repudiated (ii. 4). Of bad sins there is hardly any record in the whole Gospel. The pericope of the woman taken in adultery, which is designed to scourge pharisaic self-righteousness, and to show saving grace as superior to severe punishment, does not belong to the Gospel. The immoral behaviour of the Samaritan woman (iv. 18), which we may suppose allegorical in intention, has nothing to do with the Christian Church, even if we allow its historicity. The most it can teach is that Christ does not endure such conduct in His Churches, and that His Spirit will discover and punish it (*cf.* xvi. 8 ff.). That lying springs from the devil, and that he is the instigator of murder (viii. 44), are truths not intended as special warnings against these sins. Thus, on the whole, the Gospel bears very favourable testimony both to the author's high moral comprehension of Christianity and to the sound moral condition of the Churches concerned.

LATER CHRISTIANITY AMONG THE HEATHEN.

CHAPTER XV.

THE JOHANNEAN CIRCLE—(*continued*).

THE CHURCHES IN THE TIME OF IGNATIUS.

A PICTURE of the same Churches not more than twenty years later is given us in the letters of Ignatius. This Syrian bishop is dragged from Antioch through Asia Minor to Rome, to be thrown to the wild beasts in the circus there. On the journey the Christian Churches pay their respects to him. So far as they lie on his way, they extend hospitality to him. The remoter ones send deputations. They accompany him on parts of the journey by turns. In return he sends them letters full of thanks and counsel.

From Smyrna he writes to Ephesus, Magnesia, and Tralles, towns which he did not touch. (The Epistle to Rome does not concern us here.) Letters go from Troas to the Churches of Philadelphia and Smyrna, with which he had become acquainted, and to Polycarp, the bishop of the latter town. Ephesus, Smyrna, and Philadelphia we know from the apocalyptic letters. To estimate aright the picture of the Churches which Ignatius gives in these letters, his individuality and the situation must be brought into consideration.

Ignatius is a genuine Syrian. His diction, which,

for Greek, is almost intolerably affected, everywhere reveals the fiery rhythm of Syriac poetry with its wonderful richness of colouring and imagination. The eccentricities of his nature were in the highest degree intensified by what had befallen him in those weeks during which he was chained day and night to ten leopards, as he names his guard (Rom. v.). All the way from Antioch to Rome there was the one end before his eyes. In the burning desire to perfect his discipleship through martyrdom, he paints it with awful realism (Rom. iv., v., Smyr. iv. 2),

> Near the fire, near to God;
> Among the beasts, with God

He lives in a higher world, in a superlative sphere. The Churches meet him with honour, and worship him in a way which he himself thinks extravagant. We shall readily pardon little vanities in one who prayed expressly for humility, as knowing clearly the danger to which the martyr of Christ can be exposed in being deified by his fellows (Trall. iv.). His humility strikes us as overdone, especially where it clothes itself in Pauline phrase, as when he calls himself the least of the believers of his own Church, not worthy to be named one of them (Eph. xxi. 2, Mag. xiv., Trall. xiii. 1, Rom. ix. 2), when he will not allow himself, the captive, to be compared with any of the free Christians of Magnesia (xii.), and when he will not admit that he is a disciple of Christ at all (Eph. i. 2, iii. 1, Trall. v. 2, Rom. v. 1). His feeling of decadence, as compared with the Apostles (Eph. xii. 2, Trall. iii. 3, Rom. iv. 3), reacts naturally against the homage brought him, and seizes upon the sternest expression of personal unworthiness. It is not insincere, nor is it untruthful flattery, when he covers the Churches with loads of praise. In his very intelligible excitement, a man of his fiery nature could not speak without exaggeration.

He piles up the words. He does not say, "children of light," or "children of truth," but "children of the light of truth" (Phil. ii. 1); he is not content with "well-ordered," but must write "very well-ordered" (Mag. i.). We have only to read the untranslatable series of honorary titles which, *e.g.*, he gives to the Roman Church:—ἀξιόθεος, ἀξιοπρεπής, ἀξιομακάριστος, ἀξιέπαινος, ἀξιοεπίτευκτος, ἀξίοαγνος καὶ προκαθημένη τῆς ἀγάπης, χριστόνομος, πατρώνυμος, "worthy of God, really worthy, worthy of blessing, worthy of praise, worthy of intercession, really chaste, presiding in love, walking in the law of Christ, adorned with the name of the Father." Ignatius is so far from desiring to flatter, that he expressly says, "I know that you will not be puffed up, because ye have Jesus Christ in you: and especially when I commend you, I know that you feel shame, as it is written, the righteous man is his own accuser" (Magn. xii., *cf.* Proverbs xviii. 17). We shall, however, receive his expressions with caution, even where he repeats the judgment of others, *e.g.*, that of the bishop of Ephesus on his own Church: "Onesimus praises extraordinarily your excellent order in God, that you all live according to the truth, and no heresy lives among you, and that ye listen to no one else but Jesus Christ, Who speaks in truth" (Eph. vi. 2), a statement which is contradicted by his own exhortations. Nevertheless, in spite of all his artificiality, he is not insincere; he knows as yet nothing of that half-pathological insensibility of which later martyrs boast, and which their panegyrists admire most. He has a natural horror of death, and thinks it possible that a moment may come when he will appeal to the Romans to beg for his release.

One thing distinctly great in the man is the stern alternative which he offers: Christian or non-Christian, God or world, Life or death (Eph. xi. 1, Mag. v.). How he elaborates that, how in conflict with Docetism he asserts a very solid kind of Christological confession, how he materialises in various ways the blessings of Christianity, how in opposition to heresy he sees the whole of salvation in one hierarchy and in the strictest subordination of the Churches, are points which do not fall to be discussed here. But it is important to observe that he emphasises the truth that " They that are carnal cannot do spiritual things, nor they that are spiritual, carnal things; as also faith cannot do the works of unbelief, nor unbelief do the works of faith" (Eph. viii. 2). " No one who confesseth the faith sinneth, nor does any one who has love, hate" (Eph. xiv. 2). It is interesting to see how in this quite Catholic-minded bishop, who thinks only of the great of the Old Testament past as prophets, there yet speaks to the Churches of Asia Minor a "minister of the spirit" ($\theta\epsilon o\phi\acute{o}\rho o\varsigma$) living wholly in ecstasy and revelations (Eph. xxi., Trall. v., Philad. vii., Polyc. ii.). His words, too, bore fruit. Even while he was on the journey, these letters were collected and exchanged from Church to Church. The letter which the very differently-constituted Polycarp of Smyrna sends along with the collection to Philippi bears witness to the impression which Ignatius made. It is the echo of the letter which Ignatius sent to Polycarp himself.

This letter to Polycarp, which differs distinctly from the others, is a Mirror for Bishops, a pastoral letter in the noblest sense of the word. We learn from it better than from the letter to Timothy and Titus, the high demands which were made of the Christian bishop. Ignatius had become acquainted with Polycarp a short time before, and had observed him in his Church; all the more important are the details which he gives.

The bishop, with eye fixed on the Lord Who sustains him, praying ever for richer knowledge and clearer revelations, is to exhort all that they may be saved, to support all and to receive all. Man for man he is to talk with them to godly unanimity of mind. "If ye love only the good disciples, what profit have ye? rather seek by gentleness to subdue the more corrupt" (ii. 1). He is a physician who must heal every wound according to its nature, and cool every fever through cold fomentations. He is not to be afraid of false teachers; like a good soldier he is to withstand them. He is to provide for all sorts and conditions of people. Above all, the widows are placed in his charge. The slaves also are to be received by him, but he is to guard them from pride and desire for emancipation. In preaching he is to warn against shameful callings, and because he has also to care for the married, marriages are to be performed before him. The main concern is the unity of the Church, which Ignatius impresses on the bishop, and also on the Church itself.

Polycarp, to whose performance of the foregoing

Ignatius testifies, really bears it out. That is shown by his epistle to the Church of Philippi, from which we know him as a faithful exhorter of Christians. He is skilful in discovering defects in all ranks. He holds up the pattern of Jesus Christ and His commandments, dwelling specially on the duty of forgiveness and the giving up of revenge. Influenced by Paul and John equally, Polycarp holds fast the ideal of Christian faith, which hope follows and love precedes. Thus is fulfilled the commandment of righteousness, " Who has love is far from every sin " (iii. 3). He exposes wrong doctrine in its diabolical deceit and fortifies the Church in fidelity of confession, in unity of love, in the duties towards the world outside, and in prayer for magistrates and persecutors.

Such are the character sketches of two leading Christian personalities, who, in a ruling position, exercised influence on the moral spirit of these Churches.

What was the state of matters in the Churches themselves? In the first place we admire the living consciousness of the unity of all Christian communities, the warm interest in the success of all which is revealed in actual deed. Deputations were sent to greet the martyr-bishop, letters and news are interchanged. Through the Cilician deacon Philo, and the Syrian Rheus Agathopus, who followed him and reached him in Troas, Ignatius received the glad news that in his Church of Antioch peace is restored after the severe persecution. He wrote at once to Philadelphia and Smyrna, and because he had to proceed on his journey, and could not write to all the others, he asked Polycarp to hand his letter on. The intercessions for Antioch are now granted (Eph. xxi. 2, Magn. xiv., Trall. xiii., Rom. ix., Smyr. xi.). The Churches are to express their joy by sending deputations and are to strengthen the brethren there. It is a large demand; but Ignatius had himself learned how willing the Churches of Asia Minor were to send deputations to him (Eph. i. 1, Rom. ix. 3).

He rejoices at their escort (Phil. xi., Smyr. xii.); hurrying on before by the direct road, the Ephesians go to Rome on his behalf (Rom. x.). He knows that the nearer Churches have already sent deputations, and is convinced that the people of Asia Minor can do so also—for the name of God (Phil. x.) Who is ready to assist those who desire to do well (Smyr. xi. 3); the Christian does not belong to himself; he must have time for God (Polyc. vii. 3). As a matter of fact we see that the Philippians, the most remote, have asked the Smyrnæans to represent them also, and Polycarp, either himself or through a deputation, will on a favourable opportunity make the due arrangements (Polyc. ad Phil. xiii.). It is well known where the other prisoners are (Rom. x. 2), and there is always news (Poly. ad Phil. xiii.). If this amounted almost to a worship of martyrs it was due to pure admiration of their heroic confession of the Gospel; of the worship of relics there is as little mention as of intercession with God.

Ignatius can even express the wish that the wild beasts will be his grave, devouring him entirely, so that his burial may not be a burden to any one (Rom. iv. 2), while at the same time he hopes to rise one day in his chains (Eph. xi. 2). Other Christians also find everywhere a friendly welcome, like the two

Syrians who followed Ignatius in Smyrna (x.) and Philadelphia (xi. 1). If some treated them evilly there (ἀτιμάσαντες), that was due to personal and material differences, to which we shall return; the passionate Syrian bishop with his *ceterum censeo* " Obey the bishop," did not please every one. Greetings are sent to intimate acquaintances, and when brethren go to strange places they are to be commended to the Churches there (Polyc. ad Phil. xiv.).

Within the Churches a great alteration has taken place. Everywhere—Rome is not concerned here—there is a firmly-organised administration: a bishop, the presbytery, deacons. Of charismatics there is now no mention. When Ignatius speaks of prophets, he means the prophets of the Old Testament. Nevertheless Ignatius the bishop is himself an ecstatic, who receives lofty revelations which he cannot impart to every one (Trall. v.), who waits for such in order to write more (Eph. xx.), who with wonderful wisdom looks into hearts and makes known hidden discords. Polycarp, too, is to pray for such revelations (Polyc. ii. 2). A warning is given against those who, without a call, press in as teachers (Eph. xv.). This shows that the conflict which we saw in the third Epistle of John is settled: the Church clearly feels itself to be the only bearer of charismatic gifts. Diotrephes has prevailed over the presbyter John. But the effects of the conflict continue. The position of the bishop seems not everywhere firmly fixed. Ignatius never tires of repeating that union with him is the most important Christian duty. He represents the unity of the Church (Trall. iii. 1, Phil. iii. 2, Smyr. viii. 1). Without him nothing can happen in the Church: no baptism, no agape, no eucharist.

He who honours the bishop is honoured of God. He who does anything secretly behind the bishop's back, serves the devil (Smyr. ix. 1, *cf.* Magn. iv.). It is good when the bishop's adornment is great wisdom and his strength humility (Trall. iii. 2), yet want of oratorical gifts and youth (Magn. iii. 1) do not lessen his importance. His prayer, as the combined utterance of the whole Church, has particular weight (Eph. v. 2). Special demands, however, are made of the bishop in the moral aspect; he is to be a pattern to his Church. Ignatius can boast of the extent to which he has experienced the inexpressible love, the zeal of the entire Church in Onesimus of Ephesus, Damas of Magnesia, and Polybius of Tralles. We have already spoken of the pastoral theology of the Epistle to Polycarp. Polycarp himself, in the Epistle to the Philippians, records the requirements made of the other clerics. Ignatius brings all these under the one great commandment of obedience to the bishop. The presbyters are to be full of love and mercy toward every one, to bring back the wandering, to receive the weak, not to neglect widows, orphans, and poor. They are to be without anger, partiality, unjust judgment, far from all greed of money, not giving ready ear to any against another, not severe in judgment (vi. 1); the teachers are to be the servants of God and Christ, not of men, not slanderers nor two-tongued, free from greed of money, temperate in all things, full of pity, caring for all, following the example of Christ (v. 2).

Besides these, as we see here, there were still other

classes in the Church, who, with the exception of those virgin ascetics described as widows (Smyr. xiii.) did not belong to the clergy. As the men are to arm themselves with the weapons of righteousness, and to teach themselves to walk in the Lord's commands, so their wives are to teach themselves in faith, love, chastity, to love their husbands, and to bring up their children in the fear of God (Polyc. ad Phil. iv. 1 f.). The widows are soberly and thoughtfully to apply themselves to intercessory prayer, and remain free from slandering, evil-speaking, false witness, covetousness, and other evils (3). The young men are to guard their purity in obedience to presbyters and deacons; and the virgins to walk with unstained and chaste conscience (v. 3). These are all requirements so natural to the Christian conscience that we may not assume their prominence as a proof of failure to fulfil them. They were always repeated, and thereby with time a corresponding demeanour was bound to result.

If there ever was an offence against these demands, as happened in Philippi in the case of the avaricious presbyter Valens and his wife, it was keenly felt. Even Polycarp, the bishop of a different Church, expressed the deep pain which the occurrence caused him, and did not lose the opportunity of exhorting the whole Church once more to chastity and truth, and of steeling it against covetousness which leads to idolatry (*cf.* Col. iii. 5), yet with the express addition that he does not expect such from the Church which the Apostle Paul commended. The Church is to call those people to repentance, and so to edify itself (ad Phil. xi.).

If the one conflict of the Johannean period is set aside through firmer organisation, the conflict with false doctrine, especially docetism, continues unabated. We are not concerned here with the relation of its representatives to earlier heretics, whether the idea is still the same or a development. Nor is Ignatius the man to take pains to make that clear. He is concerned only with the great facts of Christ's death and resurrection, which are the guarantee of real salvation and which he sets forth as solidly as possible. He plays with formulæ only to lead his opponents to an absurdity; those who will admit only the appearance of suffering are themselves only appearances (Trall. x., Smyr. ii.). As they do not believe in the redeeming death, so are they themselves unworthy of belief, unworthy that they should be named (Smyr. v.). His special criticism lies in the moral domain. He declares that false teachers lack love. That is shown by the fact that they give occasion to all these debates and destroy the unity of the Church (Smyr. vii. 1). But they have no idea at all of the tasks of practical Christianity. They are not troubled about the exercise of love (Smyr. vi. 2); they keep themselves far from the eucharist and the Church's meetings (Smyr. vii. 1). Their abominable pride is to blame; they imagine themselves to be superior (Eph. v. 3). Ignatius seems unable to say anything more about them when he calls their doctrine evil (Eph. ix. 1), and speaks of their doing what is unworthy of God (Eph. vii. 1). Though the Churches are to flee from them as from wild beasts, they may still be prayed for; it will nevertheless be difficult to save them (Eph.

vii. 1). The rupture was evidently complete, although gnosticism by no means withheld from propagandism in the Churches. In Ephesus there was no schism in the Church (Heresy vi. 2). Ignatius expressly says that his warnings are intended only to guard against schism (Eph. viii. 1, Mag. xi., Trall. viii. 1).

Nevertheless he must have considered these exhortations very necessary. As a matter of fact there were false teachers in Ephesus itself (Eph. ix.), and in Magnesia there were people who, while they recognised the bishop as such, held their own assemblies without him (Magn. iv.). The Churches must draw together all the more, and the episcopal organisation, which also afforded a middle point of worship, is found to be very effective to this end (Magn. vii., Phil. iv.). Ignatius asks for more active participation in the devotional life, more frequent meetings (Eph. xiii. 1); the bishop is to summon all members by name (Polyc. iv. 2).

Docetism was not the only danger. A second threatened in Judaism, as Ignatius names it, without, however, giving us any sufficient explanation of what he understands by the term. It might almost be supposed to be only a reminiscence of Pauline controversy. But the warnings which are found only in the epistles to Magnesia (x.) and Philadelphia (vi.) are too definite. With the old agitation that proceeded from Palestine this had indeed nothing to do; its representatives are Gentile Christians, uncircumcised (Phil. vi.). It is simply biblical legalism, which, as reaction against the moral indifference of speculative theology, goes to the other extreme, burdening Christianity again with Old Testament law and setting up again the once historically-justified ideal of Jewish Christianity, the loyal fulfilment of the law under the entirely altered circumstances of Gentile Christianity.

On the other hand it is a wonderful fact that this Christianity, under the guidance of men like Ignatius and Polycarp, held fast to its own ideal. Naturally it is no longer necessary, as it was in the days of Paul, to form a new ideal through the operation of the Christian spirit, which finds unaided what is right in the moral domain. The type of the Christian moral life was already long formed. There was a regular expression for it, κατὰ χριστιανισμὸν ζῆν, to live according to Christianity, to walk according to the principles of Christianity (Magn. x. 1). It is characteristic that besides the earlier motives of the imitation of God (Eph. i. 1, Trall. i. 2), the pattern of Christ (Polyc. ad Phil. x. 1), and the thought of the end of all things (Eph. xi. 1), the most effective inducements are the recollection of the great past and their relation to the apostles (Eph. xi. 2, xii., Polyc. ad Phil. i. 2, iii. 2, xi. 2 f.). The new period, it is true, did add new features to the ideal. What, in the case of Paul, was only slightly indicated as Christian public spirit and acknowledgment of voluntary services on behalf of the Church, now appears as the external cohesion of all congregations in confession and ceremonial, and as the obedience of all members to the bishop and his clergy. But however much importance the special characteristics of Ignatius attach to this, the early Christian elements have not been disowned. It still remains the most important duty of Christians that, looking to Christ's sufferings, they should meet anger with gentleness, boasting with humility, calumnies with prayers, seductions with fixed faith, cruelty with mildness, showing themselves the brethren of their opponents with meekness. These are the works by which the heathen can be won as disciples of the Gospel (Eph. x). The Lord's words which forbid judgment and revenge, are always kept in mind (Polyc. ad Phil. 2). The Christian owes it to his Christianity that his work shall be seen (Eph. xiv. 2). A few foolish men can discredit the whole Church of God; therefore all offence in outward things is to be avoided, and all inner enmity, which only too easily gives occasion to offence (Trall. viii. 2).

The greater extension of the Churches gives rise to a much greater danger, that, viz., of a merely nominal Christianity. Ignatius exhorts Christians to be so not only in name but in deed (Magn. iv.), as he himself prays for the strength, not only to be called a Christian but also to be found a Christian (Rom. iii. 2). Christianity is not something that men can be persuaded to by art; it reveals its greatness and power, when it is met by the world with hatred (Rom. iii. 3). In Christianity Ignatius certainly places the greatest stress on the religious confession which remains constant in martyrdom, and on the common worship. But he means also the practical demonstration of morality. It is indeed remarkable that he never mentions the grievous sins of heathendom, unchastity, covetousness, and so on. He indicates in a single word that married people are to belong exclusively to one another, for in the Christian brother- and sister-hood it was just here that a certain danger lay (Polyc. v. 1). For the rest, Ignatius is disposed to view with much more suspicion the spiritual pride of asceticism (Polyc. v. 2) and the desire for emancipation on the part of the slaves, who probably even claimed that they should be redeemed with Church funds. Ignatius repeats what Paul said in regard to this. Instead of becoming to some extent puffed up as Christians, they should rather serve with greater faithfulness for the honour of God (Polyc. iv. 3). There is still a warning against dishonourable professions which are incompatible with Christianity (Polyc. v. 1).

What Ignatius is thinking of specially is not quite clear. According to later statements, we shall have to understand all that is in any way connected with idolatry, the theatre, the circus, and perhaps, also, war. The Christian himself engages in a warfare with his heavenly Lord: let none be found deserting His standard (Polyc. vi. 2).

It may be said that the fact of those questions of morals not being spoken of is due to the method of Ignatius, who emphasises only the one central point of Christianity, confession and Church unity. But even Polycarp, who is so different and so entirely practical, goes carefully through the duties of Christians in all conditions, and hardly mentions them at all. On one occasion he names, as what Christians have to avoid, injustice, over-reaching, covetousness, calumny, false witness (ad Phil. ii. 2), especially in the case of widows (iv. 3). The moral failings against which Paul warns the Corinthians (1 Cor. vi. 9 f.) he treats only as the temptations of youth. The ideal is the chastity of the young man and maid, and we do not get the impression that any great difficulty was looked for in the realisation of this. A Christian custom has been developed, and lies like a wall of protection round the individual members of the community, separating them absolutely from everything pagan. The dangers now lie in another province. There is a Christian clergy, which easily abuses its office, not in the way of false doctrine only, but also for cruel party-judgment and self-aggrandisement. The case of Valens is a sad instance of this. But this, too, is such an isolated instance that it cannot be accepted as typical.

Love and obedience—these are the two poles round which the Christian life of this circle moves. The former, standing at the beginning and right in the forefront, brings us back immediately upon the central thoughts of the Gospel. Here it was Jesus who taught John as well as Paul. The obedience which Ignatius pushes into the foreground shows, on the contrary, the spirit of later development, and points to the organisation of the Catholic Church. It is remarkable that we find both united in that letter from Rome to Corinth, which is evidently quite unaffected by this Johannean circle. We must again admit that the same spirit, though operative in very different fashion, shapes conceptions and conditions that are entirely similar.

LATER CHRISTIANITY AMONG THE HEATHEN.

CHAPTER XVI.

THE BEGINNINGS OF GNOSTICISM.

WE have already had occasion to note two influences which worked with disintegrating effect. One was the divergence between the intellectual and the moral side of Christianity, the other was the effect which the ascetic tendencies of the age had on its moral ideas. These two influences are the constituent factors of that form of Christian morality which we find in gnosticism. A very significant name for a thing hard to comprehend! We may say for certain, that it is no specially Christian phenomenon. The currents which the whole thought of the time followed attained great influence in the youthful Christianity. Speculative necessity, the desire for redemption and expiation, formed wonderful systems and rites from Oriental mythology, astrology, Greek philosophy and mysteriosophy. To these the Gospel of Christ made a more or less large contribution. From the point of view of religious history, it is of the utmost interest to see how Christianity influenced this whole world of thought in the way of clearing it up, and how this influence made itself more and more felt.

Still more important is it to observe how Christianity itself, the Gospel, suffered peculiar modification through its introduction into this world of thought, how there was first formed a doctrine of faith and morality, a theology, and how this doctrine on the basis of Greek speculation spiritualised the Gospel and volatilised its historical content. Here, however, our task can only be to test the influences which this whole tendency exercised on the moral life. We restrict ourselves purposely to the beginnings of gnosticism. The great systems of a Basilides or a Valentinus lie outside the limit which we have adopted. As a matter of fact they also offer something new and different. They are, in the first place, results of theological reflection, and, further, they show a distinct advance in the Christian factor. An express appeal was made by them to passages of Scripture and words of the Lord, and the interpretation put upon these shows that the positive thoughts of the Gospel balanced the negative thought of the common gnostic ethic. The narratives of the so-called apocryphal Acts of the Apostles are nearer to the original gnosticism than those systems. In story form these narratives set forth the fates of the apostles Thomas, Andrew, and John, in order to bring the views of gnostic circles into the Church. However late they may be, we can well use them as illustration. What they relate gives a picture of conditions and views much older than the works themselves. We renounce those systems all the more readily because we are less concerned with systematic foundations than with the actual outcome of ethical tendencies.

The beginnings of gnosticism are lost in thick darkness. Concrete figures are almost entirely wanting. Names like Hymenæus, Alexander,

Philetus, Phygelus, and Hermogenes tell us nothing (1 Tim. i. 20, 2 Tim. i. 15, ii. 17, iv. 14). Even in the case of those who are usually first treated in the history of heresy, Cerinthus, *e.g.*, we can obtain no clear picture from the contradictory sources. In the heat of the controversy some of the leaders had typical names from the Old Testament applied to them—Balaam, Jezebel, Jannes and Jambres (Apoc. ii. 14, 20, 2 Tim. iii. 8, Jude 11), and one might almost claim to learn more from these. Nevertheless we can see that the beginnings of the movement reach back into the first ages of Christianity. The tendencies combated by Paul in Phrygia are already gnostic. The Johannean writings wage a conflict with gnostics in Asia Minor (perhaps Cerinthus). The pastoral epistles and the Epistle of Jude (2 Peter) also contend with gnostics of various kinds. We must everywhere remember that gnosticism is no closed system. The word describes a variegated manifold of views, and the boundary line between it and Church Christianity is always a fluctuating one. The separation from communion with the Church, which II. John strives for, seems in I. John to be already complete. 2 Tim. ii. 20 even offers a theory for the existence side by side of true and false Christians, while Jude 23 demands the strictest separation and hardly seems to believe in the possibility of conversion. Ignatius also warns against these false Christians. They are like raving dogs, which bite secretly and leave wounds that cannot easily be healed (ad Eph. vii. 1). Thus it is not always easy to define exactly where the Catholic Christianity ceases and gnosticism begins.

Gnosticism is, in the first place, intellectualism, one-sided over-valuation of knowledge at the expense of moral activity. In this sense we have found gnosticism already among the "Strong" in Corinth. If faith was for Paul the source of the highest moral power, the two closely-connected factors, objective belief and moral conduct, diverge more and more as time goes on. Sometimes the emphasis is laid only on the one, sometimes on the other. Knowledge is the catchword on the one side and practical Christianity on the other. The hostile tendencies move always further and further apart until there is a distinct external break. We have come across such oppositions repeatedly. Sometimes they were differences within the Church, sometimes disputes with different communions which called themselves Christian. The boundary line always fluctuates.

The warning against many teachers (Jas. iii. 1) was directed against tendencies within the Church. The people mentioned in the Pastoral Epistles (1 Tim. i. 4 ff., iv. 7, vi. 4, 20, 2 Tim. ii. 14, 16, 23, Tit. iii. 9), who delighted in dialectical arts and exegetical wiles, disputes about words and mythological genealogies, are already distinct from the Churches. Their impulse towards knowledge no longer abides by the simple Christianity. Those who are combated in the Johannean epistles volatilise Christianity itself with their speculations, but are driven out of the communities (II. John 7 ff., I. John ii. 18 ff., iv. 1 f.).

Now it is characteristic of the intellectualism of all ages, that it has little understanding of, and no interest in, the practical tasks of life. Christian gnostics of the later period could not disprove the statement of the heathen Plotinus that they neglected ethics and were worse than epicureans. It was the same in the earlier period. " They profess that they know God, but by their works they deny Him, being abominable and disobedient, and unto every good work reprobate (Tit. i. 16). " They lack the fruit of righteousness" (Hermas, S. IX. xix. 2).

What the Christian circles feel most in these people is the lack of Christian consciousness and sense of community : they separate themselves from the Church even where no separation has been made on the Church's initiative. In vain self-exultation they declare themselves pneumatics, the true spiritual men, and despise ordinary people as psychic (Jud. 19). In the presumption of wisdom they boast of their superiority and have envying and strife in their heart (Jas. iii. 13 ff.). The gnostic is arrogant; he considers himself superior, he has really known God (I. John ii. 3 f., iv. 7 f.), is in communion with Him (i. 6), and is a being of light (ii. 9). In spite of that, however, he neglects the simplest duties of brotherly love, hospitality, and helping the poor (I. John ii. 9, iii. 10 f., 14, iv. 7, 20, 1 Tim. i. 5). Gnostics have no loving concern for the widow, for orphans, for the distressed, for prisoners or emancipated, for the hungry or the thirsty. They keep far from the Lord's Supper and prayer (of the Church, Ignatius ad Smyr. vi. 2, vii. 1).

And more, the gnostic shrinks from confession, while in the later period, with the increase of persecution, Christianity emphasises the Christian's obligation to confess most expressly. We might almost suppose this reproach to be a calumny of antagonists, were it not always repeated in regard to nearly all the large schools of the second century.

The gnostics must have thoroughly abominated the martyr fanaticism of the other Christians. That was in keeping with their philosophical attitude. Stoics like Epictetus and Marcus Aurelius saw in Christian boldness of confession only obstinacy. The rejection of the Christian eschatology and future hope shaped the conduct of the gnostics even more than their fundamental attitude to the state and to society. It cannot be denied that there was much unwholesome fanaticism hidden under the cloak of zeal for confession—the later Church had to adopt a policy of dissuasion in this matter. Then also the very sensuous representatives of future glory, and of the reward that awaited martyrs, which were current, led to the frequent seeking of martyrdom, as the visions of Perpetua and Saturus show. A withdrawal of the gnostics here was quite intelligible. On the other hand it is not to be lost sight of that this eminently cold attitude of theirs deeply hurt the other Christians, and was bound to strengthen the idea that gnostics lacked real boldness in confession and proper courage of the faith.

Single martyrdoms of gnostically-minded people could not alter this. "Si duo faciunt idem, non est idem"; the death of one who did not belong to the Christian Church was not considered Christian martyrdom.

In general it is difficult to decide how far this barrenness in practical moral behaviour went in single instances. Allusion must be made to the fact that in the apocryphal Acts of the Apostles there is much

THE BEGINNINGS OF GNOSTICISM 257

said of miracles of every kind, but little of the works of love. The former are simply wonderful displays, in some cases without any moral reward ; only, as a rule, the death is followed by a reanimating of the corpse, as a demonstration of divine, not diabolical, power. Where sums of money, or even whole properties, were divided among the poor, the motive is less pity of those in necessity than the effort to get away from possessions that are found to worry. But it must also be maintained that the real apostle, as distinguished from magicians, faith-healers, and itinerant charlatans, was to be recognised by goodness, healing without reward, simplicity, mildness, and joy in confession (Act Thom., ii. 20, p. 16 ; Act John, 5, p. 153, Act Andr., 12, p. 28, Bonnet). There are not lacking some fine instances of moral instruction (Act Thom., vi. 55, p. 42, ix., p. 56, and frequently), where in particular the stress laid upon the command not to return evil for evil is remarkable. Moral responsibility for the guidance of others cannot come to finer expression than in a word of the Traditions of Matthias used by Basilides: " When the neighbour of a chosen person sins, then the chosen person has himself sinned ; because had he so guided himself as the logos demanded, then the neighbour would not have sinned out of respect for his conduct." As a rule, however, they do not go beyond the repudiation of the serious heathen vices. The revelation of hell in the Acts of Thomas vi. 52 ff. describes in close touch with the Apocalypse of Peter the punishments for unnatural vices, adultery, calumniation, theft, dissolute life, while the other moral duties, like mildness, visitation of sick, burial of the dead, are only faintly indicated in negative form. The avoidance of fornication, covetousness, gluttony, is not specifically Christian. We find similar exhortations among the orphics and other pagan philosophers. The disorder (ἀταραξία, Act John 29, p. 166) also is more reminiscent of Stoicism than of the Gospel. The gnostics sought the essence of Christianity elsewhere, in absorption, in the mystery of redemption and—in asceticism.

We should do great injustice to gnostics were we to treat them as mere intellectualists, barren of practical morality. Many of them bestowed a great deal of thought upon morals: Isidorus, the son of Basilides, wrote a book on ethics, and in Clement of Alexandria highly interesting disquisitions by different gnostics can be read. Not only did they think about ethics; they made a serious endeavour to practise morality. Only their ideal lay in a totally different direction from that of the Gospel. Their ground principle is absolute dualism between spirit as good and matter or nature as evil. That man is a natural being is here felt not to involve a divinely-appointed task, but to be a consequence of human sin. Breaking away from nature is the parole. Hence the docetism of their Christology: Christ cannot belong to the four elements (Acts Thom., p. 87). Hence the spiritualism of their eschatology: the resurrection has already (inwardly) taken place (2 Tim. ii. 18). Hence also their asceticism in the moral domain. This is so far from being something originally Christian, that in view of its ground principle of dualism and its denial of the natural-human, it can be regarded as the opposite of the Christian ethic. It dominated the

THE BEGINNINGS OF GNOSTICISM

popular philosophy of the time. We find it in Philo and the later Stoics. Originally as foreign to Judaism as to Hellenism, it had assumed in Essenism and New-Pythagoreanism, Jewish as well as Greek forms. We already saw how powerfully this spirit influenced the youthful Christianity. Even a Paul could not entirely avoid the tendency of the time, however clearly he held fast in principle to the positive central thoughts of the preaching of Jesus. How much less his Churches, how much less the later-comers, to whom the close touch with the witnesses of the Gospel, and, above all, the sure foundation supplied by the prophetic religion of Israel, were wanting! Some of these, perhaps, before their conversion, had gone through the school of Greek philosophy, and had belonged to an orphic society! When Paul himself defined the moral ideal of Christianity negatively as opposition to the sins of heathendom, what was more natural than to contrast the spirituality of Christian life with the sensuality of the ancient world? We explained the early appearance of such endeavours in Corinth as due to the abhorrence of ceremonial glorification of unchastity. The gnostics, however, went further. Among them we find the body regarded as the source of all defects (Act Thom., iii. 37, p. 28). The most important task is the disciplining of the body in the sense of continually-increased asceticism (1 Tim. iv. 8); while the repression of all impulse, the restricting of all needs to a minimum, is the goal of perfection.

The fact that we, who are accustomed to measure by the supreme standard of the Gospel, see in all this something unnatural, a want of moral maturity, and even a lower stage of morality, ought not to prevent us from noting that for the time it was an intelligible utterance of moral energy. The degradation and sensuality, the shamelessness with which immorality flaunted itself, the deterioration of *naturalia non sunt turpia* into the vilest unnatural perversities were bound to call forth a reaction of the kind when moral earnestness came into sway. Only that gnosticism makes the mistake of standing still with the physical. It did not recognise morality in its special features. The confusion of the two domains is characteristic of it. The inwardness which constitutes the height of Gospel apprehension is wanting, outward things are decisive also in moral questions.

Here, too, the boundaries fluctuate. We find the ascetic tendencies both in the Churches acknowledged as Catholic, and in gnostic circles separated from the Church. By some the duty of moderation was emphasised as well as practical tasks; by others stress was laid on positive moral demands as well as on asceticism. In theory it makes indeed a great difference whether the ἐγκράτεια comes to light only as the involuntary outflow of moral earnestness, or as the consequence of a complete dualistic system: in practice it is, as a rule, only a difference of degree. To mark the boundaries better, then, we might state it thus:—where asceticism, as complete abstinence from all sensuality on ground of dualistic theories, is to be laid upon all believers, there is Sect. On the other hand, the high valuation of abstinence as a special stage only to be attained by single persons richly blessed of God, beside which the positive morality remains recognised as the ideal of average

Christianity, is Catholic. In other words, the specific Christianity rescues itself only through the theory of the twofold morality, of which we shall have to speak in the next section. Besides this, it is not to be forgotten that the majority of gnostics rejected or set aside the Old Testament basis of Christianity. They have no share in the rich treasure of moral experience and the keen moral judgment formed upon a strict monotheism, which Christianity had brought over from Judaism in the Old Testament. The ancient heathen spirit could assert itself without any limitation.

The moral ideal of gnosticism is rightly described in the requirement which Thomas makes (ii. 28, p. 21). "Refrain from fornication, from covetousness, from care for the belly." In the first of these demands, however, every sexual relationship, even within the marriage, in the second all earthly possession, and in the last, all nurture that went beyond what was absolutely necessary, is forbidden.

Paul also, as is well known, discusses the renunciation of marriage, but he speaks with remarkable restraint, and urges objections. John of Asia Minor appears in tradition as the apostle of virginity, and the glorification of virgins (Apoc. xiv. 4) confirms this view of him. But it is something quite different from this when false teachers are said in the Pastoral Epistles to hinder marriage (1 Tim. iv. 3). Procreation as such was considered sin, and the cause of death's domination. Christ came to break away from it (Satornil apud Iren., 1 xxiv. 2, Tatian, *ibid.*, xxviii. 1, Gospel of the Egyptians). Hence, on the other hand, we have the idealising of Christian motherhood

(1 Tim. ii. 15). Sexual impulse is a foul frenzy, something devilish (Act Joh., 113, p. 213). Stories of the lust of the devil and his companions after beautiful women make up the gnostic romances. The horribleness and insatiableness of the sensual passions are illustrated by all sorts of terrible tales. A converted youth slays his love because she does not consent to preserve her virginity. An unbelieving youth lets himself be carried on to violate the dead, because his love has not been listened to. And further, family life is set forth in the most direct way as a hindrance to true blessedness. Wife and children only cause worldly anxiety. As a rule the children are either ill or degenerate, in both cases the effect of demons. The family-sense becomes family-egoism. For the children's sake men rob and take advantage of one another, oppress widows and orphans (Act Thomas, i. 12, p. 11). Hence the continually-repeated exhortation, " Flee from fornication, abstain, renounce marriage," or as it reads in the parting words of Andrew to Maximilla (8, p. 41), " Be it thine henceforth to keep thyself chaste and pure, holy, unspotted, clean, free from adultery, without agreeing to dealings with our enemy, without injury, unharmed, unbroken, unwounded, undisturbed, undivided, free from anger, without participation in the works of Cain."

That such doctrines as these, when spread among a people living till then in moral disorder, and now suddenly awakened in conscience, achieved success, is quite intelligible. It may indeed have happened, as the Acts of Thomas report, that bride and bridegroom from the very marriage-day renounced wedlock, and man and wife separated from one another. In particular, the continually-recurring narratives of a converted wife avoiding common life with her unbelieving husband seem to be taken from life. We have the express witness, not only of Christian apologists, but also of the heathen physician Galen, that among the Christians many women and men abstained all their life from intercourse of sex. It is not possible for us to estimate the actual spread of this kind of absolute renunciation. That it would have caused the abolition of the sect is not correct; at the present day in Russia we still see sects of the same kind continuing from generation to generation by a system of propagandism and adoption. Self-mutilation, the proper consequence of such doctrine, was reprobated by a fortunate inconsistency. Passages like Matthew xix. 11 f., which induced the youthful Origen to take this course, are cautiously and prudently explained by Basilides.

With the rejection of the wedding goes hand in hand an uncertainty in the estimation of the female sex. On the one hand the women are little thought of. In the Clementine homilies (iii. 22) it is expressly declared that the nature of the woman is much inferior to that of man. Women, except the mother of Clement, play almost no rôle in this romance. In the Gospel of the Egyptians, Salome, on asking how long death will rule, receives the humiliating reply, "So long as ye women bear; I am come to abolish the works." In the Pistis Sophia, the disciples want to push away Mary Magdalene, so that the Lord must take her under His protection. Speculation is indulged in as to why the women were not present at the Lord's Supper, and the discovery is made that they had behaved in an unseemly fashion. On the other hand, in many circles individual women, *i.e.*, especially virgins, must have occupied a leading position. Like Mary Magdalene in gnostic writings, so in some schools prophetesses play a leading part: the (perhaps fabulous) Helena of Simon Magus, the pseudonymous Jezebel of the Nicolaitans, Philumene of Apelles, and Marcellina the Carpocratian. whose settlement in Rome under Anicetus is recorded in the oldest Roman list of bishops.

By friend and foe it was acknowledged that zealously pious women offered the best spoil for the propaganda of these gnostic circles. That follows from the biting derision of those women taken captive by false teachers, laden with sins, led away by divers lusts, ever learning, and never able to come to the knowledge of the truth (2 Tim. iii. 6), and also from the glorification of converted women in apocryphal romances. Bigoted women have always been fanatics for ascetic heroism, and have often been deceived and slighted by masters whom they admired.

In the second place complete renunciation is required in the matter of earthly possessions. Here, too, men like Luke and James can be brought in for the sake of comparison as ordinary Christian representatives of the ideal of poverty. Yet the attitude of the gnostics is different and more fundamental. They demand actual and perfect separation from all earthly relationships (Act Thom., p. 11) to restore perfect exemption from care. In this evangelical notion there is involved an indifference towards the practical tasks of life. Matt. vi. 25 f. is referred to as ground for asceticism (pp. 21, 27). The imitation of Jesus' *Life of Poverty*, plays a large part here (p. 81). The gnostic apostle boasts of his poverty: he has fulfilled the will of his Lord in being poor, needy, a stranger, a slave, despised, a prisoner, hungry, thirsty, naked, and barefoot (p. 89). He wears only one cloak (p. 60), and those who are converted by him must lay aside all outward adornment (p. 57). Even magisterial office is held to be a hindrance to blessedness, which it is best to renounce in order to share the poor itinerant life of the Apostle (Mart. Andr., i. 7, p. 50). Especial value is laid upon forsaking home for the Lord's sake: not fields, nor cattle, nor wife can excuse when the Lord's call goes forth (Act Thom., p. 43). Indeed, the principle is here clearly expressed: Possession is sin; and loss, even when involuntary, is deliverance from sin (Clem. Hom., xv. 9). Certain gnostics like Carpocrates declared the communism of Plato, with its watchword, " Private property is theft," as a demand of Christianity. How far, however, such thoughts were actually put into practice is at least very doubtful. We shall credit the Christians with voluntary poverty as readily as many a Greek philosopher who gave up his possessions in order to avoid the vexations to which the possessor was much exposed.

But it is again a fortunate inconsistence that beside the sentence which makes possession sin, we find it stated also that poverty does not make righteous, for Jesus has blessed only the believing poor (Clem. Hom., xv. 10), and that among hindrances to blessedness poverty appears as well as riches. The cynical world-contempt which deprived itself of its property by destroying it, is met by the employment of it according to the Christian view on behalf of the poor. John restores the broken jewels of two pupils of the philosopher Crates, for which they had given all their means, has them sold, and divides the proceeds among the poor (Ps. Abdias, v. 14). More strongly even than in the philosophers there here comes to light, ever and again, the ground-thought of all Christian ethics, that the important matter is not the thing but the intention: man sees what is before his eyes, God looks on the heart.

Lastly, the ascetic spirit found expression also in the domain of sustenance. This serves to strengthen the body, and thus—according to the ground-principle of gnosticism—promotes the evil in man. Therefore not only is extravagance in eating and drinking forbidden, but sustenance itself is limited to bare necessities. The strict consequence, viz., suicide by starvation, is obviated by the natural impulse of men towards self-preservation. The practical demand which remains is, as a rule, the renunciation of wine and eating of flesh: so, *e.g.*, with the false teachers of the Pastoral Epistles (1 Tim. iv. 3). Here, too, however, there are again various methods and stages of abstinence. We already found inclinations to voluntary abstinence among the Roman Christians of the first period. Almost universal within the Christian Church of this later period is the declining of meat offered to idols, and as we saw, this could occasionally be increased to the renunciation of flesh altogether. The motive is abhorrence of paganism and its diabolical powers. It coincides well with dualistic views, but is nevertheless something entirely different from the demand for the limitation of sustenance as such. Here, also, there are very different stages. The apostles of gnostic romances start as a rule from the conflict against gluttony, soon bring forward vegetarianism as a principle, and finally reduce even the eating of herbs as much as possible. In this there is still a distinction between what the heroes of asceticism do —John takes one date every Sunday (p. 154),—and what they ask of their followers (Act Thom., pp. 16, 22, 64). Here, too, Jesus appears as the pattern of complete asceticism in virtue of His fasting, while at the same time He redeems from Adam's sin, which consisted in eating.

In the interests of vegetarianism the Gospels were directly falsified. An ascetic like John the Baptist could not have eaten locusts. Accordingly, instead of ἀκρίδες (Matt. iii. 4), ἐγκρίς was written, "he ate wild honey, which tasted like manna, like oil-cake." Jesus, Who has to be explained as come to do away with the bloody sacrifice, could not have longed for the Passover, and so a μή was immediately inserted in Luke xxii. 15, "I have not desired to eat this Passover with you" (Epiph. Hær., xxx. 13, 16, 22). It is known that the disinclination to use wine was so great that even at the Lord's Supper water was employed. But it is worthy of remark that even the care of the body was neglected, the usual anointing with oil avoided, and even bathing discontinued. There have always been extraordinary people who seek to please God by their filth.

The whole idea of these gnostic circles can be best reproduced in that word of the Gospel to the Egyptians (from the Oxyrhynchus-collection), "If ye do not fast to the world, ye cannot find the Kingdom of God." This νηστεύειν τὸν κόσμον is the most pregnant expression for the turning-away from the world which Andrew in his last word of exhortation lays to the heart of men of all ages and positions: "Leave all this life, and despise everything temporal" (p. 27).

However much these views may strike us as perverted, we shall not fail to see that a great amount of moral earnestness and moral energy is demonstrated in them. To be sure, we may not overlook the other side: revolt against nature avenged itself when asceticism was transformed into the opposite. It is perhaps the most remarkable, certainly the saddest thing in our whole field, that immediately beside this power of abstinence, the wildest licentiousness prevailed. The filthiest immorality appeared, and was justified by horrible theories as the true development of the Christian spirit and Christian freedom. We can quite understand that the conflict against such a tendency in Christianity was waged with the greatest keenness. The Apocalypse, Ignatius, the Epistle of Jude and the Pastoral Epistles oppose it in the most uncompromising manner.

That consideration lets us see the need for caution. Injustice is easy to opponents who are credited with everything evil, and things are attributed to them of which they are absolutely ignorant. Thus in 2 Tim. iii. 1 ff., an apocalyptic description of the general depravity of the end of the world is evidently applied directly to the false teachers who are opposed. We cannot, following that description and without further investigation, describe them as "lovers of self, lovers

THE BEGINNINGS OF GNOSTICISM 269

of money, boastful, haughty, railers, disobedient to parents, unthankful, unholy, without natural affection, implacable, slanderers, without self-control, fierce, no lovers of good, traitors, headstrong, puffed up, lovers of pleasure, rather than lovers of God." What we can be quite certain of is that in Asia Minor, towards the end of the first century, there were Christian circles which were closely in touch with paganism, had no scruple in eating meat offered to idols, and, as it seems, preached in the domain of sex a far-going freedom. Hence the seer compares their doctrine to that of Balaam, who seduced the Israelites to eat meat offered to idols and do fornication ; hence he names their prophetess after Queen Jezebel, of whom the same was related (ii. 6, 14, 20). In the same way the Epistle of Jude speaks of people who turn the grace of God into licentiousness: like the fallen angels (Gen. vi.), and the Sodomites (Gen. xix.), they pollute their flesh ; through their vile theories, which help the bestial in man to come uppermost, they dishonour the Lord and slander the heavenly powers. They separate themselves arrogantly from the Church, and boastingly call themselves ministers of the Spirit, while they are guided entirely by their sensual impulses ; they are veritable dirtspots on the Christian Church when they share her love-feasts, murmuring the while, and railing at fate. According to the Pastoral Epistles, some have wandered away, following Satan, and have thus given the enemies of Christianity occasion to indulge in invective. The context here shows that sins against the seventh commandment are being dealt with. The same thing is indicated in the warning which

Ignatius gives against those who carry about the name of Christian only in wicked guile, while yet they practise things unworthy of God (Eph. vii. 1).

It is not right to treat all these things only as single instances of moral error, as proof that the moral spirit of Christianity even later on was not able to drive out all sin, or as parallels to the occurrence in Corinth which we have spoken of above. What meets us here is rather a system. The conduct of the Valentinians, as related by Irenæus (adv. Hæres. 1 vi. 3), reminds us of Corinthian libertinism, eating meat offered to idols, participating in banquets in the Temple, going to the theatre and circus. But they have a theory to justify it: "fleshly things for the fleshly, and spiritual things for the spiritual." It is not enough either to recall the behaviour of the Corinthian Church and find here a one-sided and exaggerated emphasising of Christian freedom. This frivolous libertinism is no more due to the Pauline teaching of freedom than the asceticism of the gnostics to the Apostle's ascetic tendencies.

Pauline formulæ, nevertheless, were constantly employed as catch-words. In the face of advancing Jewish Christian narrowness, some may have been concerned to preserve a free attitude towards paganism as well as towards Judaism. Opposition to law may have passed into lawlessness, but ultimately the phenomenon is gnostic, and is intelligible only as the result of dualism and nature-deification. The proof of this is, that even later on, when the Christian Churches were entirely free from enemies, the two practical tendencies are distinctly to be distinguished within the gnostic schools, the more strictly ascetic

THE BEGINNINGS OF GNOSTICISM 271

and the lascivious libertine. The great heads of schools, like Basilides, Valentinus, and Marcion all stand on the side of the former. Only the Carpocratians are reproached with having taken over, with Platonic communism, unrestricted intercourse with women, not only as theory, but as actual practice in horrible nightly debauches. As types of the libertines we may take the "gnostics" in the narrower sense, the Cainites and others whose dissolute orgies ceremonially glorified the obscene. In particular, Prodicus is adduced by Clement of Alexandria as a teacher of unchastity, and spreader abroad of immoral mysteries. Plotinus wages a keen conflict with similar gnostics, and the Coptic-gnostic works show how much the inconsistency of these two parties was felt.

In view of these considerations, we shall have to judge those phenomena in early Christianity as growths of early Christian gnosticism, as extravagances of the gnostic-dualistic ethic. Naturally, the opponents have a certain amount of right, when they represent the sensuality of the teachers and their loss of good conscience as the cause (1 Tim. i. 19 f., 2 Tim. iv. 3). Evil practice preceded evil theory, the latter being set up to cover the former. On the other hand, we may not undervalue the significance of the underlying idea. The whole attitude of gnosticism towards the physical, the non-Christian element of Christian gnosis, *i.e.*, the dualism between spirit and matter, and the contempt for the natural, are, to a certain degree, answerable for this degeneration. Even where a strong ascetic spirit rules, we sometimes find these natural-moral things treated with a nakedness which pains us.

The method employed by gnosticism of taking the sensual as parable for the supra-sensual leads to twin-significations which clearly reveal how easy the transition was from the strictest earnestness to the most external shamelessness. Such an occasion of transition is described in the Acts of Thomas, p. 53 : "There will come false apostles and prophets of wickedness (ἀνομία), whose end shall correspond with their doing; they preach and order people to flee from godlessness, but are themselves always found in sin clad with sheepskin but inwardly ravening wolves, who, unsatisfied with one wife, defile many women, and while maintaining that they despise children, destroy many children . . . ., who are saddened by the good fortune of others, and rejoice in their misfortune, who are not satisfied with their possessions but wish everything to serve them, whose mouth speaks otherwise than their heart desires, who advise others to guard against evil, but themselves do nothing good ; before whom adultery, theft, oppression, greed is hateful, while yet in secret they do all those things which they teach others are not to be done." What is here comprehended as pure hypocrisy appears elsewhere as an organised system. Gnosticism operates readily with the idea of a reversal of all values: "Unless you make right left and left right, over under and under over, before behind and behind before, then ye cannot obtain the Kingdom of God." "The twain must become one, the outside as the inside, the man as the woman, neither man nor woman" (Gospel of the Egyptians). That can be taken in a very serious sense, and perhaps it was so intended. But it is only a short step from that to the perversion of all moral notions.

In general it is one of the most suspicious aspects of every sort of gnosticism that it does not deal altogether strictly with truth. That, to some extent, is grounded in the distinction between esoteric and exoteric doctrine, or in its theory of interpretation to which all is "symbolic and economic." The great thought, "all earthly is only a likeness," found here perfect expression. The variety of the forms in which Christ appeared, the wealth of names under which He was known and called upon, may correspond to the various degrees of understanding which were possessed. The simplicity of early Christian conceptions occupies, in spite of its concreteness, a higher moral level; it is sincere and true, while this docetic Christology, with its showiness and elusiveness, has something deceitful in it.

When Christ appears to His beloved disciple in the hollow of the mountain, and says, "John, for the multitude there in Jerusalem shall I be crucified, pierced with lances, struck with a reed, made to drink vinegar and gall .... but nothing of that which ye shall say of me, have I endured" (Act. Joh. 97, 101, p. 199 ff.), it is almost falsehood. And that is repeated by the disciples. Thomas lies without any concern to the king; the palace is ready to the roof —and yet there is not a single stone there; he meant the heavenly palace. John even circumvents his Lord: in order to listen to Him, he pretends to sleep. The example is copied by their followers. Mygdonia gives herself out to be unwell in order to avoid her husband, and Maximilla deceives her lord by substituting a maid-servant for herself. All this shows that here truth did not enjoy the regard that was its due.

In conclusion we have to notice the attitude of the gnostic circles to the Christian Churches. Here they cannot be spared the reproach that, unconscious of the missionary task of Christianity, they settled themselves in parasite-fashion on the stem of the Christian Churches, turning their propaganda not so much on the heathen as on Christians, members of Christian communities. If we start from the apocryphal Acts of the Apostles, then the missionary interest in these circles seems to have been extraordinarily active. But that, too, is only falsehood. It is due to the adoption of the literary form of the journey-novel on the common Christian presupposition that the Apostles had been missionaries to the whole world. If we look more closely at these missionary pictures, we very soon see that they lack the experiences of actual missionary life. There never was such mission-work; missions have such successes only in fiction. The points which every Christian mission sermon must contain are made subservient, in a remarkable way, to those others in which we see the peculiar content of this popular gnosticism. The purpose of the stories as a whole is evidently no other than to form a foundation for these thoughts within the Christian Churches. The propagandism of the gnostics among the Christians must have been extraordinarily active. We may see in it an outflow of high moral inspiration, and we shall be glad to reckon this to their honour.

But on the other hand we must admit the right of their opponents, who complained that they were fond of fishing in troubled waters. Here the situation is similar to that of Judaistic propaganda. A certain moral energy is united with a want of moral knowledge, with failure to recognise the highest moral duties. To trace the whole movement to covetousness and similar passions, or lower impulses and lusts, is in many cases certainly unjust. But certainly want of love, of Christian brotherhood, and of sense of communion, lies at the bottom of it. The confining of their propaganda to the Christians after the manner of sects is only another form of the habit of thought which we have already become acquainted with as fear of confession and avoidance of suffering. Add to that the secret doings and the double-dealing. False prophets like the one described by Hermas (Mand. xi.), or like the Valentinian Mark, deceived their own followers by a sequence of magical jugglings and legerdemain. Others have at least in teaching concealed their heresies behind good Christian-sounding formulas, giving deadly poison in honey-sweet wine, as Ignatius says (Trall. vi. 2). Without doubt we have here a form of Christian morality which bears no comparison with the practical piety of Catholic Christianity. Even if the suspicions were false or exaggerated, the opponents were entirely right in their contentions that what gave itself out as higher knowledge, was, when morally valued, a lower form of Christianity, unfruitful and altered in a heathen ascetic fashion, or even perverted into frivolous libertinism.

Nevertheless gnosticism is a proof of the high morality of early Christianity. For what had Christianity to offer to attract speculative minds and to inspire reflection on the Gospel, the very Gospel which Paul called "to the Greeks, foolishness"? It had the thought of redemption on the one hand, the moral power on the other. It was a practical philosophy, a *vita philosophica* without any philosophic system. This the gnostics endeavoured to provide (Harnack). That they undertook this is proof of the extraordinary impression which the moral life of the Christians made.

LATER CHRISTIANITY AMONG THE HEATHEN.

CHAPTER XVII.

The Churches of the Transition to Catholicism.

THE great majority of Christian communities adopted an attitude of decided opposition to the form of Christianity which we have just spoken of. Conservative of all early Christian traditions, slow to adopt new thoughts and influences, and protecting the old with a system of guarantees, the average Christianity develops gradually into Catholicism. It is the Christianity of "sound doctrine," unfriendly to speculation and emphasising the practical tasks of the Christians. Instead of gnosis it demands active life; instead of asceticism it asks for brotherly love, helpful sacrifice of self for others and the community, and obedience to Church ordinances.

It is a Catholic Christianity also in so far as it betrays no essentially local colour. It is true that the individual communities, or rather the Churches of the separate provinces, are still distinguished from one another. The practical spirit of Roman Christianity is well known: it defined the character of the whole western piety of this period. Egypt at all times exhibited a great leaning to gnosticism, to contemplation and to asceticism, while Syria, in spite of its being called the home of gnosticism, is, on the whole, always more concerned with the practical life. It is perhaps possible in the difference between the Epistle of Barnabas and the Didache to observe something of the distinction between these two districts; and the Epistle of James may exhibit still more specially the nature of Palestinian Christianity. But the origin of these works is doubtful, and the great uncertainty which was felt concerning them among the literary historians of early Christianity is a clear proof that no conspicuous local peculiarities existed. No more is the so-called second Epistle of Clement, with its mixture of speculation and practice, in any way characteristic of Rome. The Pastoral Epistles belong to the whole Church. At least what is individual is outweighed by what is Catholic. It would be too bold to bring forward the various forms which we meet as local and isolated pictures.

In the first place one common feature is the Christian moral ideal in its marked distinction from that of the earlier periods. There is no more thought of leaving the Spirit of God, as Paul did, to produce His effect in the individual Christian and in the communities, and also to create something new in respect of moral forms; everything is regulated in the greatest possible degree.

Yet it is not simply the Jewish method of life. The "law of liberty" spoken of in Jas. ii. 12 is not the Old Testament law, about which a mighty conflict was once waged. Probably the new ideal was affected by the Mosaic law, and perhaps still more by the deposit of experience and knowledge contained in the Old Testament wisdom-literature. The

Christians of this period possessed a certain knowledge of the Scripture from their youth, which served in practice as instruction in righteousness (2 Tim. iii. 15 f.). Occasionally, too, the argumentation is taken directly out of the law, although, as a rule, with extensive modification of its spiritual purport (1 Tim. v. 18, Barn. x.). A Jewish moral catechism was probably used for the instruction of converts. But the leading thought in that "law of liberty" is the Gospel itself, apprehended as a complex of demands; this is what is meant in the proclamation of Christ as "the new law." The sayings of the Lord gathered in the interval become increasingly important, and enrich the traditional catechism; an appeal to them settles all possible questions as to the shaping of the life of the community and of the individual. Also externalities directly counter to the Spirit of Jesus are legitimised by them. The new law is not to be viewed as a compulsory yoke, like the old (Barn. ii. 6); yet by reference to Matt. xi. 29, it is called the yoke of the Lord, and this yoke is by no means easy; on the contrary it is so heavy that few are able to bear it altogether (Did. vi. 2).

Christianity was not able to resist the tendency of the time. To the Gospel and its free spirit are united the gloomier thoughts of asceticism. These were not allowed complete supremacy. The simple demands of a positive morality were still allowed. But the former occupy the leading place; they brought perfection. The bearing of the whole yoke of the Lord means to live an ascetic life, and at the same time to perform the duties of love and of social life. The stress is on the former. It is the more difficult, the higher, the more meritorious; only it is not to be demanded of all. Each one has his own special gifts from God. There is a gift of abstinence. He who possesses it is not to pride himself, but to thank God for it. From the man who has it not, it is not to be required; even without it he can please God and be saved.

This is the theory of the twofold morality with which the early Christian spirit, holding more strictly to the Gospel, met the gnostic demand for the unconditional asceticism of all real Christians. It is a large concession to the dominant dualism, but nevertheless it saved one of the most precious possessions of Christianity—the evangelical conception of morality.

All the dangers which the gnostic ethic brought with it can be obviated by this theory. The gross Individualism which withdrew into itself and despised others, was met by the urgent demand for common effort. The spiritual pride of asceticism could be broken by the consideration that abstinence is only a gift of God's grace, for which one ought to be grateful. The struggle to do more than was possible, which led to hypocrisy, was obviated by the exhortation to do only so much as was humanly possible. The unnatural change from exaggerated asceticism to sensual dissipation was prevented through the acknowledgment of the claims of natural needs and impulses. All the special dangers which gnosticism could not fail to bring along with its moral ideal, were, where not removed, essentially weakened. Where there is any mention of continence, *e.g.*, 2 Clem. xv. 1, what is meant is first and foremost the inward breaking loose from the goods and joys, the sins and vices of the world, the conquest and subjugation of one's sinful impulses. Above all it could only have a wholesome effect that great positive tasks were laid on a man, and that, as the member of a closely-knit community, he was under a constant discipline. It may cause remark that the moral ideal is still often clad in negative forms. To be unstained, without reproach and blameless, is still the watchword. But the Christian teachers know how to elaborate this ideal in a wonderful positive fashion (1 Tim. vi. 11 ff., 2 Tim. ii. 22, Tit. ii. 1 ff., iii. 1 f., Jas. iii. 17 f.). What we already recognised in the post-Pauline period as essential to the formation of a constant morality— viz., the existence in the communities of a kernel of morally mature Christians of fixed character—is now made much more prominent by the fixed organisation.

Insistence on fixed regulations is perhaps the most outstanding feature of this late period. We have already discovered indications of it in Clement. But nowhere do these questions play such a rôle as in Ignatius. Reliance on the free development of the Spirit had disappeared; it was sought to regulate everything. The Pastoral Epistles and the Didache supply very distinct evidence of that. Free utterances of the Spirit have become suspicious in their doctrinal aspect. Teaching and speaking, till then open to all, became confined to the clergy, whose office was entrusted only to reliable people and afforded a guarantee of the right tradition of sound, pure doctrine (2 Tim. ii. 2). In the district to which the Pastoral Epistles belonged, the only ministers of the free Spirit outside the clerical office were heretics. A teacher like the author of the Epistle of Barnabas may have had an ecclesiastical office, but even in his case we can see how clearly every effort after knowledge borders upon heresy. In other places there were still charismatics, apostles, prophets, and teachers, as the ancient trio is still called (Did. xi. 1, 3), and where there were such, they enjoyed the highest regard. To them belong all the liturgical functions without restriction (x. 7). Only as supplement to these—so it is still maintained in theory—do the officials of the single communities, bishops and deacons, act (xv. 1). They receive the Church's alms; as men of God they take precedence of the poor of the community (xiii. 4). It is something of the Old Testament priest idea, which is applied first to the ministers of the Spirit and then transferred from them to the clergy.

But the second and more threatening danger is that the early Christian prophecy is not only dogmatically but also morally discredited. The Churches have learned by experience that they were often deceived by people who pretended to speak in the name of God. An effort was made to prevent their being victimised. What makes the thing so difficult, however, is that, on the other hand, distrust of a real prophet was held as sin against the Holy Spirit (Did. xi. 7). The rule is that the prophet must possess the qualities of the Lord. This means that he must practise what he teaches; that he does not demand from the others his own special ascetic achievements, and above all that he keeps himself perfectly self-less. He can perhaps order a meal, but it must not be for himself; he can ask money for the needy, but he may himself accept no money, not to speak of asking for it in the Spirit (xi. 8 ff.).

He speaks of himself impelled by the Spirit, but not in answer to demand. He bears witness and rebukes because he cannot do otherwise, but he takes no money for it (Herm. M. xi. 5 ff.). From such rules we can learn the experiences which the Churches had had with their prophets. The earthly intention, *i.e.*, covetousness, is all the more painful, when it takes divine inspiration as its cloak. Therefore the first demand which the Pastoral Epistles make of Church officials is that they shall be free from covetousness.

Under the pretence of divine inspiration human vanity asserted itself. This is exemplified in the author of the Epistle of Barnabas, whose inordinate self-consciousness becomes only more evident under the phrasy formulas of modesty. Hence the warning not to force oneself to the vocation of teaching, in the passage where the great responsibility of this position is shown. The tongue is the member most difficult to manage, and sins of the tongue most dangerous of all. Spiritual officiousness and gossiping must have won the upper hand to a great degree, especially among the women (1 Tim. v. 13). The dispossession of the Spirit-effected teaching by the church office, strikes us at first as a limitation and a moral retrogression. When we reflect, however, that the matter is much more one of the rejection of self-chosen teachers who had no inward divine calling, we shall come to a different estimate of it. If the Spirit was no longer there, or no longer powerful and morally without reproach, then better a ministry which was regulated, controlled and responsible.

The office, too, brings new dangers. Its introduction was not effected without conflicts which often severely threatened the peace of the Churches. Charismatics, real or false, do not let themselves be easily repressed. On the other hand ambition, which can no longer shine in the mantle of the prophet, transforms itself into spiritual place-hunting. Love of domination is developed, and new doors are opened to covetousness. The management of the church treasury and the funds for widows and orphans is a temptation to dishonesty. There were actual cases where the temptation was given way to. We possess proofs of it. But we shall not fail to remark that they were isolated cases, which were at once clearly branded. All sorts of precautions were adopted against them, and if any attention was given to these precautions in the election of church officials, a clergy was bound to be formed which would conduce to the ornamentation of the Christian Church and the honour of Christianity. And what we know of men like Ignatius, Polycarp, and others fully confirms this expectation.

It is required of one who is to be a bishop that he be blameless, the husband of one wife, sober, intelligent, honest, hospitable, apt to teach, not given to wine, not quarrelsome, but mild, not contentious, no lover of money, one that ruleth well his own house, having his children in subjection, not a novice, having good testimony of them that are without (1 Tim. iii. 1 ff., Tit. i. 5 ff.). The appointment of a deacon is preceded by a probation, in order to test whether he is blameless, honest, not double-tongued, not given to much wine, not greedy of filthy lucre. Only in the event of proper fulfilling of the office of deacon is promotion to a higher office promised (1 Tim. iii. 8 ff.).

Now and then there are dispositions towards the later Catholic view which elevates the clergy out of the Church entirely and places it over the same. The man consecrated by the laying-on of hands possesses thereby an authority which is not at all affected by some degree of youth (1 Tim. iv. 12, Tit. ii. 15). A salary in the case of officials is a matter of course (1 Tim. v. 17), but the ascetic ground for it that they might not become entangled in concern for their maintenance is to be noted (2 Tim. ii. 3-7). That the bishop was allowed only one marriage, while in the case of other Christians a second marriage was permitted, is a first step on the way to celibacy, to the higher morality of the priesthood. That complaints against presbyters were made difficult, (1 Tim. v. 19) moves in the direction of exemption of the clergy from secular courts. But still these things are only tendencies which are morally motivated through and through. Perfect inoffensiveness, protection against thoughtless calumny, are a necessity to the man who, as the most prominent member of the Church, occupies a conspicuous position. And yet these men are really members of the Church; the Church elects them out of her midst (Did. xv. 1). The leading idea still is that they are to be guides of the Church in morals also, the same luminous patterns which the apostles once were (1 Tim. iv. 12, 2 Tim. iii. 10, Tit. ii. 7, 2 Clem. xix. 1).

The Church itself, however, no longer bears the simple family character. Its larger compass made a classification necessary. So a separation is made among its members according to age and sex: old men and old women, young men and young women. They remain apart at service, they have each their particular tasks, and also their particular honours. The clergy receives instruction how to behave towards each separate class: "Rebuke not an elder, but exhort him as a father; the younger men as brethren: the elder women as mothers, the younger as sisters in all purity" (1 Tim. v. 1 f.).

This whole classification of the communities was of high moral significance not only as the expression of order. It avoided the actualising of what the heathen said of the Christians, and what is so often said in the case of exclusive societies, viz., that their coming together in intimate intercourse of the sexes served for debauch; it cut the ground from under calumny.

But in another sense the family character was still actually there, as expressed in the terms brothers and sisters, fathers and mothers; the whole Church shared the fate of the individual member. We shall still have to speak of how assistance was given when one fell into any sort of necessitous circumstances. When he was sick he received visits from the presbyters as representatives of the Church (Jas. v. 14). In family events like births and deaths, the whole Church participated with intercession and thanksgiving, as we learn from the Apology of Aristides. Burials were carried out. The individual did not stand alone; he belonged to a large and wide

TRANSITION TO CATHOLICISM 287

family. He enjoyed great advantages from it. But he must comply with its regulations.

A similar state of matters prevailed in worship. Here, too, there were everywhere more fixed organisation and regulation in detail. Attention was paid to costume and deportment (1 Tim. ii. 8 f.). In this matter custom is powerful. The words of the prayers were fixed, at least for men who were not gifted by the Spirit. A definite leader in prayer not particularly powerful in the Spirit would gradually form a somewhat fixed type of prayer. Thus we have seen that the great prayer of the first Epistle of Clement grew out of the devotional exercises in the Roman divine service. This mechanical regulation takes a further step when, after the pattern of the Jewish hours of prayer, the repetition of the Lord's Prayer is demanded three times daily (Did. viii. 3). Here the moral grounds of all real prayer, perfect acquiescence and truth, must suffer. The habit of regular prayer has much educational value, but conceals great dangers. Fasting, too, is externalised to a custom which is to some extent valued as an especial service (*cf.* 2 Clem. xvi. 4); this is especially noticeable in the regulation that once more, in dependence on Jewish usage, two days in the week shall be set apart as special fast days (Did. viii. 1).

Here we get the impression that Christianity has indeed become a spoil of the Judaism so warmly combated by Ignatius, not in the sense of the increase of a Jewish Christian current, but by the simple adoption of the Jewish method, with trifling outward alterations which do not alter the spirit of the matter. The whole divine service comes more and more under the Old Testament sacrificial point of view. This involves not only the idea of the priesthood, but, above all, the conception of particular services and the power to influence God or make an impression on Him thereby. That is true also of the bringing of gifts for the supper and for the poor, and of the sacrifice of prayer and song.

Nevertheless, the ground principle that Christian worship is something spiritual and moral is still maintained. The Epistle of Barnabas sees something pagan (xvi. 2) in the Jewish localising of divine service at the Temple in Jerusalem. The idea of offering is spiritualised as much as possible to the thought of a sacrifice of praise from the lips. The priesthood appears in the main as the pattern of order. In baptism the important thing is the painful performance of every sort of external form; yet a certain measure of freedom is preserved (Did. vii.). The Lord's Supper—at least in the circle of the Didache—is celebrated in the sentiment of joyful thanksgiving for God's rich bodily and spiritual blessings, not as the awful mystery of the later period. Sunday is a day of joy, kept in remembrance of Christ's resurrection and ascension (Barn. xv. 9, Did. xiv. 1). In general, amid all the feeling of sin and guilt, the thought of praise and thanksgiving is supreme (Barn. vii. 1, xix. 2). A thanksgiving prayer sanctifies every meal-time (1 Tim. iv. 3 ff.). Thankfulness for God's rich benevolence is the leading motive of all moral dealing (2 Clem. i.). Fasting is regarded as a very wholesome exercise, but the prophetic view is clung to, that the right fasting is the exercise of righteousness and brotherly love (Barn. iii.). Confession is, above all, a confession of deed, the performance of the Lord's commands (2 Clem. iii. 4, iv. 3). It is important to note, however, that there is still a feeling for the principle that the moral duties are higher than the ceremonial (Mark vii. 11 ff.). "Pure religion and undefiled before our God and Father is this, to visit the fatherless and widows in their affliction: and to keep himself unspotted from the world" (Jas. i. 27).

The passage in Ps. li. 19 is repeated impressively: "A sacrifice for God is a broken heart; a sweet savour for the Lord is a heart that praises its Maker" (Barn. ii. 10). The Lord's teaching that reconciliation is more urgent than sacrifice is still taken seriously (Matt. v. 23 f.); only holy hands without wrath and disputing shall be raised to God (1 Tim. ii. 8). He who has a dispute with his brother may not take part in the Lord's Supper unless previously reconciled. So before the beginning of the meal a general confession of sin shall take place (Did. xiv. 1 f.). Confession of sin and intercession as reciprocal brotherly duty are usually strongly emphasised (Jas. v. 16). This, too, when practised in a merely external way becomes impure, but, in the family character of the smaller Churches especially, the exercise had without doubt a promoting and strengthening effect on the moral consciousness and steadfastness of individuals.

The Churches still form a communion answerable for the moral behaviour of every member. One member is to call the other to account and rebuke him, not in anger but in peace. One who does his brother an injustice is not to speak in the church (Did. xv. 3). He who brings his erring brother back to the right way has done a good work (Jas. v. 19 f., 2 Clem. xv. 1). Even where Church discipline is looked upon chiefly as the duty of the clergy, the same thing holds good. Public correction of sinners serves for the instruction of all (1 Tim. v. 20). The preservation of a member from moral ruin is more important than the conversion of an unbeliever (2 Clem. xvii. 1). Along with preaching of the word we have rebuking, threatening, exhorting, though with all patience and instruction, mentioned as among the chief tasks (2 Tim. iv. 2, ii. 24 f.). In certain circumstances severity is necessary (Tit. i. 13), but regard must be had for age and worth, while partiality is to be guarded against (1 Tim. v. 1, 21). The teachers, too, followed these directions, as is shown by works like the Epistle of James, the so-called second Epistle of Clement and the Shepherd of Hermas, whose leading tone is that of a scolding sermon to the Christian Churches. Indeed, in opposition to the claims advanced by single sects to represent a community of perfect saints on earth, the view that the Church is an institution, which must include both good and evil, becomes more and more common in Catholic circles (2 Tim. ii. 20). But, on the other hand, even then the Church is spoken of in the highest strain as the house of God, in order to impress upon the leaders the need for blameless conduct (1 Tim. iii. 15), and Christianity itself appears as a great divine pedagogy, teaching that, denying ungodliness, and worldly lusts, they should live soberly, righteously, and godly in this present world (Tit. ii. 11 f.).

Outwardly Christianity is still perfectly aware of her missionary duty. It is from this period that we learn properly and accurately about the extent of missionary endeavour. Everywhere there are apostles whose task is to speak to non-Christians. If these come to a place where an organised Church already exists, they may only make a short stay there. Their calling drives them further. For here in the place the Church itself does mission-work; its assemblies stand open to all. (Only to the Lord's Supper are non-baptized denied admission, Did. ix. 5.) All who come are bid kindly welcome. As in the time of Paul in Corinth, the Spirit of God as revealed in the Church still manifests itself, especially in the retributive detection of what is hid in the inmost heart of man (Herm. M. xi. 14, Ign. Philad. vii.).

But now a change of character, a worldly spirit, is revealed in the different receptions accorded to strangers, of which James ii. 1 ff. complains. Christians put themselves about for a well-dressed and rich man, and show him extraordinary politeness, but a poor man in his dusty smock is left unnoticed. We shall afterwards deal with the causes of this worldly spirit. Here we must rather emphasise that the universalism of God's saving intention was always vividly maintained in the general intercession (1 Tim. ii. 1-4, Ign. Eph. x. 1); and the immediate result of this was the universal missionary obligation of the Church.

Again, there was the duty of confession. For how can adherents be won to a cause by any one who is not himself absolutely devoted to it? So far as this is concerned, things seem to be better than in the period immediately after Paul. There is not so much complaint about apostasy and forsaking of the assemblies. But appearances are deceptive. The vigour with which the necessity of fearless confession is emphasised (2 Tim. i. 8, ii. 3) is to be explained not only by the opposition to a gnosticism which fights shy of confession. The apostle who was not ashamed of his bonds appeared to his successors as a pattern that put them to shame (2 Tim. i. 12, ii. 9 ff., iv. 6 ff.). In Timothy a fearfulness is combated which is evidently widespread (2 Tim. i. 6 ff.). The prospect of a glorious reward in the future must instil new courage (2 Tim. ii. 11, 2 Clem. xix., xx.). As a matter of fact the Christians see themselves continually threatened by persecutions.

They had to make it clear to themselves that these should serve only to preserve faith and work patience (Jas. i. 2 ff.); loss through the confiscation of property only signifies progress in the religious inner life (i. 10), and martyrdom always leads to eternal and glorious life (i. 12). The example of no less a man than the Apostle Paul shows that "all that would live godly in Christ Jesus shall suffer persecution" (2 Tim. iii. 10 ff.). "Those who wish to behold me, and lay hold of my kingdom, must through tribulation and suffering obtain me" (Barn. vii. 11).

In spite, however, of the hostility of the heathen powers as revealed in these persecutions, loyalty towards the magistrate appointed by God remains unshaken (Tit. iii. 1). It finds its expression in prayer and intercession (1 Tim. ii. 2). I do not see in this exhortation any proof of the presence of a contrary tendency. True there exists no close connection with the state. Little interest was felt in it. Except in one passage it is never mentioned. But on the one hand, the strong anti-Jewish feeling presupposes a positive regard for the Roman imperial power. Barnabas cordially acquiesces in Hadrian's action towards the Jews (xvi. 4). On the other hand the eschatology peculiar to them allows the political features of the earlier Jewish revelation to be more and more lost sight of (Did. xvi.). To be sure there were instances where a Christian on trial broke out in sharp aggressive words against heathendom and the heathen state. But so bad as Hausrath makes it, the speech of Christian apologists and martyrs was not. On the contrary, the fact that the good confession which Jesus Christ witnessed before Pontius Pilate was always kept in view (1 Tim. vi. 13), and that the long-suffering and patience of a Paul in his frequent sufferings and persecutions were pointed to as a pattern (2 Tim. iii. 10 ff.) shows how differently the proper behaviour of a Christian martyr was conceived. The provocation and abuse which a much later time considered it edifying to put in the mouth of martyrs only throws the more brilliant light on the moral earnestness of the martyrs of the older period.

Much rather could the attitude to Judaism be reproached as un-Christian. It is unjust to call Jewish custom, as such, hypocrisy (Did. viii. 1 f.), to denounce the Jewish verbal comprehension of the Old Testament as sin (Barn. ii. 9, ix. 4, x. 9, xvi. 1), and to make the one apostasy at Sinai an everlasting reproach against the people of Israel (Barn. iv. 8, xiv. 1, 4). The great delight which Barnabas takes in the recompensing of the Jews (xvi. 4), is far from kind. But we are not to forget that this unkind attitude was caused by the Jews themselves, who, in their hatred of Christians, kindled and revived persecution everywhere, and probably even won over weak Christians through the seductive prospect of a recognised and free exercise of religion. On the other hand, it was an expression of Christian self-consciousness. With conscious renunciation of the advantages enjoyed by the synagogue, Christians wished to stand on their own feet, and even if suffering should be involved, to bear it for the name of Christ. Lastly, this attitude appeared warranted and even commanded through words of holy writ, in which God rejected the Jews and legitimised the Christians and their comprehension of the Old Testament. We cannot here compare Paul's utterances of warm self-sacrificing love towards his blinded people (Rom. ix. 1 ff.), but the fanatic hatred of Jews which was characteristic of the Græco-Roman world of the time, especially in Alexandria. Placed alongside of this, the anti-Judaism of a Barnabas appears harmless and even reasonable.

We might here point out in a word that Christian generosity was extended even to those outside the Christian community. The Pauline maxim, to do good to every man, though most of all to the brethren of the faith, is strictly observed: "Give without asking to whom thou givest" (Herm. M. ii. 4, 6). And, finally, such proper regard was had to the judgment of those outside, that every effort was made to be inoffensive and to contradict all calumnies by ocular demonstration (1 Tim. iii. 7, Tit. iii. 2). A Christian preacher expresses exactly what obligations the possession of an admittedly lofty and pure doctrine of morality lays upon the Christians. "When the heathen hear the word of God out of your mouth, they admire it as beautiful and great. But they note that our works do not correspond with the words we speak, and so get occasion for slander, calling it tales and lies. When they hear from us that God says, ' It brings you no grace to love those who love you, but it brings grace when you love enemies and those who hate you,' they admire, on hearing it, the excess of goodness. But they see that we not only do not love the enemy, but not even the friend, so they laugh at us, and the name is slandered" (2 Clem. xiii. 3 f.). Thus Christianity is fully conscious that it is not only to glory in the commands of its Lord, but that it must also realise them.

The Christian self-consciousness reveals itself still more clearly in the relations of the Christians to one another. The great communion, the Church, the Ecclesia, is clearly there. Prayer is offered for its unity, that in the end it may be visible. Already, however, it is spiritually present, mediated through those wandering apostles, prophets, and teachers. The Didache gives the impression of the existence of very many itinerant brethren, who kept up comunications between community and community. More and more also there is formed an outward conformity in constitution, ceremonial, and custom. The ordinances of the Pastoral Epistles, *e.g.*, are certainly given for a larger circle of Churches (Tit. i. 5); and the "Teaching of the Apostles" applies to the Church in a whole district. When we compare these two, the fundamental features, in spite of all varieties of local development, are the same.

Within the separate Churches, however, the Christian consciousness is no less lively. When individuals withdraw (μονάζειν) from fear of suffering or in haughty self-exaltation, "as if they were already justified," they are severely reproached (Barn. iv. 10). The value of union is understood; only as a member of the community does one come to fuller knowledge of the will of God, and find the strength to really keep His commands (Barn. x. 11). The exhortation to seek the face of the saints daily, to gain life from their words (Did. iv. 2, Barn. xix. 10), may be taken over from Judaism, but here it won new significance and was inculcated afresh (Did. xvi. 2). The advice points to existing carelessness, which, however, would be confined to a section of the Church. We have already become acquainted with the gatherings for divine service as the essential means for promoting and fixing Christian morals. Here the matter is one evidently of assemblies of a more private kind, wholly for mutual edification and education.

The finest achievement of the Churches is their organisation of Christian charity. Formerly this was purely voluntary, but now, with the consolidation of the constitution, it became a Church affair—at least in great measure. Individuals, however, still enjoyed sufficient opportunity of freely exercising their desire to give. Such organising, morally estimated, may be a doubtful advance. When we look at it in general, however, it is a brilliant proof of the strong moral spirit which lived in the Churches. Through a system of giving, which does not appear to have been strictly regulated, and which left the individual room for free play, the Church was made capable of meeting the largest demands, while also very sensible measures were adopted against its being taken advantage of. According to the Didache, the members of the Churches in the country have to deliver the first-fruits of the wine-press and the threshing-floor, the firstlings of the oxen and sheep, the first of the dough-cakes, and the first of a wine or oil cask, as also of money, garments, and other possessions; the regulation reads expressly, "the first portion according to thy judgment" (Did. xiii. 7). These offerings are employed primarily for the maintenance of those who serve the community, and especially on behalf of those itinerant teachers who are entirely dependent upon it; then come the officials of the individual Churches, who, indeed, in large congregations might give all their time to the work and be dependent upon it for their livelihood, but in smaller Churches certainly had their own business and property besides. At the outset, however, it is stated that enough is to be retained to tend the poor of the Church, to provide journeying brethren with two or three days' support, and to carry out any similar obligations of love towards prisoners, sick, and needy that might arise. In particular there is a class in the Church for whom it is bound to provide. This class is composed of the widows, who, on their side, serve the Church in various ways, teaching the youth, bringing up orphans, and nursing the sick, etc. In this case the feeling of a special obligation to protect the widow, who is deprived of her proper maintenance and protection, and the special arrangements for the maintenance of the clergy, go hand in hand. Further, every newcomer who bears the Lord's name has a right to look for shelter and food, and, in case his journeying further, can claim a provision for the way. If a Christian is thrown into prison for the Lord's name, the Church maintains him, and, if possible, purchases his freedom. This concern of the Church extended even to other Churches, to companions of the faith deported to penal servitude in the mines.

An organisation of this kind dies of itself when it is shackled by the spirit of a blind enthusiasm. This reproach was made against the Christians. Lucian sneers at the touching concern which the swindler Peregrinus Proteus, who obtruded himself among them for some time, secured for himself as minister and martyr. It may have been so in single instances. The passionate willingness of the Christians tempted the unscrupulous to take advantage of them. On the whole we must acknowledge with wonder that they did not fall into this mistake. The individual was asked for absolute readiness to assist; yet as a Church institution Christian benevolence was always exercised in that sober, thoughtful spirit which, with clear vision surveys the means at hand, adopts what is practicable, and helps only where there is actual need. We possess evidence of this in the views expressed in the Pastoral Epistles on the care of widows, and in those of the Didache on the treatment of wandering brethren. If a widow has children and grandchildren, it is their business to care for her, and to give expression to the love and gratitude of children. Should it happen that a member of the Church has voluntarily accepted the care of some widows, then these are to be entirely given over to him, and no longer to take part in the provision made by the Church, in order that the Church may not be unnecessarily burdened. Further, if a Christian comes to a Church in his journeying, rest and a meal are to be provided first of all. Then he is to be tested. Here we shall have to think of the letters of commendation which at that time were probably regularly given from the home-Church. If he is only on his way through, he is to receive what further help is possible, and, in case of need, to be accommodated with quarters and maintenance for two or three days, but no longer! If he wishes to make a longer stay, he is to earn his bread himself; even here, however, the Church is to assist him by securing some work for him to do. In the case of an artisan, that is evidently not difficult; in other cases it is entrusted to the prudence of the Church to look out for a suitable occupation, to the end that in the Church no Christian live a lazy life (Did. xii. 4)—an exceedingly instructive parallel to the modern combating of vagabondism. He who declines to labour is to be considered a deceiver travelling in the name of Christ, and to be expelled. When we add to this that slaves were denied any claim upon church funds for their emancipation, unless there seemed to be special circumstances demanding it, we see that the Christian Churches were by no means blind in their management. These regulations, too, have another value than simply that of a protection against being victimised by false brethren or against mismanagement by over-zealous officials. They show also what attention was paid in the Churches to the virtues of affection towards parents and dependents, joy in labour and industry, modesty and contentment with one's position. The high valuation of the love of children, of labour, and of service shows genuine evangelical features which richly atone for any ascetic grounds that reveal themselves, and anything impersonal which accompanies the organisation.

It is, however, extremely important to observe that organised liberality does not make private charity superfluous, does not anticipate it; on the contrary, it leaves as much as possible to individual liberality. Devoted and loving toil for all in need is still considered one of the chief proofs of personal Christianity. Among the qualities which a member of the Church to be chosen as bishop must unconditionally possess, hospitality is named (1 Tim. iii. 2, Tit. i. 8). This is to be explained not by the fact that in the future he will have to exercise hospitality in name of the Church, but because hospitality is the sign of a living Christian, and only such are to be chosen to preside over the Church. The same applies to the widows, who are to be cared for by the Church. It is presupposed that, in addition to works of benevolence, training children and hospitality, they have willingly rendered the lesser services of love like foot-washing, have received the oppressed and in general done all possible good. It cannot be denied that the unfruitfulness of intellectualism in works of Christian love, which we already found among the gnostics, is revealed also in Church circles.

People who rest content with an appeal to the Pauline formula, *i.e.*, with a theoretical acknowledgment of faith, are reminded by Jas. ii. 14 ff. that faith without works is dead, that true heavenly wisdom must reveal itself among other things in abundant mercy and good works (iii. 17). With an insistence similar to that in 1 John iii. 17, and in the Gospel of the Hebrews (*vide* p. 169), the heartlessness of mere words is pilloried (ii. 15 f.). " If a brother or a sister be naked, destitute of daily food, and one of you say unto them, Depart in peace, be ye warmed and filled, notwithstanding ye give them not those things which are needful to the body, what doth it profit ? " In this connection the emphatic demand for practical, applied Christianity, which so distinctly characterises this whole conception of Christianity, is recognised (Tit. iii. 8). Christianity must bring forth fruit. The highest boast of a Christian is that he has served (2 Tim. i. 18). Faith and love are the determining signs of a Christian (1 Tim i. 15) and of a Christian Church. The author of the Epistle of Barnabas bears witness to his readers that they possess these richly (i. 4, xi. 8). Along with the hope of eternal life, with which faith begins and ends, along with the righteousness which is more than judgment, there is a bold, joyous love which is evidenced in works of righteousness, the third of the main commandments of the Lord (Barn. i. 6). It is not enough, as might be the custom of many Christians, to hear the Word of God; it must also be done (Jas. i. 22). The insufficiency of the Greek view that knowledge is the one important thing, even in the moral sphere, is clearly recognised, and stern tones are employed against it : " To him that knoweth to do good and doeth it not, to him it is sin." The oldest Christian sermon contains the warning to take home something from the assembly, and amid the seductions of the world not to forget the Lord's commands (2 Clem. xvii. 3). Among the commands which are most expressly inculcated is that of giving, and, moreover, joyous giving, which finds its pattern in God's manner of giving to all men liberally, and upbraiding not (Jas. i. 5). So the Christian also is to give to every one who asks, and not to demand anything in return; are they not gifts of the Father's grace which he designs for all (Did. i. 5, iv. 7, Barn. xix. 11)? Therefore the Christian is to share everything with the brother, and to call nothing his own: "If ye are companions in immortal, how much more in mortal things." (Did. iv. 8, Barn. xix. 8). He who gives need have no scruples if sometimes the recipient prove unworthy; the blame and punishment fall on him alone.

All this, however, as they learned by experience, was not sufficient to prevent their being imposed upon. Hence there is added (by reference to an apocryphal saying, Sir. xii. 1?), "Let thine alms sweat in thine hands, till thou knowest to whom to give" (Did. i. 6). But this limitation—perhaps not introduced till later—was not much observed. It does not appear again in any of the older works. On the contrary, unconditional charity is more and more enforced. "More powerful than prayer is fasting, and more than both, alms." "Alms abolish sins" (2 Clem. xvi. 4). This, it is true, may involve a moral externalising of the most sacred and most serious questions of life, yet it shows the energy with which benevolence was emphasised as a decisive demonstration of the Christian spirit.

The Churches have grown. They have received additions from every rank of life. At the same time, however, social contrasts have increased. True, the Churches for which the Didache is intended give the impression of being composed essentially of small mechanics and peasants. On that ground the offerings are reckoned in natural products. The presupposition that a wandering brother is usually a mechanic points to the same probability. In the Epistle of James, too, the Christians appear in most cases to belong to the poor classes, dependants who are oppressed, day-labourers on large estates whose wages are kept from them. But there are also rich members of the Church, proprietors and merchants, men and women who appear in the church in luxurious dress (Jas. i. 9 ff., ii. 2, iv. 13, v. 1 ff.; 1 Tim. ii. 9). Now a division of sentiment is to be observed. On the one hand we see the Churches take pains to win such people, and keep them; for charitable objects the presence of well-off members was invaluable. On the other hand a great danger clung to the rich. Riches were a source of worldliness. It shocks the consciences of others when men who least merit it are given preference in the Church. The rich are haughty (1 Tim. vi. 17). Business interests choke fear of God and brotherly love. The love of money is the root of all evil (1 Tim. vi. 9 f.). Merchants make plans for journeys and designs for profit, as if there were no God and they themselves had the free disposal of their lives (Jas. iv. 13 ff.).

Proprietors oppress their workmen just like their unbelieving colleagues, who have dragged poor Christians before the judge, have slandered the Christian name, have condemned and killed righteous men unjustly (ii. 6, v. 6). This at least is the opinion of the author of the Epistle of James, which we must grant has an express sympathy with poverty. For him poverty in itself is a boast with God, an "exaltation"; the rich man must rejoice when, through confiscation of his property, he is raised to this high level (i. 9 f.). The author of the Pastoral Epistles also recognises the moral significance of wealth, and only requires the spending of it in trust in God and in His intention, *i.e.*, to do good, to be rich in good works, to be generous and ready to communicate, thus to earn a treasure in the future life (1 Tim. vi. 17 ff.). The author of the Epistle of James, however, does not go so far as to excite the poor against the rich. On the contrary he gives the express warning, " Be patient—and murmur not against one another" (v. 7, 9). The poor man is not to wish to be rich, but to be content when he has food and clothing. When united with contentment, godliness is great gain (1 Tim. vi. 6 f.). Labour is valued, even toiling with the hands in the sweat of the brow; it is the Christian's duty to earn his bread (Barn. x. 4, Did. xii. 3 f.).

Opposition to false teachers led to greater stress being laid on the moral legitimacy of sustenance (1 Tim. iv. 3 ff.). The use of a little wine is approved, and even advised on grounds of health (v. 23). This Christianity desires strict habits, but no extravagant asceticism.

So also the family life. Not only is the right of marriage recognised, but maternal duties are directly idealised and included under religion. The begetting of children is a means of salvation whereby the fall of Eve is made good. To that end, however, the bringing up of children belongs to the realm of faith, love, and holiness, and is to be done in the spirit of rational mildness (1 Tim. ii. 14 f.). The young Christian married women are shown by the matrons how to love their husbands and children aright, to manage their housekeeping, and to be in subjection to their husbands (Tit. ii. 4 f.). The head of a household who does not keep his family in order can secure no leading position in the Church (1 Tim. iii. 4 f., Tit. i. 6). The duty of every family to care for its own members was already spoken of (1 Tim. v. 8). The suspicions against second marriage, which sprang from ascetic motives, had gained strength through the evangelical view of the indissolubility of marriage and (notwithstanding Mark xii. 18 f.) the Christian hope of resurrection, but they were not generally regarded in practice.

The wife, as such, receives respect. For that reason "emancipation" and public appearances after the manner of gnostic prophetesses are not tolerated. Women's duties lie in their family and in the charitable domain (1 Tim. ii. 9 ff.). That is shown by the institution of the "widows of the Church." For these there are particularly strict rules. They must have fulfilled their family duties, and their moral behaviour must be without reproach. The special danger is conceived to be gossip and drunkenness. There is no mention of unchastity among them, even where the subject is touched upon, or, indeed, in the whole literature with which we are dealing. I can explain this only by the suggestion that moral consciousness on this point had really been elevated. It goes without saying that such sins are incompatible with Christianity. Only in respect of paganism (1 Tim.

i. 9 f., Barn. x.) and the immorality of the last days, which is already anticipated by the false teachers (2 Tim. iii. 3), are these vices mentioned.

Nor in the matter of slavery am I inclined to start from Tit. ii. 9 f. The warning against stealing only mentions how the Christian slave is to be distinguished from the heathen one. The thievish slave who deceives his master when possible, was a familiar character in comedies; the Christian slave must be different. The danger here lay in a quite different domain. The theory of the inner equality of all ranks before God furthered lawlessness and desire for emancipation. That could have very evil consequences with heathen masters. The risk was almost greater where the master was a Christian, should the slave take advantage of the bond of brotherhood between them. The warnings in 1 Tim. vi. 1 f. point to such difficulties in the Churches, but show what pains were taken to remove beforehand all desire of emancipation on the part of slaves.

Within the Churches there was a feeling that the general condition of Christian morality was not at the highest level. From time to time the feeling is vented in sharp words and calls to repentance. "Cleanse your hands, ye sinners, and purify your hearts, ye double-minded, be afflicted, and mourn and weep," is the call of James to the Churches (iv. 8).

Because of their worldly-mindedness, he calls them adulteresses, and exhorts them to "Lay apart all filthiness and superfluity of naughtiness" (i. 21). As a matter of fact, it cannot be denied that the danger of secularisation was widespread. We have proof of this fact not only in the merchants and proprietors of the Epistle of James, but in Hermas especially. We can even conclude from the requirements made of church officials that the average was tolerably low. When it needs to be particularly emphasised that such an one must be no wine-bibber, no bully, it seems that the fact was not of itself quite clear to the rank and file of Christians. Next to that, it is in especial sins of the tongue, and the quarrels these give rise to, which are dreaded both by James and in the Pastoral Epistles. But, on the other hand, these are the only blemishes, and against them a hot war is waged. Then, too, there is that richness in practical activity and works of love, besides the intensity with which the moral ideal is held fast and always set forth anew in fair formulation. Taking all this together, we may well conclude that the Christianity of that period, in its preaching of repentance, had made itself worse than it was, and even this does honour to its moral feeling. In addition to this feeling of insufficiency among the Churches, we may emphasise still more strongly their perfect consciousness of separation from the heathen environment, and that not only in regard to a difference of ideal. The inward transformation, which the individuals had undergone, was felt and noted (1 Tim. i. 13, Tit. iii. 3 f.). Renewed through the forgiveness of sin, they were become a new type with the souls of children (Barn. vi. 11). The place of all forms and degrees of impiety, impurity, and falsehood (1 Tim. i. 9 f.) was taken by eusebeia, the fear of God, and with it came a new Spirit-effected life, which meant thankful and hopeful looking to God in all conditions of life (Jas. v. 13), and a confidence which, without the assurance of an oath, does the Lord's commands (v. 12), and strives for the goal of Christian perfection (Jas. i. 4). The Lord's saying (Matt. ix. 13), is still clearly remembered (1 Tim. i. 15, Barn. v. 9, 2 Clem. ii. 4), although it is weakened by a theory of excuse for sins of ignorance (1 Tim. i. 13). Out of the filth of sin they have every one of them been called to the Church : but purified through baptism, they have now the one great task of keeping the seal inviolate (2 Clem. vi. 9, vii. 6, viii. 6).

However much this may at times smack of later Catholicism, it is primitive Christian. There still blows a fresh breeze from the Gospel; still moral freedom fights against legalism, and the strong hope of the Beyond against secularisation. The idea of the Church is strongly emphasised, but it has not yet pushed its way between God and men and become elevated to an end in itself. In spite of all conflict with the beginning of gnosticism, moral knowledge is original, naive, spontaneous. The demands are set forth in their entirety, and without such compromises as the Church ethic at the very outset, *e.g.*, in Clement of Alexandria, makes. Churches which lived as these did brought the Gospel honour.

LATER CHRISTIANITY AMONG THE HEATHEN.

CHAPTER XVIII.

THE CHURCHES OF THE TRANSITION TO
CATHOLICISM.

THE CHURCH OF ROME IN THE TIME OF HERMAS.

WE conclude with a picture from the life of the Roman Church. It belongs to a considerably later period, the utmost limit of our epoch, but it has the great advantage of animation and individuality. Hermas, our authority, is no quiet and remote observer; he himself belongs to the Church. His circumstances constitute a part of it; his thoughts and feelings reflect the thoughts and feelings within it. A man of the people, naive in comprehension and broad in expression, he gives us a precious view of the inner course of the Church's life, and the life of individual Christians. His circle is indeed very limited. He confines himself entirely to the concerns of daily life. Questions of politics trouble him as little as learned speculation. Ultimately he is possessed by one sole idea, the necessity for and the possibility of a second repentance. He feels himself a prophet commissioned by God to announce the moment of grace, and sound the call to repentance (M. XII. iii. 3). That has to be taken into account in valuing what he has to say on the moral condition of the Roman Church.

His book is not the issue of a single effort. The picture which it gives of the Roman Church is no instantaneous one. Composed at different times, it reflects varying frames of mind. The gradual and conjoint development of consecutive revelations is one of the most important criteria of real prophetic writings.

The work may embrace a period of several decades; yet there is nowhere any ground to suppose a variety of authorship. Hermas is well acquainted with the general edification literature in the Christian Church of his time. From his youth he has evidently known the Old Testament in the Greek translation, and has fashioned his own speech upon it. He knows Gospels, Epistles, works like the "Preaching of Peter," and the "Teaching of the Apostles," and, above all, books of revelation. Reading was evidently not an entirely familiar art to him (V. II. i. 4), but he has so absorbed the writings which were read in the services of the Church, and in private meetings for edification, that their contents, and to some extent their modes of expression, have become his own. This relative dependence also requires to be kept in view in estimating what he has to say.

We begin with that which concerned Hermas himself most intimately, and therefore possesses greatest interest for us—his confessions. These reveal to us the actual state of affairs in a Christian who must at least be reckoned among the conscious members of the Church, though in a certain sense also he may be counted among its spiritual leaders. To hold them

TRANSITION TO CATHOLICISM 311

as a mere literary form, which he chooses in order to chastise the sins of others, does not explain them; the whole man is too naïve. On the other hand, this naïveté must also be allowed for.

Hermas has not the skill in introspection and self-torture of an Augustine, in whose confessions every emotion of the heart and every thought becomes sin. There is something non-Christian in Hermas, though he does not himself appear to have been aware of it. This is shown by the way in which he bristles against the angel of punishment, and by the declaration that he has indeed many sins, but not so many that on account of them he must be given over to that angel (S. VII. 1, 2). In two ways he shows a trace of Pharisaism. On the one hand he speaks of the small punishment of other sinners (S. VI. iv. 2), reckoning it mechanically (4). (The theory of remembrance, v., weakens this only a little.) On the other hand he calculates on the possibility of a surplus of good works (S. v. iii. 3). We cannot acquit him of a certain amount of vanity, though we may excuse it to his naïveté that he repeatedly sets forth convincing proofs of his own continence (V. I. ii. 4), his being tried in persecution (V. II. iii. 2), and his zealous prayer (V. III. i. 2, S. IX. xi. 7).

We learn from Cyprian's epistles the extraordinary self-exaltation of the confessors of the Decian period; the insubordination of ascetic saints has often enough given trouble to the Church. The vain conceit of Hermas comes very clearly to light in the sofa-scene (V. III. i. 8), where he claims the place of honour. We shall judge him more leniently because he admits that he is to blame for it; but the pointed way in which he administers a thrust to the elders on that occasion cannot be counted to him for righteousness. The cold reception which he prepares for the shepherd (V. v.) throws no specially favourable light on his own hospitality.

But all this only shows us how hard it is for men to judge themselves justly. Hermas has really a very different opinion on these things: he condemns ambition and pride, and sets a very high value upon hospitality. Undoubtedly he would have recognised and penitently acknowledged his fault as soon as he became conscious of it.

Hermas, too, has a feeling of guilt: he knows that a man must make himself responsible for every failure (M. IX. 8), that all sorts of disasters, losses, wants, sicknesses, are divine discipline to lead the sinner to repentance (S. VI. iii. 4 f.), that penitent consciousness of past sins is the pre-condition of all salvation (V. III. vii. 6, S. VI. iii. 6), and that the sinner after conversion and penitence must not murmur against God's punishment (S. VII. 4). He is conscious that his want of Christian knowledge is a consequence of his earlier sins (M. IV. ii. 1). Yet he has a greater consciousness of sin than others, a finer feeling for all that is unrighteous. This sensitiveness goes hand in hand with the greater sensibility of the prophet, confessor, and ascetic.

It appears in the very first scene, the meeting with his former mistress, V. 1. Hermas, whose own marriage was not fortunate, is aware only that he has harboured the thought, "How lucky were I, had I a wife of such beauty and character." There was nothing evil in his thought. But he has to be taught by the heavenly vision that this thought too is a sin for which he will be accused before God, a wicked impulse which is fatal to him as a just man.

We learn from this that the Lord's saying in Matt. v. 28 was taken seriously. It is true Hermas himself weakens this impression to some extent by afterwards repudiating the notion of sin here. What he was guilty of was only an evil will leading to sin—a thing which was objectionable only in a Christian so tried and practised in abstinence as Hermas the confessor and ascetic.

A second confession goes deeper. Hermas is evidently a shopkeeper. Business always causes him a great deal of worry, and that not only in the ordinary sense. What he sees in it rather is a great danger to his soul's salvation. This we can quite understand, for he admits having sadly abused the confidence of his customers. His words come choked by tears of repentance: " Never yet in my life have I spoken a true word, but have always spoken like a rogue with every one. My own lies I set before all people as the truth, and no one ever contradicted me, but my words were believed" (M. iii. 3). Though certainly exaggerated, these words show us how deeply he was touched by the exhortation to truth. The pretended ignorance of this command, behind which he tries to flee (4), makes a peculiar impression. Was so little stress laid on truth and honesty in business affairs in the Christian Church that they were never mentioned? Hardly credible! But what attitude does Hermas adopt when he knows better? He learns and resolves to make up for earlier failure by honesty in the future, and through a blameless method of business to deserve in reality the credit which he enjoyed without any claim upon it. It shows his honesty that he thus exposes himself, and his naïveté that he believes he can make up for all that has happened. This resolve is exceedingly creditable to him. For his leanings are evidently in quite a different direction. He would rather give up business altogether; it is a continual temptation to him. He finds himself eased by the deprivation of his possessions, evidently through confiscation on account of his Christianity. The world-fleeing disposition of the ascetic, the "woe to earthly possessions," is always recurring.

The worst, however, that Hermas is aware of is his neglect of his own house. Whether it is the fanatic love of the prophet for solitude that has alienated him from his own, or weakness of character that has prevented him from taking the reins in hand—he is reproached with foolish fondness of his children—he has at any rate proved wanting in the necessary discipline and in the constant exhortation of his household, and has quietly looked on while everything went to ruin in his home.

His family was evidently Christian. Not only, however, had his wife become infamous for her evil tongue, but his children too had strayed to the extent of blasphemy and denying Christ. Hermas, whose own ideas about apostasy were so strict, experienced the agony of having to count his own children among the backsliders. The circumstances, too, seem to have been particularly aggravating. If we may so construe the indications which are not quite clear, his children, impelled by a contemptible desire for gain, or, as is possible, to avoid the consequence of their father's neglect of business and the loss of means that resulted from it, denounced their own father as a Christian (V. II. ii. 2). It did not profit them. The father lost his all, while they received nothing but the reward of denunciation, which they squandered. On the other hand the father feels himself lightened by this loss, and fosters the hope that the time is now come to call his family to repentance. Gladly, therefore, does he take it upon himself to continue zealous in exhortation, holding out at the same time the promise that there shall be forgiveness for the repentant. Their names also shall be received into the book of life. It is not to be forgotten either, that all this is said to Hermas by the Church. To be sure, she appears to the prophet as a heavenly figure. But we do not err when we transfer the vision to earth. The matter touches the readmission of his children into the Christian Church, from which they have shut themselves out by their apostasy. This also explains the much-contested words about his wife, who shall be his sister. She, who was evidently already a Christian, appears to have made common cause with the children; she, too, must be accordingly received into the Christian communion again.

A new light, however, is thus thrown on these confessions. They are no private confession before the heavenly Church, but were evidently laid before the whole Church, to which the work as a whole is naturally dedicated. That reveals anew the magnificent moral earnestness of the man, and not of him only, but of the Christianity of his time, which expected so much of its adherents. What valuable training it must have been for the moral consciousness of the Church, that a man specially known for piety should not only remove the offence which he had publicly given, but also openly confess his secret thoughts and make known his own increased consciousness of sin to others. The confessions of Augustine have taught centuries to confess.

Hermas, not without sinful impulses, of doubtful business integrity, and a poor head of his house! Certainly this is no happy picture of a Christian prophet, but is it not all outweighed by the moral courage of the confession and the delight which he has in improvement?

What we have to note specially in this man, who belongs to a Christian period already showing signs of degeneration, is his moral delight in the good, the courage with which he bravely surmounts difficulties and defies the devil. Hermas is well aware that he has not himself to thank for these qualities. Joyousness is not in any way natural to him. He rather takes things seriously, has continual suspicions, and would, if it lay with himself, turn out of danger's way. He is like the two-souled man ($δίψυχος$), whom he frequently pictures. He is continually considering and doubting in his heart whether the revelations really contain actuality or not (V. III. iv. 3, cf. iii. 4), whether God really forgives sins and hears prayers (M. IX. 1, 7). He is frightened at approaching troubles; he would fain flee from them (V. iv. i. 4, 7), and through this very uncertainty he falls into new dangers (M. v. ii. 1 f., xi. 1). But there is something else in him, something which contends with this natural inclination of his, whether it assume the form of the Church or of the Angel of Repentance, whether he trace it back to an operation of the Lord or the indwelling of His Spirit. It is the criterion of the true prophet. For the essence of all prophecy consists in this inner fight between the natural weakness of man and the divine power that comes over him, compelling him to do and to speak what he himself is afraid of. In Hermas this inward contradiction is revealed with rare clearness.

He pursues the confession of sins so busily that it is almost too much for him. He makes it an integral portion of every prayer. But he is rebuked: "Cease praying continually for your sins; pray for righteousness, in order that you may obtain something of it for your house" (V. III. i. 6, *cf.* M. XII. vi. 3). Harnack is right in referring this to Phil. iii. 14, and in calling it a real evangelical counsel. It transforms Hermas from a state of melancholy and miserable wallowing in his sin to a joyous Christianity, which wins the courage to do good.

When the Angel delivers his commands, Hermas finds them great, beautiful, and glorious. Happy the man who could fulfil them! But who can do that? They are hard. Even where there is the best possible will, for which every man will surely pray to God, the devil is refractory and drags men down. So he thinks (M. XII. iii. 4, v. 1, *cf.* S. VI. i. 1). But the Angel rebukes him, "Thou fool, imprudent and double-minded! If one straightway say, 'That I cannot do,' then one has no power; but he who gladly resolves to fulfil God's commands, finds them easy." The man does not depend upon himself:

God, who has made him lord over His creation, gives him strength. Only he must have the Lord not only on the lips, but also in the heart (M. XII. iv. 4, cf. S. IX. xxi. 1). As for the devil—a Christian does not need to fear him. God is more mighty than he. God's angel drives him out, and even before the man who boldly fights against him, the devil flees conquered and full of shame. He is a fearful being, without elasticity, like a corpse (M. VII. 2, XII. vi. 2). But there is to be no word of fear! only with the whole heart hope in God! In half-empty vessels the wine perishes; in half-men the devil gets his way. It is an evangelical joyous attitude which reminds us of Luther's defiance of the devil.

In this sense Hermas keeps up a constant fight against the spirit of indecision, of half-and-halfness (διψυχία). What he requires is the whole man for Christianity, perseverance in good (V. II. ii. 7), the fast fixing of the heart, and the whole heart on God (V. III. iii. 4, IV. ii. 4, M. X. i. 6). Repentance must come from the whole heart (V. II. ii. 4, IV. ii. 5, S. VII. iv., VIII. xi. 3); from the whole heart faith; from the whole heart worship (S. VIII. vi. 2), and the confession of the Lord (S. IX. xiv. 6) even in suffering (S. IX. xxviii. 2). Where there is the right faith, all care is thrown on the Lord (V. IV. ii. 5), and the Christian is confident that he can do all (V. IV. ii. 6). That is the ground of a wonderful courage, Θάρσος (V. IV. i. 8) and a great boldness.

Among the most remarkable utterances of the whole work is the tenth of its commandments. It is directed against sadness (λυπή), the sister of double-mindedness (διψυχία), and grumbling (ὀξυχολία). James also declaimed against wavering and double-mindedness. That murmuring is un-Christian is self-evident; but the statements to the effect that sadness is the wickedest of all the spirits (M. x. i. 2), that it vexes and drives out the Holy Spirit (M. x. ii. 2), astonish Hermas. It is something quite new to him. And yet he reaches here the height of a truly evangelical conception, the joyous Christianity, certain that good will conquer, which the Lord inculcated upon His disciples in opposition to the sad countenances of Pharisaism, and which Paul at the most exalted point of his life set forth in his will to the Church at Philippi. In the case of Hermas this inward joy finds expression in outward cheerfulness. It is quite peculiar what a rôle this "cheerfulness" (ἱλαρότης) plays in one naturally disposed to sadness. We learn from it also that here we have to do with Greek, not Oriental, piety. Cheerful as the angel of lust and seduction (S. vi. i. 6) is also the shepherd, the angel of repentance (S. ix. ix. 7), and in his company Hermas himself (x. 1). The virtues are cheerful (x. 7), and with them Hermas (xi. 5). The Church appears cheerful to him (V. i. iv. 3), and will become always more cheerful as Christians grow better (V. iii. x. 4 f., cf. ix. 10). More cheerful still will Hermas be when he sees her (V. iv. ii. 2), and the Christians in general when they learn the tidings of reprieve (V. iii. iii. 1). In cheerfulness God is to be served (M. v. i. 2), and cheerfulness is given as a characteristic of forbearance, μακροθυμία (M. v. ii. 3). The Holy Ghost Whom God has presented to man is cheerful (M. x. iii. 2); the environment of men must also be cheerful (M. ii. 4, S. ix. x. 3). It is no dark apocalyptic picture that this story and these revelations give us. This, however, is not because Hermas the Encratite was naturally of a cheerful disposition, but because his faith had wrestled with him, and forced this inward joy and gladness upon him.

Hermas is as bad a moralist as he is a strong moral character. To construct his ethical system would be a task as thankless as it would be misguided. How very uncertain he is, *e.g.*, in his views on the significance of suffering!

Sometimes suffering is conceived as an impulse to repentance (V. IV. ii. 5, S. VI. ii. 6, iii. 6); sometimes he sees in it actual atonement for sin (V. II. iii. 1, S. VII. 4). Occasionally he comes to terms with it in a very external way: as the head of a family Hermas himself must suffer, because only so can his children be reached (S. VII. 3). This is an idea to which too much honour would be done by comparing it with the supreme ethical thought of the vicarious suffering of the innocent. In a definition like that of gluttony, τρυφή (S. VI. v. 5), "Everything is gluttony for a man that he likes doing," our good Hermas gets into such difficulties that he is compelled to make a very artificial distinction in order to avoid the consequence that voluntary beneficence is impermissible gluttony (v. 7). But this want of skill in method, a consequence of his want of philosophical equipment, we may put out of consideration; for it is not any system but immediate moral feeling which is concerned when we emphasise that in Hermas an insistence on inwardness is characteristic.

It is true he makes statements that savour strongly of *opus operatum*. God has to be made gracious

(V. I. ii. 1); a surplus of good works is possible (S. v. iii. 3). But they vanish entirely when we observe how much more importance he attaches to the intention than to its expression. Of the individual works of Christian love he speaks comparatively little. Very frequently, however, he enumerates what may be called the virtues and failings of intention: fear of God, abstinence, simplicity, innocence, honour, truth, purity, long-suffering, knowledge, unity, contentedness; and on the other hand, unbelief, debauchery, disobedience, lying, melancholy, wickedness, sensuality, discontent, deceit, want of understanding, calumny and hate. Sometimes Hermas attempts a classification. He chooses faith, abstinence, strength, and forbearance from the larger group as the four chief virtues. He tries to derive the one from the other, and expressly places faith, fear of God, in the forefront of all his commandments. This reveals his knowledge that the power of all morality has its ultimate basis in piety. Under this point of view everything turns on the right attitude of the heart to God. From this attitude the right intention always comes naturally; and out of this the right activity follows as an inward necessity. Hermas is so convinced of this that his preaching of repentance is continually being summed up in the exhortation to purify the heart and turn it to God.

This feature of his preaching is revealed also in the method by which he seeks to motivate his exhortations. Here he is indeed often very unskilful, and he binds together motives of very different value. Occasionally he condescends to trivialities. The rich, *e.g.*, are to be induced to give liberally by the hygienic consideration: "They are as sick that surfeit with too much, as they that starve with nothing."—*Merchant of Venice*, Act I. Sc. ii. (V. III. ix. 3). Or he takes his stand on the Christian's hope of compensation (V. III. ix. 5, v. 7, S. I. 5), and is fond of laying stress on the fact that the fulfilling of all promises as well as the hearing of special prayers (S. v. iii. 9) is connected by God with the keeping of His commands (V. v. 7, S. I. 7). It is therefore a familiar thought with him that the right Christian conduct is advantageous and useful, σύμφορον, συμφορώτερον (S. I. 5, VI. i. 3, X. iv. 2). This leads him occasionally to fall into an unintended opposition to the Sermon on the Mount and the difficulty of the right way (M. VI. i. 4, *cf.* Matt. vii. 13 f.). With all this, however, his ethic is in the highest degree religiously and inwardly grounded; he who has the Lord in his heart keeps His commandments (M. XII. iv. 3). The God-fearing man seeks after divine things, and he who has his heart directed on God, apprehends them, for where the Lord dwells there is much understanding (M. x. i. 6). Hermas takes his stand on the summit of evangelical motives and measures human obligation by divine practice (*cf.* Matt. v. 48). If the Almighty does not upbraid those who confess their sin to Him, but is merciful, should not men also forgive? (S. IX. xxiii. 4). God intended man to be the lord of creation; should not man have the power to fulfil God's intention? (M. XII. iv. 2 f.). Only tentatively does the pattern of Christ appear. In Hermas the historical person of Jesus Christ stands remarkably in the background. The readiness of Christ's humanity to serve, and to obey the indwelling Holy Spirit walking in honour and purity (S. v. vi. 5 f.) is held up to the Christians. In the Son of God, Who is preached as a law to all ends of the earth (S. VIII. iii. 2), what is thought of is not the pattern life of Christ, but the revelation of God's will through the Holy Spirit Who was in Him, and the commands which constitute the essential content of the Gospel.

Not the life of Jesus but the apostolic life is here the pattern. The apostles, whose task it is to evangelise the world, both the living and the dead (S. IX. xvi. 5 f.), are the true types of a walk in divine honour, righteousness, and truth, free from all inordinate desire, inseparable from all virtues and pattern of unity (V. III. v. 1, S. IX. xv., 4, 6, xxv. 2). Here, as in the martyrs so highly celebrated by Hermas, the first tendencies to the later hagiolatry are to be observed; but it is a remarkable criterion of the whole moral spirit of this Christianity that it is the thought of the moral pattern which lifts these men here to such exaltation.

If the motive adopted to support its demands is always a measure of the strength of moral consciousness, we shall be able to adduce good witness for the Christianity of Hermas.

It is not as Hermas that our author interests us here, but as a type of the Christianity in the Roman Church of his time. And as a matter of fact he is typical in the good as well as in the bad. He indicates this fact himself by continually generalising the exhortations and instructions directed to himself personally and applying them to all saints (V. I. i. 9), to all who have sinned (V. II. ii. 4), to all who do righteously (V. II. iii. 2), and to all who do not doubt (V. III. ii. 2). The vision of the beast which represents the approaching persecution is to be recounted to all the chosen of the Lord (V. IV. ii. 5). The commands are by no means directed solely to him, but he who always hears them and acts accordingly will live to God (M. II. 6, III. 5, IV. ii. 4, iii. 7, v. i. 7, ii. 8, VI. i. 5). The moral ideas of Hermas cannot have been peculiar to him: he reckons on a larger circle of like-minded Christians among whom his preaching shall find sympathy. On the other hand Hermas is certainly not the only one who had to make such confessions. We can see that from the short exhortations which he directs to the Church.

Even the external circumstances are typical. Hermas belongs to the commercial middle class. He had not been free from birth. Sold from his Arcadian home when a youth, he was taken to Rome and there secured his freedom. A shop—the exact nature of it we do not know—maintains him and his family. He is not well-off, but still not poor. So it may have been with the average of the Roman Church of his time. There were indeed not wanting rich people, nor those who had acquired means after their adoption of Christianity (S. VIII. ix. 1). Hermas has no particular love for them.

There were not lacking poor either, who were entirely dependent on the rich for support. About them Hermas is exceedingly concerned. They appear to him to be the really devout, without whom the rich man cannot get on by reason of his barrenness in religion. That there were many in the Church who were not free, many slaves, is nowhere indicated. The great bulk of the Church was probably made up of citizens, freedmen like Hermas himself, people who followed their trade. For it is one of Hermas' chief cares to relieve the Christians from being choked by worldly concerns.

Of the Church's relation to the state we learn practically nothing. I do not at all think that the Roman Emperor is thought of in S. i., where the right of citizenship in the world is contrasted with citizenship in the city of God, and the laws of the Lord of this city with the laws of God. It is rather the devil that is intended by the ruler of the world. The silence of Hermas in this regard can be explained by the fact that political life lay entirely beyond his field of vision. As he did not belong to the leaders of the Church, political considerations affected him very little. But indeed, if the question of the relation to the state had been really a burning one in the Church, Hermas would have assumed a definite attitude to it, and all the more because persecution and apostasy play a leading part in his thoughts. We have to conclude that, in spite of the many and varied oppressions which she had had to experience and expected again every minute, the Roman Church of that period had loyally laid to heart the Apostle's exhortation in Rom. xiii. 1–7. Hermas, the confessor, has had his own possessions confiscated, but he sees in the deprivation only a wholesome disciplining of him by God; he does not think of fostering dark thoughts of revenge nor of calling his companions of the faith in the name of God to conspire against the power of the state hostile to Him.

To the external relations of the Roman Church belongs also its relation to the Christian Churches in other places. We have already learned that this relation was very active. We shall therefore attribute it to the narrowness of our author's point of view that he has practically nothing to say on the point. The only passage is V. ii. iv. 3, which looks almost like a reference to the so-called first Epistle of Clement. Of the two copies which Hermas has to make of the special revelation given to him, Clement is to send the one to the other towns; for that has been entrusted to him. We may well consider this an indication that epistolary communication was regularly kept up with other Churches.

The Church in Rome remained true to the obligations which its position in the centre of the empire, in the metropolis, laid upon it. And even at a later date we shall find this consciousness of responsibility for the whole Church still alive in the Church and among the clergy of Rome.

The feeling of union with the whole of Christendom was maintained alive in the Church at Rome more than in other Churches through the constant arrival of strangers who were one with the Roman Christians in faith. Among the Christians of that period in general there was developed a keen desire to move about. This was due to their release from former narrow notions of home on the one hand, and to their striving after close fellowship with the scattered companions of the faith on the other. Rome offered special attractions. Here, in the place where the great apostles Peter and Paul had worked and sealed their witness with their blood, there was one of the most conspicuous and significant Christian Churches. The capital of the world offered in addition plenty that was worth seeing, even when the Christian had only the thought of becoming acquainted with the great Babylon, from which shortly there was to proceed the destruction of all existing things that was to precede the longed-for establishment of the Kingdom of God. A visit to Rome, the centre of commerce and of administration, was sometimes due to business necessities, and many had to go there in connection with lawsuits in which they themselves or others were concerned. Then there were the countless hosts brought there as slaves. Their presence laid special duties on the Christian Church: these brethren who came to them must be cared for. Here we see clearly that Christian hospitality was organised by the Church. There were special officials, the bishops, on whom it devolved to exercise this duty (hence ἐπίσκοποι καὶ φιλόξενοι, S. IX. xxvii.), just as the care of the poor is strictly regulated and entrusted to the deacons (S. IX. xxvi.); naturally neither excluded the private exercise of hospitality and charity.

How far the Church as a whole provided for her own members we learn from Hermas only in a very fragmentary way. There may have been funds for sick and dead, as in the majority of Roman societies of humbler people outwardly similar to the Christian Church. Hermas does not speak of this. He once mentions an administration of funds to be attended to by the diaconate, *i.e.*, giving relief from the funds of the church to widows and orphans. That might possibly be confined to the distribution among the poor of the offerings left over in the common meals.

We are not to wonder at finding so little on all these matters in Hermas. The preacher of repentance is in the first place an individualist. The more inwardly he apprehends religion and morality, the more importance he attaches to the laying hold of individuals. When he so strongly emphasises the duties towards the whole, as we shall presently find him doing, he reveals clearly how essential the feeling of community was to the Christianity of the period.

Firmness arises from pressure. The feeling of close connection was kept alive among the ancient Christian Churches by persecution. It was a Church of martyrs in which Hermas lived. A severe persecution which had just been experienced forms the background of his preaching of repentance, and, on the other hand, the certain expectation that very quickly a new and greater will come, gives his exhortation weight and urgency (V. II. ii. 7, iii. 4, IV. ii. 5).

The persecution had tested faith, at least in the case of a section of the Church. Some had had to seal a bold confession with death; others had had to endure all sorts of affliction—prison, torture and the like—or, like Hermas himself, had had to suffer confiscation of their goods. Naturally that served to strengthen the Christian consciousness and to increase moral power. But it also brought new dangers. We already indicated that in Hermas himself signs are to be found of that confessor-vanity which afterwards became so notorious. The martyrs were held in extraordinary esteem (S. VIII. iii. 6, IX.

xxviii.). They take their stand immediately next the apostles (V. III. v. 2). Like baptism, the bath of blood effaces without more ado all earlier sins (S. IX. xxviii. 3). The martyr is *eo ipso* well-pleasing to God (V. III. i. 9); he has a claim to the highest place of honour in heaven (V. III. ii. 1).

Yet Hermas breaks away from the tendency to conceive martyrdom as the highest and most meritorious achievement, the very apex of service. He declares it must not be thought that a great work has been done in suffering for the cause of God; for that, too, is a grace of God Who hereby offers sinners the possibility of becoming free from their guilt and entering into life (S. IX. xxviii. 5 f.). Here we see again, as so often in Hermas, two views in conflict with one another; the ordinary Catholic Christian conception, and an evangelical view which is higher both from the religious and the moral standpoint.

Otherwise the high value set upon martyrdom can be inferred from the observation that the true confessors formed no very large part of the Church. However highly Hermas and his friends praised martyrdom, many, nevertheless, preferred to preserve this earthly life and its pleasures. Hermas has a depressing feeling, that in the last persecution a very large section of Roman Christianity either avoided confession or directly denied Christ. The occasion of his whole preaching of repentance was the question whether it was possible for such as have already, through baptism, received perfect remission of sins, to be again delivered from such serious guilt? Could they again enter into the Church of the saints? Hermas has himself a very personal interest in this question, because, as we saw, he had to count his own children and wife among the apostates. He now lays hold on the mercy of God. He who has once received forgiveness of sins should sin no more but dwell in holiness; but God's great love permits Him to have mercy on the weakness of men (M. IV. iii. 2, 4 f.). Thus the thought of a second repentance originates. Hermas knows himself commissioned by God to proclaim this message of grace to Christendom: there is still a space for repentance. But yet —here the old view is at work—there is only one second repentance (M. IV. iii 6), and the time for it is short (V. II. ii. 5, III. v. 5). Following his usual practice of making everything clear, wherever possible, by a classification, he here divides Christians who have sinned into those from whom a second repentance is still to be expected, and those in regard to whom this is not the case (S. VIII. 6–11). As he distinguishes between martyrs and confessors (V. III. ii. 1), and among the former again between those who have gone joyously to death and those who have done so only after delay (S. IX. xxviii. 4), so also among the apostates he makes a distinction between those who have simply denied Christ, and those who, through express blaspheming of the name of Christ, have aggravated their apostasy. From the latter he expects no repentance (S. VI. ii. 3, VIII. vi. 4).

In general, however, he has not much hope; for one who has fallen from grace is not only become as he was before, but worse (S. IX. xvii. 5). Apostates are on precisely the same footing as heathen; they have even less of a prospect, for to the heathen repentance always remains open (V. II. ii. 5). In the case of Maximus, probably a leading member who appears to have returned to the Church after his apostasy, Hermas is exceedingly concerned lest the next storm wash him overboard again (V. II. iii. 4). For the repentant, however, a complete union with the Church and the fixed determination not to avoid the renewal of persecution are necessary. Even a momentary hesitation whether to confess or not is, if not direct sin, yet wicked. It detracts from the glory of the martyrdom (S. IX. xxviii. 4 f.).

On the other hand Hermas has now to learn that many, having once denied Christ, do not wish to become connected with the Church again (S. IX. xxvi. 3); while others who have not publicly fallen from Christianity keep far from the Church. In these isolated Christians (μονάζοντες) we have a very remarkable phenomenon which must be set parallel to the usual form of Jewish proselytism in the higher ranks of Roman society. They adopted what they thought good, the monotheistic faith and the noble moral commands, while they observed also one or other of the ceremonial laws so as not to be entirely without the guarantee of the pleasingness of such a life to God. But the attempt was made to keep far away all the discomfort, all that a closer connection with such a religious brotherhood involved. It is in every case the well-off, those belonging to better classes, of whose separation from the Christian Church Hermas complains. How was an eminent Roman, however much he was impressed with Christianity and its strong monotheism, its sure hope of the future, and its truly elevated morals, to be on familiar terms with the common people who found themselves together with him in the Christian Church and claimed to be considered his brethren? Besides, did not Christianity expose one to burdens of all sorts?

In the Church one was continually being solicited for alms (S. ix. xx. 2); the brethren were always in need of hospitality. Then, too, one was exposed to the jeers of former companions. And what was even worse, one ran danger of coming in contact with the police. For these Christian brethren did not enjoy the advantage which the synagogue had, of being recognised by the state as a lawful religious society. They were hunted as criminals of whom the very worst could be said. The very name of Christian was enough to secure condemnation (S. ix. xxviii. 3, διὰ τὸ ὄνομα). Confiscation of goods was the very least that could be looked for (V. iii. vi. 5). Scourging, prison, severe tortures, crucifixion and fighting with wild beasts in the arena were in prospect (V. iii. ii. 1). Naturally that thought alone was enough to frighten many from joining the Christian body; and when the report of an approaching persecution was spread, these would do everything they could, to blot out the slightest appearance of belonging to it.

The synagogue tolerated this ambiguous position. It was always a means of maintaining influential connections with leading people, who would otherwise be quite inaccessible. There did exist indeed among the propagandists of Judaism people of stricter convictions, as we learn from Josephus' account of the conversion of the Prince of Adiabene and his family. But Christianity could under no conditions endure such lukewarmness. The Church of confessors required a real confession and one in union with herself. Only in her midst could holiness be achieved. He who separated from her lost, while he thought to win, his life (S. IX. xxvi. 3). We have already repeatedly met with the warning against forsaking the assemblies, but nowhere does the exhortation to hold fast to the saints meet us so often as in Hermas (V. III. ii. 6, vi. 2, S. VIII. viii. 1, ix. 1, IX. xx. 2, xxvi. 3).

With the requirement of close connection with the Christian Church and all her members, goes hand in hand the demand for a strict outward exclusiveness. As a matter of fact, there must have been here a great danger for Christianity, and, in particular, for its moral character—the danger, viz., of deterioration to paganism while the outward appearance of Christianity was retained. Hermas speaks tolerably often of people who may well be Christians, who have faith, and bear the Christian name (S. IX. xiii. 2, xix. 2), but who do not in any way bear out the moral ideal of Christianity.

It is interesting to note all that Hermas regards as pagan. Not only is idolatry itself pagan, although in the deeds and works of the heathen (S. VIII. ix. 3) and the things which the heathen do (M. IV. i. 9), that is thought of chiefly. An attitude towards Christian prophets which recalled the mantic and involved the consultation of them about all sorts of things, also appears to him to be pagan. The stupid doctrines and views into which many Christians have fallen back are pagan (S. VIII. ix. 3), and also the whole system of expensive food, etc., that many adopt (S. I. 10). Pagan is the antithesis of holy and just. The heathen, along with apostates and sinners, are opposed to the Christians as the just (V. I. iv. 2,

S. IV. 4). Accordingly the worst epithet of reproach which Hermas has, is "heathen." In his judgment of the false prophets and those who honour them, the decisive and incriminating factor is that their whole behaviour has something idolatrous in it, that it is heathen mantic with the form of Christian prophecy (M. XI. 4). Wealth appears to him for the same reason equally dangerous, because it reveals a connection with paganism, to which it is ever dragging its possessor down (S. I. 10). If it does not cause direct denial, it leads to a life of wanton luxury, which brings to death or at least to the brink of ruin.

This was evidently the greatest danger of all for the vigorous moral development of personal Christianity. The old social relations, the "heathen friendships," as Hermas says in anger, were kept up (M. X. i. 4). The Christians took pains to secure favour with the heathen, especially if they had any property, or, worse still, if they had just acquired some. With no thought of falling away from Christianity, all sorts of un-Christian forms were observed in social intercourse; the tone of heathen society, with its haughtiness and frivolity, was adopted, and, without knowing it, many Christians were in danger of being altogether brought into this current and so falling from God in very truth (S. VIII. ix. 1, 3). To Hermas this is a most pernicious presumption, and he cannot warn them enough against it. The danger which here threatened the Christian Church is revealed by the fact that Hermas, who in other respects was by no means a hard man, insists with the utmost rigour on perfect separation from everything heathen.

A pagan life, participation, that is, in pagan ceremonial and pagan practices, is, like adultery, to be sufficient ground of divorce; one who continues to live with a Christian who leads such a life becomes equally guilty (M. IV. i. 9). The matter is not one of mixed marriages, but of Christian marriages in which one partner threatens to fall or has already fallen back into paganism, as was the case with the author's own wife. Everything that bears even a remote resemblance to paganism is to be avoided by the Christian. Christianity is to exhibit itself as a Church of holy, righteous, and God-fearing men, quite exclusive but bound in an internal and close union.

The Church was no longer a fortuitous conjunction of men of the same faith and aim. She had an organisation. She possessed leaders and officials. It is true we are not altogether clear on these points, but the existence of leaders (V. II. ii. 6, III. ix. 7), of presbyters as managers (V. II. iv. 3), of bishops and deacons for church work (S. IX. xxvi., xxvii.), is certain. Where there are such leaders, they are responsible not only for the outward weal of the Church, but also for her moral condition. When the angel of repentance in the form of a shepherd so strongly emphasises the responsibility of the shepherd for his flock (S. IX. xxxi. 5), we may be sure that not only he himself is intended, but all the shepherds of the Christian Churches. It seems that the leaders of the Roman Church have not by any means borne out these requirements perfectly. They must be warned to better their ways in righteousness (V. II. ii. 6); they have poison in their heart and are hardened; they will not purify their heart and be of one mind (V. III. ix. 7 f.). To be sure Hermas knows bishops who have always performed the duty entrusted to them by the Church blamelessly. They have received the journeying servants of God hospitably, seeking out and caring for the needy and the widows, and leading a pattern life and conversation (S. IX. xxvii., *cf.* V. III. v. 1). But the prominence he gives to these shows that there were others. And, indeed, he had complaints to make against officials of the Church, who vilely misused the office entrusted to them and enriched themselves on what was intended for widows and orphans (S. IX. xxvi. 2).

These utterances of Hermas must be cautiously employed, and especially so when he speaks in general terms against the leaders. The "pious" have always had some fault to find with the occupants of church office, and in this matter Hermas is not free from partisanship. The charismatic, who is also ascetic and confessor, feels himself forced to oppose the presbytery. It is a part of that great contest which runs through the whole history of the Church and the world between organisation and free spiritual movement, or, as it has been recently expressed, the Spirit under restraint and the Spirit in free play. Hermas gives his contempt for the presbytery unmistakable expression in that sharply ironic remark, "Let the presbyters first take their places," whereupon the Church answers him shortly, "What I tell you, that do; be seated" (V. III. i. 8). He calls the leaders of the Church scathingly, "the men of the first place" ($\pi\rho\omega\tau o\kappa\alpha\theta\epsilon\delta\rho\hat{\iota}\tau\alpha\iota$, V. III. ix. 7), and storms against the stupidity of quarrels as to precedence (S. VIII. vii. 4). We cannot avoid the impression, however, that with his prophetic dignity and pride of confession he was hardly a competent judge in this matter.

Here the most remarkable thing is that it is far from clear whether the matter is only one of quarrels as to precedence, or whether deeper differences do not enter into it. " The men of the first place," in V. III. ix. 7, have an undoubted resemblance to the false prophet pictured in M. XI., who sits alone on the throne while his attentive hearers occupy a form at his feet, and whose whole conduct Hermas traces to his endeavours to secure the first place (12), θέλει πρωτοκαθεδρίαν ἔχειν. To connect this with the beginnings of the gnostic movement is a view which, especially in consideration of S. IX. 22, will always have something to be said for it. Of actual false doctrine there is remarkably little said in Hermas, though it is possible to put this interpretation upon the poison mentioned in V. III. ix. 7 (*cf.* the strange, foolish doctrines, S. VIII. vi. 5, ix. 3). He lacks also the understanding which would enable him to estimate the dangers of gnostic speculation. He is concerned only with the practical. And gnostic teachers, false prophets, and ecclesiastics are not yet clearly separated in his view. Everywhere he sees among them unChristian ambition, which leads to suspicious divisions. In some cases it is still harmless, and does not make an end of their Christianity. " All the time they are believing and good, only they hanker after privileges and a certain honour " (S. VIII. vii. 4). In other cases this ambition, which manifests itself in boldness, shamelessness, and talkativeness, is united with covetousness and gluttony (M. xi. 12), constituting a twofold danger to the Church.

Gluttony seduces (M. xi. 13). In particular these lying prophets prophesy smooth things to the people (M. xi. 2). Covetousness leads to imposture (S. ix. xix. 3), as we have already more than once learned. The great dangers which accompanied the mighty impulse brought by Christianity were just that, when transferred unduly to the intellectual domain, it led to an intolerable self-conceit, an obtrusive doctrinal readiness (S. ix. xxii. 2). With persons of impure character it degenerated even into immorality, or at least into the impermissible employment of their authority for selfish ends, while in worse cases it ended in lascivious libertinism, afterwards, perhaps, palliated by antinomian theories. Hermas does not entirely despair of such people—this, too, a good sign of the strength of his own Christian conscience and the Church's belief in the might of moral good; they can still repent, and some of them will (S. ix. xix. 3, xxii. 3).

The main point, however, both for Hermas and for us, is the harm that all this caused to Church life; schisms still kill Christianity. When the leaders themselves quarrelled about precedence, when charismatics rebelled against the regular Church office, when special parties within the Church were formed round individual teachers, whether gnostics, false prophets, or ecclesiastics, it was inevitable that the sense of communion, the spirit of brotherly love, the unity should be very severely damaged. Hence we are continually coming across the exhortation to preserve peace in mutual services and discipline (V. III. ix. 2, 10), and to avoid all evil report which disturbs peace and increases confusion (M. II. 1 f.). Only when there is peace in the Church can the Lord impart further revelations to her, and the religious life be enriched (V. III. xii. 3). The building of the Church is to have the outward appearance of a monolith (S. IX. ix. 7, xiii. 5). But while in the foundation, which is built out of the pattern apostles, bishops, teachers, and deacons, this is a magnificent fact, there is still much wanting to make the upper part of the tower fit exactly. Many stones must be taken out again and be freshly hewn. The call to unity is an essential part of Hermas' call to repentance.

From this insistence of Hermas we can learn that there was present in the Roman Church of his time, some degree of the same faction-spirit which we have already seen in the Corinthian Church of Paul to be the sad accompaniment of an excessive development of power.

Hermas' almost complete silence in regard to the devotional life of the Church is due to his individualism. It might be supposed in reading his works that there was no such thing, so seldom and so vaguely does he speak of it. He says nothing about the service of the word or the Lord's Supper. It is almost entirely of the devotional exercises on the part of individuals that he speaks. But the way in which he judges these is significant for us: it throws a light on the question how far moral power asserted itself in public worship.

Evidently it was only latterly that the custom had reached the Church of frequently withdrawing into solitude for a time, for the purpose of living an entirely ascetic life. There were definite days for this called Statio, like the military outposts (S. v. i. 1). Fasting and prayer were closely associated with it. It was a spiritual exercise, not without a strong admixture of the righteousness of works. The intention was to please God thus, to do penance for past sin (V. i. ii. 1) and to achieve a definite reward of special honour in the Kingdom of God. Abstinence (ἐγκράτεια) was, as such, very highly prized: it appears to be the supplement of defective positive morality (V. ii. iii. 1 f.); it is the pre-condition of all hearing of prayer (V. iii. x. 6), and of further reception of revelations. What effects were attributed to prayer is most clearly seen in the parable of the elm and the vine. As fruit can be attributed to the elm, which is not a fruit tree, but serves to support the grape, enabling it to rise from the earth, so the prayer of the grateful poor helps the generous rich and supplies what these lack in Christian perfection. It is a remarkably external and mechanical method of handling moral things.

That, too, is only one aspect of the matter. This way of thinking, though widely spread within the Church, does not remain uncontradicted. Here we once more see at work in Hermas that prophetic spirit which represents a higher stage of moral perception, and is endeavouring to elevate Christianity to it. Hermas the prophet is constrained to bear witness against himself, the representative of ordinary Christian thinking. With all his eagerness, however, for uninterrupted prayer and strict fasting—his own designation of himself is Hermas the Encratite (V.

I. ii. 4),—he must still warn himself and others against excess. "See to it that thou dost not through much prayer injure thy flesh (thy health)" (V. III. x. 7). "Ye know not how to fast to the Lord, and your useless fasting is not a (proper) fast, is not fasting to Him. God will not have such empty fasting; for with it you make no righteousness." In the place of fasting there is to come the keeping of God's commandments, the remaining free from every wicked impulse, the trusting God, fearing Him, and abstaining from every wicked deed. That is a great fast and well-pleasing to God (S. v. i. 3 ff.). And if they are to fast in the strict sense, let them spare from their mouths to help widows and orphans and the needy. That is a pleasant sacrifice for God, a fast which he places upon record, a beautiful joyous service. Blessed the man who does it (S. v. iii. 7–9). The highest moral thoughts, as they are only occasionally to be found in the prophets of the old covenant, the central thoughts of the Gospel, here become effective as distinguished from the practice of the Christianity of the time, which threatened to sink to a sub-Christian level.

The same thing holds in regard to baptism. As a sacrament, if we may use the word, it is exceedingly highly valued. It is the necessary pre-condition of the attainment of all salvation, not only for the Christians who are now living (V. III. ii. 4, iii. 5, S. IX. xii. 4), but also for the holy men of the old covenant (S. IX. xvi.), and even for the angels (S. IX. xii. 6, 8). It blots out all past sins. This is the reason why the question as to the possibility of a second repentance after baptism is so burning and so much discussed (V. II. ii. 4 f., III. v. 5, M. IV. iii. 1, S. VIII. 6–11). But the very fact of these questions being brought up shows us how far Christianity was from resting quietly with the grace of baptism. Hermas is always inculcating anew the moral duties which this same baptism lays upon the Christian: he should sin no more, but dwell in holiness (M. iv. iii. 2), be simple, not bear a grudge, lay aside wickedness, and live in unity (S. ix. xxxi. 4). The seal of baptism must be preserved unbroken, or the sinner must repent (S. viii. vi. 3); the white baptismal garment must be kept unstained.

Baptism demands as its complement the exercise of all Christian virtues (S. ix. xiii.). The Christians, as those baptised in the name of the Son of God, are holy (V. i. i. 9, iii. 2, iii. iii. 3, vi. 2, viii. 8. 9, iv. iii. 6), but they have still sin (V. i. i. 9, ii. ii. 4, 5, iii. viii. 11). The call to repentance is directed to the saints: Cleanse ye from your sins and do righteousness. Not on the ground of baptism, but only under the discipline of the angel of repentance does Hermas know himself to be free from shortcomings (S. x. ii. 1 f.). It is no exception to this rule when we find Hermas assuming the existence of Christians who have preserved their childish innocence all life long (S. ix. xxix.); the most we can see in that is only a want of psychological depth of vision, not a neglect of moral requirement. The innocence of children set forth in the Gospel as pattern for the disciples of Jesus remains in Hermas also the ideal of every Christian (M. ii. 1.).

Moral strengthening is also the ground element of the common edification. It is true there were also dangers in the devotional domain, *e.g.*, in the nightly assemblies for prayer which were taken part in by members of both sexes, and inspired Hermas' fancy in the description contained in S. ix. xi. 7. It was in these that the well-known heathen suspicions took their rise. But we have nowhere any proof that these were in any way grounded. On the contrary, if anything can be concluded from the peculiar character of Hermas about the divine services of the Church, they were permeated throughout by a moral spirit. Probably there was an admixture of much that was unevangelical in the idea of influencing God by uninterrupted fasting and prayer. But the public repentance, the confession which the sinner, as we saw in the case of Hermas himself, made before the whole Church, was at least a very wholesome discipline. It is likely that in the meetings for edification revelations of a purely eschatological kind played a part (*cf.* V. I. iii. 4). But it is worthy of remark that Hermas communicates to us only the brief conclusion of one such, "the last words were useful and pleasing to us," "the preceding, however hard and difficult, were only for the heathen and apostates" (V. I. iii. 3, iv. 2). The other revelations which he offers (V. II. 2, III. 9) relate to the moral life of the Church and its defects. The entire preaching of Hermas is, as the commandments in particular show, less based on eschatology than on morality.

This could not have been peculiar to himself. The warning, so opposed to his own eager desire for continually-renewed revelations, against a curiosity which will know everything (S. ix. ii. 6 f.), is certainly also to be interpreted in the sense that such apocalyptic as desires to dive into all the secrets of God shall be repressed in the common edification. In this sense new significance is given to his sharp combating of a willingness to be asked questions on the part of the prophetic spirit after the manner of heathen mantic. The Spirit of God is no oracle, but of Himself speaks through the prophet's mouth, and punishes the lying spirit so that he is dumb (M. xi. 9, 13, *cf.* 1 Cor. xiv. 24).

Besides the Church's divine services there are evidently meetings of smaller circles for edification. Such is the assembly of righteous men (M. xi. 9), which Hermas places in contrast to the audience of doubters gathered round the false prophet, and in which he lays the scene of the above exposure of the lying spirit. A private assembly of this kind is probably to be thought of when Hermas is commissioned to communicate the revelation which he has received first of all to the presbyters who formed the management of the Church (V. ii. iv. 3). It was in such meetings that prophets like Hermas spoke; in the Church services this was perhaps no longer the case. There they delivered their revelations, their words of chastisement and exhortation, whether in free utterance (V. iii. viii. 11, iv. iii. 6) or from notes (V. ii. iv. 3, *cf.* 2 Clem. xix.) makes no difference. From these meetings for edification, in which also the earlier writings were read, Hermas probably acquired his knowledge of the Old Testament wisdom and proverb literature, the Teaching of the Apostles, and similar early Christian literature, which gave the decisive direction to his whole moral thought and sentiment. We are justified in assuming that the Christian Church did not leave the formation of the moral judgment of its members to the choice of the individual, to his more or less zealous participation in the public services and private meetings, but, as a Church, definitely regulated this important point of Christian education.

In two passages Hermas throws some light on Christian instruction; it is to be given to the neophytes (V. III. v. 4), and a definite person, Grapte, probably a widow in the technical sense, a churchworker, is to impart it to widows and orphans (V. II. iv. 3).

It is remarkable that there is not a word said of any instruction of the young in the special sense for all children of Christians. Evidently this was considered to be the business of the Christian family, of the Christian head of a house. Hermas himself is brought to account because of his neglect on this point (V. I. iii. 1). Only where there was no head of the household, in the case of widows and orphans, did the Church intervene in the person of some elder specially appointed for this purpose. Here, too, the eschatological element has its place. Grapte received for her instruction the one specimen of revelation set down by Hermas. The main material, however, is morality. The neophytes shall be instructed to do good (ἀγαθοποιεῖν). The nature of this instruction is revealed to us by single passages of a catechetical nature introduced by Hermas, especially in the commandments. Hermas is here evidently directly dependent on older literature of the style of the Teaching of the Apostles. This shows how constant and regular this style of instruction was. His commandments were employed for catechetical purposes in the Church of the Christian empire two to three centuries later.

The instruction commences with the belief in God, the One, the Creator and Preserver of all. But from this belief there immediately follows the requirement to exercise abstinence in the fear of God (M. I. 2), not in the encratite sense, but in the sense of keeping far from all wicked works like adultery and fornication, drunkenness, rioting, gluttony, luxury, pomp, arrogance, lying, calumny, hypocrisy, nursing of a grudge, and calumnious speech (M. VIII. 3. ff.). To the commandment of abstinence there are attached the commandments of simplicity, innocence, and honour. Under these are included the forbidding of calumny, the exhortation to communicativeness (M. II.), the commandment to love the truth, in connection with which lying and dishonesty in business are spoken of (M. III.), to be chaste (with the forbidding of evil lust, M. IV.), and to forbear (M. V.). We already saw that Hermas lays the main stress on the inward intention, and never tires of inculcating upon Christians faith, abstinence, simplicity, innocence, honour, righteousness, content, truth, knowledge, unity, love. The practical exercise of Christian works of love is conceived by him to follow naturally, even as a worldly and heathen intention leads to sinful deeds, to theft, lying, robbery, false witness, ambition, lusts, deceit, boasting and the like.

In the instruction of catechumens, the practical proofs of Christian intention were more strongly emphasised. The new Christians were exhorted " to stand by the widows, to look after orphans and needy, to deliver the servants of God out of need, to be hospitable, to set themselves in opposition to no one, to be quiet, to be humble before all men, to honour the old, to practise righteousness, to maintain brotherhood, to endure scoffing, to be forbearing, to comfort oppressed souls, not to desert people who have erred in faith, but to convert them and make them cheerful, to exhort sinners, not to oppress debtors and the necessitous, and everything similar " (M. viii. 10). The collection is remarkable; still more the order. Dissimilar things are joined together, and similar are separated. But we everywhere recognise clearly how it was especially the works of pitying love that were laid to the hearts of young Christians, and then the giving up of insistence on their own rights. The thoughts of the Sermon on the Mount touching love of enemies are here made the chief authority.

These thoughts, however, come to expression not only in instruction but also in life. We can draw that conclusion at once from the fact that Hermas has so little to say on the point. He evidently judged it unnecessary to go into detail. In the same way he took it for granted that the sins enumerated in the usual way in the catechism, required among the Christians of the Church no special explanation. That a Christian stole, pilfered, lied, and bore false witness was evidently considered something rare, while many well-off Christians did not consider it sin to allow themselves a luxurious, merry life, and to make a great show with their riches. There was no want of attention to liberal giving, but there was quarrelling as to places of honour. Hermas is concerned to show that the one depends on the other, that where the right intention is wanting the practice of Christianity must suffer. But just thereby he unconsciously gives all the more valuable witness for the actual exercise of Christian morality in the Church.

More important still is the second consideration. An occasional utterance of Hermas very well worth noting shows us that the commandments were not handled as dead catechetical material, as requirements which it was easy to set up and which sounded very beautiful, but whose impracticability relieved the hearers from any endeavours to realise them. Rather with the catechumens it was strongly insisted that this practical side of Christianity must also be taken seriously, and the commandments of God, in all their compass, be truly fulfilled.

In the building which symbolises the Church, Hermas sees stones thrown away from the tower lying near the water, without, however, being able to roll into it. These are they who have received the word and would have themselves baptized in the name of the Lord; but when they become conscious of the holiness of truth, they alter their intention and follow their evil lusts again (V. III. vii. 3). Here Christian catechumens are meant. They have been attracted by the preaching of the Gospel; they have formed the decision to be Christians, to join this community where such a message of comfort, such magnificent promises are proclaimed; they have already notified themselves for baptism. Now they are given instruction, and here it is made clear to them what the truth, what Christianity, calls for. It is something holy; it calls for a great renunciation, the complete rupture with their whole former life.

Not only must they avoid certain coarse sins like theft, fornication, adultery, murder, and others; not only must they take upon themselves all sorts of brotherly duties like visitation of the sick, hospitality, and so forth, but they are also enjoined to alter their whole trend of thought and to renounce everything that up till now has made life dear to them. This requirement is too severe. So they turn aside and fall back again into their earlier life. There is hardly one clearer proof of the energy with which the Christian Church had struggled after the realisation of its moral ideal than this witness of those who draw back. It is too hard for us! Would they have acted thus if they had seen that the requirements, as set forth in the catechism, were not intended so seriously? Would the strong impulse towards propaganda among men so nearly won, have been renounced, if the slightest yielding in these things could have made it possible to keep them? Of theoretical hesitation and dogmatic scruples not a word is here said. It was the unconditional maintenance of the moral ideal in its entire holiness which worked terror amid the undecided catechumens. Their withdrawal and the fact that no attempt was made to prevent it, show at once how seriously this matter was taken in the Christian Church.

We have this conclusion confirmed by the actual circumstances in the various moral provinces of the Christian life.

The holiness of marriage was one of the foremost moral principles of Christianity. It is rightly credited with having first awakened the feeling that not only adultery, but sexual intercourse outside of marriage, fornication, is sin. It is remarkable how seldom this is mentioned in Hermas. Would he have judged this less strictly than other Christians? That would be quite unlike the man, and is contradicted by the passages where he does speak of it (M. IV. i. 1, VIII. 3). We can explain his silence only by supposing that little occasion was given for warnings against fornication. The actual position must have been in accordance with the demands of moral teaching. Nor is there in Hermas any mention of many other sins of heathenism which go hand in hand with fornication and have their place in the Jewish Christian moral catechism. This evidently lay beyond the field of vision of the Christian Church of his time.

It is solely the question of divorce which interests Hermas, and, if we may say so, that aspect of the question which is connected with ecclesiastical law. Here the definite Christian principle contained in the Lord's saying was in direct opposition to the custom of the non-Christian world. In the Judaism of the time and in paganism, divorce for the most trifling reasons was something quite usual. Christ declares the indissolubility of marriage (Luke xvi. 18). Paul maintains the commandment in all its strictness (1 Cor. vii. 10 f.). Hermas already presupposes as ground of divorce the one exception admitted in Matt. v. 32, xix. 9, adultery. But not less rigorously than the Apostle does he maintain the duty of the innocent party to remain single, to be ready to be reconciled at all times (M. IV. i. 4-8). Hermas appears to speak as if there was an actual case of adultery in which some Christian woman was involved (4), and one might almost think it his own wife. But he quietly classes heathenism as adultery (ἐν μοιχείᾳ τινί), in order to represent this also as ground of divorce (9). This is just what suits his own circumstances; all his discussions are directed upon it. So we lack in Hermas all positive proof of the actual happening of adultery within the Christian Church. What he scourges, what he warns against when he speaks of adultery is, as the first of his confessions showed us, the wicked impulse, not yet the accomplished deed.

We must not fail to observe that the whole life of the time offered great dangers in this direction; recall only the bath scene in the first vision. Even the Church life was not entirely beyond it. To be sure the picture which Hermas gives of his nightly presence with the virgins who watched the tower (S. IX. 11) is meant quite harmlessly; it is only personified virtues who say to him, "You will spend this night with us as a brother, not as a man." But playing with these things is dangerous. And Hermas himself teaches us that an impure fancy is to be estimated equally with an impure walk.

We must note that Hermas—in sharp opposition to hyper-ascetic tendencies—commends the continual and loving thinking of one's own wife as the best means of protection against such seducing thoughts (M. IV. i. 1). Also in the then much-discussed question of the right of a second marriage Hermas takes his stand along with Paul (1 Cor. vii. 39), admitting the right unconditionally although he gives the preference to remaining single (M. IV. 4). So far he is not at all encratite, however fond he is of calling himself ὁ ἐγκρατής (V. I. ii. 4). Accordingly I do not believe that in other passages he would have preached the renunciation of marriage.

Naturally the married life of these Christians was not always in every respect ideal. Hermas knew that from his own experience. In his own naive way he shows us how marital differences arise. The discontent of the one partner (here it is to be noted that he places the wife first in accordance with his own experience) finds occasion for bitterness in the most trifling things of daily life, food, a meaningless word, a friend, the purse, or anything equally trivial. The bitterness increases to passion, which becomes anger and lasting rancour (M. v. 2). Here Hermas combats not only the evil tongue of his wife (V. II. ii. 3), but especially the spirit of discontent (ὀξυχολία), which he makes responsible for everything (M. v.). We recognise here again both the inwardness of his method, which always aims at the intention, and the strength of his moral consciousness, which always holds unconditionally by loyalty to marriage and does not let itself become embittered or strives to fight down the rising bitterness (V. II. iii. 1).

Of the position of woman there is practically nothing said. When Hermas speaks only of an assembly of righteous men (M. XI. 9), we cannot conclude that women took no active share in the divine services and meetings for edification; at most it can indicate only that they did not take any part in speaking and praying. Just from the fact that Hermas speaks always in the masculine, and makes no special mention of women, it follows that he considered them in moral relations to stand on exactly the same level as the men, and the name of "sister," ἀδελφή (V. II. ii. 3), expresses the full equality of Christian women in the religious aspect. We already saw further that the instruction of widows and orphans lay in the hands of a woman (V. II. iv. 3).

The discipline of children was held to be an important duty of the Christian household. It extended in Roman law to the sons and daughters already grown up. Hermas' own family bears witness that in this domain not everything was in order. But the way in which Hermas is brought to account for this neglect of his duties as head of a household is a proof that the Church felt such a thing to be an injury done herself and a violation of the absolute and requisite morality of Christians.

There does not seem to have been wanting, either, the feeling for outward order and cleanliness in Christian houses. When Hermas pictures to us how beautifully white the tower is and how its surroundings are swept and cleansed to dazzling whiteness (S. IX. x. 2 f.), there certainly come in thoughts of spiritual purity (cf. S. x. iii. 2, and καθαρίζειν, V. II. iii. 1, III. ii. 2, viii. 11, ix. 8, IV. iii. 4, and freq.). But inward and outward are evidently to correspond, and the vividness of the picture lets us see that what Hermas had in view was the daily life, although perhaps in the careless ordering of his own house it was the contrary picture which had stamped itself on his mind.

The slaves also belong to the house. That there were slaves among the Christians of Rome, although perhaps not in such enormous numbers as is sometimes thought, is self-evident, and has been mentioned already. It is probable that such Christian slaves were often uncomfortable enough in heathen houses. Hermas mentions once by way of comparison that the heathen beat their slaves when they deny their master. That may be the actual experience of Christian slaves. Because, though the ancient view admitted slaves the private exercise of religion, it must not come at all in conflict with the religion of the family. The exclusiveness of the Christian confession could indeed appear as denial of the master of the house, who, at the same time, was the priest of the family worship. Thus there might be cases where the Christian Church had to effect the separation of her members from heathen masters in order to protect their Christian faith. Possibly Hermas is thinking of that when he mentions the release of servants of God from oppression (M. VIII. 10). Except in cases of an oppression of faith fraught with danger to the soul, the Christian Church took no exception to the slave condition of many of her members. Here there is revealed the wonderful power of religion to equalise social conditions.

But were there also slaves in Christian houses? Hermas gives us no proof of this, though also no disproof. That Hermas had to thank Christianity, his mistress, for his freedom, is nowhere said (*cf.* V. I. i. 1). Emancipation was the reward of good service (S. v. ii. 2, 7). We should put too much into the analogy just mentioned, were we to conclude that only heathens possessed slaves. But we may well find in it an indication that the severe treatment of slaves, their terrible chastisement, was considered something heathenish. Christianity did not alter the outward conditions of life, but it filled every relationship with a new spirit. A Christian master, as we have clearly seen in Paul's directions to Philemon, could no longer treat his slaves as the heathen did, even when the slave himself was an unbeliever. In that case he was to be considered by the master as an immortal soul, whom he must win for his Lord. There would be still less danger of cruelty when the slave was a Christian and a brother in the Lord. If Hermas does not enter upon this question, then we shall again be able to conclude only that the actual moral circumstances in the Church offered nothing particular to record.

We have already spoken of social intercourse in connection with the secularisation of Christianity. Here there was real ground for misgiving in the freedom and ease with which Christians mingled with heathen, and even in their own house suffered themselves to imitate heathen luxury and extravagance.

There was, however, as it seems, another and worse danger, the risk of absorption in trade interests and dishonest business dealings. We have already had this danger exemplified in Hermas himself, and have seen that we must think of the Church as in great measure constituted of merchants and artisans of the middle class. They maintained themselves by the work of their hands, and their wages were scanty. At that time, too, the small shop and the trade were sorely held down by the factories of the great slave-holders. No wonder that there were troubles of all kinds, and that the Christian with all his piety was ever more and more deeply entangled in worldly affairs. Hermas is quite full of the dangers that await Christians here.

Now the whole commerce of the period was based on an unscrupulous and inexcusable system of fraud and imposture. How was the individual Christian to avoid this? The Christian Church, to be sure, maintained that here too the Christian should be distinguished from the heathen. But how difficult it was to accomplish this is shown us by the astonishment with which Hermas receives the exhortation (M. III. 4).

It was indeed worse, when within the Church management and the Church poor administration, cases of embezzlement occurred, as we must grant they did. These too, however, are traceable to the same spirit which led to dishonesty in commercial affairs. The new moral spirit of Christianity had evidently not permeated the whole domain, as was necessary and desirable. But that this was felt—and Hermas shows this clearly—is a sign that improvement was approaching.

Hermas is specially displeased with the really well-off, the rich in the Church. He cannot deny that even among them there are Christians of irreproachable morality, and when he counts their wealth as in itself a fault, he betrays a very one-sided and not truly moral method of judgment.

But he may have been to a certain extent right. Probably it was very often just with the rich that the fear of confession and separation from the Church originated (V. III. vi. 5), while on the other hand they would be likely to supply the impulse to secularisation. He speaks of one who boasts of his riches even among Christians (V. I. i. 8). Riches entangle in the affairs of this world (M. x. i. 4, S. IX. xx. 1 f.), entice to covetousness (M. XII. i. 2), harden against the poor (V. III. ix. 6), and steel the heart against the perception of divine things (M. XI. 4).

Hence Hermas treats earthly possessions as in reality a worrying burden. He is himself quite happy because confiscation has eased him of it. Now for the first time he is useful to his Lord (εὔχρηστος, perhaps a play on the word: a good Christian, V. III. vi. 7). So all the others who are rich must be deprived of their wealth (6). Yet it is remarkable that he limits this deprivation to the lessening of their property. He does not desire its entire removal; with what remains they are to do good (S. IX. xxx. 5).

Hermas thereby recognises a positive moral significance attaching to earthly possession. In spite of his little valuation of property, he is no pauperist, and his ideal by no means one of communism. Such an ideal would render impossible what Hermas considers the most important expression of practical Christianity.

We have already seen that the care of the poor and of journeying brethren was organised by the Church. It is clear, however, that the exercise of private generosity and hospitality was not anticipated. Much too often in Hermas there are repeated exhortations to the zealous exercising of these Christian duties. The only question is how private and public charity were differentiated.

For wandering prophets and teachers, and such brethren as were otherwise quite unknown in the place, provision was certainly made by the Church; but when a man had an acquaintance or a commercial friend, it was certainly expected that he should stay with his friend. In certain circumstances that may have made very great demands on individuals. Yet we find great readiness to show hospitality to the servants of God expressly recognised even in the case of Christians whose behaviour was not otherwise beyond reproach (S. VIII. x. 3).

Things were otherwise in the matter of benevolence. Church relief was naturally confined to the Church members, the Christian widows and orphans, and necessitous Christians. Now the Church in Rome was certainly large enough to have concealed in it sufficient poverty and misery to open a wide field for private generosity. But we may assume that Christian charity was extended to those who were not within the Church. True, it is always said that the Christian must serve the saints; he who does that in simplicity is certain of everlasting life with God (M. II. 6). Also in the case of the widows and orphans especially recommended to support (S. I. 8), we shall think of Christians first. But when Hermas speaks in praise of a class of Christians who, without discord, always rejoicing in their relations with the servants of God and full of Christian virtues, had ever pity for all and shared their earnings with every one without reproach and without delay (S. IX. xxiv. 2), he shows clearly that Christian love, in spite of all its external limitation to the fellowship of faith, did not let itself be hindered from being active in every place where necessity and misery called for help. It belonged to the most general catechetical rules that the servants of God were to be purchased out of oppression. Here not only slaves are to be thought of, but also prisoners and Christians condemned to penal servitude. But it is further required that every one is to be relieved from distress, and it is expressly emphasised that necessity and want in daily life can often be as painful as prison and drive many to death. Accordingly he who does not help one whose need he knows, is guilty of murder (S. x. iv. 2 f.). It even seems that this large support extended to necessitous non-Christians was a means of propaganda. At least the counsel "to purchase souls out of oppression" (S. I. 8), can be understood to mean that such people shall be won through material support for Christianity and so for everlasting life. The context of the parable which treats of belonging to the kingdom of God or to the kingdom of the prince of the world, confirms this explanation.

The exhortation to do good is naturally directed in the first place to the well-to-do in the Church; they are to perceive that God has given them riches only to the end that they may help the needy therewith.

Hermas appears to feel that the actual facts are here far from ideal. The rich indulge in banqueting instead of doing good. Therefore he repeats so constantly and always with new grounds for it the exhortation to charity: "Do not claim for yourselves alone what God has made, as if it were only thus poured over you; share it also with the needy" (V. III. ix. 2). God gives along with the earnings the duty of serving love (M. II. iv.); to him who joyfully gives of them, God makes them more; he will be brought into the number of the angels and with his seed dwell by the Son of God (S. IX. xxiv. 2–4). Such an one, like the good servant in the parable, not only did more than he was commissioned to do, but also gave to his fellow-servants of the food sent him for the banquet.

Hermas cannot conceal that the Christians with their unlimited liberality have repeatedly had unhappy experiences. False prophets take advantage of them, and they are often asked for help by undeserving people. But so great is the necessity to do good that it overcomes even this scruple. He who gives does not need to ask to whom; he is free from blame, because he has carried out the service laid upon him by God. Only the recipient is responsible. He who hypocritically begs and receives gifts without need will be brought to task for it by God. It is a delight in giving without parallel that blinds the eyes thus. The energy with which Hermas sets it forth becomes still clearer when we see that he points new thoughts in this way. And indeed Hermas can bear this witness to the Christians of his time, that they gave not only of their superfluity, but of what was hard-earned (S. IX. xxiv. 2, *cf.* M. II. 4). More still; what he here recommends, following an older Christian saying, viz., that they should by fasting spare from their own mouths in order to have to give to the needy (S. v. iii. 7), was without doubt put into practice.

If it is no ideal picture that we gaze upon here, yet this very fact is in itself a good witness for Hermas, and in general for the earnestness of moral judgment in the Church. The defects were not veiled. Sin was called sin. "Increase not your sin," says Hermas, in his oft-repeated call to repentance (V. v. 7, M. IV. iii. 7, S. VI. i. 4, ii. 3, VIII. xi. 3). The guilt is admitted, but at the same time improvement is vigorously striven after. However hard the preacher of penitence complains, we have not discovered any extraordinarily heinous sins. The Christian Church is not constituted of angels but of men, though Hermas praises certain individuals for an angel-like walk (S. IX. xxiv. 4, xxvii. 3). As he says himself, in this world just men and sinners cannot be distinguished (S. III. 2). But the Christian Church is still aware that she is not only a refuge for sinners, but in the first place a communion of the saints; nor has she forgotten that the Christian standing, baptism in the name of the Lord, brings its definite moral obligations. Among the defects that we found, the most conspicuous are the worldly spirit, a certain heathenish way of living, and the unwillingness to confess, the fleeing from suffering. Here, however, we must not forget that our guarantor is an ascetic and confessor, who is especially strict in his judgment of these two points. Few modern Churches would find favour in his eyes. The errors which have met us in the domains of sex and commerce ultimately bear witness only to the high demands which were made, and the earnest view which was taken of the highest principles in the evangelical apprehension of moral law. To be sure, a strong tendency to external morality and negative asceticism pervades the Church. But the Christian consciousness reacts against it with primitive power. Inwardness of method and delight in doing all good have met us as characteristic features. And how impressive is the demand for an entire Christianity? Certainly it is no ideal picture we have here before us, but as certainly it is a picture of which Christianity has no reason to be ashamed. In this Roman Church there was something that was looked for elsewhere in the world in vain: simplicity in the midst of a refined over-culture, honest effort in a world of deceit and moral degradation, and active charity which boldly resisted all selfishness.

To be sure there are black sheep in the fold: wicked people, hypocrites, slanderers, doubters, and those who yield themselves to all wickedness. But there will come a purifying judgment, and when all these evil elements are removed, the Church of God will be one body, one mind, one idea, one faith, one love; and then will the Son of God rejoice and be glad in them, when He finds His people pure (S. ix. xviii. 4).

CONCLUSION.

WE have reached the end of our survey. In the course of our review of a whole century of Christianity we have become acquainted with very different congregations. We have now to sum up. Was Aristides justified in giving such a brilliant description of the Christian life? We may confidently answer that he was. In the picture which we have reproduced from actual sources, we have found many imperfections and blemishes. These, however, do not constitute the essence of it. At the outset, before the eye is used to them, they may indeed have some disturbing effect. But as we peer into the details, the dark spots recede and all the brighter streams the light from the whole. We may even discover virtues in failings, and real, if misdirected, power in defects.

Before we pass judgment, it is important that we should be in possession of the correct standpoint. We are not entitled to start from the moral views of our own time, although even then, could we be quite honest and exclude all involuntary idealising, the comparison might conceivably result in favour of those days. Hausrath's view "that to-day, after the Gospel has worked on the human heart for eighteen centuries, the most desolate Christian Church approaches the ideal of the Sermon on the Mount more closely than the most outstanding of the second century," does justice neither to the days of the early

Church nor to our own time. Nor are we entitled to start from any sort of ideal picture of Christian communities which we have made for ourselves, even if that ideal be based upon the Sermon on the Mount. Certainly we must estimate the real Christian worth of everything by the Gospel; but the question we are dealing with is not whether the morality of the early Church was Christian, but whether there was any realisation of Christian morality in the earliest Church, and if there was, what value is to be attached to it. To that end we must employ an external standard. The morality of the early Christian Churches can be correctly judged only by comparison with the moral condition of the surrounding world. Let us attempt, in a short survey, to picture this condition for ourselves. We shall not start from St Paul's opinions of Jewish and heathen morality which we have already mentioned, Paul being open to the charge of partiality. We shall adopt results which are based upon the legitimate evidence of historians and orators, moral philosophers and satirists, the results, that is, of modern historical research, and in particular of L. Friedlander's masterly work, *Darstellungen aus der Sittengeschichte Roms.*

It was indeed a bloom-time of the highest culture, to whose magnificent services in literature and art the world owes a debt of gratitude; an age of the greatest moral refinement which looked down with contempt upon the former barbarism and upon the uncivilised peoples beyond the bounds of the Empire. Yet it was a time of moral enervation, decrepitude and decay. There is no disproof of this in the fact that it received a new impetus and experienced, in a great religious Renewal, a new moral birth—the last roses of autumn. All was swept away by the storms of national migration; only what had its origin in Christianity lasted through the winter.

The moral ideal of the ancients, the strenuous man who devotes himself to the service of the city and the state, was destroyed by the Empire. With astonishing rapidity imperialism and devotion to the imperial house took firm hold. Fostered by a kind of philosophical cosmopolitanism, an intense patriotism quickly developed. But there was no practical task for it. The Emperor, with his freedmen and slaves, managed public affairs. At Rome the Senate, and in the provincial towns the councils, found their chief occupation in passing decrees of honour. Servility was the only means of advance, often the sole salvation; independence of thought was dangerous. This was the position both in the state, with its notabilities and officials, and in the great families, with their extensive and complex gradations of servants. The great wasted their means in incredible extravagances: the poor suffered themselves to be fed.

There was no family life. Time was frittered away in the baths. Interest was absorbed in the games. Even the studies of the young nobility partook chiefly of the nature of sport. Not that there was no real work: the gigantic buildings of the time bear eloquent testimony that there was. Alongside of the troops of slaves there seems to have been a not inconsiderable array of free workers. Particularly in the smaller towns there existed a middle class which fought its way through life somehow, severely threatened indeed by the wholesale competition of slave-holders. The state did not neglect higher tasks, as the Christians of the time always recognised. It protected the frontiers and made roads. Yet the soldiers grumbled loudly if they were employed for this purpose. It made fixed laws, and set limits to the arbitrariness of officials and the robbing of the provinces by tax-collectors. Nevertheless there was no feeling of safety among the people. Many of the nobles were ruined by their riches, while the poor and insignificant had no protection against arbitrary treatment. In spite of its efforts to regard crime in its moral aspect, and to enquire into motives rather than consequences, public law was terrible in its means of obtaining evidence as well as in its punishments. Money was might—though also danger. Hence there was on the one hand striving after possessions, heaping up of riches; on the other, pauperism and beggary. As a rule the former was accompanied by hard-heartedness, the latter by envy and hate. The balance could only be preserved by the surrender of personal independence; the client was provided for, but also despised and misused. The philosopher's surrender of property is only a means of guarding his liberty on all sides, no more in the last resort than a manifestation of dominant egoism. Correct style demanded humanity. This humanity, however, was not what we understand by the word, but elegant society forms which exposed no weakness by any show of feeling, preserved a gentle and suave manner, and avoided all obscenities of speech. All that was only a varnish, and behind the smooth-turned phrase there lurked want of character and often shamelessness. This very humanity was insincere. The worst feature was morality in the strict sense. There were, no doubt, many houses where honourable family life was maintained. We do the middle classes a gross injustice, if we treat Tacitus' scandalous tales of the palace as the only expression of existent circumstances. At the same time it cannot be denied that unparalleled shamelessness had spread over wide circles. Unutterable things were done without any secrecy. Divorces were of daily occurrence, adultery common, and unchastity considered no sin. Antinous, the plaything of an Emperor, was deified. The wife was slighted and coquetted with; the upbringing of children was left to slaves. Human life was little valued. Not a few were sacrificed to magical rites. Poison removed the inconvenient. Suicide, either voluntary or compulsory, ended many a promising career. The philosophy of a Seneca reveals the moral bankruptcy even of the best. Alongside of frivolousness and satire there did not lack religion. But this also was without moral force. On the contrary, the myths, dramatised and parodied, were demoralising. The old ceremonial, renewed by Augustus, was in reality only a matter of form, the worship of the Emperor a political act. The new Oriental cults, sometimes with expensive festivals and horrible mysteries, were only superstition, a means of quieting fearful consciences by penances of all sorts, a mere outward purification with no inward value. And as the climax of all, there was the chief tendency of the time, the most impious and most immoral of all religions—Astrology.

It was into this world that Christianity entered,

gathering churches round the Gospel of God's forgiving grace. Without any imperial support, such as Judaism enjoyed, it dared to have an independent conviction as to man's nature and duty. It made no compromise with the state religion by interpreting it to suit its own ends as philosophers did. It was not satisfied, like the majority of cults, with a simultaneous participation in other forms, or, like Judaism, with the minimum of adherence. It offered its followers an alternative and demanded from them an unreserved confession even when this meant death. In return, however, it gave them what the whole world of the period lacked: peace of conscience through reconciliation with God, a new aim, and fresh moral strength.

The Christian lives to God, and finds his life in God. At the same time he lives for the brethren, for humanity at large. Christianity, so to speak, revives the now lifeless ancient ideal that the individual exists for the Polis, but the ideal assumes an extended and transfigured shape.

The whole Christian brotherhood—the whole humanity—belongs to the Christian sphere of labour. Christian activity is not the result of organised selfishness and blind hatred of all other similar bodies. It is as wide as love and entire devotion can make it. The Christian calling is not confined to any special class of enfranchised citizens. Man and woman, freed man and slave, have an equal share in it. It even abolished the fundamental distinction of the ancients, Greek, *i.e.* civilised, and barbarian. It looks with contempt on none. It aims at winning every individual by love, whatever the age, standing, sex

CONCLUSION

or race be. In a purely voluntary fashion a great organisation was developed, effecting the spread of the Gospel, the multiplication of Churches, and the preservation and education of adherents. It secured a firm footing throughout the whole Empire and beyond it. It had sentinels everywhere. all joined in living union. Even the highest officials of the state could only rarely travel by the imperial post; but every Christian could rely on the brethren to help him on his way. The net of Christian Churches spread over the Empire meant a powerful, beneficent organisation in the centre of a world of egotism. The chief object of the clergy, the main aim of their voluntary offerings, was mutual aid. Money was gathered also by the priests of Isis and the great mother of gods; but they gathered it for a luxurious ceremonial and their own well-being. With Christianity it was far otherwise. Whenever there was anyone in need, help was at hand, and no bond of life and limb was demanded. How great were the social advantages which Christianity offered, though unrecognised by the state and sometimes persecuted, we learn from the precautionary measures adopted against the intrusion of impure elements. Money was not scattered abroad as it was by the Emperor, when he entertained the mob with bread and games to keep it in good humour. An attempt was made rather to train to work and to teach the exercise of temperance and contentment. The social distinctions between rich and poor, owner and slave, existed within as well as without the Christian Church, but they had lost their sting, because the mercy, mildness, and goodness of the one side, and the grateful trust and joyful obedience of the other neutralised all distinctions. Here, too, there was no lack of "humanity." "Whatsoever things are true, whatsoever things are honourable, whatsoever things are pure, whatsoever things are lovely, whatsoever things are of good report, if there be any virtue, and if there be any praise, think on these things," was no cant phrase.

The greatest importance was laid on truth, honesty in business and conduct, honourable family life, and chastity. A complete rupture with the heathen past was demanded of new members, and they were conscious of an inward moral change. The outward form was not enough. The innermost feelings were appealed to, and sins of thought confessed. Yet with all the strict discipline of the Churches, the motive in the last instance was love. Even in the most extreme case, the invocation of God's judgment, the end aimed at was the salvation of a soul. Life had eternal worth. The body was holy, as the temple of the Lord. Suicide was as much abhorred as unchastity. While there was no avoidance on the part of Christians of violence and unrighteousness, no attempt was made to secure revenge. The highest demand of Christian morality was that injustice should be endured with forgiveness and pardon. Prayer for enemies and persecutors is the highest triumph of the moral power of Christianity. And this whole community which in certain places grew so quickly as to be dangerous to the old religion, not a new association but a new people, a state within a state, yet kept far removed from the hatred of the Romans which marked the Jews. With humble obedience it complied loyally with the existing authority of God's ordering, even where it was met by opposition, offering to every measure only the passive resistance of a faith that rejoiced in confession.

As we have seen, this is no imaginary picture. Every single fact has been supported by documentary evidence. The apologists were thoroughly entitled to represent morality in the Christian Churches as Aristides has done. Heathen like Pliny, Lucian, and Celsus were compelled, even against their will, to witness to the correctness of the picture. The Christians themselves were well aware that it was not sufficient to point to their splendid and marvellous moral teaching if its realisation in actual practice failed. This very thought is taken advantage of by a preacher to urge upon the hearts of his hearers the fulfilment of the commandments, and, above all, of that highest and hardest commandment, Love thine enemies.

It is equally clear, indeed, that the ideal was not always realised. But offences against it were exceptions, and have less significance, as they awoke at once the moral consciousness of the spiritual leaders and of the congregations.

If even one half of the Christians lived as we have described, something great was already achieved. Certainly more of them did. The discipline exerted by this majority was, apart from other considerations, an invaluable moral achievement.

This brings us to a second question.

The period we have covered is a long one, and at the close we may not exhibit a picture that lacks perspective. Changes occurred in Christianity In these young days of the Church development was most rapid. How does this affect its morals? It is a widely-spread idea that a period of deep decline follows a brilliant beginning, and that the post-apostolic age cannot be placed within sight of the apostolic. That may be right, if the concise spiritual power of St Paul's epistles are compared with the rambling spiritual poverty of the Apostolic Fathers. In our domain, however, it is a totally erroneous view. We have, on the contrary, to reckon with a real advance. Let us again picture the course of development from St Paul to Hermas in its main points. Jewish Christianity, which proceeds on widely different presuppositions, we shall not consider.

There an already existing ideal was to be realised, but with inwardness and purity. In the heathen world it was otherwise. Few of those whom St Paul's preaching won for the Gospel had received moral schooling in the Jewish synagogues. Up till now most of them imagined debaucheries of every kind—impurity and gluttony, dishonesty and imposture—to be the natural course of life. It was therefore necessary to inculcate carefully the elements of morality, that God's will is sanctification—*i.e.*, refraining from unchastity and deceit. St Paul trusted the working of the Holy Spirit to develop therefrom a steadfast moral conscience which could, in all cases, give correct guidance. From time to time he would present the moral ideal in an enumeration of Christian virtues, or he would go into the conduct befitting the various positions of life. But only as little as possible did he attempt to anticipate free development by legislation. Thus, within his

Churches Christianity developed in very different ways: markedly individualistic with all the allied merits and failings in Corinth; strongly social, emphasising order in the Churches of Macedonia; with a practical bent in Galatia; with a speculative asceticism in Phrygia.

St Paul only removed excrescences. All teachers, however, were not equally liberal. The Churches themselves desired a more rigid statement of the moral ideal. In some degree this was supplied in the Old Testament, which was read in the Pauline Churches; in some degree, also, by the words of the Lord Himself and what could be drawn from the pattern which He supplied. Jewish Christianity may also have co-operated. To some extent it developed from within as the result of the new tasks which Christianity had to face, the duty of confession, for example, in times of persecution, or of subordination and obedience in the controversy about constitution. In the post-Pauline period, without being able to distinguish clearly the various gradations, we can see the growth of the feeling of unity throughout Christendom, strengthening both communities and individuals against threats from without. In the Johannean period we have the conflict of Christianity with gnostic dualism and its negative asceticism giving occasion for the strong assertion of the practical Christianity of brotherly love. Lastly we are brought to a stand before the developed ecclesiastical Christianity, where there is the greatest possible amount of law and order, and the individual's chief duty seems to be to accommodate himself to these grooves.

There can be no doubt that this defining of the moral ideal has a compressing and curtailing significance. On the other hand, however, it means a closer approximation to realisation.

The real moral status of the Churches is raised in spite of all so-called secularisation, or, rather, to some extent in consequence of the abatement of enthusiasm. Excesses like those with which Paul had to contend in Corinth are to be met with only in quarters which the Church cut off from herself. In the later literature there is hardly any mention of the sins of the flesh, falsehood, and so forth. This was not because such were considered indifferent, but because within the Churches there was now no occasion to discuss them. (With catechumens, of course, it was different.) On the contrary, the most serious task now was to estimate at their full heinousness and to punish sins of thought. We can understand this, inasmuch as the Churches were not now mission Churches but self-supporting. Even at first these Churches possessed some few who belonged from youth to Christianity, and had imbibed Christian thought with their mother's milk. As time wore on the number of these people increased.

The thought of belonging to the third or fourth Christian generation, even where it awakes a feeling of decadence, includes also the consciousness of being heir of a great tradition. Habit, notwithstanding the danger of a Christianity of habit, has its chief educational significance exactly in the domain of morals. The preservation of something of the early freshness and inspiration, in spite of all adaptation to existing conditions, was effected by the powerful eschatological expectation which, to the end, markedly distinguished the early Christianity from that of the following period.

Goethe says: "Humanity advances continually; man remains ever the same." The Christian of the second century had to do with the same temptations as the Christian of the first, but the general tone of Christian morals had advanced and exerted a wholesome influence on the conduct of the individual. For with all the richness and variety of form that the Christian life may assume, it is ever one and the same Spirit that works in it, the Spirit of Jesus Christ.

The advance of which we have spoken is not constant. Within the early Christian period we have had fluctuations to consider, and if we glance a little beyond our period, we shall become aware, towards the end of the second century, of an actual retrogression. Christianity renounces her strict exclusiveness more and more. She enters the field of Græco-Roman culture. Justin is delighted to quote Homer, in spite of his abominable myths; a Christian Church honours the teacher whom it celebrates with a statue, without, however, the hero-worship of the gnostics; the catacombs are decorated with elegant ornaments; the moral apprehension is laxer. The Church continually throws her doors wider. The institution of penance rendered a form of discipline possible which could adapt itself to conditions. Any reaction in the direction of a stricter view is cut off as heretical. Bishops begin to deal with Church politics, becoming unduly mixed up with the influential people of the palace and quarrelling with one another—a demoralising which, according to Eusebius, received God's judgment in the Diocletian persecution. Worldliness increases in the Christian kingdom; simultaneously flight from the world grows ever more usual.

The moral decline of Christianity shows traces of the general demoralisation of the time. But while in the storms of national migration all else was lost, the moral spirit of Christianity was preserved, and presently began to demonstrate its civilising power in the Teutonic stock which now makes its appearance in the historical field. From this point onward a continuous advance can be observed.

The development of early Christian morality, however, was not completed entirely from within. At several points we have met variously effective admixtures of foreign ideas. Here we must return to the Gospel once more. Jesus was in no way an ascetic. His opponents have censured that as a defect. Any apparently ascetic traits, *e.g.*, His being without wife and home and possessions, were only conditions of His personal calling. The precepts of a similar tendency, in which He inculcated restrictions upon His apostles, and surrender of property upon individuals who wished to become His followers, were conditioned in the same way. Jesus' "Life of Poverty," as Saint Francis apprehended it, and as we found it among the gnostics of the second century, is a distortion of His picture due to a foreign spirit. It is in this very respect, in this thoroughly positive attitude to the manifold moral duty of man, that the greatness of Jesus lies. While He claims the heart for God, He yet insists on the indissolubility of marriage, acknowledges the state, and desires proper use of possessions. This immanent piety which sees a divine service in every detail of life, because everywhere it acknowledges God and is sure of Him, did exercise some defining influence on Christianity, but was never quite understood, and was not exclusively maintained. It came in contact with a powerful current of the age, the ascetic tendency, which travelled here from the Orient and triumphed on Jewish as well as on Greek soil. Originating in a physical rather than in an ethical Dualism, it could not comprehend the inwardness of Jesus' thoughts. If there was any antithesis between a Holy God and a sinful world, it seemed necessary that it should find outward expression: not a mere inward breaking with sinful desires, but also an outward separation from all evil, a renunciation of all that forms its seat, and, to some extent, its origin as well.

We possess a twofold proof that this asceticism does not rest entirely upon an increase of the moral earnestness of Christianity, but has entered Christianity from without. In the first place there is the distinctly observable conflict between the two views in a man like St Paul. The one, the negative-ascetic, which as man of his time and as former Pharisee he honours, deludes him with celibacy as the Christian ideal. The other, the positive-ethical, which constitutes his warrant as Apostle of Jesus Christ, causes him to preach Christian liberty and to exalt love above all ascetic practices. The greatness of St Paul lies in the fact that the second consideration always prevailed with him; Christ triumphs in him over the spirit of the age. In these days of ours, Paul the ascetic would have no part, but Paul the

Apostle remains still in our time, as he was of old, the world missionary.

In the second place, what we observe is not a gradual advance of ascetic tone in early Christianity, such as we should expect if it had developed from some internal source. Immediately on its appearance among the gnostics, it asserted itself with all severity, and only gradually gave place to milder conceptions. The domain of morals shared in what we may call the Christianising of gnosticism. Here also the Gospel of Jesus Christ overcame the tendencies of the age. Basilides stands nearer the Gospel than the earliest gnostics, just as Clement of Alexandria, with his condemnation of riches, is more evangelical than, let us say, Hermas. No more than Dualism can this asceticism be attributed to Christianity; the moral earnestness with which it is practised is its only Christian feature. Just as little can we trace to Christianity the excesses to which asceticism leads when it o'erleaps itself and degenerates into the opposite. Here once more we must rather emphasise the separation of the early Christian Church from both extremes, in the knowledge that the preservation of its power lay in a truly practical Christianity. It was thus that the victory was won. Galen admired the abstinence of the Christians above all, but their apologists are right in laying stress on the other considerations, chiefly brotherly love. It was as a charitable organisation that the Christian Church carried to a victorious issue its mighty contest with the Roman Empire, the heathen religions, and its own sects.

Christianity did not owe its final victory to superiority of dogma. To Neoplatonism it seemed ἄλογος πίστις, irrational faith. As a matter of fact Christianity was inferior to that system as regards speculative power and logical completeness. But Christianity possessed what the speculations of Neoplatonism lacked — the sure historical basis of Jesus Christ's person. Nor was it to a higher moral teaching that Christianity owed its victory. Stoicism and Neoplatonism after all produced moral thoughts of great beauty and purity, thoughts which are more imposing to superficial contemplation than the simple commandments of Christianity. Yet neither of them could enable artisans and old women to lead a truly philosophical life. Christianity could and did; the apologists point triumphantly to the realisation of the moral ideal among Christians of every standing. That was due to the power which issued from Jesus Christ and actually transformed men. The certainty and confidence of faith based on Him with reliance on God's grace in Jesus Christ, begot in Christians a matchless delight in doing good. Joy in good was more potent than abhorrence of evil. In the midst of an old and dying world this new world springs up with the note of victory running through it: "If God be for us, who can be against us?" "And this is the victory which overcometh the world, even our faith."

LITERATURE.

C. VON WEIZSACKER, The Apostolic Age, translated by James Millar, B.D.
V. LECHLER, The Apostolic and Post-Apostolic Times, translated by A. J. K. Davidson.
TH. KEIM, Rom und das Christentum, 1881.
O. PFLEIDERER, Das Urchristentum, seine Schriften und Lehren, 2nd ed., 1902
A. C. M'GIFFERT, History of Christianity in the Apostolic Age, 1897
E VERNON BARTLET, The Apostolic Age: Its life, doctrine, worship, and polity. Edinburgh, 1900.
A HARNACK, Die Mission und Ausbreitung des Christentums in den ersten drei Jahrhunderten Leipzig, 1902
P WERNLE, The Beginnings of Christianity, translated by Rev. G. A. Bienemann, M A. London, 1903.
G HEINRICI, Das Urchristentum, 1902.
W. LECKY, History of European Morals, 1870.
C LOHRING BRACE, Gesta Christi; or, A History of Human Progress under Christianity London, 1882
L. FRIEDLANDER, Darstellungen aus der Sittengeschichte Roms, 6th ed., 1888.
G. ULHORN, Christian Charity in the Ancient Church, 1883.
L ZSCHARNACK, Der Dienst der Frau in den ersten Jahrhunderten der christlichen Kirchen Gottingen, 1902.
O ZOCKLER, Askese und Monchtum, 2nd ed , 1897.
K. J. NEUMANN, Der romische Staat und die allg. Kirche, 1890.
H. HOLTZMANN, Das N T. und der romische Staat, 1892.
A. BIGELMAIR, Die Beteiligung der Christen am offentlichen Leben in vorconstantinischer Zeit. Munchen, 1902.
TH. ZAHN, Skizzen aus dem Leben der alten Kirche, 2nd ed , 1900.
G. WOHLENBERG, Bilder aus dem altkirchlichen Leben einer heidnischen Grossstadt, Neue Kirchliche Zeitschrift, 1900, XI
H. ACHELIS, Spuren des Urchristentums auf den griechischen Inseln, Zeitschr. f. neutestl. Wissenschaft, I , 1900
R. KNOPF, Die soziale Zusammensetzung der altesten heidenchristlichen Gemeinden, Zeitschr. f. Theologie und Kirche, 1900, X.

NOTES.

1 ANCIENT STATISTICS (p xxxiv).

LITERATURE.—R Pohlmann, Die Ubervolkerung der antiken Grossstadte, Preisschrift der Jablonowskischen Gesellschaft, 1884;—J Beloch, Die Bevolkerung der griechisch-romischen Welt, Leipzig, 1886;—Zofia Daszyńska, Stoff und Methode der historischen Bevolkerungs-statistik, Conrad's Jahrb. fur Nat -Oek, 66 (3 Series, 11), 1896, 481-506;—O. Seeck, Die Statistik in der alten Geschichte, *ibid*, 68, 1897, 161-176;—J. Beloch, Zur Bevolkerungsgeschichte des Altertums, *ibid*, 321-343, Antike und moderne Grossstadte, Zeitsch fur Sozialwissenschaft, 1., 1898, 413-423,—E Kornemann, Die romischen Censuszahlen als statistisches Material, Conrad's Jahrb, 69, 1897, 291-296,—Ed. Meyer, Art Bevolkerungswesen, Handworterbuch der Staatswissenschaften, 11[2] 674-689; Die Zahl der romischen Burger unter Augustus, Conrad's Jahrb, 70, 1898, 59-65 (combating Kornemann).

THE difficulties here are due to the meagreness and the uncertainty of the material at our disposal. We possess only a few enumerations, and these, as a rule, bear upon capitals and special periods. They record only the number of freemen (for military and excise purposes) The proportion of men, women, and children, of freemen and slaves, is problematical Statements as to the provision of corn and the extent of area built over render us considerable help, but immediately raise the further points: who are to be reckoned as the recipients of alimentation, what extent of ground is to be calculated for dwelling-houses, and what for open spaces, gardens, etc ?

After the tentative endeavours of the older scholars, of whom, *e g*, Justus Lipsius reached a total population for Rome of four millions, and Isaac Vossius of fourteen, it was Boeckh who started a systematic enquiry. His results have been adopted by one section of scholars, mostly philologists and historians. Recently, however, these have been met by a national-economic current of thought, championed by Beloch and advocated with most warmth by Edward Meyer The former rely simply on the enumerations handed down

(Boeckh), and endeavour to demonstrate their possibility by a reconstruction of corresponding conditions with no regard for probability and analogy, taking for granted the extraordinary crowding of large towns (Pohlmann) and immense accumulations of slaves belonging to single individuals (Seeck); while the others start from a general picture of the economic conditions arrived at by observation of existing circumstances, and estimate the numbers handed down on the ground of this "possibility" In addition, they lay stress on the fact that numbers very easily suffer alteration in tradition, that it is very difficult to check them, and that frequently the authorities do not combine their large figures with any concrete view (Beloch, Jahrb, 68, 322; also J Burckhardt, Griech. Kulturgesch, 1 79, 115, note 3 on $\mu\nu\rho i\alpha\nu\delta\rho\sigma$; H Delbruck, Geschichte der Kriegskunst, 1. 1900, 7 ff, against the traditional strength of armies)

Beloch gives the following numbers for the towns in which we are interested :—

Corinth, 600 B C, scarcely more than from 20,000 to 30,000; 421 B.C perhaps 100,000

Athens, 500 B C, scarcely more than 20,000; 421 B C something over 100,000 (Wachsmuth, 200,000).

Ephesus (under Augustus), not less than 200,000

Smyrna, same as Ephesus.

Pergamum (150 A D), 120,000 to 180,000

Troas (in the Roman period), far above 10,000 to 15,000

Alexandria (60 B C), 400,000 to 500,000 (300,000 freemen)

Antioch, same as Alexandria

Rome (in the time of Christ), 800,000 to 1,000,000 (1,800,000 to 2,000,000, Seeck; 2,000,000, Lanciani)

The others obtain in some cases considerably higher numbers. For while Beloch sets the numerical proportion of the sexes as equal, and that of the slaves to the freemen (both sexes) as 1 : 2, Seeck estimates the women somewhat lower and the slaves considerably higher.

The numbers of the slaves are especially hotly disputed Athenæus (Deipnos, vi 103) gives, by reference to—

(Epi)timæus, for Corinth 460,000
Ctesicles, „ Athens 400,000
Aristotle, „ Ægina 470,000

These numbers, maintained by Boeckh, Seeck, and others, are given up as totally impossible by Hume, Niebuhr, J Burckhardt,

NOTES 383

Beloch, Ed Meyer Perhaps the μ before μυριάδες is wrongly given, so that we should have 60,000 for Corinth and 70,000 for Ægina ; while in the case of Athens the figure may have fallen out (*cf.* note 2)

Till now an estimate of the earliest Christian communities has been quite impossible Even for the period of Constantine only guesses have been made, *cf* Harnack, Mission, p 537 The number of Jewish Christians in the year 58 is fixed in Acts xxi 20 at several tens of thousands In Rome, Tacitus (Ann., xv 44) records Nero's annihilation of an *ingens multitudo* of Christians in the year 64 ; *cf* πολὺ πλῆθος, 1 Clem. vi 1. [In the year 250 the Church in Rome had 154 clergy, with over 1500 widows and persons in receipt of relief, this gives us a total of at least 10,000 souls (Sohm)] Pliny tells us that in Bithynia in the year 111 a large proportion of the population was Christian. Ignatius (Eph , 1. 3) speaks of the πολοπληθία of the Church in Ephesus The total number of Christians in 95 is said (Rev. vii. 9) to be innumerable, far more, that is, than the 144,000 previously mentioned In general the primitive Christian communities are represented as too small rather than the reverse The large increase during our period also is reflected in the transition from the family character of the congregation to a form which necessitated a classification according to age and sex (*cf.* p. 286).

2. SLAVERY AMONG THE ANCIENTS (pp 33 f , 115 ff.).

LITERATURE —Wallon, L'esclavage dans l'antiquité, 1847 ,—Hermann-Blumner, Griech Privataltertumer, [3], 1882, 80 ff ,—J Burckhardt, Griech Kulturgeschichte, 1 152 ff ,—Marquardt, Privatleben der Romer, [2], 1886, 135 ff, 175 ff ;—L Friedlander, Sittengesch, 1 [6] 126 ff ,—M Schneidewin, Antike Humanitat, 206 ff. ;—Th Mommsen, Rom Geschichte, ii 74-77 ,—Ed Meyer, Die Sklaverei im Altertum, Jahrb der Gehe-Stiftung, iii 1899, 191 ff, and in several passages in Conrad's Jahrb f Nat-Oek, especially 64, 1895, 696 ff, 748 . Zur Bedeutung der Sklaverei in der Kaiserzeit ; —V Lechler, Sklaverei und Christentum 1877 f ,—Th Zahn, Sklaverei und Christentum in der alten Welt (1879), Skizzen aus dem Leben der alten Kirche, [1], 62-105, 290-296 ,—E. Teichmuller, Der Einfluss des Christentums auf die Sklaverei, 1894

As opposed to the older view of the immense expansion of slavery in the ancient world, especially under the Empire, and of the method of treating slaves as it is clearly expressed in the citation we have made *supra*, p 119, from Mommsen's Roman History (ii 77), there has of late been revealed a strong inclination both to lessen the significance of slavery in the ancient world and to set the position of slaves in a much more favourable light. Beloch and Edward Meyer maintain that free workmen were employed to a large extent in ancient industrial concerns This view finds strong support, so far as Egypt is concerned, in U. Wilcken's Ostraka, i 695 ff.; *cf.* C. Wachsmuth, Jahrb. fur Nat.-Oek., 74, 1900, 798. Edward Meyer compares the state of affairs in the East at the present day in the matter of polygamy and slavery, which are quite confined to the higher classes But it must have been somewhat different in the ancient world. To be personally waited upon and accompanied by slave attendants was a feature in the life of even the humblest people. The numbers given by Athenæus (see note 1) are possibly too high Beloch calculates for Rome (Jahrb., 68, 1897, 332 f) at most 200,000 to 300,000; Friedlander (i. 61) makes the number somewhat higher.

This view, it is true, does not harmonise with former accounts of the contempt of handicrafts and working people (*cf.* E Rohde, Griech Roman, 200, J Burckhardt, Griech. Kulturgesch., 1 152; Marquardt, Privatleben, ², 401 f; Friedlander, 1 299; also J Beloch, Griech Geschichte, 1 1893, 226) Edward Meyer (Die wirthschaftliche Entwicklung des Altertums, in Conrad's Jahrb fur Nat.-Oek., vol 64, 1895, p 721) explains this as a prejudice due to a one-sided use of the sources provided by philosophic literature, and refers to the νόμος ἀργίας, which punished all who could not make it clear that they worked for their living; *cf* P Guiraud, La main d'œuvre industrielle dans l'ancienne Grèce, Paris, 1900. It is possible that the Greek contempt for labour, the lazy idling of the proletariat in opposition to the labouring hordes of slaves, has often been exaggerated, yet it cannot be denied entirely. To place everything on the level of present-day conditions is dangerous, however valuable the comparison may be

On the question of the treatment of slaves, see especially Friedlander, 1 479 ff Slaves meet us in all possible positions and callings, as charioteers, gladiators, actors, artists, musicians (*ibid*, ii 327, 366, 468; iii. 295, 351); Hermippus of Berytus (second century A.D.) wrote περὶ τῶν διαπρεψάντων ἐν παιδείᾳ δούλων. There is an important distinction to be made between slaves within the house giving personal service to their master, slaves without in factories and independent businesses, and slaves engaged on estates. The last-named, who, without doubt, had the most miserable lot, are hardly concerned at all in Christianity, which was chiefly confined to towns Legally the slave is and remains *res corporalis*, even when he is to be counted as a personal member of the *familia* (Gaius, 2, 13, Karlowa, Rom Rechtsgesch, II 1, 100 ff) He is under quite a different set of laws, e g., trial by torture, severer penalties (Mommsen, Rom Strafrecht, 416 f, 1032) For *peculium, cf* Karlowa, *loc. cit*, 112 f, for release, 128 ff; for redemption, Dittenberger, Sylloge, ii.[2] 690 ff, 835 ff.; for the right of slaves to join a separate body *volentibus dominis*, Digesta, 47, 22, 3, § 2, *vide* Marquardt, Privatleben der Romer, [2], 189, 7; Foucart, Associations religieuses, 6 ff; Hatch-Harnack, Gesellschaftsverfassung, p 23, note 14; for the special confession of slaves and their burial according to its rites, J. Burckhardt, Griech. Kulturgesch, ii 134, Herkenrath, Studien zu den griech Grabinschriften, 49 In an epigram of Dioscorides (Anthol pal, vii. 162, Dubner) a Persian slave begs his master to commit him to earth and not to fire, lest the latter should be rendered impure; perhaps the passage in Anthol, ed Jacobs, iv p 260, No. 676, is to be understood in the same way

The influence of Christianity on slavery may in older time have often been exaggerated *Cf.* Wallon, *loc. cit*, iii.[2] 358 ff.; Marquardt, Privatleben, [2], p 194; J Burckhardt, Constantin, [2], 379 f Of abolition or even of cessation we cannot speak. Slavery continued in the Christian empire until it was removed in the Teutonic lands through a different legal form, viz, bond-service The Church did not even press for emancipation. In the Acts of Peter and Andrew, chap. 20, p 126 (Bonnet), Onesiphorus offers to release his slaves in exchange for the power to work miracles, but Peter refers him to faith The instances in Acta Petri, chap. 28, p 77, and in Acta Philippi, chap 81, p. 32, are exceptional. There is nowhere any indication that the emancipation of Hermas was connected with his or his mistress's being a Christian The following are known examples of Christian slaves: from the second century, Callixtus, afterwards bishop (Hippolytus, Refut., ix. 12); from the fourth century, Jerome's fellow-traveller Hylas (*cf* Grutzmacher, Hieronymus, i 148 f) De Rossi, Bulletino di archeologia cristiana, i. 1874, pp 49–67 (*cf.* Bull. del instituto, 1880, 10), has gathered together the neck-irons of runaway slaves; these often bear Christian emblems, and belong to the post-Constantine period, when branding was forbidden.

Edward Meyer's sentence, "Soon after Aristotle this thought (that slavery is unnatural and based on a human ordinance) came to general recognition along with the idea of humanity; Christianity only repeated and gave religious formulation to what was the common property of the whole period" (Jahrb. der Gehe-Stiftung, 1899, p 224), and the statement that slavery died out gradually and solely through the reformation of economic conditions (Conrad's Jahrb, 64, 1895, 749), exaggerate just as much on the other side They are views which are the outcome of a materialistic method of writing history, and mistake the significance of the moral considerations, the inward alteration of the condition along with the outward maintenance of the form The philosophic doctrines of stoicism did not accomplish what Lactantius (v 152) could with right say of Christianity, that there was there no distinction between poor and rich, slave and master The Epistle to Philemon gives us an example of the actual advantage which the Christian slave enjoyed The complete proof of the high valuation of the slave is supplied in the note of Aristides to the effect that the Christians take pains to win their slaves to the faith, and then straightway call them brethren. This is not done by compulsion, but by persuasion As a matter of fact, there are heathen slaves in Christian houses, e.g., in Lyons (Euseb, Hist Eccles, V 1 14)

For the repudiation of slavery in ascetic societies, *cf* Philo de vita contemplativa, pp 109 f, Conybeare In the tenth Speech of Dion of Prusa (1 107 f, v Arnim), Diogenes develops the utilitarian morality that a bad slave should rather be allowed to escape The pains taken to recover an escaped slave are often treated in comedy and satire As regards legal aspects, *cf* Marquardt, Privatleben, ², pp 184 f These show decisively that Onesimus sought out Paul directly as advocate.

Against the conception that Paul demanded legal emancipation of Philemon, *vide* Weizsacker, Jahrb. f. deutsche Theologie, xxi 20 The decisive point is that the exegesis of the ancient church here finds the very opposite. maintenance of slavery, *vide* Zahn on Chrysostom., Gesch. d N Tl Kanons, 1 637, note

The remark in Philemon 13 that Paul would have been glad to keep Onesimus for personal service is to be taken quite literally. This being served by slaves, children or young men, plays a larger *rôle* than is often admitted In this way John Mark's being a ὑπηρέτης (Acts xiii. 5) and the λειτουργία of Epaphroditus are to be understood; *cf*. also Acta Petri, chap 3, p 48, where two young men are given to Paul to accompany him to Spain "Even Virgil's fancy would have halted had he had no slave to wait on him, and no tolerable dwelling-place," says Juvenal, vii 69 ff ; Friedlander, Sittengesch , iii ⁶ p 432.

3 THE DIVINE JUDGMENT IN CORINTH (pp 44–52)

The view which I have presented above requires some justification At present there is tolerable agreement among exegetes as to the nature of the case of incest concerned ; it was marriage (not only an immoral relationship) with the stepmother (probably not belonging to the Church) after the father's death The father is not mentioned (ἀδικηθέντος, II vii 12, does not refer to him as J Lightfoot thinks), the woman is not brought to book ; the word "mother" is not employed ; γυναῖκα ἔχει means real marriage

On the other hand, the instances which have been adduced require thorough revision The more recent commentaries content themselves with references to Wettstein, Lightfoot, Schottgen,e tc , who have brought together cases of the most diverse nature without critical investigation of them The two sets of instances which follow cannot be placed in the same category .—(1) The forbidding of marriage with one's own mother, Lev xviii 7: Pythagoras, Iamblichus, Vita Pythag., chap 31, § 210, p 149, Nauck ; Lysis the Pythagorean (contemporary of Plato, if genuine , cf Zeller, Geschichte der griech Phil , ⁵, I. i p 294), ibid , chap 17, §§ 77 f p 57 ; Julian, adv Christ, i p 184, l 4, Neumann ; Aelian, Hist Anim , iii 47 (on camels), and also the admission of such a marriage among the Persians, Clem , Hom , xix 19, Sext Empir Pyrrhon Hypot , i chap 152, p 35, l 14, Bekker , cases of similar incest, e g , in the story of Œdipus and its numerous parallels, as well as its defence by Zeno and Chrysippus, Clem , Hom , v 18, Sext Empir adv Mathem , xi 191 f   (2) Instances of an adulterous relationship with the stepmother in the lifetime of the father: Reuben, Gen xxxv 22, xlix 4 , Absalom, 2 Sam xvi 21 ; Amyntor's son Phœnix, Iliad, i 447–461 ; Anchemolus, son of Rhœtus, Vergil, Aen , x 388 f., with the commentary by Servius ; Agathocles' son Archagathus, Diodorus, Siculus, XX xxxiii 5 (iv p 185, Dindorf), Anatozadus, son of Chosroes, Procop , bell gotth , iv. 10 (ii 504, Bonnet), the oft-told tale of the love-sickness of the son, to whom the father, on the advice of the physician, makes over his own wife, e.g., Antiochus, son of Seleucus and Stratonice (cf E Rohde, Griech

Roman, ¹, p. 52 and p 31, note 4) [The citation of Philip of Macedonia in Elsner, Observ Sacr., 1728, n. 90 f, rests on a misunderstanding of the text in Justin, Hist., VIII iii. 10.]

For the case before us we can properly adduce only (1) the terms of Jewish law, which in this section is only a comparatively late transformation of the ancient custom of Israel. (Nowack, Lehrbuch der Hebraischen Archaologie, i 342), in Deut. xxiii. 1, xxvii. 20; and (P) Lev. xviii 28, xx. 11 (penalty of death); cf. Philo de Spec. Leg , II. cccii 42 (Mangey): οὐδὲ προγόνῳ τελευτήσαντος πατρὸς ἄγεσθαι μητρυιὰν ἐφῆκε, Sanhedrin, vii 4 : *isti sunt lapidandi : qui coit cum matre sua . . . . et qui coit cum uxore patris sui . . . sive vivus sit pater sive mortuus* [Rabbi Akiba taught that this was allowed to the Proselyte (Maimonides, Jebamoth, 982)]; cf. Wettstein, Lightfoot, Schottgen on 1 Cor 5 ; Saalschutz, Mosaisches Recht, ², 766 f. Gregory the Great, in his instructions to Augustine for the Church of England, quotes Lev. xviii 8 *cum noverca misceri grave est facinus, quia et in lege scriptum est* (Beda, Hist Eccles , 27) Cases of transgression: Adonijah and Abishag, 1 Kings ii 13 ff. ; Ezek. xxii. 10 f (2) Roman law forbids marriage between ascendants and descendants, even in the case of adoption (Gaius, i. 59, Dig., xxiii 2, 14; Mommsen, Rom Strafrecht, 685) "The relation between parents-in-law and children-in-law and between *step-parents and step-children*, as caused by marriage and approximating to filiation, during the existence of the causing marriage, constitutes an aggravation by adding incest to adultery, and *remains incest even when the marriage is dissolved"* (Mommsen, 686, cf. Gaius, i 63 and elsewhere , Institutio, I x 7)

Concubinage with a father's concubine is *prope nefarium* (Ulpianus, Dig , xxv 7, 1 3), and marriage with her invalid since the time of Alex. Severus, C v., iv 4; cf. the Syriac-Roman Book of Law, Bruns and Sachan, § 109, pp 23 and 280 Sexual intercourse between ascendants and descendants is considered incest, whether without or with the form of marriage (Mommsen, 687); the penalty is deportation, seldomer death (688), an appeal to ignorance of the law in the case of such marriages as were already forbidden by the moral law (*moribus* or *jure gentium*) is not recognised (687). An exceptional case is that of Hermogisclus, a prince of the Varnes, who on his death-bed engaged his son Rodiger to his own second wife, a sister of the French prince Theudibert . ξυνοικιζέσθω τῇ μητρυιᾷ, καθάπερ ὁ πάτριος ἡμῖν ἐφίησι νόμος, Procopius, Bell. Gotth , iv. 20 (ii. 562, 11, Bonn). The very frequently adduced passage of Ælius Spartianus, Vita Antonini Caracallæ, x. 1-4 (*cf.* Aurelius Victor, 21, Eutropius, viii 20; Hieronymus, chron ad annum, 2232, Orosius, VII. xviii. 2), is considered by modern criticism as one of the "stupidities of the Historia Augusta" (Schiller, Rom Kaisergesch, 1 2, 754, note 8; *cf.* Spanheim, Diss de prestantia et usu numism, ii 1717, 294, Ranke, Weltgesch, in 371) We have therefore only three known cases left Of these the one in 1 Kings ii. 13 is punished not as incest but as rebellion; apart from the political aspect, Adonijah's lust does not seem to have raised moral indignation Ezek xxii. 10 f. contends, from the standpoint of advanced moral perception, against ancient popular usage, while in the case of the Varnes the legitimacy of the marriage is expressly stated In the strict sense, accordingly, we have no quite analogous instance

The strangeness of such an incest in the Christian Church has induced Trigland (de Secta Karæorum, 1715, 141 ff) to employ the terms of Jewish Proselyte law in order to explain the conduct of the incestuous person As the later Rabbis did not consider the marriage of a *Goi* as marriage, and accordingly adultery with the wife of such an one as sin (Eisenmenger, Entdecktes Judentum, 1700, 1 432 f), Maimonides declares, by reference to R Akiba, that the Proselyte is not bound by the marriage prohibitions, Lev xviii 8 (*vide supra*) With still more right, if there was any such explanation required, could cynical and stoical theories be adduced, which, throwing over the notion of incest, must occasion a complete confusion of the moral judgment The single case, however, demands no founding upon a theory T hat it was no isolated instance cannot be proved by 2 Cor xiii 2 (against Weizsacker, Jahrb. f deutsche Theol., 1876, 31)

My conception of the Apostles' attitude towards the case of incest shows two points of departure from the ordinary view

In the first place, I lay more stress on the character of the penal miracle in connection with ancient ideas of the curse and its working *Vide* Zoroastrianism and Primitive Christianity, Rev. James Moffat, D D., Hibbert Journal, vol 1, p 771, E v Lasaulx, Der Fluch bei Griechen und Romern, 1843 (only useful for the material collected, unhappily modern in theory: the curse as the will projected in word, the hypnotising power of the will, etc); K Wachsmuth, Rhein Mus, 1863, 539; 1864, 481; Kretschmar, Aus der Anomia, 1890; R Wunsch, Die sethianischen Verfluchungstafeln aus Rom, 1898; *idem* Corp inscr Attic

Append, 1897, A Schurer, Geschichte des Judischen Volkes, [3], iii p. 298. These tables, now found in great numbers, with private curses are all to be understood from the presupposition that the divinity appealed to, in case of the forbidden thing having happened, will immediately intervene, in the same way as it is often accepted that perjury causes sickness (Herodot, iv 68 f). Famous instances of PUBLIC curse are: The curse pronounced on Hippolytus by Theseus (Euripides, Hipp, 888 ff.), where, in case death should not at once occur, exile is added; the curse pronounced on Alcibiades by the Eumolpidæ (Lysias, Orat, vi 51; Diodorus, xiii 69, Plutarch, Alcib, xxii 33; Corn. Nepos, Alcib., iv 5, vi. 5; Maximus Tyr, xii 6; Suidas, *sub voce*, Ἐυμολπίδαι, i. 897). In Jewish law we have here the so-called "bitter water that causeth the curse" associated with suspicion of adultery (Num v 11 ff., *cf* Nowack, Archaol, ii 251), a practice which had its analogues in the tests of purity among the Greeks, and whose persistence is proved through its adoption in the series of legends that constitute the apocryphal gospels of the childhood (Protev. Jac 16; Ps - Matthew xii ; *cf*. Hermas, Sim., VIII i 5) Sudden judgments of God following a prophetic threat we have in Jer xxviii 16 f. Hananiah dies within two months; in 1 Macc ix 54 f : Alcimus, the temple violator, has a shock and dies; Acts xii 23 : Agrippa I. dies on account of blasphemy; Acts xiii 11 : sudden blindness; Acts v 1 ff : sudden death (Ananias and Sapphira). Sudden death is also indicated in the παραδοῦναι τῷ σατανᾷ εἰς ὄλεθρον τῆς σαρκὸς. What seems to point in the opposite direction, ἵνα σωθῇ τὸ πνεῦμα ἐν τῇ ἡμέρᾳ τοῦ κυρίου Ἰησοῦ, is not to be psychologically understood as the modern view would have it. Death itself frees the spirit (placed in Christians by God) from the flesh, and thereby saves it There can even be put to account a moral working of death on the individual himself We know too little of the views which were held on the state of the soul after death. In the Acta Thomæ (I. 6, 8, pp 7 ff, Bonnet), in the case of a miraculous punishment of sudden death there is an express statement of the prospect of forgiveness in the future world There is also a short period on earth for repentance, if the case is understood on the analogy of the miraculous punishment recorded by Marcus Diaconus in the life of Bishop Porphyrius of Gaza, chap 89 f, p 72 f, *ed*. Teubn: Porphyrius pronounces a curse on Julia, a blaspheming Manichean prophetess, who immediately begins to tremble, to alter her expression, loses the power of recollection, and dies after some hours; Act Petri c Simone, 2, p 46, Lipsius · Rufina, to whom Paul denied admission to the Lord's Supper on account of adultery, suffers a stroke which paralyses her left side and her tongue

In this deliverance to Satan (I v 4) we are not to understand any special apostolical power (Schottgen), any more than a specific Jewish formula of excommunication, the great ban (Selden, Lightfoot). The mention of God's giving Job over to Satan (Redpath, Expos , 1898, 287 ff) introduces heterogeneous material In 1 Tim. 1 20 the form is employed with different and weakened significantion : there the Apostle alone appears as agent without any help from the Church, the occasion is not a moral offence, but a question of belief, the purpose is (bodily) discipline with a view to improvement, not annihilation of the flesh This sense of *officium pœnitentiæ*, torturing of the flesh through fasting, etc , was attached by the Church to 1 Cor v 4, so early as the indulgence-edict of Callixtus (Rolffs, Texte u Unters , xi 3, 112, also 81 ff.), in which II 11 5 ff is referred to I v 4 For later ecclesiastical applications of 1 Cor v 4, *cf* Thummel, Die Versagung der kirklichen Bestattungsfeier, 1902, 82

The second point to which I attach importance is the religious-psychological significance of the non-appearance of the miraculous punishment That the operation of a curse can be prevented was the ordinary view, notwithstanding Horace, Epod , 5, 89, *dira detestatio nulla expiatur victima* Pollux, 5, 131, makes a simple classification of gods into those that undo a curse and those that fulfil it, *cf* Suidas, *sub voce*, ἀποτρόπαιος ; Photius, lexica, *sub voce*, προστρόπαιος. Only it was necessary that those who pronounced the curse should also remove it, *e g* , the Eumolpidæ in the case of Alcibiades already cited There are numerous narratives of the averting of the divine μῆνις In general the idea is one of ceremonial, as in the story of Heliodorus, II Macc iii 23 f On the basis of the prophetic religion of Israel the moral notion of conversion takes its place (Joel ii 12 ff , Jer xviii. 7–10, Ezek iii. 17–21, Dan iv 21 ff) The problem of the non-appearance of the threatened curse which Plutarch plagued himself with, *de sera num vind* (iii. 417 ff , Bernardakis) finds a simple solution in Jonah iii., iv The notion is all the more likely in Paul, because in the moral purpose of the miraculous penalty the first step towards it has been already taken.

The interpretation of 2 Cor ii 5–11, vii 8–12, which has been in vogue since the time of Bleek, and construes it as referring to some matter of offence, avoids the supposed difficulty that Paul himself undoes his own vigorous interference, but only at a twofold sacrifice, for in that case (1) we learn nothing of the issue of the incident so strictly dealt with in 1. v , and (2) we must construct a new incident built upon the one word ἀδικήσας, 2 vii. 12 How very fanciful that would be we can learn from the various interpretations of Bleek, Ewald, Hilgenfeld, Weizsacker, Schmiedel and Julicher My conception has points of contact with those of Klopper, Heinrici and Haupt (Stud und Krit , 1895, 385 f)

In spite of Hilgenfeld's objections (Zeitschr. f wiss Theol , 1899, 1 ff.), I think the acceptance of the so-called middle journey is well warranted by 2. xiii. 1 and xii 14 On the other hand, I agree with Hilgenfeld in regarding chaps. x –xiii as belonging to 2 Cor ; I cannot find any place for an intermediate letter. 2 ii 4, vii 8 ff., refer to 1 Cor , i e , to the admonitory parts of the letter—above all, chap. v The Corinthians properly felt Paul's agitation, which modern exegetes deny Hence their assertion that only Paul felt hurt by the scandal, a mistake which he sets right, 2 ii 5. In the same way 2 i 15 f points back to 1 xvi 5 ff. The confusion in this case arose in Corinth, because Timothy arrived there with the original design, which seemed better suited to the Corinthians, after the altered plan had become known from 1 xvi 5 ff This to some extent explains Timothy's want of success

4. JAMES, THE LORD'S BROTHER.

LITERATURE .—Hilgenfeld, Einleitung in das N T., 1875, 520 ff. ;— Lipsius, Apokryphe Apostelgeschichten, II. ², 238 ff ,—Lightfoot, Galatians ¹², 252 ff. ;—Th Zahn, Bruder und Vettern Jesu, Forschungen zur Geschichte des N. Tl Kanons, vi. 1900, 225 ff

Even if Acts i 14 anticipates events, James, we may say, belonged from the beginning to the Christian community. In 1 Cor. xv. 7 the appearance of the risen Lord to James, after that to five hundred brethren at once (Whitsuntide), marks a new stage On the occasion of Paul's first visit in 37–38, James stood alongside of Peter, Gal. i 19 ; when Peter fled in 44 he was the recognized head of the Church, Acts xii. 17 , at the Apostolical Conference in 51 he took precedence of Peter and John, Gal. ii. 9 The view that he was received into the circle of the Twelve after the death in 44 of his namesake the son of Zebedee is suggested by comparison of Gal. ii 9 with Mark v 37, ix 2, xiv 33 (Hort, Judaistic Christianity, 1894, 62, and, by inference, Holtzmann, Einleitung, ³, 473) Acts xii 17, however, makes it somewhat improbable, and a proper conception of the circle of the Twelve altogether so. It is further contradicted by the ancient tradition in accordance with which the Lord's brother is ordained by Peter, James, and John immediately after the resurrection (Euseb, hist eccles, II. i. 3, xxiii 4) The position of James can be explained apart from the vigour of his character and personality by the consideration that he was the Lord's brother and the eldest of the four A messianic-dynastic idea, the representation of the Messiah through his nearest relative (Caliph), alone explains, if not the historical, at any rate the legendary position of this James (Réville, Wernle, notwithstanding Loofs' contradiction), the office of ἐπίσκοπος ἐπισκόπων of the Clementines far exceeds the position of the monarchical bishop; it even goes beyond the metropolitan of later centuries and recalls the vicarius Christi.

The famous description in Hegesippus is frequently dealt with, perhaps most thoroughly by Lechler, Apost. Zeitalter, ³, 51 ff, and lately by E Schwartz in Preuschen's Zeitschrift fur die N T Wiss, iv, 1903, 48 ff Lechler divides it into five elements, but his analysis can very easily be simplified into the two constituents of Nazaritism and priesthood For Nazaritism cf. Nowack, Hebr Archaologie, ii 133 ff., Schurer, Gesch des jud Volkes, ³, iii 120. Lifelong Nazaritism appears to have been exceptional in the period, cf Luke i 15 The regulations admit of vows only for a limited time, Num. vi (P.); 30 days, Jos, Jewish War, ii 313; Mishna Tractatus Nazir Surenhus, iii 146 ff, cf. Acts xxi 23 f, xviii 18 Abstinence from the eating of flesh is not a tenet of Nazaritism, is even absolutely forbidden for the nomadic Rechabites, neither is it a tenet of Essenism (vide Note 5) οὐδὲ ἔμψυχον ἔφαγε (Jerome, carnem nullam comedit; Ruf, sed neque animal manducavit) can, it is true, be only so understood in accordance with Greek usage; but perhaps originally only abstinence from blood and flesh containing blood was meant, cf. Gen ix 4, κρέας ἐν αἵματι ψυχῆς, Deut. xii 16, Acts xv 20, 29, xxi 25, αἵματος καὶ πνικτῶν· ἔμψυχος would equal ἔναιμος (both are absent in lxx), after the parallel in Lev xvii 11, 14 Origen too, c Cels., viii 30, places ἔμψυχα and πνικτά close together That abstinence from impure flesh which was binding upon every Jew is here mentioned as a special feature of Nazaritism, finds its parallel in Judges xiii 4, 7,

14, μὴ φάγῃς πᾶν ἀκάθαρτον, and its foundation probably in the fact that the command was not quite strictly observed, as there are frequent complaints of violation: Zech. ix 7, Is lxv 4, lxvi. 3, 17, Ez xxxiii 25 M T., 1 Sam xiv. 32 f. (for these passages I am indebted to my colleague Professor Baentsch)

In the avoidance of ointment and warm baths it is usual to see traces of Essenism Both are, as a matter of fact, witnessed for the Essenes, Jos, Jewish War, ii 123, 129. But this avoidance is not specifically Essenic, and in no way connected with the special doctrine of this order It gives expression to the repudiation of civilization and its enervating effects, one of the fundamental features of both Nazaritism and Rechabitism. Celibacy—also a principle of Essenism—was first read into the picture given in Hegesippus by Epiphanius, and is probably more the result of his own ideal of sanctification than of some older source The historical James, the Lord's brother, was married, 1 Cor ix. 5 Linen garments were also worn by the Essenes at their meals, Jos, Jewish War, ii 129 But here they are associated with the priestly character of James, Ezek xliv 17, Ex xxviii. 39, 42, xxxix 28 James is conceived as priest, and further as highpriest; that lies in the privilege belonging solely to him of entering the Holy Place The view which regards it as only permission granted to one layman of saying his prayers in the temple is a totally modern evasion On the question of the equality of Nazarites and High-priest in regard to holiness in P, cf Nowack, 136 The Nazarite is called in lxx, εὐξάμενος, ηὐγμένος, Num vi 13 ff., which means, the man who has vowed, but can also be translated the man who prays, since εὔχεσθαι stands also for בעה

The name ὠβλίας, for which Fuller without any necessity would write ὠζλίαμ, following Ps xxix 11, is explained by the ancients from עפל עם, vide Suicer, Thesaurus, s v., ii, 1593, περιοχή, Eus., τεῖχος, Epiph., σκέπη, Jobius mon, Hausrath, N Tl. Zeitgeschichte, ii, ¹, 329, note 2, derives it in agreement with Lipsius, Apokr Apostelgesch, ii, 2 part, p 240, note, from חובליה, with reference to Zech xi 7, 14 (lxx σχοίνισμα), cf. Herklotz, Zeitschrift fur katholische Theologie (1903), xxvii 572

How much of all this is historical and how much an ideal picture it is hard to conclude The ὁ ὀνομασθεὶς ὑπὸ πάντων δίκαιος of Hegesippus is to be taken with as much caution as the two varying texts of Josephus, both of which, with Schurer, i, ³, 581 f, I consider interpolations In any case the formation of a legend is quite intelligible, and all the more so by consideration of the remarkable parallels which meet us in the development of tradition regarding this James, the Lord's brother, and John of Asia Minor If the oldest Kerygma names Peter as the first witness of the Resurrection, 1 Cor xv 5, the Christians of Asia Minor have placed the favourite disciple before him, John xx 4, xxi 7, while those in Palestine have given the preference to the Lord's brother, Gospel of the Hebr *apud* Jer de viris illustribus, 2. [Clemens Alex, Hypot *apud* Eus, hist eccles, II 1 4, mentions James before John and Peter among those who were entrusted with the gnosis after the Resurrection] To both also at the last supper a prominent participation was attributed (as unhistorical, I believe, in the case of James as in the case of John of Asia Minor, who is to be distinguished from the son of Zebedee) Both appear as high-priestly figures On James, *vide* Hegesippus, and in confirmation, Epiph lxxviii 14; on John, *vide* Polycrates of Ephesus, ἱερεὺς τὸ πέταλον πεφορηκώς Both are unmarried On John, *vide* the ancient prologue in Corssen, Texte und Unters, xv 1, 6, 75 ff; on James, it is true, no one earlier than Epiph (*v supra*) The special position of James as ἐπίσκοπος τῶν ἐπισκόπων finds its analogy in the extended authority of the Ephesian presbyter over all the Christian communities of Asia Minor These parallels are most instructive, because they provide us with an objective view of the origin and growth of local tradition in two important provincial Churches.

That the so-called apostolical decree really originated with this James and the presbyters associated with him I consider very probable, though I cannot accept Weizsacker's special combination with the episode at Antioch, Gal ii 11 ff, *vide* Apost. Zeitalter, [2], 180 f; M'Giffert, Apost Ages, 215 f From Acts xxi 25—a "we" section—the unprejudiced reader gains the impression that this is an entirely new experience of Paul; *cf* Harnack, Sitz-Berichte der Berliner Akademie, 1899, xi 168 f As regards the two recensions of the Apostolical decree, *cf.* against Blass, Hilgenfeld, Zahn, Corssen, Gott gelehrte Anzeigen, 1896, 442 f; Weiss, Texte u Unters Neue Folge, ii 1, 108 f; Harnack, *loc cit*, Wendt in Meyer's Commentary, [8], p 50 The later recension avoided the confusing mixture of moral and ceremonial elements discussed above (pp. 152 f) by omitting πνικτοῦ, and inserting instead at the end the so-called golden rule (Matt vii. 12 in negative form) Origen, *loc cit*, endeavours to justify the single items by a process of Christian reasoning   The non-mention of the Sabbath (Zahn, Skizzen, [1], 208) is natural when we consider the aim of the letter.

5. VEGETARIANISM AMONG THE ANCIENTS
(pp. 126–128).

The vegetarianism of Pythagoras is legendary   As a tenet of his school it can be traced to Orphic influences, *vide* Zeller, Geschichte der griech. Philosophie, 1, [5], 317 ff (espec 318, note 5).   In Empedocles (*ibid*, 806 ff) the prohibition of flesh is certainly a feature of the doctrine of transmigration   For the vita orphica, *cf.* Lobeck, Aglaophamus, 245 ff   Plutarch wrote two books περὶ σαρκοφαγίας (Bernadakis, vi 101 ff ; preceded by the Tractate περὶ τοῦ τὰ ἄλογα λόγῳ χρῆσθαι); Porphyrius four, περὶ ἀποχῆς ἐμψύχων. It was opposed in general by Peripatetics, Stoics, and Epicureans, and was advocated by the New Pythagoreans, along, however, with individual teachers of those other schools, as, *e g*, the Peripatetic Theophrastus and the Stoics Sextius and Sotion, Zockler, Askese, and Monchtum, [2], 107 ; Androcydes *apud* Clem Alex, Strom, VII vi 34; Plutarch, De Tranq. Anim, xiii, Stobæus, xxi 16   Seneca was for some time in his youth a vegetarian on the advice of his teacher Sotion   He enjoyed good health, but gave it up to avoid the suspicion of belonging to a foreign cult (Epistola, cviii. 21). For Apollonius (*cf* also his Epp, 8 and 43) and Heliodorus, *vide* E Rohde, der griechische Roman, [1], 440   Apart from the mention of Ethiopic gymnosophists (as a rule Ethiopia and India are to be reckoned as one), the rejection of the bloody-offering for a divine worship by means of incense and prayers (*cf.* on this point also Test xii Patr. Levi, iii) seems here to point to Indian influences.   For the active traffic of the countries bordering on the Mediterranean with India, *vide* Rohde, griech Novellendichtung, 57 = Roman, [2], 581   In Buddhism the slaughter of no living thing is the painfully-observed first command of the fivefold rectitude, *vide* H. Oldenburg, Buddha, 1881, 296 f.   Nevertheless vegetarianism is prior to Buddhism, Zockler, Askese, u Monchtum, [2], 36 f   The Brahmins are referred to in the Recog Clem, ix 20, and the Seres in viii 48

Vegetarianism as a principle is not attested on Jewish ground, and in view of Gen ix. 3, Deut xii 15, hardly to be expected   The prohibition of flesh and wine among the Essenes, who were divided upon the question of marriage-repudiation, is rightly disputed (notwithstanding Zockler, Askese, ², 126) by Lucius and Schurer, Gesch des jud Volkes, ³, ii. 569, because, apart from a worthless notice in Jerome, adv Jovin., ii. 14, no evidence in favour of it can be adduced, and probabilities are rather against it In 4 Ezra ix 24, xii. 51, the temporary restriction to a vegetable diet is only a small part of the complete fasting commanded as preparation for the ecstatic state, v. 13, vi 31 Similarly the limitation of Jewish priests to figs and nuts (Jos , vita, iii 14) is only a temporary and precautionary step against pollution by heathen foods Among Nazarites there was no abstinence from flesh observed, this followed from their relationship with the nomadic Rechabites When, therefore, it is mentioned in Hegesippus' description of James the Just (Euseb., hist eccles , II xxiii 5) that οὐδὲ ἔμψυχον ἔφαγε, we must understand it in the sense of flesh containing blood, *i.e* , not killed according to the Jewish method, and hence unclean (*cf* supra, note 4) The vegetarianism of the Philonic Therapeutæ (de vita contempl., p 74, 113, Conybeare) shows only influences of the Orphic circles, which were very numerous in Egypt

It is in Egypt that we discover the first traces of it on Christian soil; for the Gospel of the Egyptians (πᾶσαν φάγε βοτάνην, τὴν δὲ πικρίαν ἔχουσαν μὴ φάγῃς), *vide* Wobbermin, Religionsgeschichtliche Studien, 97 f.; Clemens Alex , Pæd , II. 1. 11, even ventures to place Paul and the Pythagoreans together. In the Gospel of the Ebionites (Epiphanius, hær , xxx., 13, 22) the locusts of John are removed and the Passover is repudiated by Jesus, Resch, Agrapha, 344, 406, in the same way as Tatian altered the seven years of Anna's marriage into seven days, Luke ii 36; *cf*. F. C. Burkitt, "St Ephraim's Quotations from the Gospel," p. 41 As regards the Encratites, *vide* G Kruger in Real Encycl., ³, v 392 f., who rightly rejects the conception of them as a sect; they represented tendencies that were to be found among the most various heads of schools (*e.g* , Tatian, Julius Cassianus), and were not foreign to the Catholic Church, although in principle this latter always opposed them, *vide* 1 Tim iv 3 ff. Musanus wrote against the Encratites, Eus., hist eccles , iv 28 (about 180) There was among the martyrs of Lyons and Vienna an Encratite Alcibiades, who gave up this mode of life on the ground of a revelation which was made to Attalus, his fellow-sufferer (Eus , hist. eccles , V. iii 2 f) In the Liber Pontif. there is a note under Eleutherus worth noticing for Rome (p 17, Mommsen; taken over in the Martyrol. Rom., 26th May), *et hoc constitutit* (P *firmavit*) *ut nulla esca* (*usualis*) *a Christianis repudiaretur maxime fidelibus, quod deus creavit, quae tamen rationalis et humana est* (*cf.* Schwegler, Montanismus, 277, note 78)

The descriptions of the asceticism of the Apostles given in the apocryphal Acts go as a rule beyond vegetarianism They live as saints and cynics like that wilderness saint Bannus, with whom Josephus in his youthful asceticism studied (vita, ii. 11) Peter says, *panis mihi solus cum olivis et raro etiam cum oleribus in usu est* (Rec Clem , vii. 6, Migne, Ser. Gr , 1, 1357; *cf* ix 6, *aqua et pane utentibus*), also Greg., Naz Or , xiv. 4, Migne, Ser Gr , 35, 861, c Πέτρος ἀσσαρίου θέρμοις τρεφόμενος, and Carm , 10, 550, Migne, Ser Gr , 37, 720; only water, bread, and one garment are allowed the Christian, Clem Hom., xv 7 Following this also, Epiph , hær , xxx 15, concerning Peter and the Ebionites Thomas himself eats nothing at the banquet, 5, p 10, 6, Bonnet , ἄρτον ἐσθίει μόνον μετὰ ἅλατος καὶ τὸ ποτὸν αὐτοῦ ὕδωρ καὶ φορεῖ ἓν ἱμάτιον, 20, p 131, 104, p. 217; to his followers he gives ἄρτον καὶ ἔλαιον καὶ λάχανον καὶ ἅλας, 29, p 46 On his journey to Rome John allows himself one date every Sunday, Acta Joh , 6, p 154, Bonnet Andrew sends the liberated prisoners of the Anthropophagi under a fig-tree, which supplies them with sufficient food, p 93, Bonnet; from his blood there spring fruit-trees, p 108 The whole part which the Anthropophagi play in the later Acts of the Apostles is connected with the vegetarian tendency

As regards the motive, the fact must not be lost sight of that the boundary lines fluctuate, and frequently there are several motives at work, as a rule not all consciously A clear distinction must be drawn, for it makes a difference whether vegetarianism is based on the doctrine of transmigration (*cf.* Zeller, Gesch der griech Philosophie, 1 [5] 449 ff , 806 ff), or on purely dietetic considerations; whether it proceeds from the repudiation of sexual intercourse, as, e g., is very clearly the case in the Katharoi (Summa fratris Raineri, Martène Thes , v. p 1761: *comedere carnes vel ova vel caseum etiam in urgenti necessitate sit peccatum mortale, et hoc ideo quia nascuntur ex coitu* , *cf* the Ebionitic view *apud* Epiph , hær , xxx 15), or from fear of the εἰδωλόθυτον. The complete abstinence from meat upon religious grounds is clearly to be distinguished from the philosophical and rationalising view expressed, *e.g* , in the proverbs of Sixtus : ἐμψύχων χρῆσις μὲν ἀδιάφορον, ἀποχὴ δὲ λογικώτερον, Origines, c. Cels , viii. 30. Frequently, too, the original motive was not understood: thus, Plutarch, De Lib. Educ , 17, shows the same

NOTES 399

spiritualising method of interpreting the Pythagorean rules of diet which we find in Barnabas, 10, applied to the Mosaic ones There is no necessary connection between abstinence from wine and vegetarianism; the former exists among the nomads who live on flesh, e g, among the Arabs of the pre-Islamic period, among the Rechabites and the related Nazarites Wine was also forbidden to the *flamen dialis* at Rome (*vide* Zockler, Aekese, ², 1 pp 93, 101) Weizsacker rightly (Jahrb f deutsche Theol , 1876, 308 f) refuses to deduce either vegetarianism or Essenism from fear of the ἐιδωλόθυτον among Roman Christians, and assigns their origin to the Orphics In that case, however, it is not easy to maintain any longer that κοινός and καθαρός (Rom xiv 14, 20) point with certainty to Jewish origin (*ibid* , 261).

6 ON THE TERMINOLOGY OF MORALITY

In what follows an attempt is made to give a survey of the terms employed in early Christian literature so far as they bear upon morality It is a chapter from the history of the rise of the devotional language of Christianity True, this is not an entirely new creation To a large extent it was fashioned earlier in the works of Greek moralists, and above all in the Greek Bible of the O.T. Still, a beginning can and must be spoken of here, and the rapid development characteristic of commencements can be clearly made out The first step is taken by Paul, at once the Hebrew and the Apostle of the Gentiles The sayings of the Lord in the Gospels are, like the O T , antecedent In both cases the Jewish-Christian method of expression remains, so far as we can recognise it But both combine also to give definiteness to the edification-speech of the later Gentile Christianity The secular spirit of gnostic Christianity comes to light in the adoption of non-Biblical ideas drawn from Greek philosophy Thus we have here repeated in a single case what we have shown above to be the course of general development

Terms, however, are more than mere mirrors of thought; they possess effective power The judgment is trained on the speech. Thus this collection belongs in a double sense to our task

I say expressly that it is only to be an attempt , no effort is made to secure completeness Proof passages have been only occasionally given, mostly from the Apostolical Fathers So far as the N.T is concerned, further assistance can be readily had from concordance or lexicon Selected examples reveal the quick growth of the edification-speech into bombast, especially in the case of 1 Clem.

For moral conduct as a whole, the Christian walk, various figurative descriptions are employed. ἀναστροφή, ἀγωγή, πορεία, πολιτεία (1 Clem), βίος (1 Clem 62, 1, ἐνάρετος ; otherwise usually = means of subsistence, earthly life) with the appropriate verbs ζῆν, ἀναστρέφεσθαι, περιπατεῖν, πορεύεσθαι, πολιτεύεσθαι, στοιχεῖν. The corresponding moral character is described by adjectives or adverbs like ἀγαθός, καλός, ὁσίως, σεμνῶς, ἀμέμπτως, εὐσχημόνως, ἀτάκτως, and prepositional phrases such as ἐν ἁγιότητι, ἐν σωφροσύνῃ, ἐν σοφίᾳ, ἐν ὁσιότητι καρδίας,—ἐν ἀσελγείαις, κατὰ τὰς ἐπιθυμίας, κατὰ ἀγάπην.

Other figures are στρατεύεσθαι (cf. δεσέρτωρ εὑρεθῆναι, Ign), ἀθλητής, ἀγών, ἀγωνίζεσθαι, ἀσκεῖν.

The religious relation is expressed in δουλεύειν, λατρεύειν (for the distinction, vide p 202), λειτουργεῖν τῷ θεῷ, ἀρέσκειν, εὐαρεστεῖν τῷ θεῷ, θεῷ σχολάζειν, Ign , Pol., vii 3.

A religious significance is also attached to the comprehensive term appearing first in Acts, 1 Clem., and especially the Pastoral Epistles, εὐσέβεια (εὐσεβής, εὐσεβεῖν) ; still more clearly but more seldom in θεοσέβεια, θεοσεβής, θεοσεβεῖν—much more frequent are ἀσέβεια, ἀσεβής, ἀσεβεῖν εὐσέβεια appears beside, and to some extent takes the place of δικαιοσύνη, a term which is conceived by Paul in a purely religious sense as right relation to God, but in the later Gentile Christianity always tends to return to the old Jewish signification of right conduct, and even of a single right action (see under)

The religious notion is often indicated by the addition of θεοῦ or θεῷ, and also by ἐν θεῷ, κατὰ θεόν, ἀξίως τοῦ θεοῦ, εἰς τιμὴν θεοῦ. Ignatius calls the Christian θεοδρόμος, Phil., ii. 2 (the same term is employed by him, Pol , vii 2 = θεοπρεσβευτής, Smyrn , xi 2, deputies of the churches), and coins the words ἀξιόθεος, θεοπρεπής, θεομακάριστος

The special Christian sense is imparted by χριστοῦ or χριστῷ, usually ἐν χριστῷ, κατὰ χριστόν, ἐν κυρίῳ, κατὰ κύριον, ἀξίως τοῦ κυρίου, κατὰ τὸ καθῆκον τῷ χριστῷ, 1 Clem. iii. 4 ; κατὰ τὴν ἀλήθειαν τοῦ κυρίου, Polyc , Phil., v 2 The Didache, xi 8, uses τρόποι κυρίου, and for the opposite χριστέμπορος, xii 5 ; Ignatius has already κατὰ χριστιανισμὸν ζῆν (opp κατὰ Ἰουδαϊσμόν), Magn x. 1, Rom iii 3, Phil. vi 1, and κατὰ χριστομάθιαν πράσσειν τι, Phil. viii. 2. The relation to Christ is especially prominent in Paul and Ignatius, while, e.g., in the Shepherd of Hermas it is almost entirely absent Here too belong forms like κατὰ τὸ εὐαγγέλιον, ἀξίως τοῦ εὐαγγελίου and πνεύματι, κατὰ πνεῦμα, also μαθητής εἶναι and μαθητεύεσθαι are used by Ignatius with an ethical colouring

Mention must also be made of the thought of the pattern applied occasionally to God, usually to Christ, but also to the Fathers of the Old Covenant, the Christian teachers like the Apostle, the leaders of the Christian community, and even the communities themselves. ὑπόδειγμα, ὑπογραμμός, τύπος, ἴχνος, and correspondingly μιμητής εἶναι, γίνεσθαι, μιμεῖσθαι, Paul exhorts the Phil, συμμιμηταί μου γίνεσθε, iii 17; and Polycarp (Phil. 1 1) calls the martyrs τὰ μιμήματα τῆς ἀληθοῦς ἀγάπης (= of Christ).

The norm of Christian practice is generally τὸ θέλημα τοῦ θεοῦ, seldomer βουλή, βούλημα, βούλησις; very frequently ἡ ἐντολή and αἱ ἐντολαί τοῦ θεοῦ and τοῦ κυρίου. νόμος, as denoting the O.T. law, is very rarely employed for the requirements of Christian morality, ὁ νόμος καὶ οἱ προφῆται, which usually describes the compass of all divine promises, is used in Matt vii 12, xxii 40, to mean the sum of God's requirements But from the time of Paul on, νόμος is applied to Christ's commandment of love, and so in James and Barnabas we find the Gospel described as the new law. Ignatius applies Χριστόνομος as a title of honour to the Church in Rome The O.T. terms νόμιμα, προστάγματα, παραγγέλματα, δικαιώματα κυρίου are frequent by the time of 1 Clement, the last-mentioned being found also in Luke, Hebrews, Barnabas Paul has παραγγελία, παράδοσις, also διατάσσειν with γνώμη and κανών; δόγματα is used to describe purely moral commands in Acts xvi 4, Ign, Magn, xiii 1; Barn, i 6, ix. 7, x 1, 9, Did, xi 3 John uses τὸν λόγον μου τηρεῖν, and we find ὑπηκόους ὄντας τοῖς ἁγιοπρεπέσι λόγοις αὐτοῦ in 1 Clem. xiii. 3 (cf. xiii 1, xlvi 7) τὰ ῥήματα τοῦ θεοῦ, 1 Clem x 1, and τὰ λογία τῆς παιδείας τοῦ θεοῦ, 1 Clem lxii. 3, refer to the O T. A church constitution with a catechism prefixed is entitled διδαχὴ κυρίου (διὰ τῶν ιβ΄ ἀποστόλων), and appeals to ὡς ἔχετε ἐν τῷ εὐαγγελίῳ, xv 3 f., ὡς κέλευσεν ὁ κύριος ἐν τῷ εὐαγγελίῳ, viii. 2 In the Pastoral Epistles ὑγιαίνουσα διδασκαλία = unspeculative, practical Christianity, is characteristic. The general description of doctrine as ὁδός, Acts ix 2 and often, which was taken over from the Rabbis, is peculiar Its figurative meaning is preserved clearly in the "two ways," Did, i 1.

In John ἀλήθεια is also used to designate the norm (cf Ign, Eph, vi. 2; Polyc, Phil, v. 2).

Other expressions are ποιεῖν τὸ θέλημα, πληροῦν ἐντολήν, τηρεῖν τὰς ἐντολάς, φυλάττειν τὸν νόμον, τελεῖν νόμον, ὑπακούειν τοῖς προστάγμασι, 2 Clem ; ὑποτάσσεσθαι θεῷ, Ign.; πειθαρχεῖν τῷ λόγῳ τῆς δικαιοσύνης, Polyc.—and correspondingly παρακούειν, παραφρονεῖν, ἀθετεῖν, ἐγκαταλείπειν, λειποτάκτειν.

The Christian ideal is τό ἀγαθόν, τὸ καλῶς ἔχον, also τὸ δίκαιον καὶ ὅσιον, ὁσίως, 1 Clem.; more religious colouring attaches to σεμνός, σεμνότης, 1 Clem, Past ;—καλὸν καὶ τερπνὸν καὶ προσδεκτόν, 1 Clem. vii. 3; τὰ εὐάρεστα καὶ εὐπρόσδεκτα, xxxv. 5. The originally purely religious notion ἅγιος (ἁγιωσύνη), "consecrated," soon assumes, if it does not actually to some extent bring with it from the O T, an ethical colouring; so especially in ἁγιασμός, ἡγιασμένος, ἁγιοφόρος, Ign ; still stronger ethical colouring attaches in the speech of primitive Christianity to the notion ἁγνός, ἁγνεία, ἁγνεύειν, ἁγνίζειν, ἀξιόαγνος.

The occurrence of the notion of ἀρετή in the ancient period is remarkably rare, only in Phil iv. 8 (of God's mighty deeds, 1 Pet. ii. 9; 2 Pet. 1 3), then 2 Pet. 1. 5, 2 Clem x. 1, and Hermas; ἐνάρετος βίος, 1 Clem lxii. 1, γνώμη, Ign, Philad, 1 2, πανάρετος καὶ σεβάσμιος πολιτέια, 1 Clem. ii 8, πανάρετος καὶ βεβάια πίστις, 1 Clem i. 2 In the same way there is a striking absence of the special ethical terminology of Greek philosophy, e g, εὐδαιμονία, vide A Carr, "The Use of Pagan Ethical Terms in the N.T, Expos., 1899, pp. 443–452 ἦθος is found only in 1 Cor. xv 33 in the quotation from Menander; there are also τὸ μεγαλοπρεπὲς τῆς φιλοξενίας ἦθος, 1 Clem. i. 2 ; τὸ ἀξιαγάπητον τῆς ἁγνείας ἦθος, 1 Clem. xxi. 7 ; cf. κατὰ ὁμοήθειαν θεοῦ, Ign., Magn., vi 2 ; Pol, 1 3.—καλοκἀγαθία, Ign. Eph., xiv. 1.

To describe the goal we find employed τελειότης, τέλειος εἶναι, ἄρτιος, ἀπ—, ἐξ—, κατ—ηρτισμένος εἶναι, ὁλόκληρος, ὁλοτελής and others.

This goal is reached on the one hand by the divine παιδεία (Hebr, 1 Clem), and on the other by human φόβος (no longer existent for Christians in the purely religious sense, Rom viii 15, 1 John iv 18, but awakened and strengthened in the moral sense, 2 Cor. vii. 11 and Phil. ii 12 and often); cf παιδεία τοῦ φόβου τοῦ θεοῦ, 1 Clem. xxi 6 ; Polyc., Phil., iv. 2 There are numerous expressions for zeal, πρόθυμος, ἕτοιμος εἶναι, προθυμία, ζῆλος (ζηλωταὶ τοῦ ἀγαθοῦ, 1 Pet. iii 13 ; περὶ τὸ καλὸν, Polyc, Phil, vi. 3), σπουδή

NOTES

(σπεύδειν), πόθος ἀκόρεστος εἰς ἀγαθοποιίαν, ἐκτενής, ἐν ἐκτενείᾳ, μετὰ πάσης ἐκτενείας. It also finds expression in the familiar figure of διώκειν (δικαιοσύνην, ἀρετήν, ἀγάπην, φιλοξένιαν, εἰρήνην, τὸ ἀγαθόν). The devotion of the whole man is described by ἐξ ὅλης τῆς καρδίας, ἐξ ὅλης τῆς ἰσχύος, etc

For the reverse we have ἀργὸς καὶ παρειμένος εἶναι, 1 Clem xxxiv 4; ἄνθρωπος κενός, Jas ii. 20; then also διψυχία (Jas, Hermas), and διπλοκαρδία, Barn xx. 1, διστάζειν, διστασμός; —ἑτερο—γνώμων, — κλινής, 1 Clem, —δοξεῖν, —διδασκαλεῖν, ἐν ἀλλοτρίᾳ γνώμῃ, Ign, are more of the nature of dogmatic terms On the other hand, there come in here expressions like ἀλλότριος καὶ ξένος τοῖς ἐκλεκτοῖς τοῦ θεοῦ, 1 Clem i 1; for a Christianity of name only. δόλῳ πονηρῷ τὸ ὄνομα περιφέρειν, Ign, Eph., vii 1, τὸ ὄνομα φορεῖν, τὴν δὲ δύναμιν μὴ φορεῖν αὐτοῦ, Herm., S IX. xiii 2; and for secularisation, περιποιεῖσθαι τὸν αἰῶνα τοῦτον, γαυριᾶν ἐν τῷ πλούτῳ, ἐμπεφυρμένος πραγματείαις, etc, in Hermas

James and Hermas retain μετανοεῖν, μετάνοια, to describe the demand made of such Christians In O T. and Gospels μετάνοια always refers to Israel's return to her own ideal, but in Paul and others is used only of the transition from paganism to Christianity Cf ἀνανήφειν, ἐπιστρέφειν, ἀνακαλεῖσθαι τὰ πεπλανημένα, Polyc

In the earlier period it is rather the maintenance of the Christian condition that is spoken of: στήκειν ἐν, κρατεῖν, κατέχειν τὰς παραδόσεις, Paul; μένειν, Joh, Barn, ii 3

Great stress is laid, especially in the later period, on the practical proof of Christianity. Frequent expressions are ποιεῖν τὸ θέλημα, τὸν νόμον, τὴν ἐντολήν, τὴν ἀλήθειαν, τὴν δικαιοσύνην, τὰ ἀγαθά, τὰ ἀρεστά, and so on; πράσσειν is used in Ignatius and ἐπιτελεῖν in 2 Cor. vii 1 and 1 Clem ἔργα is often employed (with another meaning than that which it has with Paul): ἔργα ἀγαθά, 1 Clem xxxiv. 4, xxxviii 2; ἔργα κατεργάζεσθαι, 1 Clem xxxii 4; τελειοῦν τὸ ἔργον τοῦ θεοῦ, John; τέλειον ἔργον, Ign; πρᾶξις ἀγαθή, 1 Clem xxx. 7 The range of the word ἀγαθοποιεῖν is characteristic = to do good, Luke vi. 33, 35; Acts xiv. 17 D; = to do good, Mark iii 4 (var lect, ἀγαθὸν ποιεῖν), Luke vi. 9; 1 Pet ii 15, 20, iii. 6, 17, 1 John xi, 2 Clem x 2; ἀγαθοποιός, 1 Pet ii 14; ἀγαθοποιία, 3 Pet iv. 19; 1 Clem ii. 2, 7, xxxiii 1, xxxiv 2; also ἀγαθουργεῖν, Acts xiv. 17 ℵ B, ἀγαθοεργεῖν, 1 Tim. vi 18, also καλοποιεῖν, 2 Thess. iii. 13;—along with εὐποιεῖν = to do good, and εὐποιΐα, Hebr xiii. 16, Ign Pol., vii. 3, we have εὐπράσσειν, Ign, and εὐπραγεῖν, 2 Clem. xvii. 7.

δικαιοσύνη is usually employed as right conduct = ἀγαθὸς εἶναι, Barn iv 12; hence δικαιοσύναι = good deeds, 2 Clem. vi 9 = ἔργα δικαιοσύνης, Barn i 6, ἔργον δικαιοσύνης ἐργάζεσθαι, 1 Clem xxxiii. 8; ποιεῖν, πράσσειν, πληροῦν, διώκειν, διδάσκειν δικαιοσύνην, γράφειν περὶ δικαιοσύνης, Polyc., Phil., iii 1; ὁδὸς δικαιοσύνης. So in opposition to Paul, whose formulas are still to some extent retained, there are now used ἔργοις or ἐξ ἔργων δικαιοῦσθαι, 1 Clem. xxx 3, Jas. ii 24. In this sense we must understand the short description of the Christian as ὁ δίκαιος, Barn x 11, ἀνὴρ δίκαιος, Herm V i. 18; the same term is applied to the Fathers and the Apostles, 1 Clem. The word δικαιοπραγία, 1 Clem xxxii 3 (vide p 207), is formed

In this connection the picture of the bringing forth of fruit is to be noted The figure is based on Jesus' sayings, recorded in Matt. vii 16 ff, xii 33, xiii 23, xxi. 19 Cf the Baptist's address, iii 8 ff Paul speaks in the same way of καρπὸς τοῦ πνεύματος, Gal. v 22, cf Rom vi 21 f; καρπὸς δικαιοσύνης, Phil i 11 (Hebr.. xii 11, Jas. iii 18); cf. Phil iv. 17; καρπὸς τοῦ φωτός, Eph. v 9, καρπὸς εἰρηνικὸς δικ., Hebr xii. 11—frequent in John, iv 36, xii 24, xv. 2 f, 8, 16; καρπὸς θανατηφόρος, Ign Trall., xi. 1; —μεστὴ . . . . καρπῶν ἀγαθῶν, Jas iii. 17, cf 11 f; — καρποφορεῖν τῷ θεῷ, Rom vii 4; ἐν παντὶ ἔργῳ ἀγαθῷ, Col. i. 10, cf 6, πίστις . . καρποφορεῖ, Polyc. Phil, i 2, the Christians ascend from baptism, καρποφοροῦντες ἐν τῇ καρδίᾳ, Barn xi 11; in the same way καρποφόρος, Hippolytus, Refut, ix 12, appears to be a real Christian name in the sense in which H Achelis, Zeitschr. f. neutestl. Wissenschaft, i 89, rightly defines it (it is also to be found in pre-Christian period). ἔγκαρπος καὶ τελεία ἀνάλυσις (death), 1 Clem. xliv 5, ἔγκαρπος καὶ τελεία μνεία, lvi 1;—ἄκαρπος, Matt xiii 22, Mark iv 19 (νοῦς, 1 Cor xiv. 14);—ἄκαρπα ἔργα τοῦ σκότους, Eph v 11; ἵνα μὴ ὦσιν ἄκαρποι, Tit. iii. 14; δένδρα φθινοπωρινὰ ἄκαρπα = heretics, Jude 12; 2 Pet. i. 8.

Decisive importance is laid also on the intention or mental attitude : φρονεῖν (φρόνημα) very frequently in Paul;—μέτρια καὶ σεμνὰ νοεῖν, 1 Clem i. 3;—τὴν ἔννοιαν Χριστοῦ ὁπλίσασθαι, 1 Pet. iv. 1; διάνοια καθαρά, εἰλικρινής, ἁπλή, ἀπερίσπαστος, καρδία καθαρά, ἁπλή, ἀμέριστος, ἀληθινή,—μεστοὶ ὁσίας βουλῆς, 1 Clem. ii 3;— ὁσιότης ψυχῆς, xxix 1, καρδίας, xxxii 4. Here we must include the frequent emphasising of the συνείδησις, fifteen times in Paul; συνείδησις ἀγαθή, καλή, καθαρά, ἀπρόσκοπος, ἄμωμος καὶ σεμνὴ καὶ ἁγνή, 1 Clem i 3; also ἐν   . . συνειδήσει περιπατεῖν.

NOTES 405

Among the individual virtues there is a special demand for ταπεινοφροσύνη (—φρονεῖν), ἐπιείκεια, πραΰτης (πραϋπάθεια, 1 Tim vi 11, Ign), μακροθυμία, σωφροσύνη (σωφρονεῖν), νήφειν. τὸ ἀκίνητον καὶ τὸ ἀόργητον, Ign , Philad , i 2 Here we must mention ἁγνεία and ἐγκράτεια, so far as they bear upon ἐπιθυμία, and, in the second place, on outward behaviour; εἰδὼς, very frequent in Greek moralists, is used only 1 Tim ii 9

There is a remarkable abundance of negative expressions On the one hand, we have ἀπέχεσθαι, ἀποτίθεσθαι, προσέχειν ἀπό . . ., ἀποτάσσεσθαι τῷ βίῳ, Ign , Philad , xi 1 , ἀπολείπειν τὴν ματαιοπονίαν, 1 Clem ix 1, cf xxviii 1, Polyc , ἀπορρίπτειν πᾶσαν ἀδικίαν, 1 Clem xxxv 5 ; ἀνακόπτεσθαι ἀπὸ τῶν ἐπιθυμιῶν ἐν τῷ κόσμῳ, χαλιναγωγεῖν ἑαυτὸν ἀπὸ παντὸς κακοῦ, Polyc , Phil , v 3, μακρὰν εἶναι πάσης φιλαργυρίας, vi 1 ; φεύγειν. On the other hand, there are adjectives with a privativum, e.g , ἀδιάκριτος, ἄκακος, ἀκέραιος, ἀκατάγνωστος, ἄμεμπτος, ἀμεταμέλητος, ἀμίαντος, ἄμωμος, ἀνέγκλητος, ἀνεπίλημπτος, ἀνόσιος, ἀπρόσκοπος, ἄπταιστος, ἄσπιλος, ἄφθαρτος. These terms, to be understood in Paul as the antithesis of heathenism, come later to be the expression of a negative moral sentiment , they increase and reach their climax in the gnostic writings (vide p 261) In these we also meet with ἀταραξία, ἀπάθεια, and other terms of Greek philosophy which are alien to early Christianity (vide p 258).

Sin is usually called ἁμαρτία and the single act ἁμάρτημα, παράπτωμα, πλημμέλεια, ἀνομία, ἀδικία and τὰ ἄτοπα. The sinner is ὁ ἁμαρτωλός, ὁ φαῦλος, ὁ πονηρός. ἁμαρτία as a rule = guilt, hence of various degrees . ἁμαρτία ἐστιν, καὶ μεγάλη, "sin and a great sin," Herm V i 1 8, ἁμαρτία πρὸς θάνατον and οὐ πρὸς θάνατον, 1 John v 16 f. ; there is an ἄκων ἁμαρτάνειν, 1 Clem ii 3 = ἀγνοῶν ποιεῖν, 1 Tim i 13 Other expressions are employed : ἁμαρτίας ἀναγράφειν, ἐλέγχειν, ἐξομολογεῖσθαι, ἀφιέναι, ἐξαλείφειν, ἰᾶσθαι The notion of sin attaches to ἄνθρωπος, σάρξ (Paul), κόσμος (John), to αἰὼν οὗτος or τοῦ κόσμου τούτου, ἄνομος καιρός (Barnabas). Hence ζῆν κατὰ ἀνθρώπους, σαρκικαὶ καὶ σωματικαὶ ἐπιθυμίαι, Did i 4, κόσμον ἐπιθυμεῖν, Ign , Rom vii. 1, and conversely, κόσμον νηστεύειν (vide p. 268). Evil desire is very frequently ἐπιθυμία, seldomer ἡδονή, both as a rule in the plural (with an essentially different meaning from that in the ethical philosophers). Here, too, regard is had to the intention : sins of thought are described in βουλεύεσθαι πονηρά, Herm. V. I i 8, cf. i 2 ; ἡ βουλὴ ἀναβαίνει ἐπὶ τὴν καρδίαν, διαμένει ἐν ταῖς καρδίαις, S. IX. xxviii. 4 f. The greatest sin is disobedience towards God (*vide supra*): ἀντιτάττεσθαι τῷ θελήματι αὐτοῦ, 1 Clem., ἐναντίος εἶναι τῇ γνώμῃ τοῦ θεοῦ, Ign., ἀπειθεῖν κυρίῳ, Polyc.

We cannot find room here to go into the individual virtues and vices, good and evil works

We content ourselves with calling attention to the significance which is attached to ἀγάπη, φιλαδελφία, φιλοξενία, and, in general, to duties owed to the community: ζητεῖν τὸ κοινωφελές, 1 Clem xlviii. 6, συνζητεῖν περὶ τοῦ κοινῇ συμφέροντος, Barn iv 10. As the object of this sentiment all men are thought of, but specially the Christians · ἐργαζώμεθα τὸ ἀγαθόν πρὸς πάντας, μάλιστα δὲ πρὸς οἰκείους τῆς πίστεως, Gal. vi 10, εἰς ἀλλήλους καὶ εἰς πάντας, 1 Thess v 15; for the narrowing of the idea in John, *vide* p 229 The notion ἀδελφότης comes into Christianity, 1 Pet ii 17, v 9; 1 Clem ii 4 (In 4 Macc ix. 23, x 3, it describes brotherhood in the bodily sense, in 1 Macc xii 10, 17, in the political national sense; later, it narrows down to the brotherhood of the cloister, and is employed as an honorary designation for spiritual dignitaries); then ἐκκλησία appears, Did., Herm (in the earlier period usually of the single congregation, even the house-church, and only occasionally of the ideal church); ἡ καθολικὴ ἐκκλησία, Ign., Smyr., viii. 2 To this correspond the duties of τὰ αὐτὰ φρονεῖν, ὁμόφρονες εἶναι, 1 Pet. iii 8, εἰρηνεύειν in opposition to ἔρις, στάσις, διχοστασία, ἀκαταστασία, πόλεμοι καὶ μάχαι, Jas. iv 1

The only other point is to note especially the stress laid upon the requirement μὴ κακὸν ἀντὶ κακοῦ ἀποδίδοναι: 1 Thess v 15; 1 Pet. ii 23, iii 9, Polyc., ad Phil., ii 2, Act Thom. 55, p. 42.

Instead of going into detail, let us take a short glance at the nature of moral instruction

It had two roots—one in the Greek Orphic societies, the other in the Jewish O T The former had developed an essentially negative form, the catalogue of vices; the latter possessed, along with the negations of the decalogue, rich and positive treasures in the proverb literature.

Among the Orphics ethical instruction had an eschatological form, or it was a presentment of Hades The future recompense of wickedness is pictured in single types In the Νεκυία of the Odyssey, Polygnotus introduced into the Lesche of the Knidii at Delphi two types of transgressors—one who had sinned against his father and is now strangled by him in the mire of Acheron, and a temple profaner who is tortured by a woman poisoner, Pausan, X. xxviii. 1 f. ἀσέβεια, represented in the ἱερόσυλος and the ἐπίορκος, and disrespect for parents are the ground types, from which in the course of time a rich catalogue of vices developed First of all there came in injury done to the stranger, then murder, adultery, greed, etc. With the oldest Christian form of these katabaseis we have only lately become acquainted in the apocalypse of Peter, with which a rich literature is connected, including the Acts of Thomas, 55–58, pp 171 ff, Bonnet, the Apocalypse of Paul, the Theotokos Apocalypse, and various others down to Dante's Inferno; cf A Dieterich, Νεκυία, 163 ff, with a table affixed embracing the Christian passages and also my review in the Preuss. Jahrbuchern, 77, 1894, 375 ff As a characteristic example of a heathen catalogue of vices, I adduce Lysis the Pythag., apud Iamblichus, de vita Pythag., xvii 18, p 57, Nauck : out of ἀκρασία there spring ἄθεσμοι γάμοι καὶ φθοραὶ καὶ μέθαι καὶ (αἱ) παρὰ φύσιν ἀδοναὶ καὶ σφοδραί τινες ἐπιθυμίαι, out of πλεονεξία there arise ἁρπαγαί, λῃστεῖαι, πατροκτονίαι, ἱεροσυλίαι, φαρμακεῖαι καὶ ὅσα τούτων ἀδελφά.

In the case of the Jewish instruction we must start from Proverbs, Jesus Sirach, and, above all, the Testaments of the Twelve Patriarchs, where in the twelve sons of Jacob the individual virtues and vices in their causes, their occurrences, and their consequences are set forth A typical instance is the Jewish proselyte-catechism. It is incorporated in Did. 1–6 and Barn 18–20, and is used also in Hermas, Mand 1–3 In the figure of the Two Ways, found also among the Orphics, this catechism sets forth righteousness and unrighteousness—the former in detail, chap i –iv, the latter briefly in a catalogue of vices, chap v ; vide Harnack's small edition of the Doctrine of the Apostles and the edition of the Didache by Rendel Harris, who connects the catalogue of vices here with the Jewish Viduis, the (later, occasionally alphabetically arranged) confessions of the Synagogue Special attention is due to the enumeration of sins of omission in the anonymous Jewish Apocalypse, Steindorff, Texte und Unters, Neue Folge, II iii. 152. This is related to the confessions, but, on the other hand, is strongly reminiscent of Matt xxv. 41 ff For further examples of catalogues of vices, vide Sap Sal, xiv 22 ff ; Rom 1. 28 ff, xiii 13; 1 Cor. v. 10 f., vi 9 f ; 2 Cor xii 20 f ; Gal v. 19 ff , Col iii. 5 ff ; Eph iv 31, v 3 ff.; 1 Tim. 1. 9 f ; 2 Tim. iii. 2 ff —Test , XII. patr. Reuben. 3, Levi 17 ; Enoch Slav , x. 4 f.; Baruch Gr.-slav , 4, 8, 13 ;—

1 Clem xxxv 5; Polyc, Phil, ii. 2; Act Joh. 35 f, p 168, Bonnet; Clem., Hom., i. 18, xi. 27; Clem., Recogn., iv. 36. It is worth noting that these very catalogues of vices were afterwards employed for catechetical instruction, e g, Gal v 19–21, in Charles the Great's Gr Admonitio Generalis, A D 789, chap 82, Monumenta Germaniæ, Leges, vol. ii. p 61

In the case of Paul as of Lysis, the foundation is laid in the two categories of πορνεία and πλεονεξία, 1 Thess. iv 3 ff. [where it is false to take πρᾶγμα, v 6, as a euphemism for adultery] The following out in detail is very fluctuating, as the subjoined table of the leading passages shows

1 Cor. v 10 f.	2 Cor. xii. 20	Gal. v 19.	Rom 1. 29	Col iii. 5
πόρνοι	(2) ἀκαθαρσία	πορνεία	v. 24 f.	πορνεία
	πορνεία	ἀκαθαρσία	ἀκαθαρσία	ἀκαθαρσία
	ἀσέλγεια	ἀσέλγεια	v. 26 f unnatural vice.	πάθος
πλεονέκται			ἀδικία, πονηρία	ἐπιθυμία κακή
ἅρπαγες			πλεονεξία, κακία	πλεονεξία =
εἰδωλολάτραι		εἰδωλολατρεία		εἰδωλολατρεία
		φαρμακεία		
		ἔχθραι	φθόνος, φόνος	
	(1) ἔρις	ἔρις	ἔρις, δόλος	
	ζῆλος	ζῆλος	κακοήθεια	ὀργή
	θυμοί	θυμοί	ψιθυρισταί, κατάλαλοι	θυμός
	ἐριθεῖαι	ἐριθεῖαι	θεοστυγεῖς, ὑβρισταί	κακία
	καταλαλιαί	διχοστασίαι	ὑπερήφανοι, ἀλάζονες	βλασφημία
λοίδωρος	ψιθυρισμοί	αἱρέσεις	ἐφευρεταί κακῶν	αἰσχρολογία
	φυσιώσεις	φθόνοι	γονεῦσιν ἀπειθεῖς	ψεῦδος
	ἀκαταστασίαι	φόνοι	ἀσύνετοι, ἀσύνθετοι	
μέθυσος		μέθαι	ἄστοργοι [ἄσπονδοι]	
(ἅρπαξ)		κῶμοι	ἀνελεήμονες	

It deserves notice that πορνεία with derivatives occurs about eighteen times in Paul, μοιχεία only five times, two of these being in quotations from the decalogue

To the catalogues of vices there are corresponding lists of virtues, e g, Gal v 22 ff; 1 Clem lxii 2, 64; usually as unarranged as the vices We possess examples in Hermas, V. III. viii. 3–7; M. VI. ii. 3, S IX. xv. 2; in the first of these there are seven enumerated: πίστις, ἐγκράτεια, ἁπλότης, ἀκακία, σεμνότης, ἐπιστήμη, ἀγάπη, each coming from the one preceding it, like the daughter from the mother (ἐπιστήμη in v 5 is wrongly put in between ἁπλότης and ἀκακία, which are always joined, cf V III. ix 1; M. ii 1; for the arrangement in v 7 we have the evidence of analogy in σύνεσις, S ix In the second passage only four main virtues are named, δικαιοσύνη, ἁγνεία, σεμνότης, αὐτάρκεια (cf S V 11. 9), to these are to be added the practical proofs: πᾶν ἔργον δίκαιον, πᾶσα ἀρετή. In the third passage the first has been extended to an enumeration of twelve, classified as four stronger: πίστις, ἐγκράτεια, δύναμις, μακροθυμία, and eight weaker: ἁπλότης, ἀκακία, ἁγνεία, ἱλαρότης, ἀλήθεια, σύνεσις, ὁμόνοια, ἀγάπη (σύνεσις = ἐπιστήμη, ἱλαρότης to be specially noted'; δύναμις [for which Lat Palat reads patientia = ὑπομονη, cf O von Gebhardt, Passio S Theclæ, p xcvi], probably the capability which results from πίστις to fulfil God's will).

All these enumerations are similarly unarranged and changeable. A comparison of the two recensions in Did 1–6 and Barn. 18–20 will show this

The Pauline form of the table of domestic duties is unique, Col. iii 12–iv. 2; it is imitated in Eph v. 15–vi 18; later on this kind of ethical and detailed instruction was transferred to the sermons and exhortations designed for special groups in the Church, as they are indicated in 1 Clem. i. 3; Tit. ii 2–10; 1 Tim ii 8–15, v 1 f., vi. 1 f., and in the pseudo-Clem Epistles, de virginitate, ii 4, are witnessed to for the third century; vide H Achelis, Zeitschr f. N. Tliche. Wissenschaft, i, 1900, 96

There is a wonderful wealth of forms of moral instruction and expression. From this, too, it is possible to infer the richness of the moral power which the Gospel bestowed on the primitive Christian communities

INDEX OF PASSAGES REFERRED TO OR DISCUSSED

Note 6 is not included

Gen	ii 24	183
	iii 17 ff	93
	vi	269
	vi 2 f	183
	ix 3	396
	ix. 4	393
	xix.	269
	xxxv 22	387
	xlix 4	387
Exod	xii. 11	183
	xix. 10 \} xx. 12 \}	183
	xxviii 39, 42	394
	xxxii 32	205
	xxxix 28	394
Lev	xvii 11, 14	393
	xviii 8	388 f.
	xx. 11	388
Num	v. 11 ff	390
	vi	393
	vi. 13 f	394
	xi. 16 f.	157
Deut.	xii. 15	396
	xii. 16	393
	xxiii 1	388
	xxvii. 20	388
	xxxii 15	214
Judg.	xiii 4, 7, 14	393
1 Sam xiv. 32 f		394
2 Sam xvi 21		387
1 Kings ii 13 ff.		388 f.
Job xxxi		140
Psalms i 2		140
	xv.	140

Psalms—*continued.*		
xxix. 11		394
xxxiv. 13–17		183
li. 19		289
cxix. 27		140
Prov	iii 34	193
	xviii 17	237
	xxiv 21	182
Isaiah	xi 5	194
	xliii 24	54
	lii 7	194
	liii.	185
	lix. 17	194
	lxv 4	394
	lxvi 3, 17	394
Jer	xviii. 7–10	391
	xxviii 16 f	390
Ezek.	iii. 17–21	391
	xxii. 10 f	388 f.
	xxxiii. 25	394
	xliv. 17	394
Daniel iv 21 ff		391
Hosea vi. 6		140
Joel ii 12 ff.		391
Jonah iii., iv		391
Micah vi 8		140
Zech ix 7		394
1 Macc ix 54		390
2 Macc iii. 23 ff		391
xii 42 ff		20
Sirach xii 1		302
4 Ezra v 13		397
vi. 21		397

INDEX OF PASSAGES

4 EZRA—*continued*.
   ix. 24   397
   xii. 51   397
   xiii. 24   89

TEST. OF THE TWELVE PATRIARCHS—
LEVI. iii.   396
   xiii   140
   xvii   138

MATT. iii. 4   267
   v. 16   181
   v. 17   155
   v 23 f.   289
   v. 27 f.   43
   v. 28   313
   v. 32   350
   v. 48   322
   vi. 25 f.   264
   vii. 12   395
   vii 13 f.   322
   ix 13   xxxix, 140, 308
   xi. 29   279
   xvi. 18   157
   xvii. 25 f.   131
   xviii. 17   157
   xix. 9   350
   xix. 11 f.   263
   xxiii. 15   167
   xxiii 23, 26   156
   xxv. 41 ff.   141

MARK v. 37   393
   vii. 11 ff.   289
   vii. 14 ff.   xxxviii
   ix. 2   393
   xii. 18 f.   305
   xiv. 33   393

LUKE i. 15   393
   ii. 36   397
   vi. 4   156
   xii. 14   xxxviii
   xvi. 18   350
   xxii. 15   267

JOHN i. 14, 17   231
   i 20 ff., 39   232
   i. 41, 45   232
   i. 46   232

JOHN—*continued*.
   ii 4   233
   iii. 19, 27 ff   232
   iii. 31   231
   iv. 9, 40   231
   iv. 18   234
   iv. 23   231
   v. 9 ff 17 f.   231
   v. 34, 44   232
   vi 4   231
   vi 66 ff.   233
   vii. 8, 22 ff.   231
   vii. 17   231
   vii. 18   232
   viii. 23   231
   viii. 29   231
   viii. 34   232
   viii. 44   231, 234
   viii. 51 f   231
   ix. 14 ff, 22   231
   ix. 31   231
   x 17, 25, 29   232
   xi. 16   233
   xii. 20 ff., 42   231
   xii. 43   232
   xiii. 1 ff., 12 ff.   232
   xiii 4, 12 ff.   193
   xiii. 34 f.   232
   xiii 36, 37   233
   xiv. 11, 31   232
   xiv. 15, 21   232
   xiv. 27 f.   233
   xv. 8, 16   232
   xv. 10   232
   xv. 11   233
   xv. 24   232
   xv. 27   233
   xvi 2 f.   233
   xvi. 8 f   181, 284
   xvi. 20 f.   233
   xvi. 23   231

INDEX OF PASSAGES

JOHN—*continued.*

xvi. 33	232	
xvii. 4	232	
xvii. 6 f.	231	
xvii. 6, 9, 20	233	
xvii. 13	233	
xvii. 17	231	
xvii. 21 f.	233	
xix. 26 f.	233	
xix. 35	233	
xx. 4	395	
xxi. 7	395	
xxi. 18	233	
xxi. 22 f., 24	233	

ACTS	i. 14	144, 392
	ii. 17, 18	144
	ii. 42	142
	iii. 21	141
	iv. 32, 36 f.	143
	v. 1 ff.	143, 390
	v. 6, 7 ff., 10	145
	vi. 1	144
	viii. 2	145
	ix. 2	145
	x.	150
	xii. 12	144
	xii. 17	392 f.
	xii. 23	390
	xiii. 5	386
	xiii. 11	390
	xiii. 14	99
	xv.	152
	xv. 1	162
	xv. 5	151
	xv. 13	151
	xv. 20, 29	393
	xv. 21	152
	xv. 40 – xvi. 5	99
	xvi. 6, 7 f	100
	xvi. 11 f	81
	xvi. 12, 16	82
	xvii. 1, 10, 15	81
	xvii. 2	82
	xvii. 4, 5 ff.	85
	xvii. 5 ff., 13	85

ACTS—*continued.*

xviii. 1	81	
xviii. 2	123	
xviii. 4, 6 f.	64	
xviii. 7	16	
xviii. 18	100, 393	
xviii. 23	102	
xix.	101	
xix. 1	100	
xix. 12, 13 ff, 18f	101	
xix. 21 f., 29	83	
xix 23 ff, 37	102	
xix 40	102	
xx. 1, 3	83	
xx. 2 f.	78	
xx. 4 f.	83, 85	
xx. 17–38	101	
xx. 31	100	
xxi. 18	152	
xxi. 20	383	
xxi. 23 f.	393	
xxi 25	152, 393, 395	
xxiv. 14	145	
xxvii. 2	83	

ROM	i. 7	122
	i. 8	124
	i. 9, 10, 11 ff., 15	121
	i. 18, 32	52
	i. 21 ff	133
	i. 29 ff, 30 f.	2, 3
	i. 32	49
	ii. 13 f	182
	ii 16	70
	ii. 17	122
	ii 17 ff.	140
	ii. 18	96
	ii. 21 f.	138
	iii. 9, 22	139
	iv. 17 ff.	9
	v. 1 ff.	124
	v. 5	125
	vi. 3	8
	vi. 18, 22	35

INDEX OF PASSAGES

Rom.—*continued*.

viii	2, 12, 23, 26	} 125
viii	12 ff	10
viii.	18 ff.	200
ix.	1 ff	85, 205, 294
ix.	31	139
x	2 ff	138, 167
x	4	8
xii.–xvi.		132
xii.–xiv		xxxvi
xii.	1 f	6, 132
xii	3 ff., 11, 13	} 132
xii.	2	133
xii.	1–7	325
xiii.	8 ff.	133
xiii.	11	10, 219
xiii.	12	133
xiii	13 f	132
xiii.	14	8
xiv	1–xv 13	125
xiv	1–xv. 7	133
xiv	1 ff.	210
xiv	2, 5 f.	125
xiv.	14, 20	399
xiv.	17	125
xv.	4	125
xv.	7	8
xv.	20 ff, 22	121
xv.	23	99
xv	26	84
xv.	27	9
xv.	30	121
xv	31	85
xvi	1	14
xvi	3, 7, 6	122
xvi.	4–16	9
xvi	5, 14, 15	122
xvi.	17 f.	123, 125
xvi	19	124
xvi	23	16
1 Cor.	1–iv.	113
	i. 2	15
	i 4 f.	17
	i. 12	72
	i. 13 ff.	xxx, 15
	i. 14 ff.	19

1 Cor.—*continued*.

ii	2	1
iii	16	2
iii	22	72
iv	3, 8, 10	74
iv.	12	9
iv	14 f.	63
iv.	16	9
iv	17	83
iv.	21	63
v		388, 392
v.	4	391
v	5	46, 67
v.	9	45
v.	10 f	45, 56
v	11	54
vi.	1	57
vi.	9	2
vi	9 f.	54, 249
vi.	10	56
vi.	11	55
vi	12 f.	65, 67
vi.	12, 20	52, 65
vi	15	2
vi	19, 20	35
vii.		39
vii	2, 3	39
vii.	4, 10 f, 16	} 39
vii.	6	42
vii.	8	42
vii.	8 ff.	112
vii.	10 f.	350
vii.	12 f, 14	39
vii	12–17	30
vii.	12 f.	69
vii	15	33, 39
vii.	17	9, 79
vii.	17 f.	23, 33
vii.	18	65
vii.	21	34
vii	23	35
vii.	26	112
vii	27, 28	42
vii.	32 ff	39
vii	35, 36	42
vii.	37	42
vii	39	32, 42, 351

INDEX OF PASSAGES 415

1 Cor.—*continued.*

vii 40	42	
viii. 1, 4	66, 67	
viii. 5	67	
viii 7 ff.	27, 64, 65	
viii. 9 f	65	
viii. 10–12	68	
viii. 13	69, 125	
ix. 1	76	
ix 5	394	
ix. 1–19	65	
ix. 21	8	
x. 1–11	9	
x. 15	10	
x. 16	21	
x. 20	67	
x 23 f	65, 67	
x 27	10	
xi 1	9	
xi 2	9	
xi. 2–16	37	
xi. 3 ff	65	
xi 4 f., 13, 14 f.	38	
xi 8 f.	39	
xi. 10	38	
xi. 11 f	39	
xi 16	9, 37, 38, 79	
xi 20	61	
xi 30	21, 62, 89	
xi. 34	10	
xii. 1–3	19	
xii 2 f	69	
xii 3	15	
xii. 4–30	19	
xii 9	101	
xii. 28	18, 101	
xii 31–xiv 1	19	
xiii	19, 210	
xiv. 1 ff –25	19	
xiv 13, 23 ff	19	
xiv 24	344	
xiv 26, 27 ff	16, 17	
xiv. 34–38	38	

1 Cor.—*continued*

xiv. 34, 35 36 f.	9, 37, 38	
xiv 39	69	
xv.	89	
xv. 5	395	
xv. 7	392	
xv. 29	xxx, 20	
xvi 1	105	
xvi 2	16	
xvi. 5, 10	83	
xvi 5 ff.	392	
xvi. 12	72	
xvi. 13 f.	10, 70	
xvi. 15 f. 14,	35, 57, 88	
xvi. 16	192	
xvi 20	63	

2 Cor.

i 1	14	
i 13	76	
i. 15 f	392	
i. 16	83	
ii.	48	
ii. 1	78	
ii. 4	392	
ii. 5–11	391	
ii 5	107 391	
ii 9	97	
ii. 11	67	
ii 13	59, 83	
iv. 2	76, 163	
vi 14 ff.	29, 45	
vii.	48	
vii. 5	83	
vii. 6	83	
vii. 8 ff	391, 392	
vii 12	107, 387, 392	
vii 13	59	
vii 13 f.	83	
viii 1 ff.	84, 98	
viii. 2 ff.	91	
viii. 6	59	
viii. 9	8	
viii 17	59, 83	
ix 2, 4	84	
x.–xiii	392	
x 7	75	
x. 9, 10 f.	76	

2 Cor.—*continued.*		
x 11, 12, 15	164	
x 15	164	
xi 3, 5	164	
xi 8 f	97	
xi. 9	83, 84	
xi. 13 f.	164	
xi. 16	76	
xi. 23 ff.	9	
xii. 7 ff.	9, 76	
xii. 11	76, 165	
xii. 13–15	76	
xii. 14	392	
xii. 16	163	
xii. 16–18	76	
xii. 20	2	
xiii. 1	392	
xiii. 2	389	
xiii. 11	80	
Gal. i., ii.	107	
i. 2	105, 107, 111	
i. 4	110	
i. 6	107, 108	
i 7 ff.	107, 165	
i 10	165	
i. 19	392	
i. 20	107	
i. 21	99	
ii 4	164	
ii. 6	108	
ii. 9	151, 392 f.	
ii. 9 f.	162	
ii. 11 f	107, 150, 395	
ii. 12 f.	164	
ii. 15	161	
ii. 20	8, 110	
iii. 1	107, 110	
iii 2 f.	109	
iii 4	105	
iii. 10 ff.	109	
iii 22	109	
iii. 27	8	
iv 8 f	108	
iv. 10, 12	107	
iv 13 ff	100, 102, 107	
iv 16	165	
iv. 17	111, 165	

Gal.—*continued*		
iv. 19	110	
v. 1	109, 110	
v 2	107	
v. 6	110	
v. 7	105, 108	
v. 10 ff	107, 165	
v. 11	165	
v 12	166	
v 13 ff., 15	110, 188	
v. 13	110	
v 20	104, 110	
v 21	2, 104	
v 22 f.	3, 101	
v. 25	10, 109	
v. 26	110	
vi. 1	110	
vi 2	8, 110	
vi 6	88, 106	
vi. 6 ff., 10	110	
vi. 11 ff	107	
vi. 12	165	
Eph. i 3 f.	179	
i 4	177	
i. 9, 17 f.	177	
i. 15	189	
i. 19	179	
ii 1 ff.	178	
ii. 3	178	
ii 3 f.	178, 184	
ii. 6	179	
ii. 10	177	
ii. 14 f.	177, 184	
ii. 19, 20	184	
iii. 3 ff., 17, 19	177	
iii. 20	179	
iv. 2 f., 11 ff.	188	
iv 13 f.	187	
iv. 14, 15	194	
iv. 17	186	
iv. 19	178	
iv. 20 f.	184	
iv. 25 f.	186, 187	
iv 26	188	
iv 28, 29	187	
v 2	177, 184	

INDEX OF PASSAGES

EPH —*continued*
v. 3	187
v 4	187
v 8	178
v 11	181
v. 18	177, 182
v. 21	182
v 24	184
v. 25	184, 188
v 29	184
v. 31	183
v 33	182
vi. 9	187
vi 11	194
vi. 14 ff	184
vi 18 f.	177

PHIL
i 1	96
i 5	95
i 6, 8, 9	94
i 12–18	124
i 13, 14 ff.	123, 124
i. 15 ff	86, 166
i 18	166
i. 19	94
i 23	95
i. 24	94
i. 26	84
i 27	95, 97
i 28 f	96
i. 30	9
ii. 2 f	97
ii 5 ff.	8, 97
ii 12	94, 95
ii. 13	96
ii 14, 17, 18	94, 95
ii 15	96, 135
ii. 19	84, 94
ii. 21	166
ii. 24, 25, 28	84
ii 25–30	94
ii. 29 f	88
iii. 1, 7 ff.	95
iii 2 ff	85, 96
iii. 12, 15	94
iii. 14	317

PHIL.—*continued*
iii 17	9
iii. 18 f.	123, 166
iii. 20	96
iii 21	96
iv 1	94
iv. 2 f.	85, 97
iv. 4	95
iv. 5	96, 219
iv 6	96
iv 8 f.	9, 98
iv 9	9
iv 10 ff.	83, 94
iv 15	83, 84, 97
iv 16	82
iv 22	122, 124

COL.
i 2	105
i 4	105, 189
i. 7	103
i 8, 9 ff	105, 106
i. 12 f, 23	113
ii 1	100, 103
ii. 5	105, 114
ii 7, 9 ff	113
ii. 11 ff	111
ii 16	112
ii 18	113
ii. 16, 21	111
ii 23	112, 113
iii. 1 ff	113
iii 5	2, 3, 114, 187, 244
iii 5 ff.	4
iii. 8	105, 187
iii. 13 f.	8, 114
iii 16	8, 114
iii. 18–iv. 2	4
iii 22 f.	105
iv. 5	9, 10
iv 6	105
iv 10	83, 85, 102, 103
iv 14	85
iv. 17	116

1 THESS.
i. 1	86
i. 3	90
i. 6	9, 87
i. 7	90, 98

INDEX OF PASSAGES

1 Thess.—*continued.*		
i. 9		85, 89, 91, 202
ii 5 ff.		86
ii 6 f		91
ii 7, 11		86
ii 9		9, 82
ii 10 f.		9
ii 11		88
ii 14		85, 87
ii 15 f., 17 ff.,		85
ii 19		90, 91, 94
iii 3 ff.		87
iii 6		86, 90
iii 9, 13		90, 91
iii 10, 12		86
iv. 1 ff		2
iv 3 ff		209
iv 3, 6		90
iv. 9 f.		88
iv 10 ff		86, 92
iv 12		9
iv 13		89, 91
v 1 ff.		91
v 6–8		92
v 8		90
v 11		88
v 12 f		88, 192
v 14		92
v 15		90
v 19 f.		92, 221
v 23		91
v 25, 26, 27		87
2 Thess. i 1		86
i 4		87
ii. 1 ff		91
ii 2		91
ii 15		87
iii 1		87
iii. 6		93
iii 7		9
iii. 8		91
iii 14 f, 15, 16		93
iii 17		91
1 Tim. i 3		84

1 Tim —*continued*	
i 4 ff.	254
i 5	255
i 9 f.	306, 307
i. 13	307, 308
i. 15	301, 308
i 19 f	271
i 20	253, 391
ii. 1–4	291
ii. 2	292
ii 8	287, 289
ii. 9	303
ii 9 f	305
ii 14 f	305
ii. 15	262
iii. 1 ff	284
iii. 2	300
iii. 4 f.	305
iii. 7	294
iii 8 ff	285
iii. 15	290
iv. 3	261, 266
iv 3 ff	288, 304, 397
iv 7	254
iv 8	259
iv 12	285
v 1	286, 290
v 8	305
v 13	283
v. 17, 19	285
v. 18	279
v. 20, 21	290
v 23	304
vi. 1 f	306
vi 4	254
vi. 6 ff.	304
vi. 9 f	303
vi. 11 ff.	281
vi. 13	293
vi 17	303
vi. 17 ff	304
vi 20	254
2 Tim. i. 6 ff.	292
i 8, 12	292
i 15	253
i. 18	301
ii. 2	281
ii. 3	292

INDEX OF PASSAGES

2 TIM.—*continued*
	ii. 3–7	285
	ii. 9 ff.	292
	ii 11	292
	ii 14, 16, 23	254
	ii. 17	253
	ii. 18	258
	ii 20	290
	ii. 22	281
	ii 24 f.	290
	iii 1 ff	268
	iii 3	306
	iii 6	264
	iii 8	253
	iii 10	285
	iii 10 ff	292, 293
	iii. 15 ff.	279
	iv. 2	290
	iv 3	271
	iv. 6 ff.	292
	iv 10	85
	iv 14	253
TITUS	i 5	284, 295
	i 6	305
	i 8	300
	i 13	290
	i 16	254
	ii 1 ff	281
	ii 4 f	305
	ii 7	285
	ii 9 f	306
	ii 11 f	290
	ii 15	285
	iii. 1	281, 292
	iii 2	294
	iii. 3 f.	307
	iii 8	301
	iii 9	254
PHILEM	1, 2, 5, 7	116
	13	386
	19–22	116
	24	83, 85
HEB.	ii. 1 ff.	197
	ii 2	197
	ii 17 f.	185
	iii 6, 14, 18	197
	iii. 7 ff	197

HEB —*continued*
	iii 12	197
	iv 1	198
	iv 11, 14	197
	iv. 15	185
	v 7 ff	185
	v 11 ff.	199
	v. 12	196
	vi 1	199, 200, 208
	vi 10, 11	200
	ix. 14	197, 202
	x 19, 23, 24	197
	x 25	197, 201
	x. 32 ff.	197
	x. 35	197
	xi	207
	xi. 13 ff.	199
	xi 35 ff	198
	xii 1	200
	xii 2 f	198
	xii 3	197
	xii 5 ff	198
	xii 25	197
	xiii. 1, 2, 3	201
	xiii. 4 f	203
	xiii 9	201
	xiii 13	198
	xiii. 15, 16	202
	xiii. 17, 18 f	201
	xiii. 22	196
	xiii 23	201
JAMES	i. 2 ff.	292
	i. 4	308
	i. 5	302
	i. 9 ff	303, 304
	i 10, 12	292
	i. 21	306
	i. 22	301
	i. 27	289
	ii 1 f	291
	ii 2	303
	ii. 6	303
	ii. 12	278
	ii 14 ff.	300
	ii. 15 f	301
	iii. 1	254
	iii 13 ff.	255

JAMES—continued		
iii 17	281, 301	
iv. 8	306	
iv. 13 ff.	303	
v. 1 ff.	303	
v. 6	303	
v. 7, 9	304	
v. 12	308	
v. 13	307	
v 14	286	
v. 16	289	
v. 19 f.	290	
1 PETER 1. 1, 17	179	
1 2, 14, 22	177, 178, 188	
1. 3, 21	177	
1. 6 f	189	
1. 6, 8	177	
1. 13, 22	183	
i. 14	178	
1. 15, 22	188	
11. 1	178	
11 8	177	
ii 9	178	
11. 11	178, 179	
11. 12, 15	181	
11. 13 f	182	
11. 16, 17	188	
ii 21 ff.	184	
111 1, 20	177	
111. 1 f., 3 f.	181, 183	
111. 5 f	183	
111 7	178	
111 8	188	
111. 10–12	183	
111 15 f.	181	
iii. 19 f.	178	
iv. 1	184	
iv. 3 f	178, 179	
iv. 6, 7	177, 178	
iv. 8, 9, 10 f	188	
iv. 12 ff.	189	
iv. 15	180	
iv. 16	188	
iv. 17 f.	177, 178	
v. 1 ff.	190	
v 8 f	177, 189	
v. 9	188	

1 PETER—continued		
v. 10	187	
v. 12	189	
1 JOHN 1. 1	219	
1 5	223	
1 6, 10	223, 255	
1 8 ff.	170, 229	
ii 3	222	
ii. 3 f	255	
ii. 4	223	
11. 7	219	
11 9	225, 255	
11 13 f.	220	
ii. 16	230	
11. 18, 28	219	
11. 18 ff	254	
ii. 19	222	
111 2	223	
111. 3	228	
iii. 4, 6 ff	223	
111. 7	230	
111 10	225	
111. 10 f.	255	
iii. 11, 23	219	
111 14	255	
111 16 f., 18	229	
111 17	169, 301	
iv 1 ff	221, 254	
iv. 7 f	255	
iv 7 ff, 21	219	
iv. 7, 20	255	
iv. 8	225	
iv. 20	169, 225, 229	
v 4 f	220	
v. 16 f.	229	
v. 18	223	
v 21	219	
2 JOHN 5 f.	219	
6 f.	225	
7 ff.	254	
9	223	
10 f.	224	
11	225	
3 JOHN 7	219	
9, 15	220	
JUDE 11, 23	253	
19	255	

INDEX OF PASSAGES

Rev			1 Clem —continued		
	i. 5	220	xiii 1	209	
	i. 20	226	xiv 1	215	
	ii., iii.	225	xvi 1, 17	209	
	ii. 2	226	xvii. 1	208	
	ii 4	229	xix 2 ff	209	
	ii. 5, 16	219	xxi. 3	209	
	ii. 6, 14, 20	219, 253, 269	xxi 5	215	
	ii 7, 11	220	xxi. 6	205	
	ii 9	226, 230	xxi. 6, 8	208	
	ii 13	226	xxiii –xxvii	209	
	ii. 17, 26	220	xxix 1	206	
	ii. 19	229	xxx 1	209	
	ii. 24	226	xxx 3	207	
	ii 25	219	xxxi 2	207	
	iii 3, 11	219	xxxii 3	207	
	iii 4	228	xxxiii	207	
	iii 5, 12, 21	220	xxxiii. 8	207	
	iii 8	229	xxxiv 1 f , 2	207	
	iii 9	226, 231	xxxv. 4	209	
	iii 11, 20	219	xxxv 5	209	
	iii 18	228	xxxviii. 1, 2	204	
	vi 9 ff	227	xxxviii. 2	208, 210	
	vii. 9	383	xl. f.	206	
	xiv. 3	228	xlii , xliii , xliv	206	
	xiv. 4	228, 261	xliv 3	208	
	xvii. 1 f.	228	xliv. 4	214	
	xxii 20	219	xlvi. 4	208	
			xlvi. 9	204	
1 Clem. inscr		208	xlvii. 4	208	
	i. 1	203, 215	xlviii 5	216	
	i. 2–ii. 8 f.	211, 212	xlix.	210	
	i 3	213	liii	205	
	ii 1	209, 213	liv 3	205	
	ii 8	208	lv. 2	204	
	iii 1–4	214	lvi 1	204	
	v , vi	210	lvii.	215	
	v 7	207	lviii. 1	204	
	vi. 1	383	lviii. 2	204, 208	
	vi. 2 f.	208	lix. 1	204	
	vii 1	207	lix. 2–lxi.	206	
	vii. 4–viii.	208	lix. 2	205	
	ix.–xii.	208	lix. 4	204	
	ix. 6	207	lx. 1 f.	208	
	x. 7	207	lxii. 2	208	
	xi.	207	lxii. 3	217	
	xi. 2	207	lxiii. 2, 3	204	
	xii.	208	lxiv., lxv. 2	206	
	xiii.–xx.	208			

1 CLEM —continued.			AD EPH —continued.		
lxv.		204	i 3		383
2 CLEM. 1		288	iii. 1		236
	ii 4	308	v 2		243
	iii 4	289	v. 3		245
	iv 3	289	vi 2		237
	vi 9	308	vii. 1		245, 253, 270
	vii. 6	308	viii. 1		246
	viii. 6	308	viii. 2		238
	xiii. 3 f.	295	ix		246
	xv 1	280, 290	ix 1		245
	xvi 4	287, 302	x		248
	xvii 1	290	x 1		291
	xvii 3	302	xi 1		238, 247
	xix.	344	xi. 2		241, 247
	xix. 1	285	xii		247
	xix., xx.	292	xii 2		236
BARNABAS 1. 4		301	xiii. 1		246
	i. 6	301	xiv. 2		238, 248
	ii 6	279	xv		242
	ii. 9	293	xx.		238, 242
	ii. 10	289	xxi 2		236, 241
	iii.	288	Ad Mag. i.		237
	iv 8	293	iii 1		243
	iv. 10	296	iv		243, 246, 248
	v. 9	308	v.		238
	vi 11	307	vii		246
	vii 1	288	x 1		246, 247
	vii 11	292	xi.		246
	ix 4	293	xii.		236, 237
	x	279, 306, 399	xiv.		236, 241
	x. 4	304	Ad Trall. i 2		247
	x. 9	293	iii. 1		242
	x 11	296	iii. 2		243
	xi. 8	301	iii. 3		236
	xiv. 1, 4	293	iv.		236
	xv. 9	288	v		238, 242
	xvi 1	293	v. 2		236
	xvi 2	288	vi. 2		275
	xvi. 4	293	viii. 1		246
	xviii –xx.	xxxvi	viii 2		248
	xix 2	288	x		245
	xix. 8	302	xiii		241
	xix. 10	296	xiii 1		236
	xix 11	302	Ad Rom inscr.		237
IGNATIUS—			iii. 1		204
Ad Eph i 1		241, 247	iii 2, 3		248
	i 2	236	iv 2		241

INDEX OF PASSAGES

Ad Rom inscr.—*continued.*		Ad Philad —*continued.*		
iv. 3	236	vi 1	243	
iv., v.	236	x. 1	247	
v 1	236	xi.	244	
ix.	241	xi. 2 f	247	
ix. 2	236	xiii.	241	
ix. 3	241	xiv	242	
x	241	Hermas—		
x. 2	241	Vis I 1.	312, 354	
Ad Philad. ii. 1	237	,, 1. 8	356	
iii 2	242	,, 1. 9	323, 342	
iv.	246	,, ii 1	321, 340	
vi	246	,, ii. 4	311, 341, 351	
vii	238, 291	,, iii 1	320, 345	
x	241	,, iii. 2, 3	342	
xi	241	,, iii. 3, 4	343	
xi 1	242	,, iv. 2	333, 343	
Ad Smyr ii	245	,, iv 3	319	
iv. 2	236	II. 1 4	310	
v.	245	,, ii	343	
vi 2	245, 255	,, ii 2	315	
vii 1	245, 255	,, ii. 3	352, 353	
viii. 1	242	,, ii. 4	318, 323	
ix. 1	243	,, ii 4, 5	341, 342	
x.	242	,, ii. 5	330	
xi	241	,, ii 6	335	
xi. 3	241	,, ii. 7	318	
xii.	241	,, iii. 1	352, 353	
xiii.	244	,, iii 1 f.	340	
Ad Polyc. ii.	238	,, iii 2	311, 324	
ii. 1	239	,, iii. 4	318, 331	
ii. 2	242	,, iv. 3	{ 326, 335, 344 345, 353 }	
iv. 2	246			
iv 3	249	III 1 2	311	
v. 1	249	,, 1. 6	317	
v 2	249	,, 1 8	311, 336	
vi. 2	249	,, 1 9	329	
vii 3	241	,, ii 1	329, 330, 332	
Polycarp—		,, ii 2	324, 353	
Ad Philad. 1. 2	247	,, ii. 4	341	
ii	248	,, ii 6	333	
ii. 2	249	,, iii. 1	319	
iii 2	247	,, iii 3	342	
iii 3	240	,, iii. 4	316	
iv. 1 f	244	,, iii. 5	341	
iv. 3	244, 249	,, iv 3	316	
v 2	243	,, v. 1	323, 336	
v. 3	244	,, v. 2	329	

INDEX OF PASSAGES

Vis. III —*continued.*		
,,	v. 4	345
,,	v 5	330, 341
,,	vi 2	333, 342
,,	vi. 5	332, 356
,,	vi 6	357
,,	vi. 7	357
,,	vii 3	348
,,	vii. 6	312
,,	viii. 8, 9	342
,,	viii. 11	342, 344, 353
,,	ix	343
,,	ix 2	359
,,	ix. 2, 10	339
,,	ix. 3	322
,,	ix. 5	322
,,	ix. 6	357
,,	ix. 7	335, 336, 337
,,	ix 7 f.	336
,,	ix. 8	353
,,	ix 10	319
,,	x. 4 f.	319
,,	x. 6	340
,,	x. 7	341
,,	xii 3	339
IV.	i 4, 7	316
,,	i. 8	318
,,	ii 2	319
,,	ii 4	318
,,	ii 5	318, 320, 324
,,	ii 6	318
,,	iii. 4	353
,,	iii. 6	342, 344
V		312
,,	7	322, 360
Mand I.	2	346
II.		346
,,	1 f.	349, 342
,,	4	359, 360
,,	4, 6	294
,,	6	324, 358
III.		346
,,	3	313
,,	4	313, 356
,,	5	324
IV.		346
,,	i. 1	350, 351
,,	i. 4, 4—8	350

Mand. IV.—*continued*		
,,	i. 9	333, 335, 351
,,	ii 1	312
,,	ii. 4	324
,,	iii. 1	341
,,	iii 2	342
,,	iii 2, 4 f.	330
,,	iii. 6	330
,,	iii 7	324, 360
,,	iv. 4	351
V		346
,,	i. 2	319
,,	i 7	324
,,	ii	352
,,	ii 1 f.	316
,,	ii 3	319
,,	ii. 8	324
VI	i. 4	322
,,	i 5	324
VII.	2	318
VIII	3	350
,,	3 ff.	346
,,	10	347, 354
IX.	1, 7	316
,,	8	312
X		318
,,	i. 2	319
,,	i 4	334, 356
,,	i 6	318, 322
,,	ii 2	319
,,	iii. 2	319
XI.		275, 337
,,	1	316
,,	2	338
,,	4	334, 357
,,	5 ff.	283
,,	9	344, 352
,,	12	337, 338
,,	13	338, 344
,,	14	291
XII	i. 2	357
,,	iii. 3	309
,,	iii. 4	317
,,	iv 2 f., 3	322
,,	iv. 4	318
,,	v. 1	317
,,	vi. 2	318
,,	vi. 3	317

INDEX OF PASSAGES

Sim. I			325
,,		5, 7	322
,,		8	358, 359
,,		10	333, 334
III		2	361
IV.		4	334
V.	i.	1	340
,,	i.	3 ff	341
,,	ii	2, 7	354
,,	iii	3	311, 321
,,	iii	7	360
,,	iii	7–9	341
,,	iii.	9	322
,,	vi	5 f	323
VI.	i.	1	317
,,	i.	3	323
,,	i.	4	360
,,	i	6	319
,,	ii.	3	330, 360
,,	ii.	6	320
,,	iii.	4 f	312
,,	iii.	6	312, 320
,,	iv.	2, 4	311
,,	v	5, 7	320
VII.		1, 2	311
,,		3	320
,,		4	312, 318, 320
VIII	i.	5	390
,,	iii	2	323
,,	iii	6	328
,,	vi –xi.		330, 341
,,	vi	2	318
,,	vi.	3	342
,,	vi	4	330
,,	vi.	5	337
,,	vii	4	337
,,	viii	1	333
,,	ix	1	333
,,	ix.	3	333, 337
,,	ix	1, 3	334
,,	x	3	358
,,	xi.	3	318, 360
IX.	ii.	6 f.	343
,,	ix	7	319, 339
,,	x.	1	319
,,	x	2 f.	353
,,	x.	3	319
,,	x.	7	319

Sim. IX —continued.			
,,	xi.		351
,,	xi	5	319
,,	xi.	7	311, 343
,,	xii.	4, 6, 8	341
,,	xiii		342
,,	xiii	2	333
,,	xiii.	5	339
,,	xiv.	6	318
,,	xv.	4, 6	323
,,	xvi.		341
,,	xvi	5 f.	323
,,	xvii	5	330
,,	xviii	4	362
,,	xix	2	255, 333
,,	xix	3	338
,,	xx	1 f.	356
,,	xx.	2	332, 333
,,	xxi	1	318
,,	xxii		337
,,	xxii.	2, 3	338
,,	xxiii.	4	322
,,	xxiv.	2	358, 360
,,	xxiv.	2–4	359
,,	xxiv.	4	361
,,	xxv.	2	323
,,	xxvi , xxvii		327, 335
,,	xxvi	2	336
,,	xxvi	3	331, 333
,,	xxvii		336
,,	xxvii	3	361
,,	xxviii		329
,,	xxviii	2	318
,,	xxviii	3	329, 332
,,	xxviii	4 f.	331
,,	xxviii	4	330
,,	xxviii.	5 f	329
,,	xxix		342
,,	xxx.	5	357
,,	xxxi.	4	342
,,	xxxi	5	335
X.	ii.	1 f.	342
,,	iii	2	353
,,	iv	2	322
,,	iv.	2 f.	359
Didache—			
,,	i.–vi		xxxvi
,,	i	5	302

DIDACHE—continued		
I	6	302
IV.	2	296
IV	7	302
IV	8	302
VI	2	279
VII		288
VIII.	1	287, 293
VIII	3	287
IX	5	291
X	7	282
XI	1, 3	282
XI	7	282
XI.	8 ff	283
XII	3 f.	304
XII	4	299
XIII	4	282
XIII.	7	297
XIV.	1 f.	288, 289
XV	1	282, 285
XV	3	289
XVI		293
XVI.	2	296

ACTA ANDREÆ, ed M. Bonnet, Acta apostolorum apocrypha, II, 1898, pp. 1–64—

Passio 11, p 27	268
12, p. 28	257
Acta 8, p. 41	262
Mart 1 7, p 50	265

ACTA JOHANNIS (as above)— pp. 151–216

5 p 153	257
6 p 154	267, 398
29 p 166	258
97 101 199 ff	273
113 p 213	262
Ps Abdias, v. 14	266

ACTA THOMÆ, ed M Bonnet, Suppl. codicis apocryphi, I, 1883—

I 5 pp. 10, 6	398
I 6 8 pp 7 ff.	390
I. 12 p. 11	262, 264
II. 20 p. 16	257, 267
ii 28 p 21	261, 264
II 29 p. 22	267
III 36 p. 27	264

ACTA THOMÆ—continued		
III	37 p. 28	259
VI.	52 ff	257
VI	55 p. 42	257
VI.	58 p 43	265
VIII	p 53	272
IX	p. 56	257
IX	p 57	265
IX	p 60	265
IX	p 64	267
XII	p 81	265
Mart. p 87		258
„ p 89		265

ACTA PETRI CUM SIMONE, ed. Lipsius, Acta apostolorum apocrypha, I., 1890—

2 p 46	391

ACTA PETRI ET ANDREÆ, ed. Bonnet, Acta apostolorum apocrypha, II, 1898—

20 p 126	385

HOMILIÆ CLEMENTIS—

III 22	263
XV. 7	398
XV. 9	265
XV 10	265

Recog. VII 6	398
IX. 6	398

Ep Clem ad Jac. 1	157
PROTEV JAC, 16	390
Ps MATT., XII	390

JUSTIN—

Dial. xlvii	169

IRENÆUS, adv. Hær.—

I. VI. 3	270
I. XXIV. 2	261
I. XXVI 2	171
I. XXVIII 1	261
III III. 4	224

ORIGINES, c Cels.—

III. 59	XXXIX
VIII. 30	393, 398

HIPPOLYTUS, Refut.—

IX. 12	385

EUSEBIUS, Hist. Eccles.—

II. i 3	393
II. i. 4	395
II. XXIII 4	393

INDEX OF PASSAGES

Eusebius—*continued*
II	xxiii 5	397
III	v.	168
III	xx	168
III	xxxii	168
IV.	xxii	168
IV	xxviii.	397
V	i 14	386
V	iii 2 f.	397

Epiphanius, Hær.—
xxx 13,16, 22	267, 397
xxx. 15	398
lxxviii. 14	395

Nicæa, 18 Canon 193
Marcus Diaconus, Vita Porphyrii Gazensis (Ed Teubn)—
89 p 72 f.	390

GENERAL INDEX

The leading references are printed in italics.

ADULTERY, xxv, 3, *43 f*, 138, 180, 209, 230, 257, 272, 335, 346, 349 f, 367.
Adulterers, 234.
Age classification, 286.
ἀγνόια, 178.
Alexandrine Exegesis, 198.
Allegorical Interpretation, 72, 149
ἀλλοτριεπισκοπεῖν, 181
Alms, 156, 302.
Ambiguity, 272.
Ambition, 146, 215, 221, 232, 284, 312, 338, 346.
Ananias and Sapphira, 146 ff.
Andrew, Acts of, 252, 262, 268.
Angels, 38, 112, 202.
ἀνομία, 270
Antichrist, 91.
Antinomianism, 224, 270.
Antioch, xxxiii, 99, 150, 161 f., 235, 240.
Antiochus Epiphanes, 139
Apocalypse, Jewish (Steindorff, Elias-Apok.), 141.
—— in Hermas, 343.
Apocalyptic, Jewish, 89, 130, 203.
Apollos, 52, 62, 71, 77, 136.
Apologists, xxvii, xxxii, 130, 179, 263, 293, 371, 379.
Apostasy, 190
—— from Christianity, xxvii, 186, 191, *197 f.*, 228, 233, 315, *329 f.*
—— Final, 91, 268, 306.

Apostasy from Paul, 107.
Apostates, 164, 330, 333.
Apostle, 63, 74 f., 93 f., 184, 190, 247, 257, 282, 285, 291, 295, 329, 339, 376
Apostles, Acts of the, xxix, 83, 99, 143 f., 147, 172.
—— Apocryphal Acts of the, 252, 256, 274
—— False, 164, 227.
Apostleship, 87, 107, 164.
Apostolic succession, 206.
Apostolical Council, 99, 151.
—— decree, 152, 172, 219.
Aristides, xxvii, xxxiii, 363
Armour, 184, 194
Arrogance, 255, 346 See also Pride.
Asceticism, 39, 69, 104, *111 f.*, 139, 171, 201 f, 209, 228, 249, 251, *258–268*, 277, 280, 304, 373, *376 f.*
Asia Minor, 99–120, 175–194.
Assemblies See Meetings.
ἀταραξία, 7.
Athens, 13, 36, 82.
Authority, 211
—— of the Apostle, 107.
—— of the Church Leaders, 107.
—— of Jesus Christ, 113.

BALAAM, 227, 253, 269.
βάναυσος, 92, 384.
Barbarism, 364, 368.
Barnabas, 99, 143, 150, 162, 174.

GENERAL INDEX

Barnabas, Epistle of, xxxi, 278, 282, 292 f
Baptism, xxx, 19 f., 142, 243, 288, 308, 341, 348
—— for the dead, 20, 66, 178.
Baptismal narrative in Gospel of the Hebrews, 170
Beatitudes, 156
Begging, 158, 170
Belief See Faith.
Beneficence, 141, 320 See Charity.
Beyond, The, 308
Birth, xxvi, 286
Bishops, 96, 106, 205, 239, 242 f, 282, 284, 300, 327, 335, 339, 375
Bitterness, 352
Blasphemy, charge made against Christians, 102
Blaspheming Christ, 186, 330.
Blessing and curse, 188
Blood, Eating of, 152
Body, 132, 259
—— Care of the, 267.
—— Discipline of the, 112, 259
Bond men, xxv
—— women, xxv
—— service, 202
Branding of runaway slaves, 118, 386
Brother, Name of, xxvi, 39, 54, 63
Brotherhood, The, 118, 129, 158, 182, 188, 212, 248, 286, 368
Brotherliness, 349.
Brotherly kiss, 63, 87
—— love, 86 f, 169, 188, 194, 201, 219, 229, 232, 255, 373
Burial, xxvi, 145, 241, 286
Business intercourse, 24, 90, 203, 209, 314, 356.
—— interests, 303, 356

CAIN, Cainites, 262, 271.
Calumnies, xxvii, 55, 64, 105, 130, 178, 209, 244, 249, 257, 321, 346.

Care for the belly, 261
—— other churches, 204.
—— the family, 233.
—— strange brethren, 216.
Casuistry, 139.
Catechism, 279, 345 f
Catechumens, 346 f., 374
Catholicism, 109, 174, 205, 277 ff, 308.
Celibacy, 39 ff, 69, 137.
—— Clerical, 285.
Celsus, xxxix, 371
Ceremonial See Divine Service.
—— duties, 141.
Charismatics, 211, 216, 221, 242, 282 f
Charity, Organised, 294, *296 ff*, 378
—— Works of, xxvi, 201, 357 f
Chastity, 2, 40, 42, 53, 152, 181, 210, 244, 249, 261 f., 305 f, 346, 370
Cheerfulness, 319
Child-murder, Ceremonial, 179
Children, Innocence of, 307, 342.
Christianity, 246, 332.
—— a crime, 180.
Christians, Gentile, 64 f., 122, 150, 155, 162, 171, 173 ff., 184, 230
—— Jewish, 51, 64 f, 66, 72, 84, 87, *138 ff*, 160, 168 ff, 198 f, 270 f, 372, 378.
Christology, 53, 223, 258, 273, 322
Church, The, 157, 187, 290, 295, 308, 374
—— Concern for the, 327, 335
—— Consciousness of forming a, 60, 79, *87 ff*, 96, 211.
—— constitution, xxxiii, 10, 63.
—— discipline, 157, 289 f., 370.
—— Leaders of the, 88, 97, 215, 307.
—— Meetings of the, 303, 310
—— The Primitive, 13, 141–148, 152, 184, 230
—— Unity of the, 239, 242.

430 GENERAL INDEX

Churches, Family character of, 144, 157, 286 f., 289
Circumcision, 65 f., 107, 111, 153, 162, 165, 230
Circus, 249
Cleanliness, 353
Clement of Alexandria, 258, 271, 308
—— of Rome, 1st Ep of, xxx, 195, 203–217, 250, 281, 287, 326
—— —— 2nd Ep of, xxxii, 278, 290
Clementine Homilies, 184, 265
Clergy, 192, 247, 284, 290, 369
Clothing, 153, 183, 287, 303.
Codex Cantabrigiensis, 156
Collection, The, *58 f*, 76, 105, 144, 162
Colony, Roman, 11, 82, 97
Colossæ, 102–107, 111–115, 126
Colossians, Ep to the, 3, 4 f, 174, 182
Commerce, xxv, 13, 100, 324
Communism, 56, *143 f*, 265, 271, 357
Community, Duties towards the, 279
—— Feeling of, 60, 136, 142, 188, 200, 247, 255, 275, 326, 338, 373
Compassion, 169, 257, 301, 369
Confession, 29, 156, 181, 196 f, 202, 221, 226, 238, 240, 247, 256, 289, 291, 328, 368, 373
—— Fear of, 200, 255, 275, 292, 361
—— Joyous, 145, 156, 210, 227, 256, 371
Confessors, 312 f, 328 ff.
Confidence, 307.
Confiscation, 196, 292, 314, 328, 357.
Conscience, 28, 67, 175
Constitution, 62, 88, *157 f*, 174, 189 *f*, 201, 205, *214 f*, 220 f., *242 ff*, 281 f, *335 f*., 373
Contentment, 203, 208, 321, 346

Continence, 111 f, 228, 260 ff 266, 312, 320, 340, 346.
—— a grace, 41, 202, 210, 260, 279 ff
Corinth, Church of, xxxiii, 11 ff., *11–80*, 89, 99, 106, 109, 111, 126, 129, 132, 135, 162, 175, 203 f, *210–217*, 227, 254, 259, 270, 373
Corinth, The offence in, 48, 392.
—— Town of, 11 ff, 382.
Corinthians, Eps to the, xxix, 11–80, 91, 392
Cosmopolitanism, 365.
Covetousness, 3, 249, 258.
Culture, 364
Curse, Effects of the, 46, 389 ff.
Customs, 130
Cynics, 12, 23, 49, 52, 265.

DEACONS, 96, 106, 193, 240, 282, 284, 327, 335, 339
Deaconesses, 180
Dead, Fate of the, 88, 178.
Death, Cases of, 62, 88, 286
—— Moral, 178
Decalogue, 141, 183.
Deceit, 138, 146.
Demons, 26 ff, 67.
Denial, 329, 334
Devil, 67, 194, 316, 325
διασπορά, 161.
Didache, xxxiii, xxxvi f., 278, 288, 295 ff, 310, 344
Dietetics, 127
Diligence, 92, 300
διψυχία, 316
Disciples, 150, 233.
Discontent, 321, 352
Discord in the Church, 98, 110, 148, 167, 215, 220 f.
Dishonesty, 90, 346, 355
Disinterestedness of Paul, 86.
Disobedience, 177, 197, 321.
Divisions, 125, 205.
Divorce, 32, 335, 350 ff.
Docetism, 223, 238, 245, 258, 273.

Doctrine, Disputes about, 191
Domestic duties, Table of, 2, 4 f, 174, 182
Domination, Desire for, 191, 204, 216, 284.
Doubt, 316, 349.
Drunkenness, 54, 64 f, 178, 182, 209, 305, 346
Dualism, 111, 258, 271, 280, 377
Duty, Pastoral, 88, 201
—— of reconciliation, 157, 289

EARNESTNESS, Moral, xxxviii, 137, 206 f
Ecclesiasticism, 228.
Ecstasy, 238, 242
Edification, Meetings for, 310, 345.
Education, 187, 208, 300, 304, 353, 369
—— of the Church by the apostle, xxxv ff, *1–10*, 54 f, 80, 87 f, 132, 203
—— of the individual by the Church, 213
Egoism, 165
Egypt, 126 f., 277
Egyptians, Gospel of the, 127, 261 f, 267, 272
Election, 177
Emancipation, 64
—— of women, 38, 65, 70, 183, 217, 227, 305.
—— of slaves, 118, 239, 249, 306.
Embassies, 204, 241
Embezzling, xxv, 180, 356
Emperor-worship, 100, 226, 367.
Encratism, 41, 127
Enemies, Love of, xxv, 295, 347, 370
Enthusiasm, 63, 92 f, 130, 145, 177, 215, 374.
Ephesians, Ep. to the, xxxi, 115, 175–194
Ephesus, xxxiii, *100 f.*, 226, 228, 233, 235, 245 f.
Epistles, Catholic, xxxi, 278.

Equality of master and slave, 35, 118
—— of man and woman, 36 ff.
Eschatology, *91 ff*, 181, 258 268, 293, 375
Esoteric and Exoteric, 273.
Essenes and Essenism, 112, 126, 139, 142, 145, 158, 259, 393 f.
Eternity, 128, 179
Eusebeia, 307
εὔχρηστος (117), 357
Evil-doers, 180
Excesses, 3, 137, 178, 280, 286, 320
—— in eating and drinking, 104, 132
Excommunication, 46, 93, 158, 215
Exorcists, 101
Extortioner, 54

FAITH, 109, 110, 124, 161, 177, 194, 199, 207, 211, 226, 240, 254, 301, 346 f
—— Bold, 136, 257.
—— Justification by, 166, 207.
Family, 114, 262, 304, 314, 349 ff
—— events, xxxiii, 286.
Fanaticism, 51, 179.
Fasting, xxvi, 128, 156, 268, 287, 302, 341, 360
Fast-days, 141, 287, 340.
Feeding the poor, 147.
Festivals, Jewish, 107, 111, 125, 165
Fidelity, Connubial, 352.
Fire-raising, Christians charged with, 129
Firstlings (= earliest converts), 190
First-fruits, 297.
Flesh, Sins of the, 3, 113, 132, 374
Food, Regulations as to, 107, 111, 126 f., 161 f, 165.
Forbearance, 346. See Long-suffering.

Fornication, xxv, 43 f., 68, 90, 138, 152, 170, 186 f., 227, 258, 261, 346, 349 f.
Freedom, 51, 56, 65, 111, 129, 136, 188, 270, 308, 305.
Freethinking, 64, 227 f
Funds, Church, 59, 284, 299.
—— Society, 61
—— for sick and dead, 327

GALATIA, 99 f, 102–110, 125, 136, 163 ff, 373
Galatians, Ep to the, 102 ff, 122
Galen, 263, 378
Galileans, 144.
Give, Readiness to, 60, 84, 116, 136, 143, 200, 296 f
Glossolaly, 18, 69
Gluttony, 258, 267, 320, 338, 346
γνῶσις, 66, 127, 171, 173, 193, 224, 227, 246, 251–276, 277, 280 f, 300, 308, 337, 376 f.
Gnosticism, xxxiii, 171, 173
God, Fear of, 181, 208, 307, 321, 346
Gospel, 138, 141, 251, 258 f, 275, 279 f, 308, 363, 376
Gospel of Paul, 70, 75
Gospels, xxxii, 310.
Gossip, 105, 187, 305
Greed, 102
Growth of the Churches, Outward, 174.
—— Inward, 187
Guilt, Feeling of, 198, 312.

HADES, Preaching of Jesus in, 178.
Hair, Unshorn, 153.
Hands, Laying on of, 285.
Hatred of Christians, 129 f., 196
—— of Humanity, 130
Health, 210
Heathendom, 3, *23 f*, 89, 133 f., 151 f., 161, *178 f*, 218 f., 227, 231, 269, 305 f, 333 f., 351, *364 ff*, 368

Hebrews, Ep to the, xxxi, 113, *195–203*, 207.
—— Gospel of the, xxxix, 169, 301
Hegesippus, 153, 168, 171, 393
Hellenists, 147, *149 ff.*, 218.
Heresy, 164, 171, 189, *193 f.*, 201 f, 205, *223*, 224 f, 237 f., 240, *245 f.*, 252 f, 281, 304
Hermas, Shepherd of, xxxii, 2, 290, 307, 309–362
ἡσυχάζειν, 92
Hetairæ, 37, 44, 138
Hierarchy, 189, 201, 238
Hierodules, 37, 44.
High priest, Christ as, 198
—— James as, 154
Holiness, 146, 188, 342, 348.
Holy Ghost, xxviii, 10, 15, 18, 22, 53, 55, 109, 125, 147, 194, 210, 278, 323, 372
Home, Love of, 147, 265, 326
Honesty, 2, 313, 370.
Honour, Decree of, 58.
—— Places of, 337, 347
Honourable life, 212, 321, 323, 346, 370
—— of middle classes, 179.
—— in country districts, 135
Hope, 177, 189, 197, 200, 203, 209, 301
Hospitality, 158 f, 188, 201, 207, 211, 216, 255, 299, 312, 327, *357 ff.*
House-churches, 122, 196
Household, Father of a, 305, 314 ff, 345, 352.
Humanity, 366, 370
Humility, 159, 188, 193, 208, 209, 212, 232, 236, 243, 248.
Hypocrisy, 139, 178, 272, 280, 293, 346.

IDOLS, 27 f, *66*, 89.
—— Service of, 3, 54, 178, 249.

GENERAL INDEX

Idols, Sacrifice to, xxv, *24*, 65, 69, 125, 136, 152, 161, 186, 219, 227, 266, 269.
Ignatius, xxxi, 204, 235–250, 253, 268, 284.
Ignorance, Sins of, 178, 308.
Immaturity, 136
Immorality, 69, 163
Incest, 44 ff, 52, 68.
Indecision, 318.
Indian influences, 126
Individualism, 57, 62, 73, 79, 211, 217, 280.
Industries, Great, 355.
Innocence, 321, 346
Insincerity, 139.
Insinuations against Paul, 59, 75 f, 107
—— against the Christians, 130, 179, 286, 342 f
—— against the Gnostics, 275.
Instruction, Moral, 1 ff., 104, 208, 257, 345 f
Intellectualism, 225, 254 ff.
Intercession, 194, 204, 212, 289, 291
—— for the apostle, 87, 94.
—— for enemies, 156, 370.
—— for the Jews, 154
—— for rulers, 210, 292.
—— with martyrs, 241.
Intercourse, Social, 24, 334, 355.
Inwardness, 156, 320, 347, 352
Itinerant brethren, 295.

JAMES, the Lord's brother, *151 ff.*, *168 ff.*, 174, 218, 392 ff
—— Ep of, 223, 264, 278, 289.
Jerusalem, 99, 102, 123, 141, 144, 168, 288.
Jesus, *cf.* Pattern, xxxviii f., 8, 27, 141, 149, 159, 167, 171, 178, 250, 259, 265, 273, 376.
Jews, 25, 37, 85, 127, 129, *138 ff.*, 226, 230 f., 367 f.
—— Hatred of, 293.
—— Taxation of, 131.

John, 173, 176, *218 ff.*, 233, 240, 261
—— Acts of, 252, 267, 273, 398
—— Apocalypse of, xxxi, 225 ff.
—— Eps. of, xxxi, 218 ff , 229 f.
—— Gospel of, 231 ff
—— School of, 218.
—— Writings of, 193, 253.
Joyousness, 90, 177, 197, 207, 316 f, 359.
Judaism, xxxiii, *75 ff*, 85, 104, *107 f.*, 113 f., 128 f., 136, 160–167, 172, 183 f., 198, 246, 275, 288.
Jude, Ep of, 224, 253, 269.
"Judge not," 156.
Judge, Unjust, 138, 170
Judgment, The Divine, 46, 387 ff.

KNOWLEDGE, 176, 199, 211, 321, 346

LABOUR, Moral value of, 93, 170, 299, 304.
—— Distaste for, 93, 130.
Laodicea, 103, 106, 226
Law, 9, *107–112*, 125, 139, 141 f., 156, 161 f, 169, 183 f, 198, 246, 278 f
—— of Christ, xxxviii, 110, 155, 184, 279
—— Evasion of, 139.
—— Jesus' exposition of, 142, 155
—— Roman, 118 f.
Lawsuits, 25, 29 ff., 56 f, 65, 131, 217.
Leaders, xxviii, 88, 201
Legalism, Pharisaic, 149 f.
Letter, Intercourse by, xxix, 13, 84, 102, 121 f, 204, 326.
Letters of recommendation, 117, 242, 299.
—— to the Churches, xxxi, 220, 225 ff.
Liberality, 301, 322, 347, 350 f.

28

Libertinism, 37, 64 ff., 73, 76, 227, *268 ff*, 338.
Liberty See Freedom
Liturgical functions, 282; *cf* Divine Service and Ceremonial
Long-suffering, 188, 321.
Love, 28, 115, 132 f, 140 ff, 177, 204 f, 210, 226, 229, 245, 250, 279, 301, 357, 368.
—— of husband and wife, 183.
—— of children, 183, 233, 300.
—— Works of, 257, 307, 346. See also Works of Charity.
Lovelessness, 67, 79, 139.
Lucian, 298, 371.
Luke, 142 ff, 151, 155, 264
Lukewarmness, 132, 197
Luxury, 183, 346, 355, 365.
Lying, 138, 146, 187, 234, 307, 321, 346

MACCABEES, 139.
Macedonia, 59, *81–97*, 136, 373.
Magic, 18 f., 66, 100, 367.
Magicians, 257
Magistracy, 130, 182, 210, 240, 292, 370 f
Magnesia, 236, 246.
Malice, 178
Mantic, 18 f, 333, 344
Marital relations, Renunciation of, 40 f
Mark, Gospel of, 195.
Marriage, 69, 114, 183, 203, 239, 349
—— Indissoluble, 32, 41, 305, 350, 376
—— ordained by God, 41, 304.
—— Rejection of, 40, 261 ff, 352.
—— a Second, 40, 285, 305.
Marriages, Mixed, *30 f*, 69, 161, 181, 335
Martyrs, Worship of, 236, 241, 323, 328 f
Martyr-fanaticism, 256
Martyrdom, 149, 154, 156, 168, 171, 190, 201, 210, 226, 233, 235 f, 256, 292, 328
Matthew, Gospel of, 155, 157.
Matthias, Traditions of, 257.
Meal, 144, 161, 328. See Lord's Supper
Mechanics, 303, 355.
Meetings, 180, 197 f, 296, 333.
Men-pleasing, 165.
Merchants, 303
Miracles, 257
Miracle, Penal, 46 f, 146, 387 ff.
Missions, 32, 95, 124, *158*, 162, 181, 226, 232, 274, 290 f.
Modesty, 210, 283, 300.
μονάζειν, 296.
Monasticism, 93.

Money, Love of, 191, 203, 243, 283, 284 f., 366
Monotheism, 66, 113, 197, 199, 261, 331
Morality, Ancient preachers of, 135
—— Average, 175
—— Positive, 114, 181, 279 f.
—— Twofold, 261, 279 ff
Motherhood, 233, 261, 304.
Murder, 180, 230, 234.
Mysteries, 19.
Myth, Mythology, 251, 367, 375

NAME of Jesus Christ, 15, 46, 55, 180.
Nature, Deification of, 270.
—— Order of, 38, 209
Natural and moral, 65, 259 f., 271 f
Nazarite, 154, 393
Neophytes, 345.
Nero, Persecution under, 130.
Neo-Platonism, 379
Neo-Pythagoreans, 126, 143, 259, 396
Nicolaitans, 227, 264.
Nominal Christianity, 248.
Novelty, Desire for, 209.

GENERAL INDEX 435

OATH, 308.
Obedience, 108, 124, 176 f, 192, 204, 207, 243, 247, 277, 373,
—— to rulers, 129, 210.
Offering, 202   See Sacrifice
Offerings, 62, 190, 297, 303
Office, 88, 148, 189 f, 214 f., 281 f
—— Magisterial, 265
Officials, Payment of, *cf* Office.
Officiousness, 92
Oil, Use of, 153, 267.
Opinion, Public, 92
Opus operatum, 320
Order, 22, 189, 205, 281, 353.
Ornaments, 183, 265
Orphic societies, 2, 126, 259.
Other-worldliness, 200, 204.
Outside-World, Judgment of, 92.
—— Influence of Church upon, 96

PARABLES of Jesus, 138, 170.
παρουσία, 42, 91, 95.
Parties in the Church, *71 ff.*, 111, 136, 149 ff, 211, 338 f
Passion, Christ's, 184, 212
Passover, 183, 267
Pastoral Epistles, xxxvii, 253, 261, 266, 278, 282, 295, 298
Patience, 226
Pattern, Apostle as, 292, 323
—— Clergy as, 284 f.
—— Elders as, 192
—— God as, 302, 322
—— Jesus as, 8, 97, 115, 183, 193, 209, 213, 232, 240, 243, 247, 267, 293, 322, 373
—— Macedonian Churches as, 90
—— Old Testament as, 183, 207
—— Parents as, 208
Paul, xxxv ff, 1-137, 149 f, 160 ff, 173 ff, 205 ff, 217 f, 244, 259, 270, 278, 291, 350
Peace, 93, 188, 205, 210, 212

Peculium, 385
Penance, 128
Pergamum, 226, 382
Peripatetics, 126, 396.
Persecution, 87, 129, 145, 177, 189, *196 ff*, 203, 226, 233, 256, 292, 325, *328 f.*
Peter, 145 ff., 150, 157, 162 ff, 168, 174, 190, 218, 326, 393, 398
—— 1st Ep of, 175, 181, 203, 207.
—— 2nd Ep of, 253
—— Apocalypse of, 257
—— Preaching of, 310
Petrine party in Corinth, 72
Pharisaism, 111, 114, *139 ff*, 149, 160, 210, 311, 319
Pharisees, *139 ff*, 145, 167.
Philadelphia, 226, 235, 240, 246.
Philemon, Ep. to, 115-120, 386.
Philippi, xxx, *81-86, 93-98*, 241, 244
Philosophy, xxviii, 135, 276.
Phrygia, 40, 100, *102-107, 111-115*, 136, 253, 373
Piety, 127, 147, 321.
Pliny, xxxv, 180, 185, 371
Plotinus, 255, 271.
Pneumatics, 255
Politics, 130, 181, 309, 325
Polycarp of Smyrna, xxxii, 224, 239-250, 284
—— Ep of, xxxii, 244.
Poverty, 84, 91, 144, 210, 255
—— as ideal, 264, 304
Practical Christianity, 189, 200, 207, 219, 230, 245, 301, 347, 373
Prayer, xxvii, 41, 132, 141 f, 156, 177, 194, 202, 206, 212, 230, 240, 287 f, 317, 340
—— Hours of, 141, 287
—— Lord's, 287
—— Meetings for, 245, 342.
Preaching, xxxii, 239, 290, 294, 343.
Precedence, Quarrels about, 337.

Presbyters, Presbytery, 157, 190, 214 f., 242, 285, 216, 335.
Pride, 132, 138 f, 209, 239, 245, 249, 269, 280, 312.
Priest, 282, 288, 394.
Prisoners, 196, 201, 204, 297, 359.
Procreation, 40, 127, 261
Professions, Dishonourable, 239, 249
Progress, 187, 229, 375
Progressive Christianity, 223
Propaganda See Heresy, Judaism, Missions.
Property, 56 f., 257, 261, 264.
—— Private, 56 f., 143
Prophets, Old Testament, 130, 140, 159, 183, 238, 341
—— Christian, 16 f, 69, 158, 192, 219 f, 228, 242, 282, 295, 309 f, 314, 317, 333, 340, 357 f.
—— False, 275, 337, 344.
Prophetesses, 227 f, 264, 305.
Proselytes, 2, 31, 36, 123, 147, 161, 167, 331, 388.
Proverb-literature, 149, 278, 344.
Psalms, 114.
Psychic, 255.
Punishment, Corporal, 118, 354.
Purity of heart, 159, 206.
Pythagoreans, 143

RABBINICAL theories, 31, 49, 169.
Rabbinism, Christian, 153, 161.
Rationalism, 66, 89.
Rechabites, 154.
Recompense, Future, 196, 199.
Reconciliation, Need for, 198.
Relics, Worship of, 241
Renunciation, 241.
—— of rights, 57, 347.
—— of revenge, xxv, 90, 133, 188, 240
Repentance, 48, 197, 208, 244
—— Preaching of, xxviii, 306, 309, 321, 328.
—— a Second, 330, 341.

Responsibility, 257, 289.
Resurrection, 53, 66, 89, 258, 305.
Revelations, 238, 242, 309 ff., 339, 343.
—— of hell, 257.
Rich, The, 210, 324, *356 f*, 359.
Riches, 303, 334, 347.
Righteousness, 164 f., 194, 207, 230, 301, 346.
Romans, Ep to the, 2, 5, 121 f., 182, 202.
Rome, xxxi, 83, 93, 112, *121–133*, 129 ff., 163, 166, 182, *195–210*, 235, 238, 241, 264, 266, 277, 309, 323 f., 381 f.

SABBATH, 128, 141, 149, 156, 161, 230.
Sacraments, 19 f., 341 f.
Sacrifice, 140, 156, 198, 230, 288
Sacrilege, Christians charged with, 102.
Sadducees, 139.
Saints, 67, 137, 146, 187, 200, 230, 361
Salary, 285, 297.
Salvation, Certainty of, 194, 199.
—— Economy of, 175
Samaria, 150, 231.
Samaritan woman, 233
Sanctification, 137, 166, 209, 231, 372
Satan, 46, 164. See Devil.
Sayings of the Lord, 41, *155*, 172, 185, 213, 248, 252, 279, 308, 313, 373
Schisms,
Scribes, 139, 167.
Scripture, Authority of, 183.
—— Falsifying of, 267.
—— Knowledge of, 279.
—— Reading of, 230
Sect, 127, 167, 275.
Secularisation, 96, 98, 204, 229, 291, 303, 306, *333 f*, 355, 361, 376.

GENERAL INDEX

Self-denial, 205
Self-mutilation, 263.
Sensuality, 114, 271, 321, 334.
Sermon, 207, 301   See also Preaching.
—— on the Mount, xxxiv, 133, 347.
Servants, Men- and maid-, 144. *Cf* slaves.
Service, Divine, *16 ff.*, 202, *206*, 230, 245, *286*, *339 f*
—— Personal, 83, 94, 117, 386 f
—— on behalf of the Church, 192, 215, 247, 301.
—— on behalf of the state in Athens, 57.
Seven, The, 147
Shamelessness, 260, 272, 366.
Sick, Visitation of, 201, 257, 286, 297, 349
Sickness, Cases of, 62
Simplicity, 206, 257, 321, 346
Sincerity, xxxviii, 107.
Sinlessness, 223.
Sinners, Saviour of, xxxix
Sin, Confession of, 229, 289, 310-318, 343.
—— Consciousness of, xxviii, 170, 208, 229, 288, 312, 360
—— Deadly, 229.
—— Forgiveness of, 208, 312, 307
Sister (= Christian), 39, 315, 352 f
Slaves, 11, *33 f*, 66, 105, 114, *115-120*, 144, 185, 204, 239, 249, 299, 306, 324, *353 f*, 365 f, 368, *383 ff*
—— Emancipation of, 35, 118, 354, 385
Smyrna, 226, 235, 240
Sobriety, 92, 177, 244, 284.
Social conditions, 12, 62, 90 f, 187, 368 f
—— intercourse, 24 f.
Souls, Transmigration of, 127, 390

Speculation, 177, 225, 229, 251, 277, 308
Speech, Freedom of, 15, 38, 281.
Spiritualism, 251 f., 258
State, 131, 292, 325, 364 f   *Cf.* Magistracy
Statistics, Ancient, xxxiii f., 381 ff
Stoics, 7, 33, 53, 119, 126, 258, 379.
Strangled, Things, 152.
Suffering, 87, 96, 106, 145, 189, *197 f*, 203, 226, *320*.
Suicide, 367, 370.
Sunday, 16, 58, 60, 180, 230, 288.
Superstition, 101, 180, 367.
Supper, Lord's, 22 f., *60 ff*, 217, 255, 263, 269, 288 f, 339.
Sustenance, 266 f.
Synagogue, 1, 26, 64, 75, 129, 131, 163, 185, 231, 294, 332, 372.
—— Adherents of, 131

TACITUS, xxxv, 130, 179 f, 367.
Talmud, 155, 169 ff, 170.
Taxes, 130.
Teachers, 106, 110, 201, 254, 283 f.
—— Itinerant, 282 f., 297, 357.
Temple, 149, 185.
—— -tax, 131, 156.
Testament, Old, 108, 112, 172, 189, 157, 172, 183 f, 198, 205, 213, 227, 246, 253, 261, 293, 310, 373.
Thanksgiving, 187, 288.
Theatre, 36, 249
Theft, 138, 180, 186, 257, 272, 306, 347
Theosophy, 112.
Therapeutæ, 118, 127, 397
Thessalonica, xxx, 2, *81-93*, 98, 130, 136
Thomas, Acts of, 252, 272 f, 398.
Thought, Sins of, 313, 370
Tongue, Sins of the, 307, 352.

GENERAL INDEX

Trial of Christians, 181
Truth, 187, 194, 232, 244, 273 f., 313, 321, 346, 370.
—— (Johannine), 230
Twelve, The, *141 ff.*, 145, 148, 153
"Two Ways," The, 140.

UNBELIEF, 197, 232, 321.
Unchastity, xxvii, 3, 12, 132, 187, 209, 248, 259, 367
—— Unnatural, 54, 179, 257.
Unity, Sense of, 97, 188, 205, 208, 216, 321, 323, 342, 346.
Universalism, 291.
Usages, Purificatory, 156
Usurer, 54

VANITY, 236, 283, 311.
Vegetarianism, 69, *126-129*, 137, 153, 266 f., 396 ff
Veiling, 37.
Vice, Unnatural, 48, 54, 257, 367
Vices, List of, 2, 110, 209.
Virginity, 228, 261
Visions, 163   See also Revelations.
Voluntariness, 190, 205, 296

WAR, 249
Washing of feet, 193, 232, 300
Watchfulness, 92, 177.
"Weak" and "strong," 28, *64 ff.*, 129, 210, 254

Wealth. See Riches
Widows, 42, 239.
—— and orphans, xxvi, 262, 284, 327, 336, 341, 345 f., 353, 358.
—— of the Church, 244, 297 f., 305
Wine, Abstinence from, 112, 126, 137, 153, 266, 304, 396.
Wisdom, Old Testament teachers of, 159, 278, 344
Witness, False, xxv, 244, 249, 346.
Women in the ancient world, 36, 367
—— in the Christian Church, xxv, xxx, *36 f.*, 144, 158, 183, 212, 217, 263 f., 283, 305, 352.
—— in common, Having of, 53, 271.
Works, Good, 177, 226.
—— Superfluity of good, 311, 321
World, Renunciation of the, 114, 191 f
—— The outside, 92
Worldliness, 96, 98   See Secularisation
Worship, 112.   See Divine Service
—— Old Testament, 149
—— Pagan, 367

YOUNG men (Deacons), 192
—— and young women, 286

www.ingramcontent.com/pod-product-compliance
Lightning Source LLC
Chambersburg PA
CBHW071233300426
44116CB00008B/1014